Ancient Manuscripts in Digital Culture

Digital Biblical Studies

VOLUME 3

The titles published in this series are listed at *brill.com/dbs*

Ancient Manuscripts in Digital Culture

Visualisation, Data Mining, Communication

Edited by

David Hamidović
Claire Clivaz
Sarah Bowen Savant

In collaboration with

Alessandra Marguerat

BRILL

LEIDEN | BOSTON

This book was published in Open Access with a subsidy from the Swiss National Science Foundation.

The Library of Congress Cataloging-in-Publication Data is available online at http://catalog.loc.gov
LC record available at http://lccn.loc.gov/2019013198

Typeface for the Latin, Greek, and Cyrillic scripts: "Brill". See and download: brill.com/brill-typeface.

ISSN 2452-0586
ISBN 978-90-04-34673-4 (hardback)
ISBN 978-90-04-39929-7 (e-book)

This book is printed on acid-free paper and produced in a sustainable manner.

Contents

Figures and Tables

Figures

Tables

Contributors

Sarah Bowen Savant
is a Cultural Historian and Professor at the Aga Khan University-ISMC in London. She is the PI for the Arabic DH project KITAB (kitab-project.org) and co-PI for the Open Islamicate Texts Initiative (OpenITI, <http://iti-corpus.github.io/>), a corpus building project. She publishes on early Islamic history and historiography and Digital Humanities.

Thibault Clérice
is the head of the MA program "Digital Technologies Applied to History" (Technologies Numériques Appliquées à l'Histoire) at the École Nationale des Chartes (Paris, France). He is a Classicist who served as an engineer both at the Centre for eResearch (Kings College London, UK) and the Humboldt Chair for Digital Humanities (Leipzig, Germany), where he developed the data backbone for the future *Perseus 5* (under the CapiTainS.org project). His main interests lie in data and software sustainability and Latin data mining.

Claire Clivaz
is Head of Digital Humanities + at the Swiss Institute of Bioinformatics. She is leading research projects in DH and New Testament, as the SNSF project MARK16 and her publications are in both fields, like *Ecritures digitales. Digital writing, digital Scriptures* (Brill, 2019). She is a member of the EASSH governing board and of several scientific and editorial boards and co-lead the DBS series.

Stephen J. Davis
is Professor of Religious Studies at Yale University and founder and director of the Yale Monastic Archaeology Project (YMAP). He has published five solo-authored books: *The Cult of St Thecla* (Oxford UP 2001), *The Early Coptic Papacy* (AUC Press 2004), *Coptic Christology in Practice* (Oxford UP 2008), *Christ Child* (Yale UP 2014), and *Monasticism: A Very Short Introduction* (Oxford UP 2018).

Heather Dana Davis Parker
holds an M.A. and Ph.D. in Near Eastern Studies from Johns Hopkins University (JHU). She is currently a lecturer for the Center for Leadership Education at JHU. She has extensive experience in the field of Northwest Semitic epigraphy having worked in museums, archaeological collections, and departments of antiquity throughout the Middle East and Europe. Her work on early script traditions contributes directly to the study of the origins of Levantine regional

states and kingdoms. She has co-published articles on the use of digital technologies in the research, presentation, and preservation of ancient inscriptions and artifacts in the *Bulletin of the American Schools of Oriental Research*, *Near Eastern Archaeology*, and other venues and has participated in conferences highlighting the use of modern technology in Cultural Heritage Preservation. She is the president of the Colloquium for Biblical and Near Eastern Studies and serves the American Schools of Oriental Research as a member of the board of directors and chair of the Junior Scholars Committee.

Bradley C. Erickson
is a Ph.D. candidate and teaching fellow in the Department of Religious Studies at the University of North Carolina at Chapel Hill. His research focuses on the use of digital visualization tools in archaeology. His dissertation uses digital tools to explore the ancient Jewish and Christian use of astronomy and astrology.

Brett Graham
studied Computer Science at the University of Newcastle (Australia) and wrote his honours thesis on algorithm design. After working in software development of large scale defence projects, he lectured in computer programming for five years at Nanyang Polytechnic (Singapore). Graham completed a PhD in Biblical Studies at the University of Sydney (2018).

Adeline Harrington
is a doctoral candidate in Religious Studies at the University of Texas at Austin in the subfield of Ancient Mediterranean Religions. Her principal area of focus is early Christian book culture.

James C. Henriques
is a doctoral candidate in Religious Studies at the University of Texas at Austin in the subfield of Ancient Mediterranean Religions. His principal area of focus is ancient magic.

H.A.G. Houghton
is Director of the Institute for Textual Scholarship and Electronic Editing (ITSEE) and Professor of New Testament Textual Scholarship at the University of Birmingham. The focus of his research is on the transmission of the New Testament in Latin and Greek: he serves as Executive Editor of the Pauline Epistles for the International Greek New Testament Project and has been a collaborator of the Vetus Latina Institute for over a decade. He has also been

Principal Investigator of two major European Research Council projects, the COMPAUL project on early Latin commentaries and the CATENA project on Greek manuscripts.

Brent Landau
is Senior Lecturer in Religious Studies at the University of Texas at Austin. He specializes in the Christian Apocrypha broadly, with particular interests in infancy gospels and apocryphal writings preserved on papyri.

Liv Ingeborg Lied
is Professor of Religious Studies at MF Norwegian School of Theology, Religion and Society in Oslo. Lied is the author of *The Other Lands of Israel: Imaginations of the Land in 2 Baruch* (2008) and the co-editor of *Snapshots of Evolving Traditions: Jewish and Christian Manuscript Culture, Textual Fluidity, and New Philology* (2017; with Hugo Lundhaug); and *Bible as Notepad: Annotations and Annotation Practices in Late Antique and Medieval Biblical Manuscripts* (2018; with Marilena Maniaci).

James F. McGrath
is the Clarence L. Goodwin Chair in New Testament Language and Literature at Butler University in Indianapolis, USA. He is the author of *John's Apologetic Christology* (Cambridge University Press, 2001) and *The Only True God* (University of Illinois Press, 2009), as well as numerous articles related to early Christology, monotheism, the Mandaeans, and a wide variety of other subjects.

Matthew Munson
received his Ph.D. from the Theologische Fakultät at the University of Leipzig for the application of distributional semantics to the interpretation of the Greek New Testament. He currently works as a software development engineer for the Formulae – Litterae – Chartae project at the University of Hamburg in Germany. Before moving to Hamburg, he worked a the Humboldt Chair for Digital Humanities at the University of Leipzig, in the DARIAH project at the Göttingen Centre for Digital Humanities at the University of Göttingen, and at the Scholars' Lab at the University of Virginia. His current research interests include the application of machine learning, and especially neural networks, for semantic information extraction in ancient texts, the improvement of parameter testing methods for computational semantic analysis, and the expansion of the methods used in his dissertation to other languages and to multi-lingual analysis.

Laura Salah Nasrallah
is Professor of New Testament and Early Christianity at Harvard University Divinity School. She is author of *An Ecstasy of Folly: Prophecy and Authority in Early Christianity, Christian Responses to Art and Architecture: The Second-Century Church Amid the Spaces of Empire and Archaeology and the Letters of Paul*; and co-editor of *Prejudice and Christian Beginnings: Investigating Race, Gender, and Ethnicity in Early Christian Studies* and *From Roman to Early Christian Thessalonikē.*

Peter M. Phillips
directs the CODEC Research Centre at Durham University in the United Kingdom. Peter has taught New Testament for many years, writing especially on John's Gospel and New Testament interpretation. CODEC has become a leading center for the exploration of the Biblical text through the DIGITAL HUMANITIES. Publications: "The Bible as Augmented Reality" in *Theology and Ministry Journal,* Durham University, September 2013 (with Richard Briggs); "The Woman Caught in Adultery: Nameless, Partnerless, Defenceless" in *Character Studies in the Fourth Gospel,* (WUNT 314, Mohr Siebeck, 2013, 407-421); "Wesley's Parish and the Digital Age", *Holiness* 2.3, 2016, 337-358; *Engaging the Word: Biblical Literacy and Christian Discipleship*, BRF, October 2017.

Jennifer Aileen Quigley
is Assistant Professor of New Testament and Early Christian Studies and Louisville Postdoctoral Fellow at Drew University. She holds the ThD from Harvard Divinity School. Her dissertation is *Divine Accounting: Theo-Economics in the Letter to the Philippians*, May 2018.

Paul Robertson
Ph.D. in Religious Studies from Brown University in 2013. Author of *Paul's Letters and Contemporary Greco-Roman Literature: Theorizing a New Taxonomy* (Brill 2016) and co-editor of *All Religion is Inter-Religion: Engaging the Work of Steven M. Wasserstrom* (Bloomsbury, 2019), as well as articles in *Vigiliae Christianae, Studies in Late Antiquity*, and *Method and Theory in the Study of Religion.* Past research awards include Dumbarton Oaks, the Center for Hellenic Studies, and Fondation Hardt. Currently a Lecturer in Classics and Humanities at the University of New Hampshire, specializing in ancient Mediterranean thought and the cognitive science of religion.

Christopher A. Rollston
holds an MA and Ph.D. from The Johns Hopkins University. He has published widely in the field of Northwest Semitic epigraphy and Hebrew Bible, with articles in journals such as *Semitica*, the *Bulletin of the American Schools of Oriental Research*, Tel Aviv, *Near Eastern Archaeology*, *Israel Exploration Journal*. He authored *Writing and Literacy in the World of Ancient Israel: Epigraphic Evidence from the Iron Age* (2010) which was selected the prestigious Frank Moore Cross Award from the American Schools of Oriental Research. He is the editor of entitled *Enemies and Friends of the State: Ancient Prophecy in Context* (Eisenbrauns 2018). Professor Rollston has lectured widely in the field, at institutions such as Yale University, the University of Michigan, the University of Helsinki, Brown University, Hebrew University (Jerusalem), Tel Aviv University, and Duke University. He is editor of the journal *Maarav* and the co-editor of the *Bulletin of the American Schools of Oriental Research*. He is a tenured faculty member in the department of Classical and Near Eastern Languages and Civilizations at George Washington University (Washington, DC).

INTRODUCTION

The Dissemination of the Digital Humanities within Research on Biblical, Early Jewish and Christian Studies

Claire Clivaz and Sarah Bowen Savant

This third volume of *Digital Biblical Studies* (DBS) represents a turning point in the birth of the series, as well as in the dissemination of the Digital Humanities within "Biblical, Early Jewish and Christian Studies". The title acknowledges the three research groups devoted, since 2012 and 2013, to the Digital Humanities at the annual meetings of the *Society of Biblical Literature* (SBL), the international SBL (ISBL), and the *European Association of Biblical Studies* (EABS). Our introduction will comment on the development of the Digital Humanities and offer a preview of the contents of this volume.

1 The Dissemination of DH

The DBS series is now fully established in the academic landscape. In 2013, a first volume pre-existent to the series was published through Brill edited by Claire Clivaz, Andrew Gregory and David Hamidović, *Digital Humanities in Biblical, Early Jewish and Early Christian Studies*[1]. It was entitled exactly as the first research group on the topic created at the EABS 2012 in Amsterdam, then at the SBL and ISBL 2013, and included papers presented in these research groups. After six years as co-chairs of the annual SBL DH section, Clivaz and Hamidović will pass the lead in 2019 to Garrick Allen and Paul Dilley, and join the steering committee members, as a new stage in the field begins. But it is these research groups that have brought our first articles to the DBS series.[2]

We have generally considered the title *Digital Humanities in Biblical, Early Jewish and Early Christian Studies* to be too long and quite heavy, but at the

1 Clivaz, Claire, Gregory, Andrew, Hamidović, David (eds), in collaboration with Schulthess, Sara, *Digital Humanities in Biblical, Early Jewish and Early Christian Studies* (*Scholarly Communication* 2), Leiden: Brill, 2013.

2 Volume DBS 2: Bigot Juloux, Vanessa, Gansell, Amy Rebecca, di Ludovico, Alessandro (eds.), Cyberresearch *on the Ancient Near East and Neighboring Regions: Case studies on archaeological data, objects, texts and digital archiving* (*DBS* 2), Brill, 2018.

same time, we have favoured an explicit description of our subject. Indeed, the intention in creating our research groups was to link together fields that are often distinct. Regarding the discussion about categories of *corpora* in Ancient Jewish and Christian texts, our research groups have provided since 2012 open spaces to consider the impact of the new medium of digital writing. We believe that our efforts exemplify the potential of digital scholarship as described by John Shaw: "Scholars traditionally begin projects by figuring out what the good research questions are in a given field, and connecting with others interested in the same topics; they then gather and organize data; then analyze it; and finally, disseminate their findings through teaching or publication. Scholarship in a digital environment raises questions about every aspect of this process. For example, in gathering and organizing data".[3] In other words, the Humanities studied with digital methods and sources can look quite "messy" in comparison to traditional Humanities scholarship, changing the order of the research steps, raising questions at least as often as bringing answers, and testing tools without advance knowledge of their full methodological implications.

If somebody or something has to plead "guilty" for this apparently messy way of working, the main instigator is the digital medium itself. Indeed, as Roger Chartier demonstrated, the writing medium has historically deeply influenced ideas and concepts, and the digital turn represents the greatest change since the passage from the scroll to the codex.[4] As he summarizes, "the cross between the two systems that governed previous *reading* material (the *volumen* and then the *codex*) produces, in fact, an entirely new relationship with the text. Thanks to these mutations, the electronic text is able to allow the realization of the never-ending dreams of conquering all knowledge that preceded it".[5] In this relationship to textuality, the rhythm of data production and publishing is reshaping Humanities research profoundly. The digital world allows data to be constantly updated, openly accessible online, and in various forms. Publishing formats can be short syntheses of datasets in blogs, videos,

3 Shaw, John, "Humanities, Digitized. Reconceiving the study of culture," *Harvard Magazine*, May-June 2012, 40-44, 73-75, <http://harvardmag.com/pdf/2012/05-pdfs/0512-40.pdf>, accessed on 10/04/19, here p.42.

4 See Chartier, Roger, *Les métamorphoses du livre. Les rendez-vous de l'édition. Le livre et le numérique*, Paris : Bibliothèque du Centre Pompidou, 2001, 8; Vandendorpe, Christian, *From Papyrus to Hypertext: Toward the Universal Digital Library*, trans. Scott, Phyllis Arnoff, H. [Topics in the Digital Humanities], Urbana (IL), Champaign (IL): University of Illinois Press, 2009, 127.

5 See Chartier, Roger, "Lecteurs et lectures à l'âge de la textualité électronique," *Texte-e: Le texte à l'heure de l'Internet*, Paris : Bibliothèque Publique d'Information, 2003, here p. 23 (our translation).

short posts or draft papers, social media, even before the research is completed and peer-reviewed. Peer-reviewed journals like *New Testament Studies* now allow authors to reference blogs of individual scholars.[6]

Questions relating to expertise and evaluation are consequently at stake in such a situation, and challenges are raised by open access publishing. For example, new ways of publishing are changing the speed with which data is made available, and also the ways that peer review works. Just take for example the *Journal of Data Mining & Digital Humanities*: it requests from authors that they deposit prior to peer review their articles in open repositories, such as HAL.[7] This means that, effectively, the article is available online as soon as it is submitted, with the label of the journal attached to it[8]. Such innovations in practices will require the peer-review process to evolve: it can be considered more and more as a potential multi-layered phenomenon, with different steps in time.[9]

"Rhythm" is consequently a key-word and concept to observe the changes happening in Digital Humanities research. If we look at the great but unfortunately lesser-known work of the French thinker and writer Henri Meschonnic, we can understand why rhythm is a key concept at the crossroads of written/literary production, data production and publication, and the social performances of the scholar available in talks and videos online. Throughout all of Meschonnic's work, he highlighted the importance of orality, and as a linguist

---

6 See Emmel, Stephen, "The Codicology of the New Coptic (Lycopolitan) Gospel of John Fragment (and its Relevance for Assessing the Genuineness of the Recently Published Coptic 'Gospel of Jesus' Wife' Fragment)," 22/06/2014, <http://alinsuciu.com////guest-post-stephen-emmel-the-codicology-of-the-new-coptic-lycopolitan-gospel-of-john-fragment-and-its-relevance-for-assessing-the-genuineness-of-the-recently-published-coptic-go-/>, accessed March 26, 2018; quoted by Gathercole, Simon, "The Gospel of Jesus' Wife: Constructing a Context," *New Testament Studies* 61, 2015, 292-313, here p. 292, footnote 1; <https://doi.org/10.1017/S0028688515000107>, accessed on 10/04/19.

7 <https://hal.archives-ouvertes.fr>, accessed on 10/04/19.

8 Clivaz, Claire, Schulthess, Sara, Sankar, Martial, "Editing New Testament Arabic Manuscripts on a TEI-base: fostering close reading in Digital Humanities", first published in 2016 on HAL while submitted to a special *JDMDH* number on *Computer-Aided Processing of Intertextuality in Ancient Languages*, <https://hal.archives-ouvertes.fr/hal-01280627>, accessed on 03/06/18. The accepted final version was published in 2017: Clivaz, Claire, Schulthess, Sara, Sankar, Martial, "Editing New Testament Arabic Manuscripts on a TEI-base: fostering close reading in Digital Humanities", *Journal of Data Mining & Digital Humanities, Special issue* (*Computer-Aided Processing of Intertextuality in Ancient Languages*), *Episciences.org*, 2017, 1-6, <https://jdmdh.episciences.org/paper/view?id=3700>, accessed on 10/04/19.

9 For a development on this question, see the chapter "community-based filtering" in Fitzpatrick, Kathleen, *Planned Obsolescence: Publishing, Technology, and the Future of the Academy*, New York, NYU Press, 2009, <http://mcpress.media-commons.org/plannedobsolescence/one/community-based-filtering/>, accessed on 10/04/19.

as well as a poet, he considered that writing is not opposed to orality, just as signification is not opposed to sound. Notably influenced by the reading and translation of Hebrew biblical texts, he was struck by the numerous marks of orality inscribed within Hebrew texts, and in 1995, he wrote an essay about the notion of "rhythm" in writing, *Politique du rythme, politique du sujet*.[10] The subject who is speaking always remains related to a performance, to a social act. The speaking subject is a "body-social-language", in writing as well as in speaking. Consequently, rhythm constitutes the principal operator of sense in the discourse, and it produces the meaning: "Le sens étant l'activité du sujet de l'énonciation, le rythme est l'organisation du sujet comme discours dans et par son discours".[11] If, as he argues, rhythm organizes and animates discourse, either written or spoken through the subject who is always involved in a social performance (whatever means of expression he/she uses), the same should extend to other forms of discourse. This suggests that the concept of rhythm can also be usefully employed to map transformations within the Humanities and digital culture, including the rhythm that animates data production, data mining, and data editing and publishing.

Given the rather fast rhythm of digital culture, it might appear surprising to initiate a series that includes traditional paper books, a process that requires time. But we believe that Humanities knowledge still benefits from the reflection built into the processes of paper book production, and likewise, that paper books will endure. Still, our practices are in deep transformation, and, without wishing to be the Pythia, we hope that the day will soon come when scholars no longer think in terms of a distinct field called the "Digital Humanities," but rather expect the Humanities to be studied using digital methods and sources. We only have to consider the history of computing. No one today would speak about a "digital computer", an expression that we would consider to be redundant, whereas it once was common to speak about a "digital computer". The first written trace of this expression can be found in the scientific report written in 1942 by George Robert Stibitz, according to Bernard Williams' inquiry.[12] In 1950, Alan Turing also used it in his famous article "Computing Machinery and Intelligence".[13]

10 Meschonnic, Henri, *Politique du rythme, politique du sujet*, Lagrasse : Verdier, 1995.

11 Meschonnic, Henri, *Critique du rythme. Anthropologie historique du langage*, Lagrasse : Verdier, 1982, 217.

12 Williams, Bernard, *Computing with Electricity, 1935-1945, PhD Dissertation, University of Kansas, 1984*, USA: University Microfilms International, 1987, 310. See also the monograph of Dennhardt, Robert, *The Term Digital Computer (Stibitz 1942) and the Flip-Flop (Turner 1920)*, Norderstedt: Grin Verlag, 2016.

13 See Turing, Alan, "Computing Machinery and Intelligence", *Mind* 49, 1950, 433-460, <http://phil415.pbworks.com/f/TuringComputing.pdf>, for example p. 50, accessed on 10/04/19.

Indeed, we can expect the Humanities to be entirely digitized within some years, at which point we will no longer need to mention "the digital" as such.[14] With this volume, we therefore affirm that the Humanities will persist in its core areas of enquiry since knowledge, social interactions and political challenges continue to require deep practices of interpretation. As the French thinker Yves Citton underlines it, *interpretation* is the key skill that our societies urgently need: "J'aimerais suggérer que nos 'sociétés de la connaissance' méritent d'être analysées comme étant avant tout des *cultures de l'interprétation* – et que la remise au premier plan des questions d'interprétation doit nous conduire à revoir profondément à la fois notre vision des interactions sociales, notre cartographie des savoirs, la structuration de nos institutions d'éducation supérieure et la formulation de nos revendications politiques".[15] Let's hope that digitized Humanities will listen to such a call and play their important cards in the knowledge play an important part in needing societies' needs.

2 Content of the Volume

The volume presents articles enlightening the "the availability of manuscripts to paradigms and practices of textual scholarship" (Liv Ingeborg Lied)[16]. Her essay and this entire volume can be approached as part of the so-called "Third Wave Digital Humanities Studies", "perceived as studies exploring the effect of the digital turn on the practices, epistemologies and paradigms of Humanities scholarship".[17] The maturation of data visualization and mining represents a current media shift that can be contextualized within long-term media history, "seeing the turn to digital images as yet another remediation of materially extant texts in manuscripts", as Ingeborg Lied explains[18]. To illustrate this turn toward digital images, the reader should not be surprised to find a special emphasis on manuscripts in this volume. Indeed, as pointed by Claire Clivaz in 2016, religious studies in Antiquity remain mainly textual Humanities: their "focus is clearly on texts and textuality, which have been the center of Jewish and Christian studies for centuries, while archeology and art history were

14 For a full discussion of this point and the general meaning – in French – of *Humanités*, see Clivaz, Claire, "Lost in translation? The odyssey of 'digital humanities' in French", *Studia UBB Digitalia* 62, 2017/1, 26-41, <http://digihubb.centre.ubbcluj.ro/journal/index.php/digitalia/article/view/4/18 1>, accessed on 10/04/19.

15 Citton, Yves, *L'Avenir des Humanités. Économie de la connaissance ou culture de l'interprétation ?,* Paris : La Découverte, 2010, 21.

16 See p. 17.

17 See p. 17.

18 See p. 17.

considered side disciplines. Data visualization and the resulting digital storm will surely contribute to progressively transforming" their content.[19]

Such an evolution will still take time, and it can already be considered as an important step to present a volume that proposes to *look* at the manuscript data, at the same time or even may before *reading* them. Even for the Humanities considered in general, the merits of data visualisation are not evident. For example, Johanna Drucker has qualified in 2011 the graphical tools as a "Trojan horse": "As digital visualization tools have become more ubiquitous, humanists have adopted many applications such as GIS mapping, graphs, and charts for statistical display that were developed in other disciplines. But, I will argue, such graphical tools are a kind of intellectual Trojan horse, a vehicle through which assumptions about what constitutes information swarm with potent force. These assumptions are cloaked in a rhetoric taken wholesale from the techniques of the empirical sciences that conceals their epistemological biases under a guise of familiarity".[20] Exploring this tricky aspect of visualisation for the textual Humanities, Pete Phillips' article in our volume puts the Ancient religions readers in front of what becomes everyday more obvious: the fragility of the text.

Phillips maps the power of visual culture for Christianity, including recent input in the life of the Churches: "both Vatican II and the contemporary papacy of Pope Francis signal, in different but consonant ways, a powerful shift back to the gestalt experience of the visual – that moment of recognition when the visual reveals something profound about wider culture".[21] The role of perceptions, senses, emotions is indeed important, according to David Morgan: "Visual culture refers to all the means of constructing life-worlds – attitudes, conceptual schemata, emotion, social dynamics, institutions. In addition to images, it is ways of seeing as well as the practices that deploy images. The study of visual culture is not just about pictures, but also powerful forms of embodiment, that is, the gendered, sexual, racial, ethnic, sensuous characteristics of perception and feeling that constitute primary forms of organizing human values".[22] In the transformation provoked in Biblical, Early Jewish and

---

19 Clivaz, Claire, "Introduction. Digital Humanities in Jewish, Christian and Arabic traditions", *Journal of Religion, Media and Digital Culture* 5, 2016,1-20, here p. 5-6, <https://brill.com/downloadpdf/journals/rmdc/5/1/article-p1_1.xml>, accessed on 10/04/19.

20 Drucker, Johanna, "Humanities Approaches to Graphical Display", *DHQ* 5, 2011/1, §1, <http://www.digitalhumanities.org/dhq/vol/5/1/000091/000091.html>, accessed on 10/04/19.

21 See p. 32.

22 Morgan, David, *The Embodied Eye, Religious Visual Culture and the Social Life of Feeling*, USA: University of California Press, 2012, 31, quoted p. 33 below.

Christian studies by the wave of the data visualization and mining, this volume represents only a piece of the mosaic, but hopes to help the readers to appreciate the richness of this turn.

Our volume is built in three sections. The first section presents two overview articles on the topic (Ingeborg Lied and Peter M. Phillips) and two articles that illustrate specific cases (Brent Landau, Adeline Harrington and James C. Henriques, and Stephen J. Davis). The second section is focused on data mining, with two articles on quantitative analysis and comparison (Thibaut Clérice and Matt Munson, and Paul Robertson), one article about natural language processing (Brett Graham) and one article about electronic transcription (H.A.G. Houghton). Formally speaking, it can be noticed that these articles solicit visualisation not only at the conceptual level in their texts, but also practically through tables and patterns, that present other ways to look at the data. The third section focuses on communication, with two articles on teaching (Heather Dana Davis Parker & Christopher A. Rollston, and Jennifer Aileen Quigley & Laura Salah Nasrallah), one article about communication inside of scholarship and the notion of forgery (James F. McGrath), and finally a project report (Bradley C. Erickson). The three sections together illustrate Paul Dilley's definition of digital philology, as "new scholarly interpretive practices that both produce and are enacted by the transfer of texts from manuscripts and the printed page to digital files subject to computational analysis and visualization"[23].

In Part 1, Lied and Phillips present overviews about of a visualization and its epistemological consequences on textuality. In "Digitization and Manuscripts as Visual Objects: Reflections from a Media Studies Perspective", Lied explores the outcome of digitization of manuscripts in libraries as an ongoing media shift. She considers the increased presence of online manuscripts and the changes they provoke in editing practices. She ponders what are "the academic reader's expectations to the content and format of critical editions?".[24] At the end of the article, the reader will have an overview of editing practices and readers' expectations when manuscripts can be seen online. In "The Power of Visual Culture and The Fragility of the Text", Phillips dares to raise the ultimate question that stands behind visualisation: the fragility – and potentially the diminution or even disappearance – of the text itself. He evokes the European social imaginary and the "pictural turn" in contemporary society. Three visual

23 Dilley, Paul, "Digital Philology between Alexandria and Babel", in: *Ancient Worlds in Digital Culture* (Digital Biblical Studies 1), ed. Clivaz, Claire, Dilley, Paul, Hamidović, David, in collaboration with Apolline Thromas, Leiden: Brill, 2016, 17-34; here p. 18.

24 See p. 20.

explorations of the Biblical text are discussed: an exhibition of the Lindisfarne Gospels, celebrity tweets that countain biblical references or verses, and the recent Hollywood blockbuster film, *Noah*, directed by Darren Aronofsky.

Next, the reader will find two articles concerning the latest manuscript visualization technologies. In "'What no eye has seen': Using a digital microscope to edit papyrus fragments of early Christian apocryphal writings", Brent Landau, Adeline Harrington and James C. Henriques present the technology of the digital microscope that can "take high-resolution photographs of individual letters under magnification, and some models also allow for photography in the ultraviolet and infrared light spectra"[25]. This technology is applied to three fragmentary early Christian writings: *P.Oxy.* 210 (a possible fragment of an apocryphal gospel); *P.Oxy.* 4009 (which may or may not be part of the Gospel of Peter); and *P.Oxy.* 4469 (an amulet containing part of King Abgar's letter to Jesus). The co-authors consider the importance of interdisciplinary teams and the inclusion of members with such professional skills. Next, in "Manuscripts, Monks, and Mufattishīn: Digital Access and Concerns of Cultural Heritage in the Yale Monastic Archaeology Project", Stephen Davis introduces readers to digital methods and Egypt's monasteries: what does it mean exactly to *see* monastery manuscripts and to make them visible for everybody online? Procedures, access, photos: all steps are evoked in this article that presents the cases of fragments in the Church of St. Shenoute at the White Monastery near Sohag, and the cataloguing Coptic and Arabic manuscripts at the Monastery of the Syrians in Wādī al-Naṭrūn.

Part two of the volume illustrates the developments of data mining in the study of Ancient Jewish and Christian manuscripts and electronic transcriptions and/or edited texts. Clérice and Munson and Graham's articles concern recent developments in manuscripts data mining. In "Qualitative Analysis of Semantic Language Models", Thibaut Clérice and Matt Munson aim to "make this widely used and accepted task [of automatically extracting semantic information] more useful outside of purely linguistic studies by considering how one can qualitatively assess the results returned by such algorithms".[26] They claim that the critical projection of algorithmic results belongs to the Humanities core skills, an affirmation that will surely be debated in the following works on the topic, as it deserves. In "Using Natural Language Processing to Search for Textual References", Brett Graham presents a part of his PhD research "how recent advances in NLP technology can be harnessed to search for

25 See p. 118.

26 See p. 87.

allusions and influences"[27]. He presents a generic NLP algorithm, including a set of syntax rules for textual references, "that can be used to detect any type of textual reference in any type of text (or even an oral allusion to an oral speech)".[28]

The following two articles focus on New Testament writings. In "Electronic Transcriptions of New Testament Manuscripts and their Accuracy, Documentation and Publication", Hugh Houghton describes and discusses the main transformations of digital editing as embodied in the *Novum Testamentum Graecum Editio Critica Maior*.[29] He points to the automatically generated apparatus and to new procedures involved in Greek New Testament editing: "In particular, [this article] considers the accuracy and transparency of the current transcription process for this edition, suggesting that proofreading is an important stage even if a double-blind approach has been used for the initial transcriptions and arguing for a fuller use of the TEI Header to describe the source and limitations of the transcription".[30] In a creative way, he explains the recent choice of the consortium to apply Creative Commons Licenses to its work. In "Visualizing Data in the Quantitative Comparison of Ancient Texts: A Study of Paul, Epictetus, and Philodemus", Paul Robertson focuses on Paul's letters, Epictetus' *Discourses*, and Philodemus' *On Piety* and *On Death*. He explores and applies the notion of "polythetic classification" classification to these corpora: "These forms of visualization then allow for an empirical, transparent form of comparison between texts. Qualitative analysis can productively supplement this quantitative analysis, matching specific literary and conceptual context with second-order data analysis".[31]

The third part, finally, considers communication of digital methods through teaching and other channels. Two articles focus on teaching challenges for ancient artefacts in a digital culture. In "Teaching Epigraphy in the Digital Age", Heather Dana Davis Parker and Christopher Rollston, treat Semitic epigraphy as delineating "certain aspects of the history of this field and discuss

27 See p. 118.

28 See p. 118.

29 The *Novum Testamentum Graecum Editio Critica Maior* designates the main editing project of the Greek New Testament: "The first installment of this edition appeared in 1997. The 'Catholic Epistles' (the Epistles of James, Peter, John, and Jude) are now in print. The Acts of the Apostles and – in cooperation with the renowned 'International Greek New Testament Project' – the Gospel of John are currently under preparation. The entire *Editio Critica Maior* is to be completed by 2030. This project is being supported by the Union of the German Academies of Sciences and Humanities", <https://www.academic-bible.com/en/home/current-projects/editio-critica-maior-ecm/>, accessed on 10/04/19.

30 See article's abstract on <https://brill.com/abstract/title/34930>.

31 See article's abstract on <https://brill.com/abstract/title/34930>.

the traditional means of studying ancient texts in light of new technological innovations".[32] Ancient texts and palaeographic script charts are considered in teaching, and valuable for diverse epigraphic fields. In "HarvardX's Early Christianity: The Letters of Paul: A retrospective on online teaching and learning", Jennifer Aileen Quigley and Laura Salah Nasrallah consider the effect of a MOOC (Massive Open Online Course) on New Testament teaching about the Pauline letters. It has achieved success and the authors describe what it means for teachers to be *seen* online in a classroom of thousands of people. The authors present quantitative and qualitative data about course attendance, but the main point is that "MOOCs should keep as a key goal the crafting of a public, free, and critical space for students who express a desire, no matter their location on the globe, to learn about and to discuss the Bible".[33]

With James McGrath, what is here to be *seen* are the complex relationships of scholars with their objects of study. In "Learning from Jesus' Wife: What Does Forgery Have to do with the Digital Humanities?". McGrath comes back to the hard disputed episode of the so-called *Gospel of Jesus' Wife*. He "sets aside as settled the question of the papyrus' authenticity, and explores instead what we can learn about the Digital Humanities and scholarly interaction in a digital era from the way the discussions and investigations of that work unfolded, and how issues that arose were handled"[34]. He offers readers the opportunity to consider at a distance what has been at stake in polemics by helping them to *see* the scholarly debates. Finally, we welcome in this DBS 3 volume a novelty: a project report. We consider that, in the series, it is particularly important to welcome projects reports, because of the rhythm of DH dissemination. Before a project has ended or reach its maturity and can fully be analyzed, there are several steps: the inputs of colleagues, the scholarly discussion is required at each step, and consequently the format of "project report" is acquiring a growing-up dimension in the DH scholarly process. Erickson, with "Synagogue Modeling Project Report: A Multi-faceted Approach to 3D, Academic Modeling", is the first one to test the new format. He "presents a report to address the problems of access, scale, and dimensionality that scholars face when working with material culture".[35] The readers will find information about photogrammetric and 3D models of the ancient synagogues of Beth Alpha, Sepphoris, and Hammath Tiberius.

32 See p. 189.

33 See p. 218.

34 See article's abstract on <https://brill.com/abstract/title/34930>.

35 See p. 262.

We thank warmly all our authors for offering an impressive overview of the topic and the potential of visualisation with/over textuality, and the Swiss National Science Foundation for its open access support to this volume. We express our deepest debt to our editorial assistant, Alessandra Marguerat, who prepared with so much patience and care this volume. Last but not least, our gratitude extends to Brill for its support throughout the birth of this new series, and in particular to Marjolein van Zuylen, Loes Schouten and Liesbeth Hugenholtz.

References

Bigot Juloux, Vanessa, Gansell, Amy Rebecca, di Ludovico, Alessandro (eds.), *Cyberresearch on the Ancient Near East and Neighboring Regions: Case studies on archaeological data, objects, texts and digital archiving* (DBS 2), Brill, 2018.

Chartier, Roger, *Les métamorphoses du livre. Les rendez-vous de l'édition. Le livre et le numérique*, Paris : Bibliothèque du Centre Pompidou, 2001.

Chartier, Roger, "Lecteurs et lectures à l'âge de la textualité électronique," *Texte-e: Le texte à l'heure de l'Internet*, Paris : Bibliothèque Publique d'Information, 2003.

Citton, Yves, *L'Avenir des Humanités. Économie de la connaissance ou culture de l'interprétation ?*, Paris : La Découverte, 2010.

Clivaz, Claire, Gregory, Andrew, Hamidović, David (eds), in collaboration with Schulthess, Sara, *Digital Humanities in Biblical, Early Jewish and Early Christian Studies* (*Scholarly Communication* 2), Leiden: Brill, 2013.

Clivaz, Claire, Schulthess, Sara, Sankar, Martial, "Editing New Testament Arabic Manuscripts on a TEI-base: fostering close reading in Digital Humanities", *Journal of Data Mining & Digital Humanities, Special issue* (*Computer-Aided Processing of Intertextuality in Ancient Languages*), Episciences.org, 2017, <https://jdmdh.episciences.org/paper/view?id=3700>, accessed on 03/06/18.

Clivaz, Claire, "Lost in translation? The odyssey of 'digital humanities' in French", *Studia UBB Digitalia* 62, 2017/1, 26-41, <http://digihubb.centre.ubbcluj.ro/journal/index.php/digitalia/article/view/4/181>, accessed on 10/04/19.

Clivaz, Claire, "Introduction. Digital Humanities in Jewish, Christian and Arabic traditions", *Journal of Religion, Media and Digital Culture* 5, 2016, 5-6, <https://brill.com/downloadpdf/journals/rmdc/5/1/article-p1_1.xml>, accessed on 10/04/19.

Dennhardt, Robert, *The Term Digital Computer* (*Stibitz 1942*) *and the Flip-Flop* (*Turner 1920*), Norderstedt: Grin Verlag, 2016.

Dilley, Paul, "Digital Philology between Alexandria and Babel", in: *Ancient Worlds in Digital Culture* (Digital Biblical Studies 1), ed. Clivaz, Claire, Dilley, Paul, Hamidović, David, in collaboration with Apolline Thromas, Leiden: Brill, 2016, 17-34.

Drucker, Johanna, "Humanities Approaches to Graphical Display", *DHQ 5*, 2011/1, <http://www.digitalhumanities.org/dhq/vol/5/1/000091/000091.html>, accessed on 10/04/19.

Emmel, Stephen, "The Codicology of the New Coptic (Lycopolitan) Gospel of John Fragment (and its Relevance for Assessing the Genuineness of the Recently Published Coptic 'Gospel of Jesus' Wife' Fragment)," 22/06/2014, <http://alinsuciu.com////guest-post-stephen-emmel-the-codicology-of-the-new-coptic-lycopolitan-gospel-of-john-fragment-and-its-relevance-for-assessing-the-genuineness-of-the-recently-published-coptic-go-/>, accessed on 10/04/19.

Fitzpatrick, Kathleen, *Planned Obsolescence: Publishing, Technology, and the Future of the Academy*, New York, NYU Press, 2009, <http://mcpress.media-commons.org/plannedobsolescence/one/community-based-filtering/>, accessed on 10/04/19.

Gathercole, Simon, "The Gospel of Jesus' Wife: Constructing a Context," *New Testament Studies 61*, 2015, 292-313.

Meschonnic, Henri, *Politique du rythme, politique du sujet*, Lagrasse : Verdier, 1995.

Meschonnic, Henri, *Critique du rythme. Anthropologie historique du langage*, Lagrasse : Verdier, 1982.

Morgan, David, *The Embodied Eye, Religious Visual Culture and the Social Life of Feeling*, USA: University of California Press, 2012.

Shaw, John, "Humanities, Digitized. Reconceiving the study of culture," *Harvard Magazine*, May-June 2012, 40-44, 73-75, <http://harvardmag.com/pdf/2012/05-pdfs/0512-40.pdf>, accessed on 10/04/19.

Turing, Alan, "Computing Machinery and Intelligence", *Mind 49*, 1950, 433-460, <http://phil415.pbworks.com/f/TuringComputing.pdf>, accessed on 10/04/19.

The Union of the German Academies of Sciences and Humanities", <http://www.academic-bible.com/en/home/current-projects/editio-critica-maior-ecm/>, accessed on 10/04/19.

Vandendorpe, Christian, *From Papyrus to Hypertext: Toward the Universal Digital Library*, trans. Scott, Phyllis Arnoff, H. [Topics in the Digital Humanities], Urbana (IL), Champaign (IL): University of Illinois Press, 2009.

Williams, Bernard, *Computing with Electricity, 1935-1945, PhD Dissertation, University of Kansas, 1984*, USA: University Microfilms International, 1987, 310.

PART 1

Visualising the Manuscripts

CHAPTER 1

Digitization and Manuscripts as Visual Objects: Reflections from a Media Studies Perspective

Liv Ingeborg Lied

1 Introduction

At the time of writing this essay, libraries and collections worldwide are slowly, but steadily, in the process of digitizing their manuscript collections and making them available online.[1] The *Bibliothèque nationale de France* in Paris, the Vatican Library in Rome, and the British Library in London have been in the process of digitizing their manuscript repositories for quite a while.[2] In recent years, several other holders of large manuscript repositories have announced that they will digitize their collections, in whole or in part; among them the National Library of Greece in Athens.[3]

In addition to the growing digital repositories of major libraries and collections, a series of other online sites have also provided digital images and new tools for exploring manuscripts. Sites, such as E-ktobe, aim to provide digital images and searchable information for all Syriac manuscripts[4] and the Hill Museum & Manuscript Library (HMML) has recently launched an online read-

1 The main ideas of this essay were first formulated in the blog post "Digitization and Manuscripts as Visual Objects: Effects of a Media Change" posted on *Religion – Manuscripts – Media Culture*: (<http://livlied.blogspot.no/2015/01/digitization-and-manuscripts-as-visual.html>), accessed on 10/04/19. The revised version of the essay was presented as an oral paper at the "Data Visualization, Digital Paleography and Images-session" of the SBL *Digital Humanities in Biblical, Early Jewish, and Christian Studies* at the *Annual Meeting* in Atlanta, Tuesday November 24, 2015. The paper version is available on *Academia.edu*: (<https://www.academia.edu/24937072/Digitization_and_Manuscripts_as_Visual_Objects_Reflections_from_ Media_Studies_Perspective_SBL_Paper_2015_>), accessed on 10/04/19. Thanks are due to John Durham Peters for his input on a draftversion of the revised essay.

2 See: <https://www.bnf.fr/fr>; <https://www.bl.uk/manuscripts/>; <http://digi.vatlib.it/news/#news-0>, accessed on 10/04/19. For an example of a large scale, cross-institutional digitizing project, cf. the Swiss e-codices project. See: <http://www.e-codices.unifr.ch/en>, accessed on 10/04/19.

3 See: <http://www.csntm.org/News/Archive/2015/1/12/CSNTMtoDigitizeManuscriptsattheNationalLibraryofGreece>, accessed on 10/04/19.

4 See: <http://syriac.msscatalog.org/>, accessed on 10/04/19.

 | DOI:10.1163/9789004399297_003

ing room for scholars.[5] Yet other sites may serve as online collaborative workshops where manuscripts are transcribed, translated, or edited, or they may serve as combined archives and connecting tools for scholars working on specific manuscript materials. In effect, although large repositories of manuscripts are still not digitized, these and other recent projects are turning more and more manuscripts into digital objects online.[6]

Images of manuscripts are not only there for scholars who actively seek them in their new online locations. In their capacity as digital objects, manuscripts may be seen as among the winners of the new, hyperconnected academic world, being the perfect combination of old mystery and venerable aesthetics in sharing cultures online. Manuscripts have become academic clickbait, images of manuscripts are favored objects of tweeting and retweeting,[7] Facebook groups are dedicated to them,[8] and specialized blogs update their followers regularly.[9]

Due to the ongoing digitization of manuscript collections as well as the steady flow of images in social media communication, scholars in the relevant fields are now more regularly exposed to manuscripts and they will become more familiar with the visual aspects of text-carrying manuscripts than ever before. And as time goes by and more libraries will experience the growing demand for digitization of their collections, scholars will probably expect to find manuscripts available online.

Today, scholars are increasingly and to a large degree living digitized lives. The generations of scholars who now make up the faculty at various universities live that life as "digital immigrants" – they did not grow up with it/there. However, the generations that are students at universities now, and those who will become students during the next decades will be "digital natives."[10] If the

5 See: <http://www.hmml.org/news--media/sneak-peeks-of-vhmml-reading-room-now-available>, accessed on 10/04/19.

6 In the present essay, I use the term "digital" to refer to the outcome of transforming an object into a digital code, mediated, and made available, graspable, and socially relevant through a computational device.

7 See: @DamienKempf, 26599 followers the 25th of October 2016. For a critical engagement with this phenomenon see: <http://www.historytoday.com/kate-wiles/monetising-past-medieval-marginalia-and-social-media>, accessed on 10/04/19.

8 When accessed on October 26, 2016, *Sexy Codicology*, for example, had 10479 followers, and Alin Suciu's *Coptic Literature and Manuscripts* had 5335 followers.

9 Roberta Mazza's blog *Faces and Voices* (<https://facesandvoices.wordpress.com/>), Adam McCollum's *HMML Orientalia*. See: <https://hmmlorientalia.wordpress.com> and *The British Library Medieval Manuscripts Blog*. See: <http://blogs.bl.uk/digitisedmanuscripts/index.html>, accessed on 10/04/19, just to mention a few.

10 Expression coined by Marc Prensky, "Digital Natives, Digital Immigrants", *On the Horizon* 9:5, 2001, 1-6.

process continues as it does now, looking up a manuscript online will be the intuitive thing to do for these generations of new scholars and they will do it with the skill and literacy of a native.[11]

In this essay, I wish to present and reflect on some possible effects of the ongoing digitization on scholarly engagement with manuscripts and the texts contained in them. I wish to approach this process in terms of a media shift, and I will be drawing on insights from the field of media studies – media history/media archaeology, and studies of digital and visual media in particular – in order to hypothesize about its possible effect on scholarly practices. I will explore the digitization of manuscripts as a case study, discussing how digitization may change scholarly practices in fields that apply manuscripts and their texts as their primary sources. As such, this essay can be approached as part of, or at least inspired by, the so-called Third Wave Digital Humanities Studies, perceived as studies exploring the effect of the digital turn on the practices, epistemologies and paradigms of Humanities scholarship.[12]

This current media shift could fruitfully also be contextualized in perspective of the *long durée* of media history, seeing the turn to digital images as yet another remediation of materially extant texts in manuscripts. Manuscripts are themselves old media. Their folia mediate both the text inscribed in the writing area of the pages and the verbal, as well as non-verbal, notes inscribed in the margins and elsewhere. Furthermore, manuscripts and their texts have been remediated throughout history in the form of, for instance, subsequent manuscript copies, as well as through printed critical editions, facsimiles, microfilms, and analogue photos. In this sense, the most recent digital turn is but one in a series of "turns" that have remediated the texts found in manuscripts.

It should be noted that the current essay is explorative and forward-gazing in nature. This essay asks questions and presents hypotheses: it does not provide fixed conclusions based on empirical research. The questions that are posed in the following are:

---

11 At the time being, one of the challenges to a fruitful engagement with digital manuscripts is that it is difficult to get an overview of the available resources. See: <http://www.dotporterdigital.org/>, accessed on 10/04/19, HT Caroline T. Schroeder on Facebook. Recently, portals offering ordering tools and lists of digitized collections are starting to appear, e.g., the overview of digitized manuscripts in Syriac, Arabic and Garshuni at *Syria.ac*. See: <http://syri.ac/digimss>, accessed on 10/04/19.

12 Berry, David M., "The Computational Turn: Thinking about the Digital Humanities", *Culture Machine* 12, 2011, 1-22, particularly p. 4 and 9.

How may the increased presence of manuscripts online contribute to a change in editing practices, as well as the academic reader's expectations to the content and format of critical editions? How may the increased presence of digitized manuscripts online affect studies of manuscripts beyond editorial practices? (How) will the digitization of manuscripts change the needs of scholars to access manuscripts in libraries and collections?

2 Media Change, Digital Turn, Visual Media

During the last 50 years, media scholars have given much attention to media changes and their effects, from the introduction of writing in largely oral societies in Antiquity to the contemporary digital and connective turn. These turns and their effects have been theorized differently across the broad field of media studies, and beyond.[13] The ways in which the relationship between humans and technology is construed differ, including: the degrees to which technology is ascribed agency; and, the extent to which a human person is regarded a discrete entity or better understood as networked, distributed, extended, or something the world flows through. Likewise, the interconnectedness of various media and the ways in which the relationship between media and cultural change (and vice-versa) are viewed are among the aspects that vary. The following sketch is an eclectic and heuristic presentation of some points of particular relevance to the discussion of the present essay.

A first, often stressed, feature that serves as a fundamental point of departure in the field of media history/media archaeology is the shared basic contention that media matter, and that changes in technological media will influence human sensation, experience, knowledge, and/or practice.[14] This widespread and foundational claim has typically been formulated as a response to other academic perspectives on history that are deemed blind to the role of media, or accused of seeing media only as tools. Instead, in these fields media technology has been approached, for instance, as embedded in human experience, or gradually creating new human environments, opening up for extended sense perception, and thus changing the way in which we think and

13 The assumption of a digital turn has of course also been criticised. See, for instance, Mitchell, W.J.T., *Image Science: Iconology, Visual Culture, and Media Aesthetics*, Chicago and London: The University of Chicago Press, 2015, 115.

14 It almost goes without saying that academic cultures and practices should be regarded just as any other human practice. Academic practices are not beyond or above these shifts, coolly looking down on them: they are integral parts of them.

act. Thus, in some oft cited, emblematically used references, it is hypothesized that media technology will create epistemic changes. It will change the perception, memory, communication, and social practices surrounding the mediated object, and as such it is held that we cannot understand human history without also exploring the materialities of communication; that is, the media of historical and cultural transmission.[15]

A second point, drawn from discussions in the fields of media aesthetics, visual media and visualization studies is the current increasing importance of the computer medium, the screen interface, and the mode of the image.[16] With the growing privileging of computational devices as society's main medium of communication, it has been held that information will increasingly be visually formatted and displayed, and subsequently digested through the sense of sight. Such a development would bring the image into the center of communication and add weight to the role of visual perception as a cognitive activity, also in academic pursuits.[17]

For sure, the claim as to the increasing dominance of the visual and the mode of the image is contested.[18] Current debates on digital images and digital materiality discuss the aspects of referentiality and of realism, which point to more complex views on the role of the visual.[19] On the one hand, these debates respond to assumptions that the digital images of objects are less real than the objects themselves, or "unreal" altogether. On the other hand, they respond to the notion that an image is a one-to-one representation, a stand-in or simulation based on the idea of an indexical relation between image and the object represented in the image.[20] It is of particular importance to the current essay that these debates have pointed out how a digital image is, in crucial ways,

15 Emblematically and representing the variety of perspectives involved: Kittler, Friedrich, *Nedskrivningssystem 1800-1900*, Göteborg; Glänta production, 2012, esp. 379. Originally in German: *Aufschreibesysteme1800-1900*, München: Fink, 1985. McLuhan, Marshall, *Understanding Media: The Extensions of Man*, New York: McGraw Hill, 1964, 5-6, 21. Lyotard, Jean-F., *La condition postmoderne*, Paris: Les éditions de minuit, 1979. Altheide, David, Snow, Robert, *Media Logic*, Beverly Hills, CA: Sage, 1979. Latour, Bruno, "Visualization and Cognition: Thinking with Eyes and Hands", *Knowledge and Society 6*, 1986, 1-40. Kress, Gunther, *Literacy in the New Media Age*, Literacies; London and New York: Routledge, 2003, 1-7.

16 In particular, Rudolf Arnheim, *Visual Thinking*, London: Faber and Faber, 1970. Mitchell, W.J.T., *Image Science*, and confer the main ideas and foci of Kittler, Friedrich, *Nedskrivningssystem* (Aufschreibesysteme) *1800- 1900*.

17 Kress, Gunther, *Literacy in the New Media Age*, 1-7, 9-10.

18 Mitchell, W.J.T., *Image Science*, esp. 115, 125, 130.

19 Ibid., 49-64.

20 Ibid., 53 and Bolter, David, Grusin, Richard, *Remediation: Understanding New Media*, Cambridge, MA: MIT Press, 2000.

"another thing" that deserves to be studied and understood in its own right and in its own context. Although related and intermingled with the object it portrays, a digital image is not a mere representation of the physical object appearing in the image, and hence not reducible to that object. Being a digital image, the image is part of a new constellation and dependent on a new interface. Digital images become part of and are dependent on the digital space in which they appear. They share in a specific configuration that instantiates the information that is there for us to study.

The implications of this theoretical nuancing of the ontology and epistemology of the visual mode are important to the current discussion of digital images of text-carrying manuscripts, because they highlight the multimedial access to the texts in manuscripts and the multisensory approach necessary for studying them. On the one hand, the digitization of manuscripts makes them visually available as digital objects and thus produces different and complementary possibilities of study. On the other hand, even though the increasing availability of digital images privileges the sense of seeing and the visual aspects of manuscripts and their texts, this does not mean that the media that are represented in such images (the manuscripts) will be superfluous, that other aspects of these media are rendered uninteresting, or that other modes of interaction will be considered dated. Rather, the image in its digital space and the palpable, material manuscript in its given physical location are different constellations and different mediations of a text. As such, the visually available digital object is an addition to the media and modes of interaction that we already have. It invites different forms of sensation and usage, it is part of different practices, and it tends to produce different sets of stories connected to it.[21] If we want to explore the potential effects of the scholarly use of digital manuscripts, then we need to study how this new mediation may create new perceptions and practices and how it may be related to, differ from, and/or intertwined with interactions with other, "old," modes of mediation.

3 Digitized Manuscripts, Editorial Practices, Readers' Expectations

In the light of these theoretical musings, it is time to pose the first question: how may the increased presence of visually available manuscripts online contribute to a change in editing practices, as well as the academic reader's expectations to the content and format of critical editions?

21 Røssaak, Eivind, "Archive in Motion: An Introduction", in *The Archive in Motion: New Conceptions of the Archive in Contemporary Thought and New Media Practices*, ed. Røssaak, Eivind, Oslo: Novus Press, 2010, 18, 22. Mitchell, W.J.T., *Image Science*, 56.

To suggest some possible answers to this question, I will start by reiterating how scholars of biblical studies, as well as scholars of other fields specializing in the editing and interpretation of ancient texts, have typically become acquainted with manuscripts during the last centuries. I will also discuss how that in turn may have affected the imaginations and expectations of these scholars.

Until recently, manuscripts have been physical artifacts that are kept, for instance, in monastery storage rooms, on library shelves, or in private collections – and, of course, they still are, since "old media rarely die."[22] Although many manuscripts are certainly lost, papyrus, parchment and paper have proven to be relatively durable materials that are apt for communicating texts to posterity. However, for various reasons, these physical artifacts have typically been seen and engaged only by a select few.[23] Some collections have restrictive access policies. Some scholars are never able to visit special collections due to economic, communicational, or technological limitations. Importantly, in many fields, such as New Testament Studies, a traditional division of labor between those who edit texts and those who interpret them has shaped a contention that only the editors have a real need to study manuscripts.[24]

In addition to being tangible artifacts in their physical locations, manuscripts have been remediated via microfilms, analogue photos and facsimile editions. However, for a long time the main medium of acquaintance with manuscripts has been print editions of the texts contained in the manuscripts. Hence, its major presence in the everyday life of most academics has been this remediated form where the manuscript is represented symbolically as a *siglum* in the apparatus. It is likely that this remediation has affected the way that manuscripts have been imagined. As Brent Nongbri has pointed out, the manuscript, *qua siglum*, has been part of a symbolic academic language that scholars of ancient texts have had to learn – in addition to Greek, Hebrew and other ancient languages.[25] In this context of use and mediation, the manuscript has been of interest primarily due to the text found in the writing area. It has been

22 Peters, John Durham, *The Marvelous Clouds: Towards a Philosophy of Elemental Media*, Chicago and London: University of Chicago Press, 2015, 23.

23 "[The archive] used to be the abode of secrets, silence, of dust", Røssaak, Eivind, *Archive in Motion*, 16.

24 Hurtado, Larry, *The Earliest Christian Artefacts: Manuscripts and Christian Origins*, Grand Rapids, MI: Eerdmans, 2006, esp. the introductory pages. In other fields, such as the study of the Dead Sea Scrolls, scholars have so far been working on manuscript materials to a much larger degree.

25 Nongbri, Brent, "A Very Brief Introduction to the Critical Apparatus to the Nestle-Aaland", revised 2006, 3. Available online at: <https://www.marquette.edu/maqom/ApparatusGuide.pdf>, accessed on 10/04/19.

discoursed in the vocabulary of a text critical paradigm in terms of a "text witnesses," first and foremost pointing away from itself and its own materiality and cultural context towards an ancient text.

However, when manuscripts are increasingly available as digital objects, they have now become visually accessible in all their unruly glory. They are only "a click away," and as suggested initially, when more libraries digitize their collections, the manuscripts will subsequently be expected to be no more than a click away. Hence, during the next decade(s) manuscripts may be visually available to the groups of scholars who already have the necessary language competences and who know the contents of the texts from editions very well through their exegetical work on texts, but who have traditionally not engaged much with manuscripts.

How will this situation change editing? Scholars who have worked on texts based both on studies of the manuscripts and the use of print editions know how different the visual impression of a manuscript page and a page of a critical edition may be. Scholars acquainted with manuscripts also know how poorly the critical apparatus may sometimes represent the various features on the manuscript page. The hand may, for instance, be difficult to read, words and letters may be open to interpretation, texts may be lacunose, the script may be continuous, or there may be no paragraph- or other division markers on the page. Manuscript pages may be messy too. They typically contain notes, glosses, corrections and erasures. They may also contain other paratextual features, study and memory aids, designed to communicate between text and reader.

In traditional print editions, some of these traits have been treated in the apparatus or in footnotes and commentary. Others have been overlooked, regarded as irrelevant, or as clutter. It might also have been regarded difficult or too expensive to reproduce paratextual features such as these in a printed book. However, now, when the manuscripts are available online, the unruly elements of a manuscript page are there for everyone to see. These elements may even come as a surprise to those who did not know of their existence.

This media change may constitute a challenge to dominant editorial practices *per se* because it will affect scholars' imagination of and acquaintance with, manuscripts. When academic users of print editions know that the manuscripts are there for them to consult online, will the representation of the messy variability present on manuscript pages in the form of a critical apparatus be satisfactory to them? And when editors and their publishers know that readers will be able to consult pictures of the manuscripts, will they change the way that they represent the manuscripts and the various elements found on manuscript pages, knowing that the elements of the manuscript page are visually available for their readers?

A look at some examples of ongoing projects online may suggest both how current editorial practices are already changing due to and alongside new media technology, and display how digitized manuscripts and the scholarly discourse about them are explicitly part of and formed by new media constellations. Digital manuscripts do not circulate in a void: they are often part of a larger online media package – sometimes in ways that are not traditionally associated with academic genres.

A look at the so-called Homer Multitext Project shows some of the opportunities of a current digital edition.[26] In this critical edition of Homer, the editors bring in marginalia and annotations in addition to the text in the writing area by digitally annotating the manuscripts. In this way, they use the possibilities provided by technology to make the interplay of these text units, which share the page in the manuscript, visible also in the edition. As a result, the text of the writing area is not privileged in the same way as it was previously.

Other examples can be seen in the online sites Ancient Lives and the New Testament Virtual Manuscript Room.[27] These sites show, among other things, how constellations and genres known to users from other media contexts have been brought in and are allowed to shape the engagement with the manuscripts. These sites typically include a blog or chat function, or they may include a Wiki. They connect their users "social media style" and the users apply social media language genres in their communication. The sites make engagement with manuscripts take place online and as a collaborative effort, and they are in this sense archive and communication *in tandem* – which from a theoretical and historical perspective is an interesting combination.[28] Hence, digital manuscripts are part of complex online media packages. It is likely that the entire package, not only individual digital images, may shape the way that we imagine manuscripts, how we conceptualize editorial practices and our involvement in them, and what we expect from a critical edition.

26 See: <http://www.homermultitext.org/>, accessed on 10/04/19. See also, Clivaz, Claire, "Homer and the New Testament as "Multitexts" in the Digital Age", *Scholarly and Research Communication* 3/3, 2012, 1-15. Schroeder, Caroline T., "The Digital Humanities as Cultural Capital: Implications for Biblical and Religious Studies", *Journal of Religion, Media and Digital Culture* 5/1, 2016, 21-49.

27 See: <https://www.ancientlives.org/> and <http://ntvmr.uni-muenster.de/>, both accessed on 10/04/19. Thanks are due to Alin Suciu for pointing me to these sites.

28 See: Røssaak, Eivind, *Archive in Motion*, 12, 19. Further, Kress, Gunther, *Literacy in the New Media Age*, 5, 9 10. Berry, David M., "Computational Turn", 8.

4 New Perspectives, New Studies, New Media Literacies

It is time now to address the second question: how is it likely that the increased presence of digitized manuscripts online may affect studies of these manuscripts, beyond its effects on editorial practices?

A still hypothetical answer may be that when manuscripts become visual objects online they will appeal to other categories of scholars and lend themselves to other kinds of studies than the ones we have commonly seen so far. As pointed out above, many subfields under the larger umbrella of biblical studies have been characterized by a division of labor between editors and exegetes, which has produced a division between scholars who are trained in working on manuscripts and scholars who are not. With the increased visual availability, scholars who have been exegetes may bring new interpretative tools to the study of manuscripts and their various texts, beyond those their colleagues have traditionally taken interest in, and hence giving rise to new approaches. During the last few decades, we have seen a general surge of interest in the materiality of artifacts, in the role of the medium, as well as in aesthetics, scribalism and scribal cultures, paratexts and marginalia, and reader practices in these fields. Digitized manuscripts have become an available source material for scholars who are influenced by these recent research debates.

If this proves correct, we may expect to see more studies of the various relationships between text and manuscript, and between text, manuscript and their active readers. There will probably be more studies of the role and importance of manuscript layout and aesthetic elements, as well as scribbles, doodles, notes and other text units sharing the manuscript pages. Studies of these elements in manuscripts are certainly not a novelty in the Academe,[29] but digitization and online availability will probably feed this rush, which will also be felt in biblical studies, since there is still much more to discover. We may, for instance, see more studies of manuscript pages as discursive and dialogical spaces, as spaces where the text in the writing area is sometimes contested and negotiated by later readers.[30] We may also see more studies of manuscripts

29 See, for instance, and emblematically, Carruthers, Mary, *The Book of Memory: A Study of Memory in Medieval Culture, Cambridge Studies in Medieval Literature 70*, Cambridge: Cambridge University Press, 1990. Derrida, Jacques, "This is Not an Oral Footnote", in: *Annotation and Its Texts,* ed. Stephen A. Barney, New York: Oxford University Press, 1991, 192-205. Camille, Michael, *Image on the Edge: The Margins of Medieval Art*, London: Reaktion Books, 1992.

30 Penn, Michael Philip, "Monks, Manuscripts, and Muslims: Syriac Textual Changes in Reaction to the Rise of Islam", *Hugoye: Journal of Syriac Studies 12:2*, 2009, 235-257; Penn, Michael Philip, "Moving Beyond the Palimpsest: Erasure in Syriac Manuscripts", *Journal of Early Christian Studies 18:2*, 2010, 261-303.

that were transformed and given new and different functions by later readers than the functions envisioned by the producers of the artifact.[31]

A prominent example of such a project is the ongoing, Munich-based *Paratexts of the Bible-project*, headed by Martin Wallraff and Patrick Andrist. This project explores Greek biblical manuscripts, aided by new digital imaging, focusing on the roles of individual manuscripts as textual objects that were read and interpreted, tracing paratextual elements and their mediating functions.[32] Such studies of manuscripts as culturally situated artifacts will probably both add to and challenge studies that primarily take interest in the text of the writing area and the manuscript's function as text witness or text carrier.

The increasing visual availability of manuscripts is also likely to give rise to some new challenges. There is no such thing as an easy, carefree media shift. What was once a question of availability may now increasingly become a question of media literacy – both in terms of being able to maneuver digital sites and being trained in reading manuscripts. Even though the manuscripts are in principle available, scholars must be able to retrieve the relevant materials, master the technology and understand what they see on manuscript pages. Reading Late Antique and Medieval manuscripts requires proper training. Consequently, the need for interdisciplinary cooperation will be evident and new types of literacy will be in demand.[33]

4.1 *Palpable Media, Visual Media, Mixed Media*

The third and last question that I posed above was: (how) will the digitization of manuscripts change the needs of scholars to access the manuscripts in libraries and collections?

One of the motivations behind ongoing digitization of caches of manuscripts is the preservation of vulnerable artifacts. The assumption is that when manuscripts are digitized and available online, the need for consulting the physical artifact will decrease. Due to assumptions like this, the digitization of manuscripts has already led to – and will probably continue to lead to – changes in access policies in libraries and collections. The wish to protect the

31 Childers, Jeff, "'You Will Find What You Seek': the Form and Function of a Sixth-Century Divinatory Bible in Syriac", in: *Snapshots of Evolving Traditions: Jewish and Christian Manuscript Culture, Textual Fluidity, and Material Philology*, eds., Lied, Liv Ingeborg, Lundhaug, Hugo, *Texte und Untersuchungen zur Geschichte der altchristlichen Literatur 175*, Berlin: De Gruyter, 2017, 242-271.

32 See: <http://paratexbib.eu/index.html>, accessed April 21, 2017.

33 Further, Lied, Liv Ingeborg, "Bible as Notepad: Exploring Annotations and Annotation Practices in Biblical Manuscripts", in: *Bible as Notepad*, ed., Lied, Liv Ingeborg, Maniaci, Marilena, *Manuscripta Biblica 3*, Berlin: De Gruyter, 2018.

manuscripts is noble and sometimes an absolute necessity. Furthermore, accessible digital images of a manuscript are clearly much better than having no access to the manuscript in question at all. Yet, it would be a fundamental misunderstanding of the role of media, and the intermingled processes of scholarly sensation, perception and practice, to assume that the availability of online digital images will do away with the need to consult the palpable, material manuscript.

In terms of practical research, at least three types of challenges are likely to occur. First, images, also high-resolution digital images, may hide or misrepresent features of the manuscript. Folds in the parchment may for instance hide letters that remain inaccessible in an image. Likewise, fly droppings and ink are frequently hard to tell apart in digital images. The ability to discern between the two may matter both to interpretation of words in pointed scripts as well as to delimitation criticism. Second, depending on the aim and profile of the research project, some studies will still be dependent on an exploration of the physical artifact. There is more to the manuscript than its visual features. Its texture, weight, and smell may for instance matter to studies of manuscripts as ritual objects. These features do not reach us through the computer screen. Third, it is crucial to keep in mind that images are far from neutral representations of the manuscript page. The remediation of manuscripts in digital images is also paradigm driven. The focus and framing in images may for instance be driven by, and mirror, the practices and needs of textual critics. Some digitization projects have produced high quality images of the text in the writing area, but have kept text units in the margins of the pages, fully or in part, outside the picture frame. Texts inscribed in the first and last folios and flyleaves of a codex are sometimes not included at all.

In theoretical terms, these insights can be rephrased like this: just as the traditional print edition and its apparatus is but a limited representation of the text and the manuscripts that contain it, a digital image of a manuscript is another limited representation of the text contained in physical, tactile (and smelly) artifacts. There is no doubt that digital imaging provides new opportunities and that high quality images are invaluable tools for scholars,[34] but imaging still remains a particular type of mediation, which may be apt for some types of scholarly practices and some research questions but not for all. The

34 This essay does not deal with advanced imaging, which promises to provide opportunities of research beyond the features that are described here. Advanced imaging may for instance bring out the texture of the writing surface in ways not otherwise accessible through sight and touch. In this way, images may provide opportunities that the physical object cannot. I am thankful to Todd Hanneken, as well as to one of the anonymous reviewers, for this observation.

images are not identical with the manuscripts, and the visual mode does not grasp or account for all of the qualities of a manuscript: digital images should be seen as a "deepening of the referent, not its disappearance."[35] We need to acknowledge the need for a multimedial approach to manuscripts. We should also recognize the limitations and opportunities of different media technologies. Those who work on manuscripts will frequently need to approach them across interfaces and formats – both as physical artifacts, as *sigla* in critical editions, and as visually available digital objects. One is not necessarily reducible to the other in scholarly practices.

5 Concluding Remarks and an Outlook

This essay has barely scratched the surface of a complex, ongoing, transformation of academic practices that has been ushered in by the digital turn. In this essay, I have aimed to point out how ongoing digitization projects and their resulting creation of digital repositories of manuscripts have the potential to change the ways in which scholars of manuscripts and their texts may engage with their source materials. Manuscripts, which to many have primarily been approached as "witnesses" to an older text and which have been available symbolically as *sigla* are now increasingly present as visually available artifacts. The media packages that frame the engagement with manuscripts are also changing. New technology and new interfaces enable editors to represent the text units present on manuscript pages in new ways, and academic practices of translation, transcription and commentary are becoming enmeshed with widespread social media practices.

There is potential to further explore how digitization may influence the perceptions of the physical artifacts manuscripts arguably are, including how media have historically shaped the way that we study texts and will probably do it again, how editorial paradigms and media technology have been and are intertwined, as well as how new mediations of manuscripts may provide new areas of research.

Importantly, future explorations of such aspects of scholarship may also open up for further deliberations on scholarly epistemologies and practices. For one, it is likely that the digital turn may affect the notion of the competent professional. For instance, the imagination of the biblical scholar in the new generation of "digital natives" will probably include other components than the image of the ideal biblical scholar of the past. Engaging the biblical text for

35 Mitchell, W.J.T., *Image Science*, 52.

scholarly purposes will increasingly demand a high degree of digital literacy and the longstanding division of labor between editors and exegetes will probably be challenged and crisscrossed as well. Such reevaluations of key professional expectations may subsequently, or simultaneously, involve a potential change of the discipline itself.

Another interesting aspect that clearly demands more attention in future study is the ways in which the digital turn may influence scholars' notions of the very books and texts that constitute much of their main focus. If, and when, print editions of texts are no longer the dominant medium through which scholars get acquainted and engage with books and texts, we open the floor for the unruly realities of the manuscript page. It remains to be seen how the visual availability of the manuscript page, in all its messy glory, may influence the textual imagination of the next generation.

References

Altheide, David, Snow, Robert, *Media Logic*, Beverly Hills, CA: Sage, 1979.

Arnheim, Rudolf, *Visual Thinking*, London: Faber and Faber, 1970.

Berry, David M, "The Computational Turn: Thinking about the Digital Humanities", *Culture Machine* 12, 2011, 1-22.

Bolter, David, Grusin, Richard, *Remediation: Understanding New Media,* Cambridge, MA: MIT Press, 2000.

Camille, Michael, *Image on the Edge: The Margins of Medieval Art*, London: Reaktion Books, 1992.

Carruthers, Mary, *The Book of Memory: A Study of Memory in Medieval Culture, Cambridge Studies in Medieval Literature 70*, Cambridge: Cambridge University Press, 1990.

Clivaz, Claire, "Homer and the New Testament as 'Multitexts' in the Digital Age", *Scholarly and Research Communication 3/3*, 2012, 1-15.

Derrida, Jacques, "This is Not an Oral Footnote", in: *Annotation and Its Texts,* ed., Stephen A. Barney, New York: Oxford University Press, 1991, 192-205.

Hurtado, Larry, *The Earliest Christian Artefacts: Manuscripts and Christian Origins*, Grand Rapids, MI: Eerdmans, 2006.

Kittler, Friedrich, *Aufschreibesysteme 1800–1900,* München: Fink, 1985.

Kittler, Friedrich, Friedrich, *Nedskrivningssystem 1800–1900*, Göteborg; Glänta production, 2012.

Kress, Gunther, *Literacy in the New Media Age*, Literacies, London and New York: Routledge, 2003.

Latour, Bruno, "Visualization and Cognition: Thinking with Eyes and Hands", *Knowledge and Society* 6, 1986, 1-40.

Lied, Liv Ingeborg, "Bible as Notepad: Exploring Annotations and Annotation Practices in Biblical Manuscripts", in: *Bible as Notepad*, ed., Liv Ingeborg Lied, Maniaci, Marilena, *Manuscripta Biblica 3*, Berlin: De Gruyter, 2018.

Lyotard, Jean-F., *La condition postmoderne,* Paris : Les éditions de minuit, 1979.

McLuhan, Marshall, *Understanding Media: The Extensions of Man*, New York: McGraw Hill, 1964.

Mitchell, W.J.T., *Image Science: Iconology, Visual Culture, and Media Aesthetics*, Chicago and London: The University of Chicago Press, 2015.

Nongbri, Brent, "A Very Brief Introduction to the Critical Apparatus to the Nestle-Aland", revised 2006, <http://www.marquette.edu/maqom/ApparatusGuide.pdf>.

Penn, Michael Philip, "Monks, Manuscripts, and Muslims: Syriac Textual Changes in Reaction to the Rise of Islam", *Hugoye: Journal of Syriac Studies 12:2*, 2009, 235-257.

Penn, Michael Philip, Michael Philip, "Moving Beyond the Palimpsest: Erasure in Syriac Manuscripts", *Journal of Early Christian Studies 18:2*, 2010, 261-303.

Peters, John Durham, *The Marvelous Clouds: Towards a Philosophy of Elemental Media*, Chicago and London: University of Chicago Press, 2015.

Prensky, Marc, "Digital Natives, Digital Immigrants", *On the Horizon 9:5*, 2001, 1-6.

Røssaak, Eivind, "Archive in Motion: An Introduction", in: *The Archive in Motion: New Conceptions of the Archive in Contemporary Thought and New Media Practices*, ed., Eivind Røssaak, Oslo: Novus Press, 2010, 11-26.

Schroeder, Caroline T., "The Digital Humanities as Cultural Capital: Implications for Biblical and Religious Studies", *Journal of Religion, Media and Digital Culture 5/1*, 2016, 21-49.

CHAPTER 2

The Power of Visual Culture and the Fragility of the Text

Peter M. Phillips

1 Visual Culture

In his reflections on Bible engagement in medieval Europe, Dr Eyal Poleg focuses on the centrality of the mediated bible:[1]

> Taken at face value, the dietary laws of Leviticus, the love lore of the Song of Songs, or the visions of Revelation had little to do with the values of Christian (or Jewish) medieval culture. Keeping these archaic narratives relevant and alive was thus a necessity. This led to a high degree of creativity in expounding and exploring the Bible, making biblical mediation a dynamic part of society, ever changing and bringing new texts, tunes, objects, and monuments into its ambit. The Bible was made all things to all people, in a process that was often veiled and hidden.

Poleg focuses on liturgical processions, sermons and on the Bible as a talisman, but he could have looked as well at songs, poetry, art, mystery plays, festivals and rites. Medieval society was centered around the Bible as a sourcebook for the European *imaginarium*[2], forming the basis for civic administration, law codes, and cultural expression of all kinds. The wealth of the Church and its social standing within the aristocracy, of course, meant that this was not an open process of cultural influence but one of cultural domination, the product of the Church's hold on wealth and influence throughout Christian Europe. In an age of limited literacy, Poleg shows that "the majority of men and women experienced the Bible through a carefully structured array of rituals and images, sermons and chants."[3] Indeed, one could argue that this audio-visual, aesthetic experience of the Bible has dominated Bible engagement over the last two thousand years. In our own day, the material text of the Bible is also being

1 Poleg, Eyal, *Approaching the Bible in Medieval England*, UK: Manchester University Press, 2013, 2.

2 Charles Taylor refers to the social imaginary as a gathering together of the set of values, laws, conventions and symbols common to a social group. See Charles Taylor, "Modern Social Imaginaries", *Public Culture 14*, Number 1, Winter 2002, 91-124.

3 Poleg, *Approaching the Bible*, 1.

mediated through apps and websites, through digitised manuscripts and all manners of digital expressions. We are witnesses of the ongoing mediation of the Biblical text now through contemporary expressions of visual and material culture.

The various products or artefacts of both medieval and contemporary cultural influence work together to amplify the individual impact of any one artefact. The sheer weight of biblical material across all the modes of artistic and practical expression in the medieval period witnesses to the power and dominance of the Church and creates a powerful aesthetic experience – that Christianity is normative within the European *imaginarium*. Moreover, time and again, medieval examples show oral, visual, textual and material means of dissemination converging together to multiply their effect: liturgy and preaching performed at the same time, sharing the same space and actors; visual imagery reflecting dramatic reenactments; exegetes and preachers, often the same people, mixing interpretation and homiletics; and literary narratives employing biblical and liturgical tags interchangeably.

Biblical texts, of course, themselves tend to speak in visual language, in metaphors and similes, in arresting visual stories, in parables and narratives – inviting the reader to see the events being described, to come and see Jesus, to watch the events being narrated. So, Jo-Ann Brant has skillfully explored the dramatic structures within John's Gospel, complete with prelude and epilogue, with scenes made up of Jesus as protagonist, a potential disciple as antagonist, and a chorus of disciples or local spectators.[4] At conferences of the Society of Biblical Literature, as at other gatherings of the Biblical guild, there are whole programmes exploring the Bible as a mediated and performed text.

The Bible as a whole, as well as its constituent texts, have always been part of visual culture: as stone tablets, or scrolls, or codices; as texts scrawled in graffiti or painted on murals; as mosaics embedded in villas or texts on walls. With few people able to engage with texts through reading (although perhaps significantly more than some have argued[5]), Bible engagement had to be facilitated in any way it could – usually through the mediated Bible. The advent of moveable-type print shifted the emphasis towards greater precision and accuracy and perhaps, as we shall see, created a passing domination of text over image, of precision over aesthetics. But there is a rapid shift away from such dominance. In today's digital world, the Bible remains a mediated text. Despite

4 Brant, Jo-Ann, *Dialogue and Drama: Elements of Greek Tragedy in the Fourth Gospel*, USA: Hendrickson, 2004.

5 See, for example, Wright, Brian J., "Ancient Literacy in New Testament Research: Incorporating a few more line of enquiry", *Trinity Journal* 36, 2015, 161-189.

historically superb literacy rates, the Bible is still a text engaged through visual and material culture, through performance and exhibition as well as through devotion and interpretation. So, we note the importance of Katie Edwards' edited collection exploring the role of the arts and media in contemporary biblical literacy[6], and of the work of all those who bridge the gap between culture and the Bible.

Today's exploration of the Bible through digital media is therefore a contemporary spin on a much older relationship between visual technology and the Biblical text/Biblical tech. In his exploration of Christianity and the Culture Machine, Vincent Rocchio picks up the shift from the visual/aesthetic gestalt within medieval experience of Christian practice, to the text immanence dominated by clerical authority throughout modernity/the Enlightenment. He argues strongly that both Vatican II and the contemporary papacy of Pope Francis signal, in different but consonant ways, a powerful shift back to the gestalt experience of the visual – that moment of recognition when the visual reveals something profound about wider culture. Rocchio extends his argument not so much through a discussion of the papacy but through the shifting paradigms within contemporary cinematography. Often, the tropes of mid-twentieth century Bible epics followed the lines of text/clerical dominance, but these have gradually shifted towards a more diverse exploration of biblical engagement through visual experience/gestalt.[7]

In his introduction, Rocchio explores *A Charlie Brown Christmas* (CBS, 1965), which includes a fifty- second recitation from Luke 2:8-14 from the King James Bible.[8] This section of the programme was highly controversial at the time in that it stripped away all of the usual accompaniment to the Bible on screen and instead gave the words to a contemporary child, without backing track, additional visuals, or humour. Instead, the audience is invited "to imagine – however briefly – the sacred in a post-sacred world, without resorting to a return to the past. Rather, in a message similar to Pope Francis, the narrative suggests that attending to 'the least of these' can accomplish transcendence."[9]

Mediation of cultural artefacts through visuality is at the very centre of digital culture. Contemporary society seems to have a love affair with all things visual: all manner of flashing screens; the tiresome wit of animated gifs; the vocabulary and syntax of the emoji; the ubiquity of video. David Morgan, of course, spends most of his two recent books (*The Sacred Gaze* and *The*

---

6 Edwards, Katie, *Rethinking Biblical Literacy*, UK: Bloomsbury, 2015.
7 Rocchio, Vincent, *Christianity and the Culture Machine*, Eugene: Cascade Books, 2016.
8 Rocchio, Vincent, 7-15.
9 Rocchio, Vincent, 15.

Embodied Eye) arguing strongly that 'seeing' performs religious action, or 'seeing' constructs or enacts a situation called sacred.[10] In other words, our gaze enables the construction of the sacred by investing attention and time on a given artefact or experience. We make the object the center of our attention and so sacralise it. Or as Rocchio would put it: "art and media can bring us into contact with the experience of revelation and the transcendent itself."[11]

In both books, Morgan seeks to define visual culture as both the act of seeing and the communicative sociology of that act:[12]

> Visual culture refers to all the means of constructing life-worlds – attitudes, conceptual schemata, emotion, social dynamics, institutions. In addition to images, it is ways of seeing as well as the practices that deploy images. The study of visual culture is not just about pictures, but also powerful forms of embodiment, that is, the gendered, sexual, racial, ethnic, sensuous characteristics of perception and feeling that constitute primary forms of organizing human values.

In a world of image, advertising and the apparent dominance of the visual over the textual, it is important to realize that visual culture is, in Thomas Mitchell's words, "the visual construction of the social, not just the social construction of the visual".[13] Indeed, it is not that visual culture is a social construct but that our very social arrangements take the form they do because we are seeing animals.[14] We map our world by visual construals – quite literally using maps based on Mercator's projection or Peeters', knowing that neither fully expresses geographical reality. In the information age, we increasingly seek to grapple with unfathomable amounts of data through visualization, modeling and infographics.

But none of this is new. Contemporary culture is in fact no more fixated with the visual than any other culture, as Mitchell points out, ours has been a visual culture since God looked down upon creation and saw that it was good (the repeated refrain in Gen 1:4, 10, 12, 18, 21, 25, 31) – or perhaps even when God

---

10 Morgan, David, *The Embodied Eye, Religious Visual Culture and the Social Life of Feeling*, USA: University of California Press, 2012, xiii; Morgan, David, *The Sacred Gaze: Religious Visual Culture in Theory and Practice*, USA: University of California Press, 2005.

11 Rocchio, Vincent, *Culture Machine*, 15.

12 Morgan, David, *The Embodied Eye*, 31.

13 Mitchell, W.J.T., "Showing seeing: a critique of visual culture", *Journal of Visual Culture*, Vol. 1(2), 2002, 1 166.

14 Mitchell, W.J.T.,"Showing seeing", 171.

chose to separate the light from the darkness (Gen 1:4)[15] In other words, we are not moving into a visual age: we never left the visual age. When Derrida famously declared "il n'y a pas de hors-texte" – 'there is no outside-text' – perhaps he should have said something like "il n'y a rien en dehors de l'image",[16] (although, as most of us postmodern deconstructors were shown by Roland Barthes, the Derridean text might include anything which conveys meaning, which is really anything you want it to be).

Increasingly, though, in a world which celebrates the subjective turn, or what Mitchell calls the "pictorial turn",[17] while we objectify the act of seeing into a reification of culture itself, we cannot but see that culture turning its gaze upon us – like the piercing and apparently critical gaze of Derrida's cat in *L'animal que donc je suis*.[18] Mitchell reminds us of the work of Lacan, Derrida and Bal, in which they analyze the power of the image to challenge me, the spectator:

> that images look back at us ... the eidolon talks back to us, gives orders, demands sacrifices ... why vision is never a one way street ... why the question to ask about images in not just what they mean, or what they do? But what is the secret of their vitality – and what do they want?[19]
>
> The turn towards images ... is a turn towards the acceptance of the proposition that images can speak and tell as much as they can show and represent.[20]

We need to remember that we cannot necessarily split off visual culture from textual culture, visual representations from textual representations. Textual representations themselves are visual artefacts – ink marking difference on paper, signifying meaning, screens full of programmed pixels. We need to "come

15 Mitchell, W.J.T.,"Showing seeing", 174.

16 Derrida, Jacques, *Of Grammatology*, trans. Spivak, Gayatri Chakravorty, USA: The John Hopkins University. Press, 1976, 158-159.

17 Grønstad, Asbjørn, Vågnes, Øyvind, "What do pictures want? An interview with W.J.T. Mitchell" *Images: Journal for Visual Studies*, accessed 12.7.2016: <http://www.visual-studies.com/interviews/mitchell.html>.

18 Derrida, Jacques, *Le Animal que donc je suis*, Paris: Éditions Galilée, 2006.

19 Mitchell, W.J.T., "Showing seeing", 176; to be fair, Mitchell focuses on Lacan's classic concept of the cat's cradle encompassing the screen, but there are links to arguments in Derrida's *L'animal que donc je suis* where the observed cat seems to observe and critique the author's nakedness.

20 Purgar, Krešimir, "Visual Studies and the Pictorial Turn: Twenty Years Later", *Images No.2*, 2014, accessed 12.7.2016: <http://www.visual-studies.com/images/no2/purgar.html>.

to terms with reality in its multifaceted, multimodal, multimedia forms."[21] At the same time, as Rocchio argues, the various methodological shifts in pedagogy, philosophy, and cultural practice mean that we no longer have a monolithic approach to the text of the Bible. Instead, different models are being explored through what he terms "trans-disciplinary" aesthetics. Rocchio points to three different engines for that change in semiotics, psychoanalysis and critical theory.[22] Clearly, cultural exegesis has for a long time been moving down those trajectories, shifting away from the certainties of modernist interpretation and critique, to a much more nuanced understanding of both the potentialities and imperfections of our interpretations.

This paper seeks to ask what is happening when powerful, vibrant visuality engages an apparently fragile text – when the culture machine is let loose on the Bible. Is Rocchio correct in arguing that attention to the visual, to transdisciplinary aesthetics, will enable us to see more of the text, to see the text in new light? Or will the text be suborned by the visual, lost among the contemporary whorl of imagery? If text is as much about visual culture as anything else we see, if text itself is icon or eidolon or sign, does its expression within visual culture offer a re-representation, a re-packaging, a re-signification of the text to the reader? Indeed, such questions could be asked about the effect of digitizing the text – does the process of digitalization, the rendering of material texts into digital form, transform the audience's engagement with the Bible and with its manuscripts? Do we read Biblical texts the same on screen? Do we understand the paratextuality of digital forms?

Although we don't have the space here to grapple with some of these larger issues, we will explore the interaction between visual culture and the Bible through three brief examples: the Lindisfarne Gospels exhibition, the list of most retweeted bible verses of 2015, and Darren Arnofsky's Noah. The former allows us to explore the physical display of a material artefact; the second to explore social media engagement and the impact of visual additions to the text; the third to explore the culture machine at full power as the Bible is embraced by Hollywood. We will need to explore what happens, but also what models are developed to guide the audience in their aesthetic interpretation of the synthesis between the text and visual culture.

---

21 Purgar, Krešimir, "Visual Studies".

22 Rocchio,Vincent, *Culture Machine*, 17-25.

2 Lindisfarne Gospels

In the Summer of 2013, the Lindisfarne Gospels were exhibited at Durham University.[23] The Gospels are an exquisitely illustrated Anglo-Saxon manuscript of the four gospels created on Holy Island, Northumberland (also known as Lindisfarne) some 1300 years ago. The texts have a close relation with Durham: Lindisfarne is about 100 miles north of the city and the Gospels were carried there with the remains of St Cuthbert when the monks fled the island after sustained Viking raids in the ninth century. The Gospels remained at Durham until the Dissolution of the Monasteries under Henry VIII and eventually became part of the British Library's collection of ancient manuscripts.

The Gospels were exhibited in Durham with a number of other biblical texts, including St Cuthbert's own copy of St John's Gospel (formerly known as the Stonyhurst Gospel), the earliest known surviving example of Western bookbinding. As part of the exhibition, you could see the Gospels themselves – open on different days on different pages – as well as several other artefacts of the Northern Celtic saints and Anglo-Saxon spirituality, all carefully laid out under glass, in carefully controlled atmospheric conditions. You could visit the gallery rooms and see how the gospels were made and excel in the craftsmanship of Eadfrith's textual work, Aethelwald's binding, and Billfrith's ornamentation[24] (although the existing cover is a modern replica – the Vikings stole the original!). You could even engage in writing out your own version of the Gospels.

The Lindisfarne Gospels were and are an exquisite visual experience – a cultic artefact, a processional relic, symbolizing reverence for both the text it contains and the saint whom it commemorates. The text was used through its history as a liturgical focus for worship and as a community focus for Lindisfarne's monks and then for the Benedictine community at Durham. The Gospels are also a visual reminder of the wealth, power and artistic brilliance of 8th century Anglo-Saxon Northumbria. But, the text is written in Latin. Just as few modern readers can read its archaic text, it seems that even the monks of

23 <http://www.bbc.co.uk/news/uk-england-tyne-24329431>, accessed 10.4.19.

24 Eadfrith was the Bishop of Lindisfarne at the end of the seventh century and is believed to have illustrated the Gospels. Aethelwald and Billfrith were presumably members of the Lindisfarne community involved in binding the book and ornamenting the cover. For more information on the Gospels see <https://www.bl.uk/collection-items/lindisfarne-gospels>, accessed 10.4.19; and for more information on the exhibition, see <https://www.dur.ac.uk/palace.green/whatson/details/?id=18081>, accessed 10.4.19. The British Library provides an online visualisation of the Gospels: <http://www.bl.uk/onlinegallery/ttp/lindisfarne/accessible/introduction.html>, accessed 10.4.19.

Lindisfarne seemed to have needed assistance. Written in the gaps between the beautiful Latin text is a tenth century Anglo-Saxon translation/gloss, in fact the earliest translation of the Gospels into an English language. The gloss was inserted onto the Gospels by Aldred, Provost of Chester-le-Street (ten miles north of Durham) sometime in the tenth century, perhaps as a pedagogical tool for his fellow monks or as a cultural statement on the increasing importance of English. Could this, perhaps, provide a hint that the Gospels were a working text, a cultural text as well as a visual artefact?

Robert Stanton's assertion is that the gloss is not pedagogical and that the text itself was not used in regular pedagogy within the community not least since the manuscript does not show multiple frequent usage.[25] Its size and ornamentation suggest that its place is on the altar rather than the workbench. As such, the gloss, completed as part of an economic transaction, may well be more of a cultural process of glossing Latin texts into English that follows on from the practice of both Bede and Aldred in translating texts into the vernacular. In a way, it is a process of co-opting the Latin text into the support of English. Stanton goes on to argue that such texts were self-referential. Aldred goes to some lengths to ensure that the text is understood in the very context of tenth century Britain. When Mary is introduced, Aldred provides four glosses to explain Joseph's relationship with Mary prior to the birth – betrothed, entrusted, troth-plighted or pledged ("biwoedded", "beboden", "befeastnad", "betaht") – desperate to avoid any sense that Jesus was Joseph's natural child. In fact, contemporary Anglo-Saxon scholars can no longer see the specific differences between those four words. Later, in his gloss of Luke 6:22, Aldred seems to make a huge mistake. The Beatitude in Luke 6:22 warns that "men shall cast out your name as evil for the son of man's sake". Aldred glosses "evil" as "yfel / apoltre" (evil/apple-tree). He knows that "evil" is the correct gloss for "malum', but he also adds a gloss linked to the Latin word for "apple", "mãlum" (with a long "a") and gives "apple tree". Is Aldred being lax? Or is he being too clever – creating a literary link between evil and the fruit tree, the apple tree, in Genesis and the Fall, the source of all evil? Does he expect his reader to recognise the schoolboy error but to see the over-clever pun beneath? If so, this seems to be more of a self-aware cultural exercise than a pedagogical tool for Northumbrian monks.

The role of the Aldred's gloss perhaps was to remind his pupils or those reading from the manuscript that there is a beauty that goes beyond the visual.

25 This section draws on Stanton, Robert, *The Culture of Translation in Anglo-Saxon England*, Boydell and Brewer: 2002, 9-55 and on a public lecture given by Professor Eric Stanley on 30th April 2013.

But, more likely, the gloss is part of a wider cultural assimilation of Insular manuscripts (compare the independent glossing of the Rushworth Gospels) into the increasingly confident world of Anglo-Saxon Britain. The visual splendour, Aldred knows, is dependent on the wonder of the words contained within it. But that splendor needs to be translated into Anglo-Saxon words for the new nation to align itself with the glory of its faded past. Aldred amends and resignifies the visual beauty because he sees something much more important in this text – the importance of the message it conveys, as well as the cultural opportunity to appropriate something of the past glory of the North to the service of the emergent Anglo-Saxon present.

In the terms of transactional aesthetics, what is happening here? In the present, none of the complexity about Aldred's gloss or the meaning of the original text surfaced in the exhibition. The Gospels were portrayed/exhibited as a visual, material artefact. The other activities around the exhibition pointed to this visuality and materiality. You could make your own Gospel but were never told about the contents of the Gospel. As a reader of ancient languages, I was able to gaze in wonder at the perfect script of the Gospel of John in red ink on white vellum. But for many visitors, the text was perhaps unintelligible, and no translations were provided. As such, the medium of interpretation focused wholly on the visual rather than the textual – the book became something to see rather than something read. Indeed, it might even be that in terms of critical theory and ideological criticism, the voice of the Gospels was silenced by the hegemony of secular humanism within contemporary academia – the actual words of the Gospel silenced in preference to the visual experience of a work of art. Instead, the exhibition focused on cultural and material issues about the Gospels to exclusion of the text's actual meaning. Such a focus was facilitated by the texts' otherness – the use of Latin, Greek and Anglo-Saxon – and so replicated only the visual/material importance of the text rather than its linguistic content that was largely ignored through the process. Is this an example of the image dominating the text? Of visual culture denying the place of text? Of materialism celebrating its own materiality in denying the presence of the other?

It goes without saying that there is a huge gap between the visual culture of late seventh century Northumberland and that of contemporary Western digital culture. The Lindisfarne Gospels' exhibition provided a visual expression of a text, but an exhibition which actually minimized the reading of the text, the deciphering of the words, counter to the artefact's own history. We now move to another contemporary exhibition – the use of the Bible in celebrity tweets, which include Bible references. What's the dynamic here between visual culture and the Biblical text?

TABLE 2.1 The Bible on Twitter in 2015, © Openbible Info

	Verses, RTs, Source Account
1	Phil 1:3: "I thank my God every time I remember you." (33,476 RT @mainedcm)
2	1 Cor 13:13: "And now these three remain..." (13,365 RT @allybrooke)
3	Ps 16:11: "Walk on his path..." (11,474 RT @camerondallas) *altered text
4	Rom 8:18: "I consider that our present sufferings..." (10,755 RT @camerondallas)
5	Prov 27:2: "Let someone else praise you..." (10,206 RT @RealCoryMachado)
6	Jer 29:11: "For I know the plans I have for you..." (10,279 RT @ddlovato)
7	Jn 1:5: "The light shines in the darkness..." (7,308 RT @allybrooke)
8	Ps 120:1: "I call on the Lord in my distress..." (7,550 RT @MannyPacquiaoTR)
9	Col 3: (no verse specified!) (6,700 RT @siwon407)
10	Eph 4:32: "Be kind to one another..." (5,731 RT @TimTebow)

3 Celebrities Tweeting Biblically

In his regular sharing of biblical data on the OpenBible website, Stephen Smith made available a list of the most retweeted Bible verses of 2015 given in Table 2.1.[26]

The tweets originate from and reflect aspects of an interesting mix of different cultures. They are visual artefacts that appear in Twitter's livestreams as brief text messages always accompanied by the avatar representing the celebrity who has issued the tweet and sometimes with additional images appended to the tweet. They are permanent, though ephemeral artefacts – although every tweet remains part of the digital archive, the nature of Twitter livestream display means that they can be very ephemeral – passing through on the way to digital obscurity. Notification and listing protocols can allow tweets to "survive" longer in the public's awareness, as also happens with retweeting and commenting, but generally tweets fly by pretty quickly. They are digital artefacts and part of the ephemerata of digital culture, meant to be viewed on wearables, smartphones, tablets, laptops, or computers of any kind.

26 <https://www.openbible.info/blog/2015/12/the-bible-on-twitter-in-2015/>, accessed 10.4.19.

The ephemeral nature of the tweet and its reliance on digital delivery means that each tweet competes to be seen – to be maximized for impact. As such, there are clear strategies for maximizing the visual impact to gain the required readership. Tweets contain only 140 characters but a picture paints a thousand words.[27]

First of all, it is important to note that many of the tweets in the list are tweeted by celebrities within the millennial generation, sometimes only by the inclusion of a Bible reference, and are often classic expressions of a therapeutic form of Christian spirituality known as moralistic therapeutic deism (MTD).[28] It is also important to note the different elements of the tweet – both textual and visual. So, Demi Lovato's tweet in position six includes only her avatar and the text "Jeremiah 29:11" (an archetypal millennial MTD text) and Cameron Dallas' tweet in position four includes his avatar and the text "Romans 8:18" accompanied by a smiling (flushed?) face emoji.[29] In these tweets, the textual baggage of the tweet is minimal. It is perhaps assumed that the reader will know the text cited through their own devotional engagement with the Bible. This may well point to the tweeter's own devotional engagement as well. The addition of the emoji also enhances the tweet by adding some kind of emotional signature to the text – although this particular emoji is quite ambiguous.

Some tweets often contain a paraphrase of the text as well – so Dallas' other retweet in the list, referencing Psalms 16:11, contains a specific and rare translation of the verse, which is found only: in retweets of his original tweet of 2 Jun 2015; on a Dutch photoblog in Nov 2015[30] since removed from public viewing; a now lost instagram on a teenager's site from Mexico; and by a tweet on 4 June 2015 from the Neesa Ratzenburg Foundation accompanied by hashtags about David and a picture of a rabbi – probably an unattributed and amended retweet of Dallas' tweet.[31] It is probable that the verse arises from prosperity/holiness spirituality, but the source is unknown. The paraphrase enables a specific emphasis to be placed on the tweet, which may well appeal to the tweeter

27 For a discussion of the role of tweets within digital religion, see Cheong, Pauline, "Twitter of Faith: Understanding Social Media Networking and Microblogging Rituals as Religious Practices", in: *Digital Religion, Social Media and Culture: Perspectives, Practices and Futures*, Cheong, Pauline, ed., Switzerland: Peter Lang, 2012, 191-206.

28 Smith, Christian, *Soul Searching: The Religious and Spiritual Lives of American Teenagers*, UK: Oxford University Press, 2009.

29 Dallas has a very large Twitter following (5.22m), his Vine account is the 11th most popular, and he has a further 8.1m followers on Instagram.

30 No longer searchable.

31 The author has reached out to both Cameron Dallas and the Neesa Ratzenburg Foundation without success.

or to the assumed cultural paradigms of the expected audience. In this instance, the text becomes more dominant than the visual – not least in the choice of specific paraphrase.

The second and seventh largest retweets (1 Cor 13:13 and Jn 1:5) were both sent from Ally Brooke Hernandez's account. Ally Brooke Hernandez is a member of a popular band Fifth Harmony.[32] Both tweets include the text of the Bible verse and the citation. The tweet citing 1 Corinthians 13 also includes a heart emoji. Manny Pacquiao, a boxer well known for his political and social activism in the Philippines, tweets Psalm 120:1 in a similar format of Bible verse (reference and text, including capitalization of the divine name). Again, Tim Tebow, American football athlete renowned for being disciplined over painting Jn 3:16 on his face before a football match, cites Ephesians 4:32 with the full text of the Bible verse. These last three celebrity tweeters, Brooke, Pacquiao and Tebow provide normally unaccompanied verses and references in a style very close to or identical to that of verses shared from the major Bible websites and mobile applications – it is almost as if these verses are highlighted in and shared from a Bible app. The emphasis is much more on the text in these instances – as emphasized by the use of quotation marks. The only visual elements are the avatar and the use of the heart emoji in one of the tweets.

Siwon Choi, a devout Korean Christian and boyband member/moviestar, tweets a reference to a whole Bible chapter – "Colossians 3" – and accompanies this with a picture of himself riding a police motorcycle. The picture was taken as part of a film shoot for Dai Hup Guk – apparently the bike was towed by a special effects vehicle.[33] But the connection with Colossians 3 seems tenuous – perhaps a reference to new clothes? The dominance and impact of the picture seems to affect the potential for retweeting here rather than the ambiguity of the Bible reference. Indeed, one might ask why the Bible reference is included at all, since it seems to bear little weight in this context. The Bible verse may well be being used as an evangelical hook – seeking to encourage Siwon Choi's fans to read the larger text? But the driver for this text is certainly the image rather than the text.

The top retweet (Phil 1:3) was originally tweeted from the account of a Philippine actress, best known for her viral Dubsmash video and now a successful television personality, Maine Mendoza. Mendoza has 3.3 million followers on Twitter. The (now deleted) tweet puts together a reference to Philippians 1:3 (no text) with a picture of Mendoza with fellow actor Alden Richards and the

32 <https://fifthharmony.com>, accessed 10.4.19.

33 <https://afspot.net/forum/topic/788138-choi-si-won-is-just-for-show-on-a-motorcycle/>, accessed 10.4.19.

rather cryptic hashtag #ALDUB5thMonthsary. The hashtag and picture refer to the hugely popular onscreen relationship between Mendoza and Richards ("Aldub"). If we therefore put together the different aspects of this tweet, we begin to see why it is so popular – a popular celebrity, playing a popular character, celebrating love, by using a Bible verse in a deeply biblical culture. However, the lack of a direct quotation undermines the Bible reference, makes some vague reference to a text which is assumed to be known by its intended audience. The reliance on visual culture suggests that people were retweeting the picture and its hashtag, and that the verse came along with it as a passenger, so as to speak, much like the previous tweet from Siwon Choi.

All of these tweets seem to reflect aspects of the personal faith response of celebrities to various contexts within societies favourably disposed towards the Bible. The number of retweets seems to be linked not to the specific Bible verses but to an image associated with the tweet, even if it is only the avatar of the celebrity, and the number of followers potentially willing to retweet the verse. Sometimes, especially with those celebrities seemingly tweeting from within Bible Apps, the text takes precedent. However, in other, not least in the last two, which are accompanied by pictures, the bible text seems to be a passive component, or a passenger, within a predominantly visual culture. The visual content in these dominates over the text and the texts ride undercover, perhaps cultural hints or markers.

Tweeting the Bible seems to be quite a popular form of engagement in contemporary American religious life. But here we see the difficulty of separating out textual messages from celebrity culture and visual imagery. One is left with the impression that fans tend to retweet because of the celebrity rather than because of the Bible verse quoted. Indeed, does the Bible verse add to the "squeaky clean" image of the celebrity and so add even greater appeal to their celebrity status? On the other hand, those texts which cite the Bible and which have little visual input also signal a different approach to celebrity tweeting – potentially giving some perspective into the devotional life of the celebrity.

In a way, this is clearest in Rocchio's comments about the way that Pope Francis makes use of social media in order to show his own acknowledgement of contemporary culture. Rocchio talks of the Pope's humility in asking for prayer when he was revealed for the first time on the balcony overlooking St Peter's Basilica. One could call this an acceptance of contemporary culture signaled within a contemporary medium to show a shift away from stereotypical patterns of ecclesial domination.[34]

34 Rocchio, Vincent, *Culture Machine*, 1.

We have seen that celebrities make use of the Bible in different ways within their tweets – to connect more closely with various Biblically-aware cultures, to project a specific (Christian) morality to their readers, perhaps even to make use of their tweeting as a form of evangelism. In our final test case, we move to Hollywood and explore the adaptation of a Biblical story in Darren Aronofsky's Noah.

4 Aronofsky's Midrashic Imaging of Noah

One of the potential problems of making a film out of the Noah story is not how much material there is but how little. Eight verses of historical background (Gen 6:1-7, 11-13), a few verses saying that Noah was a good man (Gen 5:30-32, Gen 6:8,9,22, Gen 7:1), a few to describe Noah's boat-building task (Gen 6:14-16) and the coming deluge (Gen 6:17, 7:4, 11-12, 17-20) with interspersed snippets of those to be saved – namely Noah's family (Gen 6:10, 18, 7:1, 13, 23) and the chosen fauna (Gen 6:19-20, 7:2-3, 8-9, 14-16). But none of these micro-themes are developed in any detail. The three main strings of the narrative (warnings of impurity, a family to be saved and the animals) are wrapped around the ark and the impending doom – a bible story contorted within itself like a bowl of spaghetti.

But there is no rich sauce to accompany the convoluted pasta. Many details are missing: we just have scant measurements, numbers of animals, a family. There is no explanation of the boat-building task, sources for building supplies (how do you build a boat in a wilderness?), or the necessary provisions and technology; no exploration of theological nuance; no details to help make anything really understandable. Even going into other traditions, such as Noë's story in the Qu'ran (Suras 57, 11 and 23), offers little solid context to draw on apart from some speculation about Noah's lost son (Sura 11:42-46) and the suggestion that Noah grew his own trees! The rest depends on later speculation.

So much more detail has to be added for a blockbuster – certainly a blockbuster to fit our contemporary needs. Aronofsky's Noah is a proper, multimillion dollar, Hollywood blockbuster complete with special effects, blood and gore, even robot-like angels. It grossed $362m dollars.[35] To some extent the film seems to have more connection with post-apocalyptic thrillers than with Bible epics. Noah is a mean street fighter in a toxic, dying world, protecting his family and striving for what is right. The opening scenes have more in common with

35 For details of the film including plot synopsis, see IMDB: <http://www.imdb.com/title/tt1959490/synopsis?ref_=tt_stry_pl>, accessed on 10.04.19.

the Book of Eli or Mad Max. We are presented with a post-industrial world that faces imminent destruction because of the cost of unchecked technological development – a strange mix of technological urban culture vs environmental rural isolation.[36] The ambiguity of a film set many years before industrialization but with industrial sites and processes at its heart allows the audience to find their own place in the film – the film draws them in and suggests that the narrative is not just a quaint stone age documentary.

Part of the ambiguity is also to pull away from the Biblical narrative. The film provides a kind of alternative space – neither the Bible we know, nor the Biblical tropes that we expect in a Biblical epic, and nor a deconstruction of those.[37] Instead, Aronofsky makes the decision to portray the 'nephilim' of Gen 6:4 in terms of the Watchers from the Enoch traditions, as fallen angels encrusted, imprisoned, by the very rocks of the earth, as pseudo-robotic allies and enemies at the same time – sometimes pet-like in their support, at others, formidable fighting machines. In creating what he called the least biblical film ever, Aronofsky takes Lamech's son, the maker of tools in bronze and iron, Tubal Cain (Gen 4:22) as a foil, or a counterpart for Noah. Tubal Cain represents the chaotic, industrial, brutish, worldly antithesis to Noah's ascetic, environmental, family-orientated goodness. Cain fights, builds, rules, slaughters; he embodies the very horror of the world which Yahweh has determined must end. But gradually through the film, Aronofsky forces the viewer to ask whether this antithesis is real. Both men are seeking to save their own people. Both men are horrified by God's silence. Both men are seeking both justice and mercy. Indeed, in the second half of the film, as we move from the expansive terrain below Methuselah's mountain to the claustrophobic confines of the Ark, Noah seems to become more and more like his mortal enemy – technologized, isolated, bent on destruction as he creates his own forge in the heart of the ark: his murderous intent becomes the exact opposite of a 'good man'. Indeed, we have already seen Noah's tendency for irrational behaviour in his decision to go through the industrial zone at the beginning of the journey – a decision which allows them to find Ila (one of the key characters of the film who married Shem and has twin children, who are threatened by Noah's violence) but which almost leads the family into destruction first at the hand of strangers and then at the whim of the Watchers.[38]

Noah has to face his own demons and come to terms with his own monstrosity – indeed even towards the end of the film, he remains convinced that

36 Rocchio also provides a detailed narratological analysis of the film: *Culture Machine*, 36-46.

37 Rocchio, Vincent, *Culture Machine*, 38; 43.

38 Rocchio, Vincent, *Culture Machine*, 39.

he has failed God. The solution comes not by an appeal to Noah's fundamentalism, nor through the brutality of industrialization but rather through the wisdom and grace of Naameh, Noah's wife, and Ila, Noah's daughter-in-law. Both women offer a wisdom which Noah ultimately cannot ignore and which for the viewer "constructs a rift between secular humanism and its most vociferous opponent in contemporary American culture: Christian fundamentalism."[39] Rather than the Bible epic pivot between the two, like *The Last Temptation of Christ* or *The Passion of the Christ*, this Bible epic chooses to create a via media, a choice for wisdom and collaboration and creativity rather than for destruction. There is a definite transformative aesthetic at the heart of the production.

To some extent, what Aronofsky seems to be doing is a classical way of engaging with the Biblical text – he's creating a midrash, or an interpretative reading of the text. Aronofsky believes that at the heart of the Noah story is an unsolved question about justice and mercy. How does a God who wishes to destroy all creation, to start again, not decide to destroy all humanity and create a world without human beings at all? Indeed, Noah argues himself into exactly the latter position and seeks to destroy his own family. Naameh and Ila persuade him, eventually, that this is not God's purpose. In the end, Noah chose to save the lives of Ila's children, "You chose love", she says.[40] After exploring Genesis, Jubilees, Enoch and the Zohar, after a creative process of moulding the traditions together and finding a synthesis between text and imagination, Aronofsky declares his Noah to be an exercise in midrash: "the text exists and is truth and the word and the final authority. But how you decide to interpret it, you can open up your imagination to be inspired by it."[41]

What lies at the heart of Aronofsky's midrash, Aronofsky's Noah, is the exploration of *hamas* (destruction/separation) – the *hamas* of Tubal Cain's industrial brutality, the *hamas* of Noah the radicalized loner, the *hamas* which the Creator inflicts upon his own creation in response. But that *hamas* is reinterpretated by Naameh and Ila in terms of God's wider provision for love. *Hamas* is the preferred route for the men (perhaps representing Western culture's expressions of both secular humanism and fundamentalism). On the other hand, the women represent an alternative path of community integration, of social creativity, of embodied love, in stark contrast to the men (reflecting contemporary communitarian approaches to social integration and inclusion). As such, the film's characters offer a biblical reinterpretation of

39 Rocchio, Vincent, *Culture Machine*, 41.

40 Rocchio, Vincent, *Culture Machine*, 44.

41 Darren Aronofsky quoted in Peter Chattaway's "The Genesis of 'Noah'", *Christianity Today*, March 27 2014 [web article], available at: <https://www.christianitytoday.com/ct/2014/march-web-only/genesis-of-noah.html>, accessed 10.4.19.

contemporary cultural divides which have become even more extreme since the film's release.

The film arrives at this point by debunking many of the accepted ways which Hollywood deals with Bible epics. Moreover, Aronofsky makes use of many different tools to make clear his aim to think theologically though the issues rather than just carry on with the normal visual and materials forms expected in the medium. Whether the film was a success is therefore immaterial since the work it was doing was to break a pattern of how to deal with the Bible on screen rather than to retell the Noah story.[42]

5 Conclusion

The three examples furnish us with different images of the Bible's encounter with visual culture, or the existence of the mediated Bible in contemporary culture.

In one of them, the text succumbs to the dominance of visual/material culture. At the same time, the text underwrites what happens in the Bible's mediated form. The glory of the Gospels creates a sumptuous Insular illuminated manuscript. But at the same time, the audience's lack of familiarity with the text and the languages in which it is written means that the text is uncoded, illegible, latent. What we know of the text and its importance has to be gleaned from the visual and material culture, which the text then rides as a passenger. In the context of the Lindisfarne Gospels, the text rides in a sumptuous vehicle and we, the audience, cannot but note its power and importance.

Tweets are a much more humble form of transport. But the tweets are also much more diverse. Sometimes the Bible rides along with the celebrities, ambiguously part of their cultural appeal, perhaps part of their media messaging to their audience. Sometimes, the Bible eclipses the celebrity fully quoted and cited and perhaps even "emoji-ed". But even here, the Bible is dependant on the celebrity transport. The celebrity is doing the tweeting and it is much more likely that the fans are retweeting the messenger rather than the message. And in others, the Bible seems to act as a footnote, an evangelistic hook perhaps, an addendum to visual culture. I am intrigued that both of the tweets where pictures dominate are from Asian TV/Movie stars. Here, the tweets are conveying imagery first and foremost and the Bible references seem to be a sideline to the main message – virtue signaling perhaps?

---

42 Rocchio, Vincent, *Culture Machine*, 46.

Although Aronofsky aimed to create the most unbiblical epic ever, he seems to have created a theologically rich form of midrash. Of all of the examples, this is the most visual, the most culturally engaged exploration of the visual text. It is a bit like the Lindisfarne Gospels but also different from them. Both the Gospels and Aldred's gloss seem to be part of the power dynamics of the Church/State in early medieval Britain. Both point to the power of the text and the need for a fledgling state to draw upon that power, to appropriate its power. But Noah rejects former norms and the potential powers-that-be in our contemporary world and seeks to develop a via media through social constructivism. In this the Biblical text, scant as it may be, plays a full part. And indeed it may well play a fuller part because of its own fragility. The text is able to be developed and explored and queried in order to set up a transformational alternative to both historical and contemporary issues. This example undertakes some serious theological heavy lifting and apparently succeeds.

Indeed, contrary to the suggestion in the title of this paper, visual culture seems to magnify the voice of the text rather than to minimize it. In each of the examples, we see a kind of symbiosis between the Biblical text and visual culture in which each seeks strength from the other, and each seeks to make its communicative task complete through the other.

Of course, that could just be a reflection of the examples I have chosen. There are other ways in which visual culture queries, contests, and challenges the text. But perhaps even there, the appropriation of the biblical text into visual culture is yet another form of enhancement rather than negation. Katie Edwards has proposed that we need to be less anxious about the warnings of decreasing biblical literacy in Western culture[43] and instead notes that "biblical stories are woven into the very fabric of contemporary culture".[44] We should, she suggests, be discussing the "ubiquity of the bible in popular culture and its impact on biblical literacy".[45] The questions raised by this paper relate to the meaning and effect of what Edwards calls the Bible's ubiquity in contemporary culture. Our tentative findings point to the power of a fragile text to maximize its presence within visual culture and continue to transmit its message. The Bible remains as a mediated text and able to maintains its identity as such even within a culture where a picture can paint a thousand words.

43 *pace* Field, Clive, "Is the Bible Becoming a Closed Book? British Opinion Poll Evidence" *Journal of Contemporary Religion* 29.3, 2014, 503-528, and then many other polls arguing for a decline in biblical literacy in the West.

44 Edwards, Katie, *Rethinking*, ix-x.

45 Edwards, Katie, *Rethinking*, x.

References

Brant, Jo-Ann, *Dialogue and Drama: Elements of Greek Tragedy in the Fourth Gospel*, USA: Hendrickson, 2004.

Chattaway, Peter, "The Genesis of 'Noah'", *Christianity Today*, March 27 2014 [web article], <https://www.christianitytoday.com/ct/2014/march-web-only/genesis-of-noah.html>.

Cheong, Pauline, "Twitter of Faith: Understanding Social Media Networking and Microblogging Rituals as Religious Practices", in: *Digital Religion, Social Media and Culture: Perspectives, Practices and Futures, Cheong*, Pauline, ed., Switzerland: Peter Lang, 2012, 191-206.

Derrida, Jacques, *L'Animal que donc je suis*, Paris: Éditions Galilée, 2006.

Derrida, Jacques, *Of Grammatology*, trans. Spivak, Gayatri Chakravorty, USA: The John Hopkins University Press, 1976, 158-159.

Edwards, Katie, *Rethinking Biblical Literacy*, UK: Bloomsbury, 2015.

Field, Clive, "Is the Bible Becoming a Closed Book? British Opinion Poll Evidence" *Journal of Contemporary Religion 29.3*, 2014, 503-528.

Grønstad, Asbjørn, Vågnes, Øyvind, "What do pictures want? An interview with W.J.T. Mitchell" *Images: Journal for Visual Studies*, accessed 12.7.2016: <http://www.visual-studies.com/interviews/mitchell.html>.

Mitchell, W.J.T., "Showing seeing: a critique of visual culture", *Journal of Visual Culture*, Vol. 1(2), 2002, 166.

Morgan, David, *The Embodied Eye, Religious Visual Culture and the Social Life of Feeling*, USA: University of California Press, 2012, xiii.

Morgan, David, *The Sacred Gaze: Religious Visual Culture in Theory and Practice*, USA: University of California Press, 2005.

Poleg, Eyal, *Approaching the Bible in Medieval England*, UK: Manchester University Press, 2013.

Purgar, Krešimir "Visual Studies and the Pictorial Turn: Twenty Years Later", *Images No.2*, 2014, accessed 12.7.2016: <http://www.visual-studies.com/images/no2/purgar.html>.

Rocchio, Vincent, *Christianity and the Culture Machine*, Eugene: Cascade Books, 2016.

Smith, Christian, *Soul Searching: The Religious and Spiritual Lives of American Teenagers*, UK: Oxford University Press, 2009.

Stanton, Robert, *The Culture of Translation in Anglo-Saxon England*, Boydell and Brewer, 2002.

Wright, Brian J., "Ancient Literacy in New Testament Research: Incorporating a few more line of enquiry", *Trinity Journal 36*, 2015, 161-189.

List of Internet Ressources

<http://www.bbc.co.uk/news/uk-england-tyne-24329431>, accessed 10.4.19.

<https://www.bl.uk/collection-items/lindisfarne-gospels>, accessed 10.4.19.

<https://www.dur.ac.uk/palace.green/whatson/details/?id=18081>, accessed 10.4.19.

<http://www.bl.uk/onlinegallery/ttp/lindisfarne/accessible/introduction.html>, accessed 10.4.19.

<https://www.openbible.info/blog/2015/12/the-bible-on-twitter-in-2015/>, accessed 10.4.19.

<https://fifthharmony.com>, accessed 10.4.19.

<https://afspot.net/forum/topic/788138-choi-si-won-is-just-for-show-on-a-motorcycle/>, accessed 10.4.19.

CHAPTER 3

"What no eye has seen": Using a digital microscope to edit papyrus fragments of early Christian apocryphal writings

Brent Landau, Adeline Harrington and James C. Henriques

1 Introduction

Scholars working with ancient papyri are often confronted with manuscripts that are challenging to read. Aside from the basic fact that papyri are often preserved in fragmentary condition, the deciphering of letters in the portions that remain frequently presents challenges. Sometimes only small parts of letters are preserved; at other times the ink may have faded away to near invisibility; and at still other times the letters are rendered almost unrecognizable by blotches of ink. Papyri may also be covered with an obscuring layer of silt as the result of inadequate conservation or a lack of conservation altogether, leaving scholars unclear as to what is ink and what is dirt. Faced with such challenges, editors still labor valiantly to produce accurate transcriptions of ancient texts. Nevertheless, uncertainties in readings still remain, and texts that have been edited more than once will sometimes have very different transcriptions. The difficulties in deciding which readings to prefer may even lead to the conclusion that such decisions are hopelessly arbitrary.

A relatively new technology, however, may be able to resolve some of these papyrological impasses, at least in part: digital microscopes. Although some of the leading repositories of papyri collections have had analog microscopes available for use by researchers for some time, digital microscopes have three significant advantages over analog microscopes. First, a digital microscope can be connected to a computer via a USB port, allowing for the image to be seen on a computer screen, rather than straining through a tiny eyehole. Second, a digital microscope can take photographs of the manuscript under magnification, allowing an editor to provide key photographic evidence in favor of one reading over another – and this paper will include a selection of photographs taken with a digital microscope. Third, some digital microscopes – including the one used by the authors – have the added feature of ultraviolet and infrared lighting modes, and these different light spectra can greatly improve the legibility of ink in some cases.

In publishing a paper devoted specifically to the application of a digital microscope to ancient manuscripts, the authors hope that this will encourage more scholars in this subfield to utilize this tool. We are not the first specialists in early Judaism and Christianity to use a digital microscope, however. By means of some informal crowd-sourcing on Facebook, the lead author determined that a small number of scholars in biblical studies and cognate fields started using digital microscopes in the past five years or so, independently of one another, and shared their recommendations of the technology with other colleagues through word of mouth. This means that some scholars are familiar with this technology, but many others, including some of the most prominent researchers in ancient manuscript studies, are not. This study thus aims to transform an oral tradition into a written document.

Before describing the circumstances under which my colleagues and I have used a digital microscope, it is important to address one preliminary matter: the possible pitfalls of utilizing such technologies. New tools of digitization have not only enabled manuscripts to be viewed upon the internet halfway around the world, but also, in the cases of technologies like digital microscopes and multi-spectral imaging, have allowed scholars to see features of the manuscripts that would be impossible otherwise. As a result of these developments, some scholars have emphasized the potential drawbacks of overreliance on digital images of manuscripts at the expense of direct observation of the physical manuscript itself.[1]

Three remarks about how the use of a digital microscope contributes to this conversation are pertinent. First, the digital microscope is in an interesting middle position between an in-person autopsy and the remote viewing of digital surrogates of a manuscript. Unlike a technician taking a photograph of a fragment in its entirety, a digital microscope is most effectively used by a scholar who is directly observing the manuscript, and is taking images of those portions of the text that he or she finds most difficult or problematic. Thus, it is much more "interactive" – at least for the initial observer – than simply examining from afar a digital surrogate whose producer may or may not have been particularly knowledgeable about or interested in the manuscript in question. Second, there is definitely the potential for overreliance upon the images produced by a digital microscope (to say nothing of other digital surrogates), since it can potentially produce "false positives," such as ink traces that are only

1 See especially Terras, Melissa M., "Artefacts and Errors: Acknowledging Issues of Representation in the Digital Imaging of Ancient Texts," in: *Kodikologie und Paläographie im Digitale Zeitalter* 2, Fischer, Franz, Fritze, Christiane, Vogeler, Georg, eds., Norderstedt: Books on Demand, 2010, 43-61.

shadows and the like. The in-person observer, thus, has a responsibility to ensure that what he or she is examining is really there, by taking multiple photographs in different types of light, at different angles, and from both sides of the fragment. Third, there is absolutely nothing that replaces having the actual physical manuscript present for observation with the naked eye, even if one is also utilizing a digital microscope at points during this process. In the case of the manuscript that the lead author has examined most extensively with a digital microscope, he returned to his home institution with several thousand images taken under the microscope – and yet, there were, perhaps inevitably, cases where he could not see the feature of the manuscript he wanted to with the photos.

The settings for this use of a digital microscope were the Sackler Library of Oxford University, the main repository for the Oxyrhynchus Papyri, and also Cambridge University Library, where several manuscripts from the Oxyrhynchus collection now reside. The microscope was used by the lead author and his colleague Geoffrey S. Smith, as well as by several of our graduate students at the University of Texas at Austin, two of whom are co-authors of this article. The digital microscope used was manufactured by Dino-Lite, and the model number is AD4113T-I2V. Its specifications include: a combination of LED, UV, and IR lights; a USB cable that allows images to be projected onto a computer screen so that the quality of the photos can be immediately analyzed; an adjustable magnification range of 20-200x; and a 1.3 Megapixel camera with 1280x1024 resolution.[2]

In this study, three specific papyri manuscripts will be discussed; two of the three fragments are probably apocryphal Christian texts, and the third definitely is. Brent Landau examines *Papyrus Oxyrhynchus* II 210, a possible apocryphal gospel fragment. Adeline Harrington examines *Papyrus Oxyrhynchus* LX 4009, whose identification as part of the *Gospel of Peter* has been debated among scholars. James C. Henriques examines *Papyrus Oxyrhynchus* LXV 4469, an amulet containing part of King Abgar's letter to Jesus. Unfortunately, it will not be possible to present in this article revised transcriptions of these three fragments. In the case of *P.Oxy* 210, a new transcription and thorough study will appear elsewhere;[3] in the case of the other two fragments, new transcriptions are planned, but more research needs to be undertaken prior to these being published.

2 Its suggested retail price is €350-550 or $629.00. The authors are immensely grateful to the Egypt Exploration Society, the Syndics of Cambridge University Library, and Dr. Ben Outhwaite of Cambridge University for their permission to use images taken with this microscope in the present study.

3 See note 8 below for publication information.

2 Papyrus Oxyrhynchus II 210

P.Oxy. 210 consists of a single fragmentary leaf from a codex, currently housed at Cambridge University Library and measuring 17.4 by 9 cm, dating perhaps to the third century.[4] It is incomplete enough that its precise contents can only be guessed at; however, the verso almost certainly has Jesus speaking about good and bad trees and fruit, as well as stating that he is the "image" and "form" of God; it thus contains an intriguing blend of Synoptic, Johannine, and Pauline features. The recto mentions an angel several times, and although previous scholars have suggested that it is an infancy narrative, the other reconstructable words appear to make better sense as part of an apocalyptic or paranetic discourse, whether spoken by Jesus or someone else. Three particularly important editions of 210 have been published by pre-eminent papyrologists: Grenfell and Hunt in 1899,[5] C.H. Roberts in 1987,[6] and Stanley E. Porter in 2001.[7] The editors have disagreed markedly about its transcription at a number of points. A new transcription and study of this enigmatic fragment by the lead author of this article has been published.[8]

Although the use of a digital microscope for examining *P.Oxy.* 210 has been beneficial in general, there are a number of places where a digital microscope has been invaluable in adjudicating between readings upon which previous editors disagreed. The digital microscope has also, on occasion, helped to point toward readings that no previous editors suggested. This presentation will not discuss every one of these instances, but will instead highlight several of the more striking and consequential examples. The instances will be presented sequentially, starting with the *recto* (in the direction of the fibers).

4 There do not seem to be any images of *P.Oxy.* 210 available online, though color plates can be found in: Wayment, Thomas A., *The Text of the New Testament Apocrypha (100-400 CE)*, New York: Bloomsbury, 2013, 402-403.

5 Grenfell, Bernard P., Hunt, Arthur S., "210. Early Christian Fragment," in: *The Oxyrhynchus Papyri*, Volume 2, London: Egypt Exploration Society, 1899, 9-10.

6 Roberts, Colin H., "An Early Christian Papyrus," in: *Miscellània papirològica Ramon Roca-Puig*, Janeras, Sebastià, ed., Barcelona: Fundació Salvador Vives Casajuana, 1987, 293-296.

7 Porter, Stanely E., "POxy II 210 as an Apocryphal Gospel and the Development of Egyptian Christianity," in: *Atti del XXII Congresso internazionale di papirologia: Firenze, 23-29 agosto 1998*, Isabella Andorlini et al., eds., Florence: Instituto papirologico G. Vitelli, 2001, 1095-1108.

8 Landau, Brent C., "A Re-transcription and Analysis of a Possible Apocryphal Gospel Fragment, *Papyrus Oxyrhynchus* II 210, Utilizing a Digital Microscope," in: *Ephemerides Theologicae Lovanienses*, 94/3 (2018): 427–80. At present, the most widely available transcription of the text appears in Ehrman, Bart D., Pleše, Zlatko, *The Apocryphal Gospels: Texts and Translations*, New York: Oxford University Press, 259-265; it basically reproduces the transcription of Roberts. A PDF of Grenfell and Hunt's *editio princeps* is available at: <https://archive.org/details/in.ernet.dli.2015.283588>, accessed on 10.04.19.

FIGURE 3.1
P.Oxy. 210. Possible *omicron* in line 3, *recto*; ©BRENTLANDAU

At *recto* line 3, all previous editors have read the first letter of the line as a *rho*, with or without an underdot. Since the next three letters can be easily read as σιν, this allowed C.H. Roberts to reconstruct the word as κάθαρσιν – quite a sensible reconstruction, since very few Greek words end with the sequence ρσιν. However, with the digital microscope, it can be seen that the top of the oval in the first letter is unclosed (Figure 3.1).

The *rhos* of this scribe all have a closed, more circular top, and on at least two other occasions, the scribe has failed to close the circle of an *omicron*. Although certainty in this instance is difficult, I have chosen to read the first letter as an underdotted *omicron*. This yields the sequence οσιν, which is unfortunately far more common than ρσιν but probably the correct reading. The fragmentary nature of this portion of the papyrus makes reconstruction impossible, but this is nevertheless an instance where the use of a digital microscope has provided an entirely new reading for a letter upon which all previous editors were in agreement.

Line 7 of the *recto* is very fragmentary, and the transcriptions of the three major editions have significant divergences. Grenfell and Hunt read it as τ̣ι̣[.]c ημε̣ι̣ν τ̣α̣ αβ[; Roberts read it as ε[...]cημ.... ρ[.]..[; and Porter read it as .. .cημ.[±3/4]...[. The transcriptions are thus quite diverse, both in terms of which letters they regard as capable of being read and the identities of the letters that are extant. Yet the stakes for this line are quite high, since Roberts and then Porter reconstructed the line to render an infancy narrative context plausible, particularly when combined with the references to an angel in the two previous lines. Porter reconstructed the line as ἐ̣c̣τ̣ὶ̣ cημε̣[ῖον τῷ̣] λα[ῷ̣ δυ-, which he interpreted to mean that the infant Jesus "is a sign for the people."[9]

9 Porter, Stanley E., "POxy II 210 as an Apocryphal Gospel", 1101-1102.

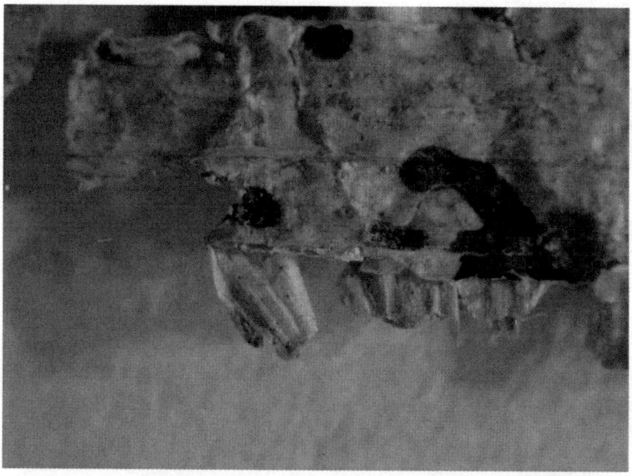

FIGURE 3.2
P.Oxy. 210. Part of *tau* in line 7, *recto*, papyrus partially twisted; ©BRENTLANDAU

My transcription has key differences from previous editions: τι̣α̣cημω̣ντ..β[. For virtually every letter in this line, I relied on a combination of the digital microscope and an inventorying that I created of all the letter forms in 210. There were, however, two instances in which an extremely uncertain letter was confirmed by the digital microscope. For the fourth letter from the end of the line, the digital microscope reveals it to be a *tau*. There is only a tiny horizontal stroke visible on the *recto*, but the microscope shows that a fiber has been twisted around. When the same fiber is examined on the *verso*, we find more of the *tau*'s crossbar, as well as the beginning of its vertical downstroke (see Figures 3.2 and 3.3).

The final letter of the line was read quite confidently by Grenfell and Hunt as a *beta*, but no subsequent editors adopted this reading. Although there are no other *betas* in the manuscript with which this letter can be compared, the digital microscope makes clear that *beta* is the correct reading. There is a loop at the top of the letter that led Roberts to read it as a *rho*, but the beginning of the bottom loop of the *beta* does indeed begin before the manuscript breaks off (Figure 3.4).

The two letters between the *tau* and the *beta* have distinctive top hooks that are only found in the scribe's *alphas*, *deltas*, and *lambdas*. Although I have marked these two letters in my transcription as underdots, the Greek is only intelligible if the letters are both *alphas*. It is quite plausible to read the sequence ταaβ as τὰ Ἀβραάμ – that is, as "the things (perhaps τέκνα, "children," similar to Matt 3:9/Luke 3:8, John 8:39, and Rom 9:7) belonging to Abraham." When we combine this potential reading with the two earlier references to an angel, a verb of command (-ταξε in line 5), and the infinitive of the verb "to endure" ([υ]πομεῖναι in line 4), the admittedly fragmentary *recto* reads more

FIGURE 3.3
P.Oxy. 210. Remainder of *tau* in line 7, recto, twisted onto *verso* side; ©BRENTLANDAU

FIGURE 3.4
P.Oxy. 210. *Beta* in line 7, *recto*; ©BRENTLANDAU

like an apocalyptic or paranetical discourse given by an angel, and less like an infancy narrative.

If we move over to the *verso* side, the digital microscope provides several other insights. In the very fragmentary line 8, all previous editors agree that all that can be seen is]το[. Yet not only is there a visible ink trace at the end of the line that merits an underdot, but even a letter before the *tau* is able to be read with some confidence. Visible to the naked eye is the curving bottom of a letter; the digital microscope reveals the faint trace of a curving top, and there is also a faint trace of a horizontal stroke extending from the middle of the letter (see Figure 3.5).

Therefore, I have read an underdotted *epsilon* before the *tau*. This line is so fragmentary that an underdotted *epsilon* does not provide much help in

FIGURE 3.5
P.Oxy. 210. Possible remainder of *epsilon* in line 8, *verso*; ©BRENTLANDAU

FIGURE 3.6
P.Oxy. 210. Possible remainder of *pi* in line 9, *verso*; ©BRENTLANDAU

deciphering it. Even so, this is an instance where the digital microscope has enabled the possible identification of an additional letter recorded by no other editors.

Line 9 of the *verso* is also quite damaged, but it seems possible to read a rather distinctive word in it, identified by no previous editors. After a tiny ink trace at the beginning of the line, the first letter is read by Grenfell and Hunt as an underdotted *pi*, by Porter as an underdot, and is strangely not recorded at all in Roberts's edition. Yet it is quite likely (though not certain) to be a *pi*. There is a bottom curve that is characteristic of the scribe's second leg of the *pi*, and where we would expect the first leg of the *pi* to be, the digital microscope reveals that several fibers have been folded over (see Figure 3.6).

FIGURE 3.7
P.Oxy. 210. Remainder of *phi* in line 9, *verso*; ©BRENTLANDAU

Thus I read it in my edition as an underdotted *pi*, followed by a *rho* and an *omicron*, about which all editors are in agreement. Editors are again divided about the identity of the final letter: Grenfell and Hunt read it as an *iota*, Porter reads it as an underdotted *phi*. Porter recognized that there was a circle in the middle of the vertical stroke; it is possible to see this with the naked eye somewhat, but it is particularly clear with the digital microscope, so much so that I do not regard an underdot as necessary (see Figure 3.7).

Taken together, we have a reasonably secure sequence π̣ροφ; in the more than 200 instances of this sequence found in the NT, all but a few are the noun προφήτης or cognate terms. It thus is possible that the *verso* includes a dispute about whether or not Jesus is a prophet, or perhaps one in which Jesus is either citing a prophet or telling a story about one.

As a final example of the contributions of the digital microscope to the deciphering of 210, at line 25 of the *verso*, all editors have agreed on the sequence ιδενοτι, but disagreed on how to interpret several ink traces at the beginning of the line. Grenfell and Hunt and Porter regarded the ink traces above the *iota* as a *diairesis* marker (i.e., trema), while Roberts instead apparently read an underdotted *epsilon* before the *iota*, saying nothing about the presence of a *diairesis*. With the aid of the digital microscope, it is clear that there are two separate dots above the *iota* serving as a *diairesis*, but there is also a separate mark to the left of the *iota* (see Figure 3.8).

This mark is very high and appears to be the end of a horizontal stroke, which is presumably what Roberts read as an *epsilon*. The mark appears to be too high for an *epsilon*, however, and since line 26 has ιδεν as an iotacism for εἶδεν, it would be unexpected for an *epsilon* to be used in the same verb form one line above. The height of the horizontal stroke, followed by a verb in the

FIGURE 3.8
P.Oxy. 210. Dots of *diairesis* marker and possible remainder of *nomen sacrum*, line 25, *verso*; ©BRENTLANDAU

third-person singular, suggests that it may be a supralinear stroke indicating a *nomen sacrum* – presumably the name Jesus (the *nomen sacrum* for Jesus is almost certainly present in *verso* line 13). Thus, my transcription of this line is:] ̣̅ ϊδενοτι; enough of the hypothesized *nomen sacrum* is missing that its identity cannot be certain, thus I have underdotted it. Yet if I am correct in my transcription, this line would contain the phrase "Jesus saw that…," perhaps indicating that what we have here is a pronouncement story of some kind.

In concluding our discussion of the enigmatic fragment *P.Oxy.* 210, it is no exaggeration to say that the use of a digital microscope has been invaluable for creating a new and more accurate transcription of this text. The examples presented above are but a sampling of the instances in which the digital microscope either confirmed one possible reading among several or demonstrated the viability of a reading suggested by no previous editors.

3 Papyrus Oxyrhynchus 4009

P.Oxy. LX 4009 is a small fragment (2.9 by 9 cm) dating to the second or early third century that has received a significant amount of attention over the past two decades.[10] In 1993, Dieter Lührmann identified the text as a possible fragment of the *Gospel of Peter*.[11] In the following year, he and Peter Parsons published a transcription and reconstruction of the text and connected one side of

10 Images of *P.Oxy.* 4009 appear on the Oxyrhynchus Papyri website. The following shortened link directs to the page containing images of the fragment: <http://tinyurl.com/poxy4009>, accessed on February 28, 2018.

11 Lührmann, Dieter, "POx 4009: Ein neues Fragment des Petrusevangeliums," *NovT* 35, 1993, 390-410.

the fragment with passages parallel in Matt 10:16, Luke 10:3, *Gospel of Thomas* 39, and 2 Clem 5.2-4 about Jesus sending his disciples out as sheep among wolves.[12] Lührmann's identification of the text as a section of *Gos. Pet.* has been further supported by Matti Myllykoski. In a recent article, Myllykoski goes one beyond Lührmann's work by providing a full reconstruction for the less intelligible side of the fragment, which he says narrates the pericope of the sinful woman in Luke 7:36-50 in agreement with the Western text type.[13]

Recently, however, Lührmann's reconstruction of the text and its connection to *Gos. Pet.* has been criticized by Paul Foster.[14] In Foster's opinion, Lührmann's reconstruction contains two major weaknesses. First, Foster notes that 4009 does not bear any resemblance to the other two possible fragments of *Gos. Pet.* that we have (*P.Oxy.* 2949 and the Akhmîm codex).[15] Second, he is skeptical of Lührmann's reconstruction; both sides of the papyrus, Foster says, are too fragmentary to be certain of any direct connection to another text, much less an early apocryphal gospel of which we have no verified copy.

With the use of a digital microscope in the Sackler Papyrology Room at Oxford, the author was able to take a closer look at 4009 and produce a revised transcription of the text. After isolating and capturing high-resolution images of each letter within the manuscript, the author was able to identify several questionable letters in the body of the text with more certainty. Moreover, by comparing the fragmentary letters along the edges of the papyrus to the more definitive and visible letter forms in the body, I was able to determine the most plausible letters in the sequence. At a few key points these letters do not match the previous reconstructions by Lührmann/Parsons and Myllykoski.

The extant text of the fragment is fairly legible. The hand is neat, and thus scholars generally agree about the identity of most letters along the center of the fragment. It is the letters on the edges of the fragment that deserve further

12 Lührmann, Dieter, Parsons, Peter J., "4009. Gospel of Peter?" in: *The Oxyrhynchus Papyri*, vol. 60, London: Egypt Exploration Society, 1994, 1-5. The most widely available transcription is in Ehrman and Pleše, *Apocryphal Gospels*, 289-293.

13 Myllykoski, Matti, "The Sinful Woman in the *Gospel of Peter*: Reconstructing the Other Side of P.Oxy. 4009," *NTS* 55, 2009, 105-115. See also Myllykoski's follow-up article on *P.Oxy.* 4009, which provides an interpretation of his own reconstruction, "Tears of Repentance or Tears of Gratitude? P.Oxy. 4009, the Gospel of Peter and the Western Text of Luke 7.45-49," *NTS* 55, 2009, 380-389.

14 Foster, Paul, "Are There Any Early Fragments of the So-Called Gospel of Peter?" *NTS* 52, 2006, 1-27.

15 While Kraus and Nicklas are not as critical of Lührmann's reconstruction as Foster is, they too take issue with the lack of connection between this text and the Akhmîm codex. See Kraus, Thomas J., Nicklas, Tobias, *Das Petrusevangelium and die Petrusapokalypse: Die Griechischen Fragmente mit deutscher und englisher Übersetzung*, Berlin: W. de Gruyter, 2004, 59-64.

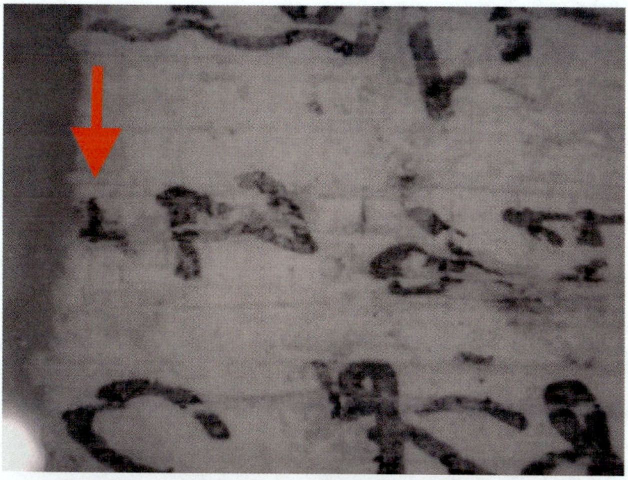

FIGURE 3.9
P.Oxy. 4009. Remainder of tailed letter preceding a *nu* in line 16, *recto*; ©ADELINEHARRINGTON

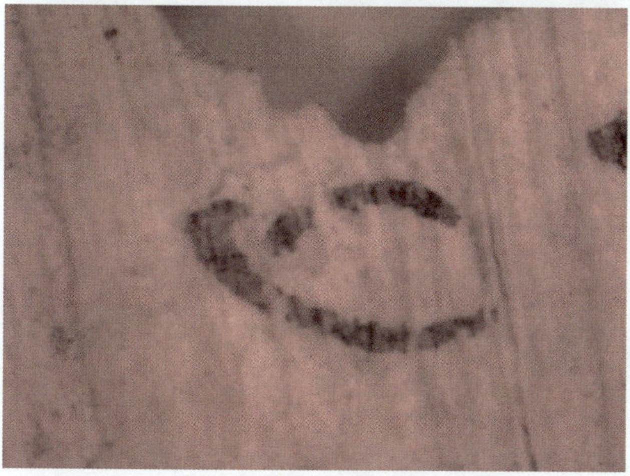

FIGURE 3.10
P.Oxy. 4009. *Omicron* in line 4, *verso*; ©ADELINEHARRINGTON

consideration. There have been a few speculative attempts at these fragmentary letters in earlier editions, but for the most part, they have been left untouched by researchers. It is these fragmentary letters to which I paid the most attention in my autopsy of the manuscript. I do not present a full transcription here, but instead some select readings of the text ascertained with the infrared lighting mode of the digital microscope.

We begin with several instances in which the digital microscope helps to determine that previous editors transcribed letters incorrectly. At the beginning of line 16 on the *recto*, there is a trace of a letter with a visible tail leading out of it (Figure 3.9).

I have transcribed it as an underdotted *alpha*, but it could be one of several other letters written with a final tail. This tailed letter, however, Lührmann's

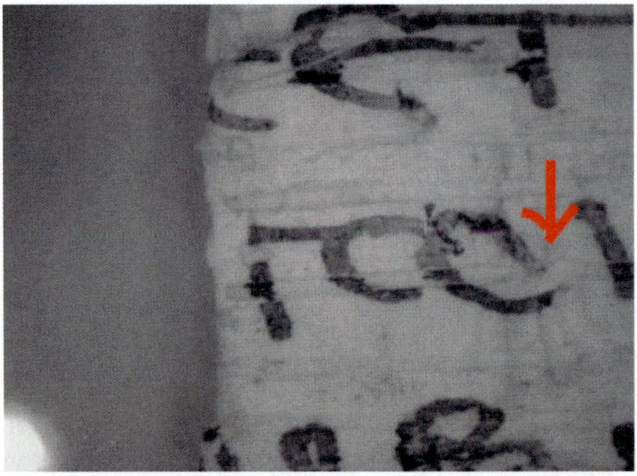

FIGURE 3.11
P.Oxy. 4009. Similar *omicron* in line 16, *recto*; ©ADELINEHARRINGTON

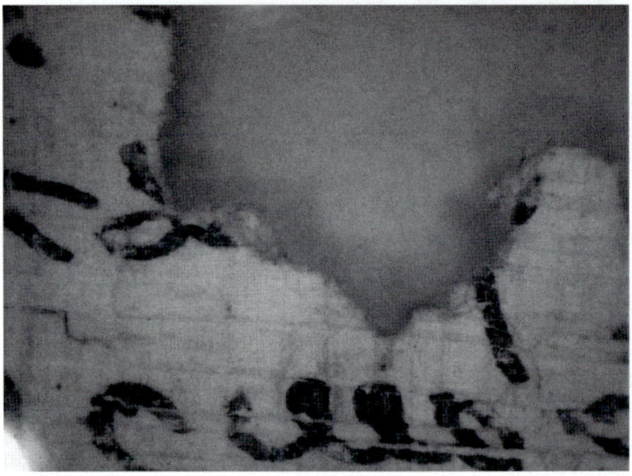

FIGURE 3.12
P.Oxy. 4009. Possible remainder of *phi* in line 3, *recto*; ©ADELINEHARRINGTON

transcription of an omega very improbable. The omegas in this manuscript are looped and closed (cf. *recto* line 8).

As a second example, the letter that begins line 4 of the *verso* is odd in that it appears, upon first glance, to be formed by two round strokes. Given the opening apparent on the right side of the curved letter, Lührmann read it as an underdotted *sigma* and Myllykoski as a *sigma* with no underdot. Upon closer inspection with the microscope, however, it appears that a single stroke formed the closed loop of an *omicron*, although partially faded (Figure 3.10). This is not unlike the wear on the *omicron* we also see in recto line 14 (Figure 3.11).

The author's in-person autopsy with the digital microscope also allowed her to identify several letters that had only been transcribed as underdots by previous editors. At the end of line 3 of the *recto*, Lührmann records an underdot, indicating that traces of ink are present but that not enough of the letter remains to discern its identity. Yet under magnification it is possible to determine the

FIGURE 3.13
P.Oxy. 4009. *Phi* and *rho* written next to each other in line 6, *recto*;
©ADELINEHARRINGTON

FIGURE 3.14
P.Oxy. 4009. Previously untranscribed *upsilon* and *rho* in line 19, *verso*;
©ADELINEHARRINGTON

letter with a reasonable degree of confidence. With a partial loop and a vertical line it has the potential to be read as a *rho*. This letter form, however, is more consistent with the other *phis* within the manuscript than with the *rhos* (Figure 3.12).

This is especially apparent when *phi* and *rho* are viewed next to each other (see Figure 3.13). With the exception of some *iotas* (cf. *recto* line 14), *phis* dip down further than any extant letter in 4009 (cf. *verso* line 8). Thus, this letter is more likely to be a *phi* than a *rho*, although its identity cannot be determined with absolute certainty.

The final lines of the *verso* are faded and damaged, and are thus particularly challenging to read. With the aid of the digital microscope, however, several letters previously transcribed only as underdots can now be read. In line 19 of the *verso*, the high-resolution images clearly capture an *upsilon* gliding into a *rho* (Figure 3.14).

FIGURE 3.15
P.Oxy. 4009. Looped *alpha* visible in line 20, *verso*; ©ADELINEHARRINGTON

The final line of the text (line 20, *verso*) is especially deteriorated. With an enhanced zoom, however, the top loop of an alpha is visible here (Figure 3.15). This looped alpha is consistent with other alphas in the manuscript (cf. especially *recto* lines 16 and 17).

Although a full transcription has not been offered here, the use of a digital microscope has made it clear that a more accurate transcription and more plausible reconstruction of 4009 is needed. Whether this text is indeed part of *Gos. Pet.* will likely not be resolved anytime soon due to its fragmentary condition, but a new examination may help to determine the contents of this enigmatic apocryphon.

4 Papyrus Oxyrhynchus 4469

P.Oxy. LXV 4469 is a copy of the letter of Abgar, King of Edessa, to Jesus, in the form of an amulet.[16] Whereas the "original" letter requests that Jesus come to Edessa to heal Abgar, 4469 replaces Abgar with the name of the amulet's petitioner, Epimachus.[17] The amulet is 5.3 cm wide by 15 cm long, with several

16 Images of *P.Oxy.* 4469 appear on the Oxyrhynchus Papyri website. The following shortened link directs to the page containing images of the fragment: <http://tinyurl.com/poxy4469> (accessed on February 28, 2018).

17 For the Abgar legend, see Doctrina Addai, *De Imagine Edessena = Die Abgarlegende, das Christusbild von Edessa*, Illert, Martin, ed., Turnhout: Brepols, 2007. For more on the use of the Jesus-Abgar correspondence in amulets, see von Dobschütz, Ernst, "Der Briefwechsel Zwischen Abgar und Jesus," *ZWTh* 43, 1900, 422-487; Youtie, Herbert C., "A Gothenburg Papyrus and the Letter to Abgar," *HTR* 23, 1930, 299-302; Youtie, Herbert C., "Gothenburg

lacunae on the left side. The text is written along the fibers, with each line of text running at an ever-increasing downward diagonal slant to the right. The reverse side is blank. Mostly written in Greek, the text switches to Coptic at line 21, and continues for four lines before returning to Greek. Franco Maltomini, who first published the fragment, dated it to the late fifth century CE, based on paleographic evidence.[18] In addition to the slant of the lines, the script itself is small and uneven, making this a rather difficult text to read.

Re-examining this text under the lens of a digital microscope was both a blessing and a curse; a blessing because the high resolution of the camera and the ability to manipulate digitally the images provided far greater ease in recognizing boundaries between letters that had blended together, viewing ink traces around lacunae, and examining less legible areas where the scribe had run out of ink. These very improvements, however, were also a curse in that they only provided a wider range of possibilities for deciphering the scribe's poor handwriting. In other words, being able to adjust the contrast on a blob of ink to make it more visible and defined does not change the fact that it is still a blob of ink, and is therefore inherently ambiguous in its identity.

The most useful feature of the microscope was the infrared mode, which helped the ink to stand out on the page in a way that a simple high contrast black-and-white image could not. This tool clarified some of the ambiguities that apparently plagued Maltomini in his transcription and translation of this frustrating fragment. The most notable observation, missed by Maltomini, is that the scribe inconsistently switched between two forms of the letter *eta*. The first form resembles a backwards Roman capital "N," with the top of the upward diagonal stroke and the second vertical meeting at an angle as high as the

---

Papyrus 21 and the Coptic Version of the Letter to Abgar," *HTR 24*, 1931, 61-65; Peppermüller, Rolf, "Griechische Papyrusfragmente der Doctrina Addai," *VC 25*,1971, 289-301; Salomons, Robert P., "The Correspondence between Abgar and Jesus: A re-edition of a Bodleian Papyrus," in: *Land of Dreams: Greek and Latin Studies in Honour of A.H.M. Kessels*, Lardinois, Andre P.M.H., van der Poel, Marc G.M., Hunink, Vincent J.C., eds., Leiden: Brill, 2006, 299-307; Caseau, Béatrice, "La lettre de Jésus à Abgar d'Édesse: appropriations et transformations," in: *Remanier, métaphraser, Fonctions et techniques de la réécriture dans le monde byzantin*, Marjanović-Dušanić, Smilja, ed., Belgrade: Faculté de Philosophie, Université de Belgrade, 2011, 13-43; Sanzo, Joseph E., "Brit. Lib. Or. 4919(2): An Unpublished Coptic Amulet in the British Library," *ZPE 183*, 2012, 98-100; Emmenegger, Gregor, "Der Abgarbrief und seine Verwendung in koptischen Amuletten," in: *Das Christusbild, Zu Herkunft und Entwicklung in Ost und West, Das östliche Christentum*, Dietz, Karlheinz, Hannick, Christian, Lutzka, Carolina, Maier, Elisabeth, eds., *OeCh 62*, Würzburg, Echter, 2016, 121-134; Given, J. Gregory, "Utility and Variance in Late Antique Witnesses to the Abgar-Jesus Correspondence," *Archiv für Religionsgeschichte 17*, 2016, 187-222.

18 Maltomini, Franco, "4469. Letter of Abgar to Jesus (Amulet)." *The Oxyrhynchus Papyri*, vol. 65, London: Egypt Exploration Society, 1998, 122-129.

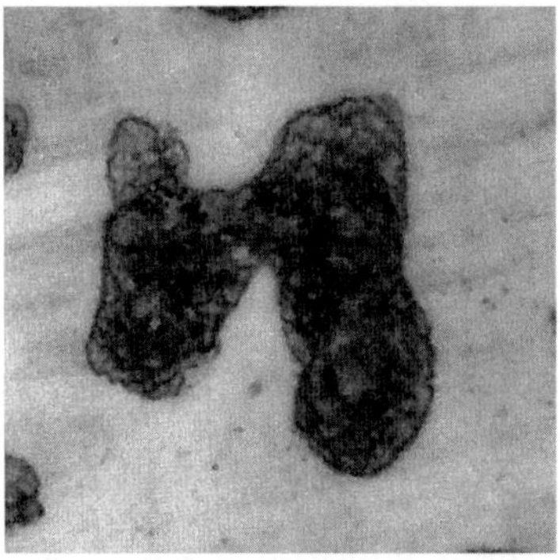

FIGURE 3.16
P.Oxy. 4469. First form of *eta,* resembling a backwards Roman capital "N"; ©JAMESHENRIQUES

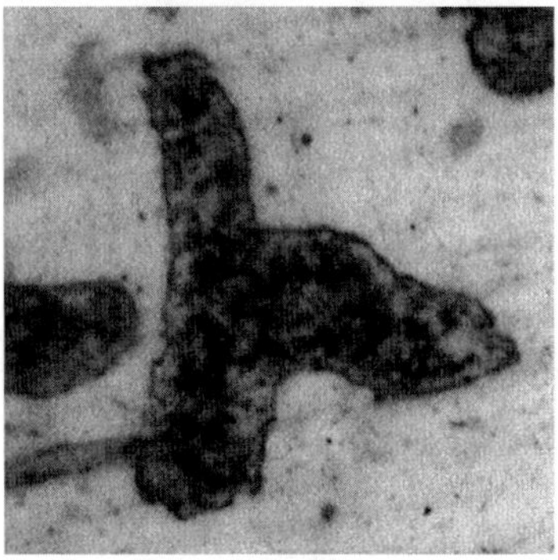

FIGURE 3.17
P.Oxy. 4469. Second form of *eta,* resembling a lower-case Roman "h"; ©JAMESHENRIQUES

first vertical stroke, while the bottom of the second vertical stroke drops below the line (see Figure 3.16).

The second form more closely resembles a lower-case Roman letter "h," beginning with a high vertical stroke which then curves upward at a narrow angle, but rises only about half as high as the first vertical stroke before curving downward again at a wider angle, often terminating at a point higher than the bottom of first vertical stroke (Figure 3.17).

While the scribe alternates inconsistently between both forms throughout the Greek text, he uses the latter exclusively when writing in Coptic. Furthermore, given the gradually increasing slant of each line, the scribe had a tendency to sometimes (but not always) slant the letters in relation to the gradient of the line, thus sometimes making the latter form of *eta* look like his *upsilon,* which in his hand resembles the Roman letter "v," and vice-versa.

This confusion is nowhere more evident than in line 19, where Maltomini has transliterated the text as σκηλλῆναις, regarding it as a gross misspelling of σκυλῆναι ("to disturb"). Yet closer inspection has revealed that first *eta* to actually be an *upsilon,* making the word indeed σκυλῆναι (which the scribe misspelled as σκυλλῆναις).

FIGURE 3.18
P.Oxy. 4469. *Upsilon* or *omicron* incorrectly transcribed as *theta* in line 17;
©JAMESHENRIQUES

Σκυλῆναι is in fact the form presented in the version of the Letter of Abgar to Jesus preserved by Eusebius in his *Ecclestiastical History* (1.13).

Closer examination under the digital microscope also suggested a corrected reading of line 17, which Maltomini had read as θ̣̅ς̅ εἶ τοῦ θ̅υ̅ ("you are the God of God"), which he noted was an error on the part of the scribe, who likely intended the correct reading υ̅ς̅ εἶ τοῦ θ̅υ̅ ("you are the son of God"). Much of the first half of the line is fragmentary, but close inspection reveals traces of ink around the lacunae that should likely alter Maltomini's reading. At the very least, the letter that Maltomini had identified as a *theta* cannot be one, since the scribe's *thetas* have a crossbar that extends outside of the central part of the letter, something that this fragmentary letter definitely lacks (Figure 3.18).

The identity of the fragmentary letter is not entirely clear: it could be an *upsilon*, in which case the scribe did indeed write the appropriate *nomen sacrum* of υ̅ς̅. But it is also possible that it is an *omicron*, which would suggest that the scribe spelled out the full υ̅ἱ̅ό̅ς̅ rather than the abbreviated while curiously still retaining the superlinear stroke that denotes *nomina sacra*.

Although Maltomini's transcription of 4469 in general was excellent, the digital microscope has nevertheless clarified some of the most difficult portions of this very challenging fragment.

5 Conclusion

This study has demonstrated how the transcription of three fragmentary early Christian papyri can be corrected and refined through the use of a digital microscope, particularly one having an infrared lighting mode. There are, of course, limitations to the applications of this technology; some letters will still remain stubbornly illegible even under high-resolution magnification and infrared lighting. Even so, the number of early Christian and other papyri, both edited and unedited, that can benefit from editors including digital microscopes in their toolkits is truly staggering.

References

Brent C. Landau, "A Re-transcription and Analysis of a Possible Apocryphal Gospel Fragment, Papyrus Oxyrhynchus II 210, Utilizing a Digital Microscope," *Ephemerides Theologicae Lovanienses* 94/3 (2018): 427-80.

Caseau, Béatrice, "La lettre de Jésus à Abgar d'Édesse: appropriations et transformations," in: *Remanier, métaphraser, Fonctions et techniques de la réécriture dans le monde byzantin*, Marjanović-Dušanić, Smilja, ed., Belgrade: Faculté de Philosophie, Université de Belgrade, 2011, 13-43.

Doctrina Addai, *De Imagine Edessena = Die Abgarlegende, das Christusbild von Edessa*, Illert, Martin, ed., Turnhout: Brepols, 2007.

Ehrman, Bart D., Pleše, Zlatko, *The Apocryphal Gospels: Texts and Translations*, New York: Oxford University Press, 259-265.

Emmenegger, Gregor, "Der Abgarbrief und seine Verwendung in koptischen Amuletten," in: *Das Christusbild, Zu Herkunft und Entwicklung in Ost und West, Das östliche Christentum*, Dietz, Karlheinz, Hannick, Christian, Lutzka, Carolina, Maier, Elisabeth, eds., *OeCh 62*, Würzburg, Echter, 2016.

Foster, Paul, "Are There Any Early Fragments of the So-Called Gospel of Peter?" *NTS 52*, 2006, 1-27.

Given, J. Gregory, "Utility and Variance in Late Antique Witnesses to the Abgar-Jesus Correspondence," *Archiv für Religionsgeschichte* 17, 2016, 187-222.

Grenfell, Bernard P., Hunt, Arthur S., "210. Early Christian Fragment," in: *The Oxyrhynchus Papyri*, Volume 2, London: Egypt Exploration Society, 1899, 9-10.

Kraus, Thomas J., Nicklas, Tobias, *Das Petrusevangelium and die Petrusapokalypse: Die Griechischen Fragmente mit deutscher und englisher Übersetzung*, Berlin: W. de Gruyter, 2004, 59-64.

Landau, Brent C., "A Re-transcription and Analysis of a Possible Apocryphal Gospel Fragment, *Papyrus Oxyrhynchus* II 210, Utilizing a Digital Microscope," in: *Ephemerides Theologicae Lovaniensis*, forthcoming.

Lührmann, Dieter, "POx 4009: Ein neues Fragment des Petrusevangeliums," *NovT* 35, 1993, 390-410.

Lührmann, Dieter, Parsons, Peter J., "4009. Gospel of Peter?" in: *The Oxyrhynchus Papyri*, vol. 60, London: Egypt Exploration Society, 1994, 1-5.

Maltomini, Franco, "4469. Letter of Abgar to Jesus (Amulet)." *The Oxyrhynchus Papyri*, vol. 65, London: Egypt Exploration Society, 1998, 122-129.

Myllykoski, Matti, "Tears of Repentance or Tears of Gratitude? P.Oxy. 4009, the Gospel of Peter and the Western Text of Luke 7.45-49," *NTS 55*, 2009, 380-389.

Myllykoski, Matti, "The Sinful Woman in the *Gospel of Peter*: Reconstructing the Other Side of P.Oxy. 4009," *NTS 55*, 2009, 105-115.

Peppermüller, Rolf, "Griechische Papyrusfragmente der Doctrina Addai," *VC 25*,1971, 289-301.

Porter, Stanley E., "POxy II 210 as an Apocryphal Gospel and the Development of Egyptian Christianity," in: *Atti del XXII Congresso internazionale di papirologia: Firenze, 23-29 agosto 1998*, Isabella Andorlini et al., eds., Florence: Instituto papirologico G. Vitelli, 2001, 1095-1108.

Roberts, Colin H., "An Early Christian Papyrus," in: *Miscellània papirològica Ramon Roca-Puig*, Janeras, Sebastià, ed., Barcelona: Fundació Salvador Vives Casajuana, 1987, 293-296.

Salomons, Robert P., "The Correspondence between Abgar and Jesus: A re-edition of a Bodleian Papyrus," in: *Land of Dreams: Greek and Latin Studies in Honour of A.H.M. Kessels*, Lardinois, Andre P.M.H., Van der Poel, Marc G.M., Hunink, Vincent J.C., eds., Leiden: Brill, 2006, 299-307.

Sanzo, Joseph E., "Brit. Lib. Or. 4919(2): An Unpublished Coptic Amulet in the British Library," *ZPE 183*, 2012, 98-100.

Terras, Melissa, "Artefacts and Errors: Acknowledging Issues of Representation in the Digital Imaging of Ancient Texts," in: *Kodikologie und Paläographie im Digitale Zeitalter 2*, Fischer, Franz, Fritze, Christiane, Vogeler, Georg, eds., Norderstedt: Books on Demand, 2010, 43-61.

Von Dobschütz, Ernst, "Der Briefwechsel Zwischen Abgar und Jesus," *ZWTh 43*, 1900, 422-487.

Wayment, Thomas A., *The Text of the New Testament Apocrypha (100-400 CE)*, New York: Bloomsbury, 2013, 402-403.

Youtie, Herbert C., "A Gothenburg Papyrus and the Letter to Abgar," *HTR 23*, 1930, 299-302.

Youtie, Herbert C., "Gothenburg Papyrus 21 and the Coptic Version of the Letter to Abgar," *HTR 24*, 1931, 61-65.

CHAPTER 4

Manuscripts, Monks, and *Mufattishīn*: Digital Access and Concerns of Cultural Heritage in the Yale Monastic Archaeology Project

Stephen J. Davis

1 Introduction

The Yale Monastic Archaeology Project (YMAP) currently sponsors work at two monastic centers in Egypt: at the Shenoutean federation of monasteries near Sohag in the south, and at Wadi al-Naṭrūn (ancient Scetis) in the north. The study of manuscripts at these sites has presented exciting possibilities – and has raised complex challenges – related to digital access and cultural heritage. My contribution to this volume has two parts, and two associated goals. First, I will report on our work at the White Monastery, the central foundation in the Shenoutean federation, where excavations in December 2011 yielded the discovery of manuscript fragments in the Church of St. Shenoute. This discovery served as a catalyst for a series of research steps that began with archaeological analysis and photo-documentation and culminated with the publication of the fragments online through Yale's Egyptological Institute website. Second, I will report on my work cataloguing the Coptic and Arabic manuscripts in the library at the Monastery of the Syrians in Wadi al-Naṭrūn, a project started in December 2013 that has evolved to include discussions about the possibility of scanning the collection and making its contents available for online access.

In the case of the White Monastery, we are supported by the local community's monastic leadership and by a team of inspectors (in colloquial Egyptian Arabic, *mufattishīn*) representing the Egyptian Supreme Council of Antiquities, also known as the SCA. The Supreme Council of Antiquities is the body that grants and renews our archaeological permissions on an annual basis, and the local *mufattishīn* implement the SCA's policy at the local level. The situation at the Monastery of the Syrians is different. There, because my research is not archaeological in nature, but rather archival, my cataloguing work in the library is facilitated through a private arrangement with the abbot and head librarian. In this article, my goal is to discuss not only our digitization practices, but also the ways in which these local relationships and institutional structures contextualize and complicate such plans. In so doing, I hope to stimulate

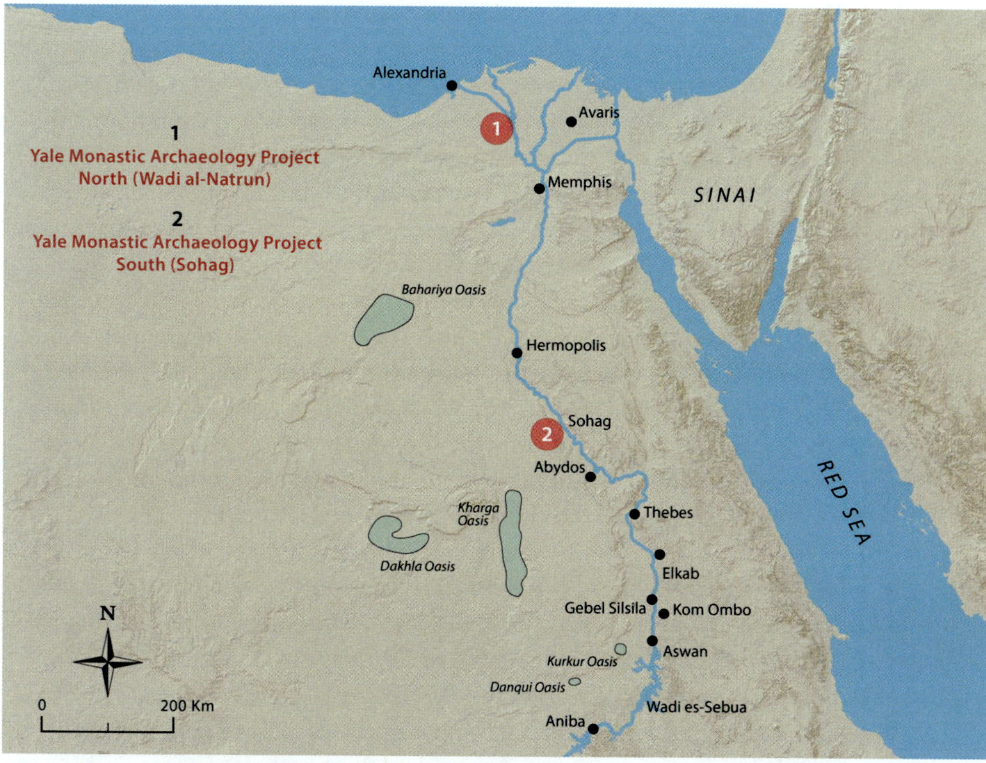

FIGURE 4.1 Map of Egypt, showing the location of the Monastery of the Syrians (Wādī al-Naṭrūn) and the White Monastery (Sohag). Map created by Alberto Urcia for the Yale in Egypt website: <http://egyptology.yale.edu/expeditions/current-expeditions>. Davis for this publication, accessed on 10.04.19; ©STEPHENDAVIS

conversations about cultural heritage, the legacy of colonialism, and the control of manuscript content in the digital age.[1]

1 In the field of cultural heritage management and preservation, there has been a recent upsurge of interdisciplinary reflection on the ethical dimensions of archaeological and archival work, including matters of digitization and digital access: Sandis, Constantine, *Cultural Heritage Ethics: Between Theory and Practice*, Cambridge: Open Book Publishers, 2014. Ireland, Tracy, Schofield, John, "The Ethics of Cultural Heritage, Ethical Archaeologies," *The Politics of Social Justice 4*, Gnecco, Cristobal, Ireland, Tracy, eds., New York: Springer / World Archaeological Congress, 2015. Murphy, Bernice L., *Museums, Ethics and Cultural Heritage*, New York: Routledge, 2016. Such reflection, however, has been noticeably absent in the publications of scholars and projects working with monastic cultural heritage in Egypt, where living religious communities (as well as government agencies) exert claims on historical sites and texts. I hope to draw on the perspectives of "indigenous" and "post-colonial" archaeologies to break this silence.

2 Manuscript Fragments at the White Monastery

2.1 *Infrastructural Challenges from Photography to Digital Database*

During our December 2011 season, the YMAP team conducted excavations in an upstairs space called the "Candle Room" within the monumental fifth-century church at the White Monastery. Located above and to the north of the sanctuary, the room had been used in recent times as a storage space for candles (hence the name). Along with fragments of candles, charcoal, floor plaster, brick, newspaper, cardboard, and modern prayer petitions, our excavations in the room yielded numerous small fragments of parchment and paper with Coptic or Arabic writing, along with pieces of textile and leather associated with book bindings. The following year, I oversaw the photo-documentation and cataloguing of the fragments on site. A co-authored article published in the *Journal of Coptic Studies* documented our archaeological methodology and presented an initial report on the contents of this find, including one identified fragment from the *Canons* of Shenoute, the fifth-century head of the community. That article placed the fragments within the context of a long history of manuscript dissemination when the White Monastery library was "dismembered and sold off piecemeal over a span of 125 years, during the eighteenth, nineteenth, and twentieth centuries."[2]

The process of photographing the fragments in December 2012 was made more difficult because of local tensions within the SCA inspectorate and because of changes in our physical working conditions. Prior to the 2012 season, based on a locally negotiated arrangement, we had been able to conduct finds analysis on a regular basis in a dedicated workspace within our rest house. But that year, tensions developed within the local inspectorate, prompted by the visit of a regional inspector who tried to implement a more stringent set of policies (one more closely aligned with written SCA statutes). As a result, prior to our planned photo-documentation we were required to relocate our entire finds magazine to a building adjacent to the inspectorate and to perform all our subsequent finds analysis and photography in the inspectorate office space, where the lighting was poor and variable. At the time, these local dynamics made it uncertain what kind of access and authorization we might be granted in the future, and so we felt pressed to complete an entire set of photographs within the short span of that season, despite the suboptimal conditions. I completed this work with the assistance of three graduate students, Elizabeth Davidson, Daniel Schriever, and Mary Farag.

2 Davis, Stephen J. et al., "Left Behind: A Recent Discovery of Manuscript Fragments in the White Monastery Church," *Journal of Coptic Studies 16*, 2014, 69-87, quote p. 79.

We faced a different set of infrastructural challenges in moving from photography to the development of an online database. Making the images of the Candle Room fragments freely available to other researchers online was understood to be part of our contractual responsibility to the SCA and part of our partnership with the monastery in preserving its cultural heritage. To this end, our aim was to create an accessible, uniform interface through the Yale in Egypt website. With this objective in mind, I worked with Mary Farag and with the website's designer and manager, Bjorn Akselsen, to format the images and to find software that accommodated different user environments, taking into account variables introduced by hardware, operating systems, mobile devices, browsers, etc.

We had 1850 images in total, and to format them we decided to juxtapose each separate recto and verso in a single, unified image file. The result was 925 slides instead of 1850. Due in part to the suboptimal photographic conditions on site, the images revealed certain variations in quality, lightness/contrast, and proportion. Thus, to prepare the composites required a multi-step approach: we adjusted lightness and contrast, and then resized and reconfigured images to achieve uniformity across the entire collection. Once the composites were prepared, the resulting images were optimized in Photoshop. Finally, the high-resolution images were reduced to about ten percent of original size, without reducing image quality for online viewing.

In preparation for making the images available to the general public, we ran tests and decided on a simple yet advanced "slide-show" gallery presentation using an application called SimpleViewer-Pro.[3] This software had a pleasing interface, allowed for Universal Playback, and provided a considerable amount of control and flexibility. The system went live in December 2014. Unfortunately, however, we subsequently were forced to change the delivery method as Yale University moved to a different content management system called Drupal™.[4] The built-in "slide-show" capabilities of Drupal™ proved to be less customizable than SimpleViewer, and as a result we had much less control over the image display. Despite this temporary setback, Bjorn Akselsen worked

3 For more information on the SimpleViewer-Pro application, see: <https://www.simpleviewer.net/simpleviewer/pro/>, accessed 10.04.19.

4 Drupal™ is an open source software platform used to create websites and online applications, see: <https://www.drupal.org>, accessed November 22, 2017, and Nick Abbott, Richard Jones, Matt Glaman, and Chaz Chumley, *Drupal 8: Enterprise Web Development* (Olton, UK: Packt Publishing, 2016).

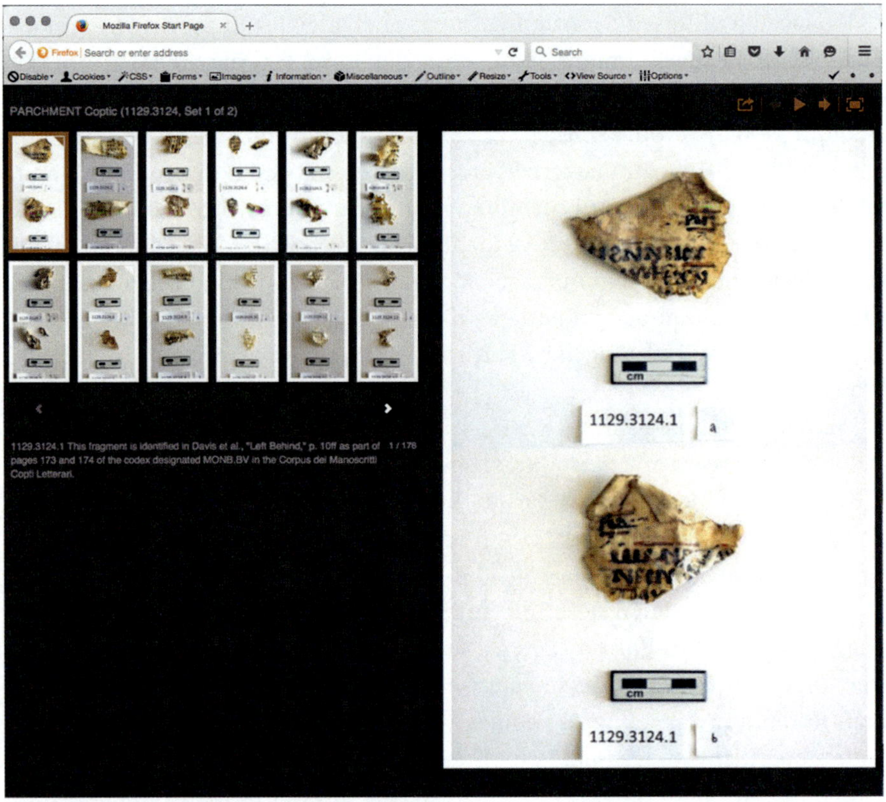

FIGURE 4.2 Screenshot of the former interface for the Candle Room Manuscript fragments in SimpleViewer-Pro. <https://egyptology.yale.edu/current-expeditions/yale-monastic-archaeology-project-south-sohag/white-monastery/candle-room-manuscript-fragments>. Accessed on 10.04.19; ©STEPHEN DAVIS

with Yale's technology department to transfer our content to the new system and in the end managed to approximate its original functionality.[5]

3 The Manuscript Library at the Monastery of the Syrians

3.1 *Cultural Heritage and Local Concerns about Digitization*

Having reviewed the process by which the White Monastery Candle Room fragments were digitized, I now turn to a second case study: the manuscript

5 I want to thank Bjorn Akselsen for his expertise in website development and his assistance in reporting on the details of this process, and Mary Farag for her invaluable help in formatting the images.

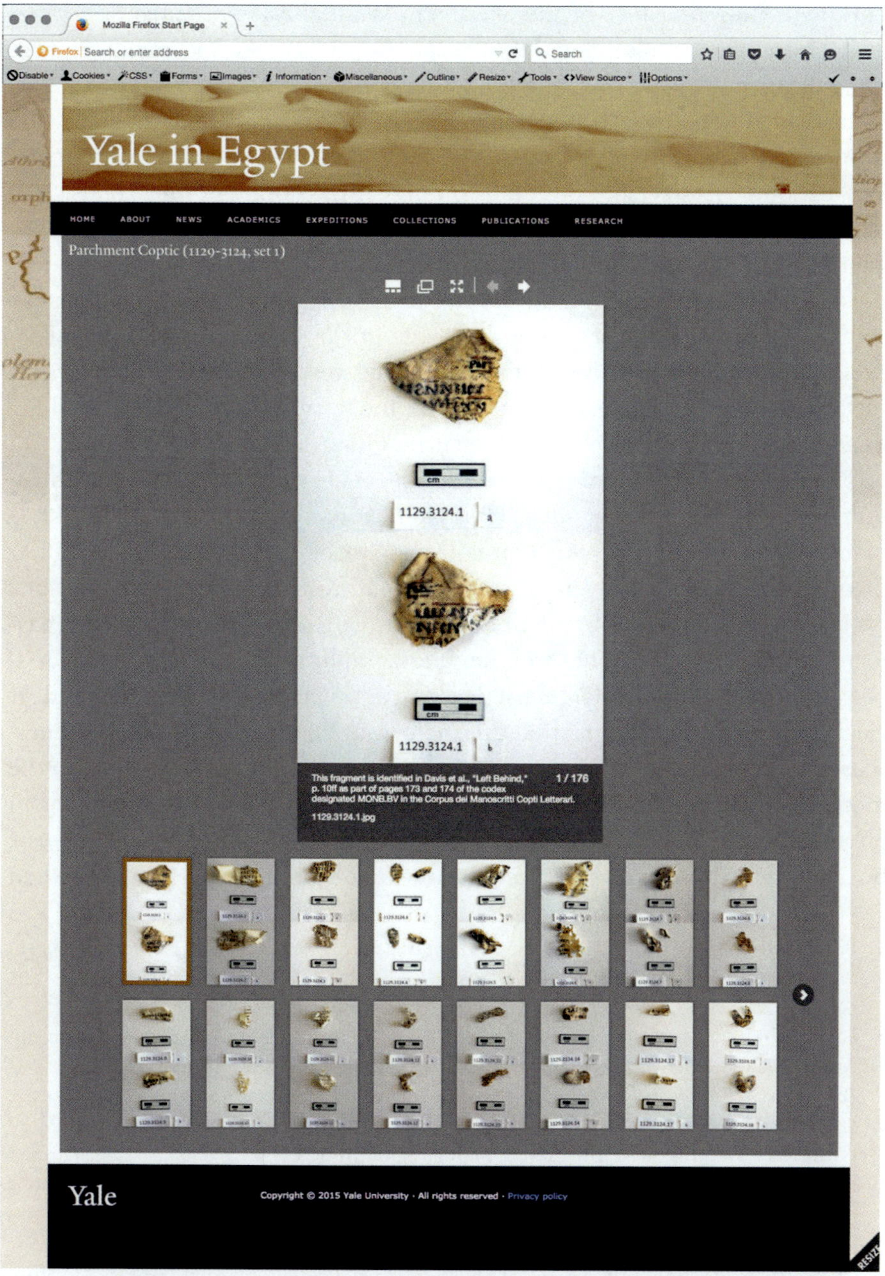

FIGURE 4.3 Screenshot of the current interface for the Candle Room Manuscript fragments in Drupal™. Drupal™ <https://egyptology.yale.edu/archaeological-expeditions/white-monastery-project/candle-room-project/parchment_coptic_1129-3124_set_1>, accessed on 10.04.19; ©STEPHENDAVIS

library at the Monastery of the Syrians in Wādī al-Naṭrūn. Since December 2013, I have been cataloguing the corpus of Coptic and Arabic manuscripts in the collection. This work follows a previous project by Sebastian Brock and Lucas Van Rompay to catalogue the Syriac manuscripts and fragments, the results of which were published in 2014 by Peeters Press.[6] Taken together, the Syriac, Coptic, Arabic, and Ethiopic holdings of the library number more than 1000. Of these, approximately 800 manuscripts are Coptic, Arabic, or a bilingual mix of Coptic and Arabic. As of June 2017, my team and I have logged almost 2000 person-hours in the library and have produced comprehensive catalogue entries for over 300 manuscripts in the Coptic and Arabic collections. This work has been facilitated by the kind hospitality of Bishop Mattā'us, the abbot of the monastery, Father Bigoul, the former head librarian, and Fathers Amoun and Azer (Lazarus), the current librarians.[7]

The hospitality of the monastery and especially my conversations with Father Bigoul provide the context for my reflections here on cultural heritage management and digitization. Our conversations evolved in stages, as Father Bigoul moved from a posture of suspicion and resistance to one of cautious optimism and cooperation. When I began my cataloguing work at the monastery, I initially inquired about whether photography and/or digitization should be considered part of my larger project, and at that time Father Bigoul made it clear (in no uncertain terms) that this topic was effectively off limits. To underscore his objection, he shared with me two stories about recent visitors to the monastery who had betrayed his trust. In one case, he had allowed someone to photograph a manuscript with the promise that it was only for personal use, but a few months later another visitor came to the monastery with a CD he had

6 Brock, Sebastian, Van Rompay, Lucas, *Catalogue of the Syriac Manuscripts and Fragments in the Library of Deir al-Surian, Wadi al-Natrun (Egypt)*, Orientalia Lovaniensia Analecta 227, Louvain: Peeters, 2014.

7 For a preliminary summary of this work, see Davis, Stephen J., "Cataloguing the Coptic and Arabic Manuscripts in the Monastery of the Syrians: A Preliminary Report," in: *Studia Patristica XCII: Papers Presented at the Seventeenth International Conference on Patristic Studies*, held in Oxford 2015, Volume 18, Markus, Vincent, 2017, Louvain: Peeters, 179-185. More recently, I have presented three reports updating our progress, with a special focus on the biblical collection and on historical information gleaned from scribal and readerly insertions in those manuscripts, at the Eleventh International Congress of Coptic Studies (Claremont, CA, July 2016), at the 2016 Society of Biblical Literature Annual Meeting (San Antonio, TX, November 2016), and at the Oxford seminar, New Perspectives on Mediterranean History (Balliol College, Oxford University, June 2017). These presentations formed the basis of a new article entitled "Marginalia Coptica et Arabica: Traces of Scribes, Patrons, Restorers, and Readers in the Biblical Collection at the Monastery of the Syrians (Dayr al-Suryān)," to be published in: *Proceedings of the Eleventh International Congress of Coptic Studies*, Claremont, CA, July 25th-30th 2016, Louvain: Peeters, 2019, forthcoming.

acquired containing the same images. In another case, a scholar visiting the library for manuscript study had pledged not to take photographs, but later Father Bigoul returned to find the person snapping pictures. These anecdotes are part of the monks' shared cultural memory of a colonialist history in which the monastery has lost agency over large portions of its manuscript collection: the majority of its Syriac holdings were purchased and carted away by the Vatican in the eighteenth century and by the British Library in the nineteenth century.[8]

Over our first year of work, it became clear that the number of manuscripts in the collection would require multiple volumes, and during this period Father Bigoul and I spoke frequently about the format, organization, and logistics related to our publication plans. As part of this ongoing conversation, in December 2014, I asked about the possibility of photographing sample folia for inclusion as illustrative figures in those volumes, just as Brock and Van Rompay had done for their Syriac catalogue. Father Bigoul was happy to facilitate this, and to my surprise he also broached the subject of digitization, telling me that making the collection available online was now a priority of his.

When I asked why his mind had changed, he told me that he had been cautious earlier because of his experiences of being "burned" by betrayals of trust. He also revealed that he had been approached in the recent past by another North American academic institution interested in entering into a contract with the monastery to digitize the collection. But the terms of the proposed contract caused him considerable discomfort, primarily because of the way copyright control was construed. While the American institution offered to provide equipment, and to undertake all the digitization work itself, it wanted to charge a fee to anyone requesting use of the images. This fee would be payable not to the monastery but to the partner library in the United States. Father Bigoul did not feel comfortable with this kind of financial structure: instead, he

8 On the history of the library at the Monastery of the Syrians, see Father Bigoul al-Suriany, "The Manuscript Collection of Deir al-Surian in Wadi al-Natrun," *Journal of the Canadian Society for Coptic Studies 2.1*, January 2011, 51-62 (available online with a subscription at <http://lockwoodonlinejournals.com/>, accessed on 10.04.19. See also Sebastian Brock and Lucas Van Rompay, *Catalogue of the Syriac Manuscripts and Fragments*, xiii-xxii. For examples of manuscripts from the Monastery of the Syrians now housed in other collections, see Wright, William, *Catalogue of Syriac Manuscripts in the British Museum acquired since the year 1838*, 3 vols., London: British Museum, 1870-1872. Wright, William, *Notulae Syriacae*, London: Gilbert and Rivington, 1887. Assemani, Joseph Simeon, Assemani, Stephanus Evodius, *Biblioteca apostolicae vaticanae codicum manuscriptorum catalogus in tres partes*, vols. 2-3, Paris: Maisonneuve, 1926. Tisserant, Eugenius, *Specimina Codicum Orientalium,* in: Lietzmann, J., *Tabulae in Usum Scholarium*, Bonn: Marcus and Weber, 1914. Hatch, William H.P., *An Album of Dated Syriac Manuscripts*, Boston: The American Academy of Arts and Sciences, 1946.

preferred to facilitate free access. The proposed contract also stipulated that copyright ownership would be shared between the American institution and the monastery and that each would possess a copy of the digital database, but Father Bigoul was concerned that in practice the agency of the monastery would be trumped by the American institution if there was a disagreement on terms of permission. As a result, Father Bigoul had come away with significant reservations about entering such partnerships.

In this context, I want to draw on some helpful insights from scholars working in the area of digitization and cultural heritage studies. As I alluded to earlier, Father Bigoul's reservations are in fact deeply embedded in cultural memories of "epistemic violence" and "the loss of Indigenous control over use and access."[9] As Joshua Bell, Kimberly Christen, and Mark Turin note in their introduction to a volume on "Digital Repatriation and the Circulation of Indigenous Knowledge," it is "precisely because [digital] materials can exist in multiple locations" that there has been a shift of emphasis from "issues of *access* to *access and control*." It is because "digital objects can co-exist in Indigenous archives and websites as well as in institutional databases (online or off)" that communities like the Monastery of the Syrians raise valid "concerns over who makes decisions about how materials are accessed, circulated, and understood across multiple settings."[10] As Kate Hennessy and her colleagues working on "The Inuvialuit Living History Project" have recognized, this is where "forging relationships" and "establishing the groundwork for clear and meaningful communication" lay the foundation for "trust, respect, and solidarity," and for the kind of "openness and flexibility that is grounded in ... the value of curatorial collaboration with originating communities."[11]

---

9 Anderson, Jane, Christen, Kim, "'Chuck a Copyright on It': Dilemmas of Digital Return and the Possibilities for Traditional Knowledge Licenses and Labels," *Museum Anthropology Review* 7.1-2, Spring-Fall, 2013, 105-126, p. 113. In drawing on the category of "Indigeneity" and applying it to the Coptic community in Egypt, I employ it not as an absolute category, but as "relational," "variable," and "defined relative to encounters with people newer to a place": see Colwell-Chanthaphonh, Chip, "Archaeology and Indigenous Collaboration," in: *Archaeological Theory Today*, Hodder, Ian, ed., second edition, Cambridge: Polity, 2012, 267-91, p. 279; quoting in part from Wobst, Martin H., "Indigenous Archaeologies: A Worldwide Perspective on Human Materialities and Human Rights," in: *Indigenous Archaeologies: A Reader on Decolonization*, Bruchac, Margaret M., Hart, Siobhan M., Wobst, Martin H., eds., Walnut Creek, CA: Left Coast Press, 2010, 17-27, p. 19.

10 Bell, Joshua A., Christen, Kimberly, Turin, Mark, "Introduction: After the Return," *Museum Anthropology Review* 7.1-2, Spring-Fall, 2013, 1-21, p. 7.

11 Hennessy, Kate, Lyons, Natasha, Loring, Stephen, Arnold, Charles, Mervin, Joe, Elias, Albert, Pokiak, James, "The Inuvialuit Living History Project: Digital Return as the Forging of Relationships Between Institutions, People, and Data," *Museum Anthropology Review* 7.1-2, Spring-Fall 2013, 44-73, at 59 and 62. Here, the authors draw on the work of Jürgen

In my case, I had forged a longstanding relationship with the Monastery of the Syrians over the course of almost a decade of archaeological and archival work in the region. Starting in 2006, during our excavation seasons nearby at the site of the Monastery of John the Little, the Monastery of the Syrians had housed our Egyptian workers, and the nearby Monastery of St. Bishoi provided space for our finds magazine. Beginning in 2013, as part of the cataloguing project, Father Bigoul and I began working intensively side-by-side in the library and engaged in many conversations on personal and professional matters. Thus, when I asked him why his mind had changed, he told me that this durative experience of collegiality and mutual investment was what allowed him to overcome his initial reservations about the prospect of collaborating on a digitization initiative. For my part, any such discussions had to hinge on an appropriate sensitivity to the enduring effects of Egypt's colonialist legacy, including the need to acknowledge and act responsibly in the face of institutional inequities when it comes to financial resources, and above all to ensure and preserve the monastery's agency in determining how best to manage its own cultural heritage.[12] This is consistent with the wider disciplinary goal in cultural heritage management of "equalizing power relationships and creating mutually beneficial projects"[13] and of attending to the "ethical implications… [and] politics of fieldwork, and collaborations with local people, descendants, indigeneous groups, and other communities of connection."[14]

After the December 2014 season, we began a process of careful deliberation involving experts from Yale, from the Bibliotheca Alexandrina, and from the Monastery of the Syrians. From April 27 to May 1, 2015, Father Bigoul paid a visit to Yale University in New Haven, CT, for a week of consultations. During

---

Habermas' interlinked concepts of "communicative action" and "communicative space". See: Habermas, Jürgen, *The Theory of Communicative Action*, 2 vols., McCarthy, Thomas, trans., Boston: Beacon Press, 1984-1989; McCarthy, Thomas, *Between Facts and Norms: Contributions to a Discourse Theory of Law and Democracy*, Rehg, William, trans., *Studies in Contemporary German Social Thought*, Cambridge, Mass.: MIT Press, 1996.

12 On the importance of cultivating and maintaining "an awareness of colonial histories, in terms of both their material and economic impacts and of the forms of thought which the colonial world produced," see: Gosden, Chris, "Post-Colonial Archaeology," in: *Archaeological Theory Today*, Hodder, Ian, ed., second edition, 251-266, quote p. 252.

13 Colwell-Chanthaphonh, Chip, "Archaeology and Indigenous Collaboration," 273.

14 Meskell, Lynn, "The Social Life of Heritage," in: *Archaeological Theory Today*, Hodder, Ian, ed., second edition, 229-250, p. 235. On the ethical dimensions of fieldwork, see also Hall, Martin, "Situational Ethics and Engaged Practice: The Case of Archaeology in Africa," in: *Embedding Ethics: Shifting the Boundaries of the Anthropological Profession*, Meskell, Lynn M., Pels, Peter, eds., Oxford: Berg, 2005, 169-184. Zimmerman, Larry J., Vitelli, Karen D., Hollowell-Zimmer, Julie, eds., *Ethical Issues in Archaeology*, Walnut Creek, CA: AltaMira, 2003.

his stay, he met with Beth Beaudin, a librarian with extensive experience in the digitization of Middle Eastern library collections, including prior collaboration with the Bibliotheca Alexandrina. He also paid visits to the photography lab at Yale, the Beinecke Rare Book and Manuscript Library, and the Manuscripts and Archives department of Sterling Memorial Library, including a meeting with Robin Dougherty, the curator for the Arabic language collection. The result of these appointments was deeper knowledge of the different methodologies and equipment utilized at Yale for digitization projects. In the end, Father Bigoul decided that a high-resolution scanner with an adjustable cradle would best suit his needs at the monastery, since it would allow for maximum efficiency and scanning speed, while preserving the integrity of the physical manuscripts, many of which have fragile bindings. During our subsequent cataloguing season at the Monastery of the Syrians, in June 2015, Father Bigoul also hosted a consultation with representatives from the Bibliotheca Alexandrina, who agreed to provide technical expertise, training, and supervision, once the equipment has been purchased (not a small task given that the desired scanner costs upwards of $50,000). Since then we have been exploring possible avenues for funding that would allow the monastery to purchase this equipment and begin the work of digitization, although Father Bigoul's recent retirement in the fall of 2016 has meant that these plans will need to be reassessed and reinitiated under the new library leadership.

4 Conclusion

What I hope to have conveyed in this article is the importance of context for determining the limitations and potentialities of digitization efforts connected with archaeological and archival work in Egypt. The Candle Room fragments discovered in the White Monastery church and the manuscripts in the library at the Monastery of the Syrians are not simply texts studied in an empirical vacuum; they are also "objects embedded in a nexus of social relations."[15] The cultural heritage of these sites is tenuously balanced among three stakeholders: the monks themselves, the Egyptian government (represented by team of *mufattishīn* at the local inspectorate), and the foreign institutional partner

15 Bell, Joshua A., Christen, Kimberly, Turin, Mark, "Introduction: After the Return," 3. In their article, the authors are interested in mining the "relational" aspect of museums, collections, and objects – what Tim Ingold has termed "meshworks", see: Ingold, Tim, *Lines, A Brief History,* London: Routledge, 2007 also Gosden, Chris, Larson, Frances, Petch, Alison, *Knowing Things: Exploring the Collections at the Pitt Rivers Museum, 1884-1945*, Oxford: Oxford University Press, 2007.

or partners. In the case of the White Monastery, the Candle Room fragments themselves are a material product of the colonialist history of dissemination I referred to earlier: they were literally "left behind" when the manuscripts were removed for sale. The process of photographing and digitizing those same fragments was conditioned by present-day relational tensions in the local inspectorate and by shifting infrastructural conditions, both on site and off. In the case of the Monastery of the Syrians, Father Bigoul's concerns that digitization might result in a loss of control over cultural heritage were shaped by a similar colonialist legacy. To avoid the many pitfalls of this legacy is not an easy task, but there is one *desideratum* that must certainly guide the ongoing conversations between monastery and university. Energy and attention must be given not only to making decisions about important technical details related to equipment and online presentation, but also to cultivating a mutually responsible relational context – one in which universal access is facilitated, and in which the monastery retains agency over its own collection in both its physical and digital forms.

References

Anderson, Jane, Christen, Kim, "'Chuck a Copyright on It': Dilemmas of Digital Return and the Possibilities for Traditional Knowledge Licenses and Labels," *Museum Anthropology Review 7.1-2*, Spring-Fall, 2013, 105-126.

Assemani, Joseph Simeon, Assemani, Stephanus Evodius, *Biblioteca apostolicae vaticanae codicum manuscriptorum catalogus in tres partes*, vols. 2-3, Paris: Maisonneuve, 1926.

Bell, Joshua A., Christen, Kimberly, Turin, Mark, "Introduction: After the Return," *Museum Anthropology Review 7.1-2*, Spring-Fall, 2013, 1-21.

Brock, Sebastian, Van Rompay, Lucas, *Catalogue of the Syriac Manuscripts and Fragments in the Library of Deir al-Surian, Wadi al-Natrun (Egypt)*, Orientalia Lovaniensia Analecta 227, Louvain: Peeters, 2014.

Colwell-Chanthaphonh, Chip, "Archaeology and Indigenous Collaboration," in: *Archaeological Theory Today*, Hodder, Ian, ed., second edition, Cambridge: Polity, 2012, 267-291.

Davis, Stephen J. et al., "Left Behind: A Recent Discovery of Manuscript Fragments in the White Monastery Church," *Journal of Coptic Studies 16*, 2014, 69-87.

Davis, Stephen J. et al., "Cataloguing the Coptic and Arabic Manuscripts in the Monastery of the Syrians: A Preliminary Report," in: *Studia Patristica XCII: Papers Presented at the Seventeenth International Conference on Patristic Studies*, held in Oxford 2015, Volume 18, Vincent, Markus, ed. 2018, Louvain: Peeters, 179-185.

Davis, Stephen J. et al., "Marginalia Coptica et Arabica: Traces of Scribes, Patrons, Restorers, and Readers in the Biblical Collection at the Monastery of the Syrians (Dayr al-Suryān)," in: *Proceedings of the Eleventh International Congress of Coptic Studies*, Claremont, CA, July 25th-30th, 2016, Louvain: Peeters, 2019, forthcoming.

Father Bigoul al-Suriany, "The Manuscript Collection of Deir al-Surian in Wadi al-Natrun," *Journal of the Canadian Society for Coptic Studies 2.1*, January 2011, 51-62 (available online with a subscription at <http://lockwoodonlinejournals.com/>), accessed on 10.04.19.

Gosden, Chris, "Post-Colonial Archaeology," in: *Archaeological Theory Today*, Hodder, Ian, ed., second edition, 251-266.

Gosden, Chris, Larson, Frances, Petch, Alison, *Knowing Things: Exploring the Collections at the Pitt Rivers Museum, 1884-1945*, Oxford: Oxford University Press, 2007.

Habermas, *The Theory of Communicative Action*, 2 vols., McCarthy, Thomas, trans., Boston: Beacon Press, 1984-1989.

Habermas, *Between Facts and Norms: Contributions to a Discourse Theory of Law and Democracy*, Rehg, William, trans., *Studies in Contemporary German Social Thought*, Cambridge, Mass.: MIT Press, 1996.

Hall, Martin, "Situational Ethics and Engaged Practice: The Case of Archaeology in Africa," in: *Embedding Ethics: Shifting the Boundaries of the Anthropological Profession*, Meskell, Lynn M., Pels, Peter, eds., Oxford: Berg, 2005, 169-184.

Hatch, William H.P., *An Album of Dated Syriac Manuscripts*, Boston: The American Academy of Arts and Sciences, 1946.

Hennessy, Kate, Lyons, Natasha, Loring, Stephen, Arnold, Charles, Mervin, Joe, Elias, Albert, Pokiak, James, "The Inuvialuit Living History Project: Digital Return as the Forging of Relationships Between Institutions, People, and Data," *Museum Anthropology Review 7.1-2*, Spring-Fall 2013, 44-73.

Ireland, Tracy, Schofield, John, "The Ethics of Cultural Heritage, Ethical Archaeologies," *The Politics of Social Justice 4*, Gnecco, Cristobal, Ireland, Tracy, eds., New York: Springer / World Archaeological Congress, 2015.

Meskell, Lynn, "The Social Life of Heritage," in: *Archaeological Theory Today*, Hodder, Ian, ed., second edition, 229-250.

Murphy, Bernice L., *Museums, Ethics and Cultural Heritage*, New York: Routledge, 2016.

Sandis, Constantine, *Cultural Heritage Ethics: Between Theory and Practice*, Cambridge: Open Book Publishers, 2014.

Tisserant, Eugenius, *Specimina Codicum Orientalium*, in: Lietzmann, Johannis., *Tabulae in Usum Scholarum*, eds., Bonn: Marcus and Weber, 1914.

Wobst, Martin H., "Indigenous Archaeologies: A Worldwide Perspective on Human Materialities and Human Rights," in: *Indigenous Archaeologies: A Reader on Decolonization*, Bruchac, Margaret M., Hart, Siobhan M., Wobst, Martin H., eds., Walnut Creek, CA: Left Coast Press, 2010, 17-27, at 19.

Wright, William, *Catalogue of Syriac Manuscripts in the British Museum acquired since the year 1838*, 3 vols., London: British Museum, 1870-1872.
Wright, William, *Notulae Syriacae*, London: Gilbert and Rivington, 1887.
Zimmerman, Larry J., Vitelli, Karen D., Hollowell-Zimmer, Julie, eds., *Ethical Issues in Archaeology*, Walnut Creek, CA: AltaMira, 2003.

PART 2

Data Mining and Visualisation

CHAPTER 5

Qualitative Analysis of Semantic Language Models

Thibault Clérice and Matthew Munson

1 Introduction

The task of automatically extracting semantic information from raw textual data is an increasingly important topic in computational linguistics and has begun to make its way into non-linguistic humanities research.[1] That this task has been accepted as an important one in computational linguistics is shown by its appearance in the standard text books and handbooks for computational linguistics such as Manning and Schuetze Foundations of Statistical Natural Language Processing[2] and Jurafsky and Martin Speech and Language Processing.[3] And according to the Association for Computational Linguistics Wiki,[4] there have been 25 published experiments which used the TOEFL (Test of English as a Foreign Language) standardized synonym questions to test the performance of algorithmic extraction of semantic information since 1997 with scores ranging from 20% to 100% accuracy.

The question addressed by this paper, however, is not whether semantic information can be automatically extracted from textual data. The studies listed in the preceding paragraph have already proven this. It is also not about trying to find the best algorithm to use to do this. Instead, this paper aims to make this widely used and accepted task more useful outside of purely linguistic studies by considering how one can qualitatively assess the results returned by such algorithms. That is, it aims to move the assessment of the results returned by semantic extraction algorithms closer to the actual hermeneutical tasks carried out in the, e.g., historical, cultural, or theological interpretation of texts. We believe that this critical projection of algorithmic results back onto the

1 Munson, Matthew, *Biblical Semantics Applying Digital Methods for Semantic Information Extraction to Current Problems in New Testament Studies*, Theologische Studien, Aachen: Shaker Verlag, 2017.

2 Manning, Chris, Schütze, Hinrich, *Foundations of Statistical Natural Language Processing*, Cambridge, MA: MIT Press, 1999.

3 Jurafsky, Daniel, Marin, James H., *Speech and Language Processing: An Introduction to Natural Language Processing, Computational Linguistics, and Speech Recognition*, Second Edition, Prentice Hall Series in Artificial Intelligence, Upper Saddle River, NJ: Pearson Education, 2009.

4 <https://aclweb.org/aclwiki/TOEFL_Synonym_Questions_(State_of_the_art)>, accessed on 10.04.19.

hermeneutical tasks that stand at the core of humanistic research is largely a desideratum in the current computational climate. We hope that this paper can help to fill this hole in two ways. First, it will introduce an effective and yet easy-to-understand metric for parameter choice which we call Gap Score. Second, it will actually analyze three distinct sets of results produced by two different algorithmic processes to discover what type of information they return and, thus, for which types of hermeneutical tasks they may be useful. Throughout this paper, we will refer to the results produced by these algorithms as "language models" (or simply "models") since what these algorithms produce is a semantic model of the input language which can then help answer questions about the language's semantics. Our purpose in doing this is to demonstrate that the accuracy of an algorithm on a specific test, or even a range of tests, does not tell the user everything about that algorithm. We assert that there are cases in which an algorithm that might score lower on a certain standardized test may actually be better for certain hermeneutical tasks than a better scoring algorithm.

Much of the impetus for this study comes from the insights in Schnabel, et al. "Evaluation methods for unsupervised word embeddings", especially their assertion that an algorithm's performance on a standardized test does not reveal everything about that algorithm.[5] They demonstrate convincingly that the correct choice of an algorithm depends upon the type of task that it is expected to perform. They then go on to demonstrate that some algorithms are better at some tasks than other algorithms that are better at other tasks. In this study we suggest that one very effective way to determine whether an algorithm produces results that are useful for a certain task is to do a close reading of a portion of the results to determine whether these results will actually be valuable for the task at hand.

Another way that this Schnabel, et al., article is useful for the present study comes from the fact that the Gap Score metric we present here relies heavily in its conception on the "Coherence" task explained there.[6] In the Coherence task, three closely related words and one outlier are chosen from different language models. In their study, they then tested the results using crowdsourcing techniques, asking the crowdsourcers to choose the outsider and then measuring how often that outsider was the same as the one chosen by the algorithm. Gap Score presents a way to perform this task without crowdsourcing if one

5 Schnabel, Tobias, et al., "Evaluation Methods for Unsupervised Word Embeddings," in: *Proceedings of the 2015 Conference on Empirical Methods in Natural Language Processing, September 17-21, 2015, Lisbon, Portugal*, 2015, 298-307, <http://www.aclweb.org/anthology/D15-1036>, accessed on 10.04.19.

6 Schnabel et al., 302-303.

has an external categorization of semantically related words for a language or a specific corpus.

This study is broken down into two parts. The first part introduces the Gap Score metric and applies it to the results produced on the Greek Biblical corpus by the Word2Vec machine learning algorithm. In this study, we produced several language models based on different parameters using Word2Vec as implemented in the Python Gensim package and evaluated each of these using both simple distance measures and Gap Score. The second part of the study considers the most similar words according to the best scoring Word2Vec models and a different semantic-extraction algorithm, which is similar to that used by Bullinaria and Levy.[7] We chose these two algorithms because Word2Vec is widely considered to be one of the most effective algorithms for discovering word relationships and the algorithms that Bullinaria and Levy used produced the highest published accuracy on the TOEFL Synonym Questions task as reported by the ACL Wiki (see link above). We will analyze the patterns of these three models to discover what light the similarities and differences between these two lists shed on the type of semantic information returned by the two different algorithms.

2 Word2Vec and Gap Score

2.1 *Word2Vec*

The basic theory that underpins most methods for automatic extraction of semantic information is the distributional hypothesis. The most widely used explanation of this hypothesis is a pithy quote from British linguist John Rupert Firth, who wrote, "You shall know a word by the company it keeps!"[8] But two citations that explain the theory a bit better are from the American linguist Zellig Harris, who coined the term "distributional" to describe this phenomenon. In 1954 he wrote, "If we consider words or morphemes A and B to be more different in meaning than A and C, then we will often find that the distributions of A and B are more different than the distributions of A and C. In other

7 Bullinaria, John A., Levy, Joseph P., "Extracting Semantic Representations from Word Co-Occurrence Statistics: A Computational Study," 2007, <https://www.cs.bham.ac.uk/~jxb/PUBS/BRM.pdf>; Bullinaria, John A., Levy, Joseph P., "Extracting Semantic Representations from Word Co-Occurrence Statistics: Stop-Lists, Stemming and SVD," 2012, <http://www.cs.bham.ac.uk/~jxb/PUBS/BRM2.pdf>.

8 Firth, John Rupert, "A Synopsis of Linguistic Theory 1930-1955," in: Firth, John Rupert, *Studies in Linguistic Analysis*, Oxford: Blackwell, 1957, 11.

words, difference of meaning correlates with difference of distribution."[9] The most developed expression of this hypothesis came in a series of lectures that Harris did in 1986 in which he stated, "The most precise way of determining a word's meaning is by investigating the meanings of the words that occur along with that word."[10] Both the Word2Vec method presented here and the "Log-Likelihood" method, which we briefly explain in section 3 below, depend on Harris' distributional hypothesis to extract semantic representations of the words in a corpus.

The Word2Vec model is a shallow neural network model that was built by a team at Google headed by Tomas Mikolov in 2013[11] that has been used and studied very heavily since then. We will not undertake a technical, complex, or in-depth explanation of Word2Vec as we believe that this is beyond the scope of this paper. Instead we would refer the reader to the several articles published by Mikolov and his team[12] or any of the less technical explanations one can find in traditional publications[13] or on the internet.[14] Instead, the discussion here will focus on a basic, non-technical description of neural networks in general and Word2Vec's place within them.

A neural network is essentially a machine-learning method that has one or more hidden layers of "neurons" between the input layer and the output layer. The input layer, in the case of Word2Vec, is the textual material that we feed to it and the output layer is the result vectors that are produced. A neural network can "learn (progressively improve performance) to do tasks by considering

9 Harris, Zellig, "Distributional Structure," *Word* 10, no. 23, 1954, 156.

10 Harris, Zellig, "How Words Carry Meaning", Language and Information: The Bampton Lectures, Columbia University, 1986, <http://www.ircs.upenn.edu/zellig/3_2.mp3>, accessed on 10.04.19.

11 Mikolov, Tomas et al., "Distributed Representations of Words and Phrases and Their Compositionality," *CoRR* abs/1310.4546, 2013, <http://arxiv.org/abs/1310.4546>, accessed on 10.04.19.

12 Mikolov, Tomas et al., "Efficient Estimation of Word Representations in Vector Space," *CoRR* abs/1301.3781, 2013, <http://arxiv.org/abs/1301.3781>, accessed on 10.04.19; Mikolov, Tomas, Yih, Wen-tau, Zweig, Geoffrey, "Linguistic Regularities in Continuous Space Word Representations," in: *Human Language Technologies: Conference of the North American Chapter of the Association of Computational Linguistics, Proceedings, June 9-14, 2013, Westin Peachtree Plaza Hotel, Atlanta, Georgia, USA*, 2013, 746-751, <https://www.aclweb.org/anthology/N13-1090>, accessed on the 10.04.19; Mikolov et al.,"Distributed Representations."

13 Goldberg, Yoav, Levy, Omer, "Word2vec Explained: Deriving Mikolov et Al.'s Negative-Sampling Word Embedding Method," *CoRR* abs/1402.3722, 2014, <http://arxiv.org/abs/1402.3722>; Wikipedia, *Word2vec – Wikipedia, The Free Encyclopedia*, 2017, <https://en.wikipedia.org/w/index.php?title=Word2vec&oldid=785880094>, accessed on 10.14.19.

14 <https://youtu.be/D-ekE-Wlcds>, accessed 02-Feb-2018, <http://mccormickml.com/2016/04/19/word2vec-tutorial-the-skip-gram-model/>, accessed on 10.04.19.

examples."[15] In the case of this article, the "examples" that we provided to Word2Vec were the texts themselves and the training involved Word2Vec progressively testing sets of neurons to see how well these neurons could predict the contexts of the words in the corpus. So, for instance, if the phrase Ἰησοῦς Χριστός occurs frequently in our corpus, Word2Vec will try to find a set of transformations that will often predict Χριστός when it sees Ἰησοῦς, and vice versa.

It is helpful to imagine the neurons that sit between the input and output layers as neurons in the human brain. The neurons in our brain have heard enough of our own native language that when it receives the input of a certain sentence, say "Every day I drink apple ???", a certain set of neurons fires and produces, as output, the expected word represented by "???" in the sentence. A very likely result for the word to fill this context would be "juice". But if the person speaking the sentence finished it with the word "car", we would assume that they made a mistake and ask them whether they actually meant "juice". You could also picture these neurons as being related to certain concepts. So, for instance, there could be a "fruit" neuron that would be activated when it sees the word "apple" or "orange". And then there might be a "citrus" neuron that would be activated when it sees the word "orange" or "lemon". And these two neurons together would be able to tell you that "orange" is more similar to "lemon" than it is to "apple". Word2Vec tests during the training whether the corpus actually needs a neuron for fruit and one for citrus. If having these two neurons improves the results, then it will keep them. Then during the training process Word2Vec trains certain neurons to fire when given an input context so that the output word that is produced will match as closely as possible to the input texts that it has been given. And it tries to do this for *all* of the input contexts in the corpus at once!

Once the training process is finished, the results vectors are essentially the record of precisely which neurons fire and how strongly they fire for each of the words in the corpus.[16] So, in our fruit and citrus example above, it would record that the fruit neuron fires strongly for "apple", "orange", and "lemon", while the citrus neuron fires strongly only for "orange" and "lemon". The intuition then is that words that have similar neuron firing pattern vectors in the

15 Wikipedia, *Artificial Neural Network – Wikipedia, The Free Encyclopedia*, 2017, <https://en.wikipedia.org/w/index.php?title=Artificial_neural_network&oldid=787575153>, accessed on 10.04.19.

16 And the length of these vectors is determined by the size of the neural network, i.e., the number of neurons it has. So, for instance, if we have a corpus with a 1M word vocabulary and we use 1,000 neurons to describe its semantics, our results matrix is only 1M × 1K cells instead of a 1M × 1M that would be produced in, e.g., the Log-Likelihood method: 1/1000 the size.

results will have similar meanings. This means that one should be able to determine the similarity of two words by calculating the similarity of their results vectors using some similarity metric (typically cosine similarity). This whole explanation is a vast oversimplification of the actual process and, as with any such oversimplification, is not completely accurate in its description. For instance, we would not expect any of the neurons to have functions as well-defined as "fruit" or "citrus". Their functions and what causes each one to fire is actually much more complex and always dependent on the corpus that we give it. We believe, however, that this oversimplification is useful to understand what is happening during the training process of Word2Vec and, thus, to help to understand better the results that Word2Vec produces.

2.2 *Gap Score*

The Gap Score metric is our contribution to the evaluation of vector-space models for semantic domain extraction. It is based on the intuition that the difference (i.e., the "gap") between the mean similarity scores for a target word of the X most similar words as computed by a certain algorithm and the Y most similar words from an external testing set, i.e., the "in-domain" words (e.g., a list of words in a semantic domain), will be smaller than the difference between the mean similarity scores of that same target word of the X most similar words computed by an algorithm and one or more words (the "out-of-domain" words) that do not fall into the target word's external testing set. As noted above, we follow Schnabel, et al., in that we allow the algorithm to produce its own semantic category by taking the X most similar words to the target word. Then we compare candidates from externally produced categories to the algorithmically produced category to see how well the internal and external categories match each other.

Mathematically, the Gap Score metric is represented by the following equations:

$$WordScore(w, W) = \frac{\sum_{w_n \in W} \left(\left[\frac{\sum_{w_t \in T_{wn}} \mathrm{SIM}(w_t, w_n)}{|T_{wn}|} \right] - \max\left(\mathrm{SIM}(w, w_n), 0\right) \right)}{|W|} \tag{1}$$

where

- w represents a single word from a semantic domain
- W represents a set of words w is tested against
- T_{wn} the set of top X most similar words to wn according to some algorithm
- w_n represents each individual word from W that is tested

- w_t represents each individual word from T_{wn} to which w_n is compared
- SIM is the similarity metric that is used to compare the words with each other (e.g., Word2Vec)

$$DomainScore(W) = \frac{\sum_{w_n \in W} WordScore(w_n, W)}{|W|} \tag{2}$$

where W represents a set of words.

And the objective of this testing is to find a set of parameters P that results in maximizing $|DomainScore(W \cup O) - DomainScore(W)|$ where W represents a set of words from a semantic domain and O represents a set of words from a disconnected semantic domain. This result in a Gap Score is positive if the in-domain words are more similar to each other but is negative if the out-of-domain words fit better. Also the distance of the Gap Score from 0 reflects the difference between the in-domain and out-of-domain words. If the in-domain words are significantly more similar to the X most similar words, then the score will be significantly above 0, whereas if the out-of-domain words are significantly more similar to the same X words, then the score will be significantly below 0. The code to carry out the gapscore algorithm was written in Python and, along with thorough documentation on its use, is openly available on Github at <https://github.com/hipster-philology/param-bias>.

2.3 *Evaluation Procedure*

Once one has one or more vector-space language models of the corpus under investigation, the next task is to evaluate how these models performed. As semantic categories, we have used the semantic sub-domains from the Louw-Nida lexicon, which can be found online.[17] This online data represents the domains and sub-domains of the printed edition of this lexicon[18] and is based on the theoretical work done by the authors of the lexicon.[19] When we say "sub-domains", we mean the collections of words represented by, e.g., domain "1A Universe, Creation" as opposed to using the whole primary domain, e.g., "1 Geographical Objects and Features". And we have only included sub-domains that have at least 10 words whose primary meaning belongs to

17 <http://www.laparola.net/greco/louwnida.php>, accessed on 10.04.19.

18 Louw, Johannes P., Nida, Eugene A., *Greek-English Lexicon of the New Testament: Based on Semantic Domains*, Second Edition, 2 vols., New York: United Bible Societies, 1989.

19 Nida, Eugene A., *Componential Analysis of Meaning*, The Hague: Mouton, 1975; Nida, Eugene A., Louw, Johannes P., Smith, Rondal B., "Semantic Domains and Componential Analysis of Meaning," in: *Current Issues in Linguistic Theory*, ed. Roger William Cole, Bloomington: Indiana University Press, 1977, 139-167.

that sub-domain. In the online version of the Louw-Nida lexicon, the primary meaning of a word is represented either by a "Gloss" that has no letter before it (for words with only a single gloss) or that is preceded by the letter "a". We have also not included words that are only represented by a phrase in a certain domain. Take, for instance, the domain "4A Animals".[20] In this domain, the first two words, ζωή and ψυχή appear only in the phrase ψυχὴ ζωῆς (living creature) and thus are excluded from the words in our cleaned sub-domain. Also, the word υἱός is excluded from this domain since the prefixed "d" means that this is actually the quaternary instead of the primary meaning. And then we selected only the first 10 words in each sub-domain since, according to the Louw-Nida organizational scheme of placing the words that are most generally related to the sub-domain first, these should be the words that best represent the sub-domain as a whole. These filters resulted in a cleaned sub-domain 4A that contains only the ten words ζῷον, θηρίον, τετράπους, θρέμμα, κτῆνος, ὑποζύγιον, ἀγέλη, ἀλώπηξ, λύκος, and ἄρκος.[21]Once we had cleaned all Louw-Nida sub-domains, we were left with 56 sub-domains that had at least 10 members. We then randomly produced 100 sub-domain pairs for testing and then, for each of these pairs, we produced a list of words that was made up of 3 words from the first domain and a single word from the second domain.[22] We chose to use sets of 3 in-domain words and 1 out-of-domain word in order to mirror the Coherence test in Schnabel, et al.[23] Then we evaluated these lists of words in two ways. First, we allowed Gensim's `doesnt_match` function on its Word2Vec model[24] to pick the single word in this list that fits worst. This function calculates the mean similarity for all of the given words with all of the other given words and chooses the one word that is least similar to the other words. So, for instance, if we gave the `doesnt_match` function the list of words "breakfast cereal dinner lunch", we would expect it to return the word "cereal" as the non-matching word.[25] For our tests, if this word was the out-of-domain word, then that whole list of words received a score of 1. If it was actually one of the in-domain words, the list received a score of 0. We then also computed the Gap

20 <http://www.laparola.net/greco/louwnida.php?sezmag=4&sez1=1&sez2=37>, accessed on 10.04.19.

21 We also excluded the domains "89 Relations", "90 Case", "91 Discourse Markers", "92 Discourse Referentials", and "93 Names of Persons and Places" as domains whose primary relating factor is syntactic rather than semantic.

22 This list of test sets can be found in the Appendix.

23 Schnabel et al., "Evaluation Methods," 302-303.

24 gensim.models.keyedvectors.KeyedVectors#doesnt`match

25 <https://radimrehurek.com/gensim/models/keyedvectors.html#gensim.models.keyed vectors. KeyedVectors.doesnt_match>, accessed on 10.04.19.

Score for each list of words, using the top 5 most similar words as computed by Word2Vec for each word.

In our tests with Word2Vec, we manipulated four different parameters: the size of the context window, the text chunk sizes we used for input, the dimensionality of the resulting feature vectors, and whether we started the training process with a pre-trained model or not. We will explain these parameters in order. The size of the context window determined how many words to the left and to the right of the target word would be counted as valid co-occurrents. As explained above, Word2Vec depends on word co-occurrence counts for its calculations. So if we chose a window size of 5, all words within 5 words to the left and 5 words to the right of the target word would be counted as co-occurrents. The premise behind manipulating this parameter is that co-occurrents that tend to be semantically important to the target word will tend to occur closer to that word. But it is unclear precisely where the cutoff in a corpus comes where increasing the window size will result in an increase in random noise as opposed to an increase in semantic information. A higher performance for a smaller window size would lead to the conclusion that semantic information tends to be tightly focused within a corpus, e.g., with short, to-the-point sentences. While a better performance for a larger context window would suggest larger distances between semantically related items within the corpus, e.g., long, complex sentences. We tested window sizes of 5 words and 10 words.

The text chunk sizes determined how large the input text chunks were. We tested as input texts single biblical verses, single chapters, single books (e.g., Genesis or the Gospel of Matthew), and the whole Septuagint and New Testament as a single large text. In conjunction with the window size above, the text chunk size acted as a limit on the words that would be counted as semantically important. No matter what the window size used, the counting of co-occurrents could never extend beyond the boundary of the text chunks we used. So if we used the verse as the chunk size, all of the words within that verse would be considered co-occurrents with the target word if they fell within the window size. But no words from the next verse could possibly be chosen simply because they were not considered to be part of the text that we were testing. The thinking behind the manipulation of this parameter is similar to that for context window size above except instead of testing the relationships of single words to each other we were more testing how chunks of text were related semantically. So if, e.g., the chunk size of verses performed the best, that would mean that semantically related ideas are most concentrated on the level of the verses as opposed to the level of the chapter or the book. So if the performance would decrease for the larger text chunks, such as the chapter, that suggests that, as above, expanding to this larger chunk adds more noise to the model than it adds information.

The size of the resulting feature vectors determined how many values the vectors for each word in the vocabulary contain. As explained above, Word2Vec learns the most salient features (the neurons) of a corpus by making repeated training runs over the corpus using different feature sets. Once the training is over, Word2Vec then chooses the set of neurons that does the best job in predicting word occurrence given a certain verbal context. By manipulating the size of the feature vectors, we were exploring how many neurons best described the corpus at hand. We tested vector lengths of 30, 50, 80, 100, and 200 neurons.

Finally, the parameter of starting with a pre-trained model or not meant that we either trained a brand new model based only on the biblical text chunks or we started with a model that had been trained on another, larger corpus and changed that model based on the new information in the biblical text chunks. If we started from scratch, the model that results would be based only on the biblical text and thus would theoretically represent a purely biblical Greek language model whereas starting with a model trained on a general Greek corpus would produce a more mixed model. The primary question we wished to answer by manipulating this parameter is whether there is enough data in the biblical corpus itself to produce a useful language model or not. So if the pre-trained models performed better, that suggests one of two things. Either there is not enough data in the biblical corpus to produce a good model OR that the training data that we are using (the Louw-Nida Lexicon) is based to a large extent on general Greek evidence as opposed to purely biblical evidence. The Louw-Nida Lexicon uses what they call "extratextual contexts",[26] i.e., evidence from outside of the biblical corpus, to assist in its definitions and its categorization because, as they assert, "the Greek of the New Testament should not be regarded as a distinct form of Greek, but rather as typical Hellenistic Greek."[27] The extent to which they have used such evidence, however, is difficult to measure. This parameter will then, at least in part, help us to see how prevalent non-biblical semantics are for Louw-Nida.

2.4 *Discussion of Results*

Table 5.1 below shows the top ten highest scoring parameter sets ordered by the mean Gap Score for all of the 100 input word sets. All of the table headings should be self-explanatory except perhaps "Size", which represents the number

26 Louw, Nida, *Greek-English Lexicon of the New Testament: Based on Semantic Domains*, xvi.
27 Louw, Nida, xvi.

TABLE 5.1 Top 10 best performing language models, NT and LXX: Mean gap score; ©CLERICEMUNSON

Text chunk size	Pre-trained?	Context window size	Size	Gap score correct	Gensim correct	Average gap score
Verses	Yes	5 Words	30	82	56	0.1428
Verses	No	5 Words	30	81	60	0.1352
Chapters	Yes	5 Words	30	78	63	0.1281
Verses	No	10 Words	30	78	57	0.1258
Chapters	No	5 Words	30	80	60	0.1250
Books	Yes	5 Words	30	75	54	0.1174
Books	No	5 Words	30	76	56	0.1134
Verses	Yes	10 Words	30	75	49	0.1113
Verses	No	5 Words	50	78	57	0.1083
Full Bible	Yes	5 Words	30	74	54	0.1081

of neurons in the result vectors, and "Gap Score Correct" and "Gensim Correct". "Gap Score Correct" measures how many times the Gap Score for a set of test words was positive, meaning that the in-domain words are, on average, closer to each other than they are to the out-of-domain word. "Gensim Correct" is how many times the Gensim `doesnt_match` function chose the correct out-of-domain word. These scores both have a possible maximum of 100, so "82" would mean that Gap Score correctly categorized 82 out of 100 test sets. Also note that for this paper, we used the Continuous Bag of Words (CBOW) method for Word2Vec, which is the default in Gensim.

For reasons of space, we will restrict the discussion here to the four test parameters listed in section 2.3 above. First notice that the most important parameter appears to be the size of the neural network. Nine out of the top ten results came from the smallest network of only 30 neurons. While this may seem surprising at first, we explain it as resulting from the thematically focused nature of the corpus. Both the Septuagint and the New Testament deal primarily with God's relationship with Israel and thus it requires fewer neurons to describe than a general English language corpus would require. The next most important parameter is the context window size. Eight of the top ten results had a context window of only 5 words as opposed to 10 words. This means that, in our corpus, the semantically important words tend to concentrate themselves within 5 words of the target word. Adding word numbers 6 to 10 to these calculations tends to add information that is not as closely related to the semantics of a word as the first 5 words are.

TABLE 5.2 Top 10 best performing language models, NT and LXX: Gensim; ©CLERICEMUNSON

Text chunk size	Pre-trained?	Context window size	Size	Gap score correct	Gensim correct	Average gap score
Chapters	Yes	5 Words	30	78	63	0.1281
Verses	No	5 Words	30	81	60	0.1352
Chapters	No	5 Words	30	80	60	0.1250
Full Bible	Yes	10 Words	30	73	59	0.0882
Chapters	No	5 Words	50	74	58	0.0829
Verses	No	10 Words	30	78	57	0.1258
Verses	No	5 Words	50	78	57	0.1083
Verses	Yes	5 Words	50	76	57	0.0978
Verses	Yes	5 Words	30	82	56	0.1428
Books	No	5 Words	30	76	56	0.1134

The next most important parameter is the text chunk size, with 5 of the top 10 being Verses, 2 each being Chapters or Books, and the Full Bible appearing at number 10. This suggests, as did the small context window size, that semantic information related to the words in a biblical verse tends to be more concentrated within that verse. And, finally, the choice starting with a pre-trained model or not appears to have very little effect on the results, with 5 of the top 10 having used a pre-trained model and 5 not using one.

Those were the results ordered according to Gap Score Average. Table 5.2 represents the top 10 best performing parameter combinations ordered according to Gensim's ability to correctly identify the outlier word.

In this table, we see that the most important parameter for Gensim appears to be the context window size. Eight of the top ten used 5-word context windows, just as we saw above in the Gap Score results. The next most important was the size of the neural network, with 7 of 10 using a 30-neuron network and the other 3 a 50-neuron network. The next most important was the text chunk size, with 5 having used Verses, 3 having used Chapters, and then 1 each having used Books or the Full Bible. And, finally, the least important was whether a pre-trained corpus was used. Four of the top ten used a pre-trained corpus while 6 did not.

The next two tables are organized the same way as the two tables above but, instead of using the whole Old and New Testament to train their language models, these are based on models trained using just the New Testament. We include these here for two reasons. First, we wish to discover whether there are

TABLE 5.3 Top 10 best performing language models, NT only: Mean gap score; ©CLERICEMUNSON

Text size	ChunkPre-trained?	Context window size	size	Gap score correct	Gensim correct	Average gap score
Verses	No	10 Words	30	65	45	0.0715
Verses	Yes	5 Words	30	71	43	0.0688
Books	Yes	5 Words	30	61	43	0.0635
Verses	No	5 Words	30	61	47	0.0625
Chapters	Yes	5 Words	30	63	44	0.0617
Books	No	10 Words	30	61	36	0.0592
Verses	Yes	10 Words	30	68	40	0.0574
Chapters	No	10 Words	30	62	35	0.0509
Verses	Yes	5 Words	50	67	46	0.0488
Books	No	5 Words	30	59	42	0.0467

any differences in the best parameters based on corpus size. The New Testament is approximately one-fifth the size of the Septuagint and, thus, it could require different parameters to produce the best model. The second reason is that we need data on the best models for only the New Testament so that we can more easily compare the results in section 3 below. Table 5.3 represents the top ten according to Average Gap Score and Table 5.4 according to Gensim's `doesnt_match` function.These tables show the same preference for smaller input text chunks as the previous two tables, with the second, Gensim table actually having 7 of the top ten relying on the verse-level chunks. They also both show no preference for pre-trained data, with the Gap Score table having 5 pre-trained and 5 not pre-trained and the Gensim table with 4 and 6, respectively. This is perhaps a bit surprising since we might expect that a corpus as small as the New Testament (about 130,000 words) might benefit from a model that has already been pre-trained for general Greek. However, the results suggest that one can get just as good a language model without such pre-training. The Gap Score table still shows a marked preference for fewer neurons, with 9 out of the 10 having only 30. The Gensim table, however, prefers larger networks, with only 5 of the ten having 30 neurons, 3 having 50, and 2 having 80. This suggests that the `doesnt_match` function requires a more complex representation of the corpus in order to produce good results. Finally, the Gap Score results show more preference for the larger, 10-word context window than did the previous two tables, 4 of 10 depending on this window size. The

TABLE 5.4 Top 10 best performing language models, NT only: Gensim; ©CLERICEMUNSON

Text size	ChunkPre-trained?	Context window size	size	Gap score correct	gensim correct	Average gap score
Verses	No	5 Words	30	61	47	0.0625
Chapters	No	5 Words	50	66	47	0.0422
Verses	No	10 Words	80	59	47	0.0341
Verses	Yes	5 Words	50	67	46	0.0488
Verses	No	10 Words	30	65	45	0.0715
Verses	No	10 Words	50	63	45	0.0429
Verses	No	5 Words	80	64	45	0.0379
Chapters	Yes	5 Words	30	63	44	0.0617
Verses	Yes	5 Words	30	71	43	0.0688
Books	Yes	5 Words	30	61	43	0.0635

Gensim results also showed a slightly higher preference than the previous two, with 3 of 10, but still less so than Gap Score. This last observation about the preference for larger context windows for the New Testament probably comes from the corpus size of the New Testament. The larger context window collects more information for every word and thus makes up for the lack of evidence coming from the number of words in the corpus.

We should also point out that both evaluation metrics tended to score lower on the New Testament than on the combined Old and New Testaments, with the top number of correct predictions from Gap Score for the combined corpus being 82/100 and for the New Testament only 71/100. Gensim showed a similar pattern with 63/100 on the combined corpus and 47/100 on the New Testament alone. All of these scores, however, are significantly better than chance, which would result in a score of 25/100. So there is useful semantic information being captured for both corpora, which we will examine in more detail below.

This brief analysis of the top results has shown that both Gap Score and Gensim tend to prefer the same parameters for the full biblical corpus, i.e., a small neural network (30 neurons) with a small context window (5 words) and small chunks of text (verses). And pre-training on a general Greek corpus does not appear to affect performance at all. The number of neurons and the size of the context window tended to increase when we trained on only the New Testament, though the preference for the verse-sized chunks of text remained constant. We will perform a more in-depth comparison of the results of these two evaluation metrics below when we actually compare the lists of the top 20 most similar words for the top performing parameter combinations for these two metrics, as well as the results from a different semantic extraction method that is based more closely on the method used by Bullinaria and Levy and that will be described in more detail below.

3 Semantic Information Extraction

The purpose of this part of the paper is to actually go in-depth into the results produced by three different language models for the extraction of semantic information from the Greek biblical corpus. The first two language models were discussed above and both were produced by Word2Vec, one being the top scoring model according to Gap Score and the other the top-scoring model according to Gensim's `doesnt_match` function. The third model was produced using a different method for semantic information extraction, though one that is still based on the distributional hypothesis, and thus word co-occurrences, for its results.

First we will briefly describe this differing method, which we will call the "Log-Likelihood" method, based on the hypothesis testing algorithm that sits at its heart. A fuller description can be found in Munson's dissertation[28] and in the 2007 article from Bullinaria and Levy.[29] This method is a simpler one than Word2Vec in that it simply counts the co-occurrents for each word in the corpus, then measures the statistical significance of these co-occurrence values using Dunning's Log-Likelihood ratio,[30] and then compares these resulting statistical significance vectors using the cosine similarity algorithm. The step of calculating statistical significance using the Log-Likelihood ratio is important to normalize the data for high and low occurrence words. If we did not do this step, the top co-occurrent for every word in the Greek New Testament would be ὁ, since this is the most frequent word in the corpus. By implementing a significance measure, this method is able to correct somewhat for extremely frequent and extremely infrequent words.

One major downside of the Log-Likelihood method is that the resulting matrices are extremely large, being N × N squares, where N is the size of the vocabulary in the corpus. So if you have an imaginary corpus that has a vocabulary

28 Munson, *Biblical Semantics*, 5-33.

29 Bullinaria, Levy, "Extracting Semantic Representations from Word Co-Occurrence Statistics: A Computational Study."

30 Dunning, Ted, "Accurate Methods for the Statistics of Surprise and Coincidence," *Computational Linguistics* 19, 1993, 61-74.

of 1M (1 million) words, the resulting matrix would be 1M × 1M, or 1 trillion, cells. Such a matrix, if it were filled with 64-bit floating point numbers in every cell, would take up 8TB of space, either in memory or on disk, making them very difficult to work with. Whereas a Word2Vec matrix that is 1M × 1K cells would only take up 8GB of space and, thus, could be handled easily by a modern computer.

Munson, in his dissertation, carried out extensive parameterization of this Log-Likelihood method and determined that the context window that best predicted the Louw-Nida semantic sub-domains was a weighted window of 12 words left and right. The term "weighted" here simply means that words that co-occurred closer to the target word were given more weight than those that occurred farther from the target word. Notice that this window is larger than the optimal window shown in our tests of Word2Vec above, which tended to prefer a 5-word window. It is also interesting to note that while the Log-Likelihood method performs better with a weighted context window, the Continuous Bag of Words algorithm used to produce the language models for Word2Vec actually uses an unweighted context window, i.e., weighting every word that co-occurs within the context window the same. Also, the text chunk size used to produce the language model for the Log-Likelihood method was the biblical book as opposed to the smaller biblical verse that was preferred by Word2Vec. And, finally, we should note here that for this study we ran the language model produced using these parameters by the Log-Likelihood method through Gap Score in order to compare it with the other two methods.[31] According to Gap Score, it was able to select the correct out-of-domain word 47 times out of 100. This was significantly worse than the performance shown in Table 5.3.[32]

But now we would like to move on to the comparison of the results from these three language models. To do this, we have chosen to focus on a single word from the New Testament, δαιμόνιον, which is typically translated as "demon" in English. We have chosen this word for several reasons. First, it is an interesting word that holds an important, though not central place in the New Testament. It occurs fairly frequently, though not too often (63 occurrences). And it has a single, well understood meaning. We will start with the table of 20 most similar words based on the Log-Likelihood model. This table, as well as Table 5.6 and Table 5.7, are sorted according to the word's similarity with δαιμόνιον as calculated by the appropriate algorithm. The glosses that we are

31 Note, however, that the Gap Score method was not the method used to assess the result in Munson's dissertation. Munson, *Biblical Semantics*, 15-17.

32 Note that we have no basis for comparison of this language model with the Gensim's doesnt`match function since that function requires a Gensim Word2Vec language model to work.

TABLE 5.5 Top 20 most similar words to δαιμόνιον: Log-likelihood model; ©CLERICEMUNSON

1	βεελζεβούλ (7)	Beelzebub	11	κριτής (19)	Judge
2	ἐκβάλλω (81)	throw out	12	ἑλληνίς (2)	Greek
3	ἄρχων (37)	ruler	13	φθάνω (7)	come to
4	ἔξω (62)	outside	14	ὀλιγοπιστία (1)	poverty of faith
5	κωφός (14)	mute	15	τράπεζα (15)	Table
6	διαβλέπω (3)	see clearly	16	δαιμονίζομαι (13)	to be demon possessed
7	συροφοινίκισσα (1)	Syrophoenician	17	νόσος (11)	Sickness
8	θανάσιμον (1)	deadly	18	σός (25)	Your
9	ἔννυχα (1)	at night	19	δοκός (6)	beam (of wood)
10	θεραπεύω (43)	heal	20	βασιλεία (162)	Reign

using for the Greek word are based on the primary gloss that is given for each word.[33] The number in parentheses after each Greek word is the number of occurrences that word has in the New Testament.

The group of words in Table 5.5 is very clearly about demons, demon possession, and exorcism. βεελζεβούλ, ἄρχων, and βασιλεία all refer to the kingdom and rulers of demons while ἐκβάλλω, θεραπεύω, and δαιμονίζομαι all refer to demon possession and exorcism. συροφοινίκισσα and ἑλληνίς refer to the specific exorcism story in Mark 7:24-30 while τράπεζα is used in this same story both here and in Matthew 15:21-28. Almost all of the other words in this list refer to the miracles that Jesus performed in the Gospels: κωφός and νόσος refer to the sickness that is healed, διαβλέπω and (again) θεραπεύω refer to the miraculous healing, and ἔξω and φθάνω all set the scene for the miracle (φθάνω refers to the people coming to Jesus). And, finally, κριτής, ὀλιγοπιστία and θανάσιμον are on this list because they occur in the context of miracle stories or exorcisms in general. The first is used when speaking of exorcism in Matthew 12:27 and Luke 11:19, the second in the exorcism story at Matthew 17:20, and the third is used in Mark 16:18 in a verse that mentions miracles that Jesus' disciples will do. δοκός appears on this list because in all of its occurrences (Matthew 7:3-5 and Luke 6:41-42) it co-occurs with ἐκβάλλω, a word that is closely related to δαιμόνιον.[34]

The relationship of the words σός and ἔννυχα with δαιμόνιον is unclear. The former could show up because it appears with the word ἐκβάλλω in Matthew

33 <http://www.laparola.net/greco/louwnida.php>, accessed on 10.04.19.

34 See Munson, *Biblical Semantics*, 41-42, for deeper analysis of the related case of δοκός and δαιμόνιον.

TABLE 5.6 Top 20 most similar words to δαιμόνιον: Gap score model; ©CLERICEMUNSON

1	λεπρός (9)	leper	11	φραγέλλιον (1)	Whip
2	ἀμφότεροι (14)	both	12	λιβανωτός (2)	Censer
3	τόξον (1)	bow	13	χρεία (49)	what is needed
4	ἐκμυκτηρίζω (2)	ridicule	14	Ἰεριχώ (7)	Jericho
5	δαίμων (1)	demon	15	εὐθύς (59)	straight, immediately
6	χωλός (14)	lame	16	ὡσαννά (6)	Hosanna
7	κακῶς (16)	evil	17	Ἰάϊρος (2)	Jairus
8	νεανίσκος (10)	young man	18	ὀρθῶς (4)	correct(ly)
9	νομή (2)	pasture	19	ἀνάχυσις (1)	Excessive
10	τρίτον (1)	third part	20	γενετή (1)	Birth

7:3 and three times with ἐκβάλλω and δαιμόνιον in Matthew 7:22, though it is questionable whether only 4 out of the 25 occurrences of this word should so powerfully affect its semantic vector. The latter, however, would require more analysis to detect its relationship.

This list demonstrates, as shown more fully in Munson's dissertation,[35] that the Gospels set demons firmly within the context first of demon possession and exorcism and more generally into the context of Jesus' miracle stories in general. As Munson asserts, the role of demons in the New Testament is not so much as evil otherworldly beings but more so as a foil to demonstrate Jesus' power as a wonder worker. And this is the focus of the semantics that this semantic extraction method captures. Now we will consider the top 20 most similar words for the best New Testament Word2Vec model according to Gap Score (in Table 5.3: text chunks are verses, not pre-trained, 10-word context window, using 30 neurons).

In Table 5.6, it is interesting to notice the number of times each of these words occurs. This list of words has an average occurrence of 10.1 times in the New Testament and there are only two words, χρεία and εὐθύς, that occur more than 20 times. This is in contrast to the number of occurrences in Table 5.5, where the average number of occurrences is 25.55 and there are 5 words that occur more than 20 times. Though this is only a small sample size, looking only at the single word δαιμόνιον, it is interesting to consider perhaps that Word2Vec, or at least the best Word2Vec model according to Gap Score, might prefer less frequent words to the Log-Likelihood model enumerated in Table 5.5. We

35 Munson, Biblical Semantics, 40-44.

will wait until after we have analyzed the words in this table and Table 5.7 to comment further on this.

While this list of words may, at first glance, seem more random than that in Table 5.5.5, we actually see several of the same themes in this table as we saw there. First, the obvious words: δαίμων and κακῶς are related to δαιμόνιον in that the former is another word that refers to the same entity while the latter refers to their nature. We also see two words related to sickness, and thus probably to Jesus' miracles, in λεπρός and χωλός. But if we look closely at the contexts in which the other words appear on this list, we actually see that many of them actually appear in stories about Jesus' miracles, both demon exorcism and healing miracles. First there is εὐθύς. Of the 59 times that this word occurs in the New Testament, 42 of them are in the Gospel of Mark. And of these 42, it appears 17 times in the context of a miracle story[36] with a typical usage describing the immediacy of the healing (1:42, 2:12, 5:29, 5:30, 5:42 (2x), and 10:52). So εὐθύς is closely related to miracle stories. But it is also occur three times independently of any miracle story along with the word πνεῦμα (spirit), which is also the word used in the phrase πνεῦμα ἀκάθαρτον ("unclean spirit", e.g., Mark 3:30) to describe demons. So there appear to be two different usages of εὐθύς that tend to bring it into the distributional semantic space of δαιμόνιον: miracles and spirit.

Other words appearing often in miracle stories are ἀμφότεροι, which appears in a demon possession story in Acts 19:16, while νεανίσκος (Luke 7:14 and Acts 20:12), Ἰεριχώ (Matthew 20:29, Luke 10:35, Mark 10:46), Ἰάϊρος (Mark 5:22), ὀρθῶς (Mark 7:35), and γενετή (John 9:1) all appear in the context of healing miracles. And since all of these words occur fairly infrequently (the most frequent word is ἀμφότεροι, which occurs only 14 times), these occurrences within miracle stories carry a lot of weight in determining the semantics of these words. So, in the New Testament, all of these words have close verbal (though not necessarily semantic) relationships with miracle stories and are thus considered to be similar to demons because demons are also closely related to miracle stories. We could also perhaps include νομή in this list of miracle words since in one of its two occurrences (2 Timothy 2:17) it is used next to the word γάγγραινα, which names a certain class of diseases.

And then we see three words that appear to show up on this list because they co-occur with words that tend to co-occur with δαιμόνιον: τρίτον, φραγέλλιον, and ὡσαννά. The first two words occur with ἐκβάλλω (in Luke 20:12 and John 2:15, respectively), which is the word used in the New Testament for exorcising demons. And ὡσαννά because it is used in Mark 11:9, Matthew 21:9, and

36 1:30, 1:42, 1:43, 2:8, 2:12, 3:6, 5:2, 5:29, 5:30, 5:42 (2x), 6:54, 7:25, 9:15, 9:20, and 10:52.

TABLE 5.7 Top 20 most similar words to δαιμόνιον: Gensim model; ©CLERICEMUNSON

1	ἀμφότεροι (14)	both	11	εὐθύς (59)	straight, immediately
2	λεπρός (9)	leper	12	φραγέλλιον (1)	Whip
3	ἄλαλος (3)	mute	13	δαιμονίζομαι (13)	to be demon possessed
4	τόξον (1)	bow	14	Ἰάϊρος (2)	Jairus
5	ἐργασία (6)	behavior	15	ἱμάτιον (60)	Clothing
6	ὀρθῶς (4)	correct(ly)	16	ἕτερος (97)	Different
7	κωφός (14)	mute	17	ἡμιθανής (1)	half dead
8	βλασφημία (18)	reviling	18	μαλακός (4)	Soft
9	παιδίον (52)	child	19	ὅμως (3)	Although
10	χωλός (14)	lame	20	ἀγράμματος (1)	Uneducated

Matthew 21:15 along with the verb κράζω and in John 12:13 with the verb κραυγάζω, both of which mean "to cry out" and both of which are used to denote the action of demons in Mark 5:5, Mark 9:26, and Luke 9:39 (for κράζω) and in Luke 4:41 (for κραυγάζω). So these three words are included on this list because they co-occur with words that also co-occur with δαιμόνιον and, thus, according to the distributional hypothesis, share some semantic relationship with δαιμόνιον.

With the other 5 words, τόξον, ἐκμυκτηρίζω, λιβανωτός, χρεία, and ἀνάχυσις, we could find no discernible pattern as to why these words might be closely related to δαιμόνιον, though it is interesting to note that τόξον and λιβανωτός occur only in Revelation and both in the context of the action of heavenly being in relation to the seven seals (Revelation 6:2 and Revelation 8:3 and 8:5, respectively). With the words ἐκμυκτηρίζω, which is used in Luke 16:14 and 23:35 to describe people who are ridiculing Jesus, and ἀνάχυσις, used in 1 Peter 4:4 in conjunction with blasphemy, we might tentatively suggest that this group of four words might have to do with sin and judgment. But we think that this is far too tenuous a connection to really assert it at this point.

Table 5.7 shows the top 20 most similar words for the best scoring model according to Gensim's `doesnt_match` function: verse-sized text chunks, not pre-trained, 5-word context window, and 30 neurons. In this list of words, there are 9 that also show up in Table 5.6, and we will allow the explanation above to relate to the words in this table as well. We also see three words here that can be readily categorized according to the categories already mentioned in the two tables above: δαιμονίζομαι for demon possession and ἄλαλος and κωφός as sicknesses that Jesus heals. Then we have several words that occur regularly in miracle stories: ἐργασία appears in an exorcism story in Acts 16:16

and 16:19, παιδίον is often the object of a healing miracle (Mark 5:39, 5:40 (x2), 5:41, 9:24; Luke 7:28, 7:30; John 4:49), ἱμάτιον is used quite often as the object through which Jesus' power is channeled for healing (Matthew 9:20, 9:21, 14:36; Mark 5:27, 5:28, 5:30, 6:56) and it is mentioned in the miracle stories at Mark 10:50, Luke 8:27, Luke 8:44, and Acts 9:39. Then we see βλασφημία and ὅμως, which probably appear because they are both used with words that are closely related to δαιμόνιον: the former co-occurring with πνεῦμα in Matthew 12:31 and Mark 3:28 and the latter with ἄρχων in John 12:42. So the relationship of these two words with δαιμόνιον-related words brings them closer to δαιμόνιον. Then we have two words that co-occur with miracle-related words: ἡμιθανής in its only occurrence appears along with Ἰεριχώ which, as we saw in the explanation of Table 5.6 above, is closely related to miracle stories, and ἀγράμματος, which occurs in Acts 4:13 along with the verb θαυμάζω (to be amazed), a word which is regularly used to describe the amazement of the witnesses to a healing miracle (Matthew 8:10, 9:33, 15:31; Mark 5:20; Luke 7:9, 9:43, 11:14). So these words are related to δαιμόνιον because they all are related to miracles.

Of the last two unexplained words on this list, μαλακός has an even more tenuous connection to δαιμόνιον than the previous four words. Three of the four occurrences of μαλακός come in Jesus' description of John the Baptist as one who does not wear "soft" clothes. And John the Baptist is closely related to two other words that are related to δαιμόνιον: πνεῦμα, in that the "spirit" comes to rest on Jesus after he is baptized by John, and εὐθύς, because John speaks of making "straight" the paths of the Lord (e.g., Matthew 3:3 εὐθείας ποιεῖτε τὰς τρίβους αὐτοῦ). So at least with these two words, the semantic fields of δαιμόνιον and John the Baptist overlap with each other, which appears to be enough to make the rare word μαλακός appear in the most similar words for δαιμόνιον. The final word, ἕτερος, is used too diversely to easily recognize the reason it is considered similar to δαιμόνιον. More analysis would be required to determine this relationship.

If we look at these results in relation to the previous two tables, we should first notice that the average number of occurrences of the words in this list is 18.8, which falls about halfway between the average for Table 5.5 and Table 5.6. Though this number is still below the 25.55 average occurrences from the former table, it is close enough that it would require a broader analysis of other most-similar-word lists before coming to any conclusions about the types of words preferred by these two semantic extraction methods.

We should also note that the last two tables, which were the results of Word2Vec, have significantly more words that appear to be more tenuously related to δαιμόνιον than in the first table. If we look at the words in Table 5.5, we would consider 8 of the twenty words to have a real semantic relationship with δαιμόνιον, either directly (βεελζεβούλ and ἄρχων), through being semantically related to the idea of exorcism (ἐκβάλλω and δαιμονίζομαι), or through being semantically related to the idea of miracle stories and sickness (κωφός, διαβλέπω, θεραπεύω, and νόσος). The other 11 words from that table for which we were able to find a distributional relationship to δαιμόνιον had this relationship because they just happened to occur within the context of exorcism or miracle stories or because, in the case of δοκός and σός, they co-occur with a word that is closely related to δαιμόνιον: ἐκβάλλω.

In the last two tables, however, we found only 4 words in Table 5.6 (λεπρός, δαίμων, χωλός, κακῶς) and 5 words in Table 5.7 (λεπρός, ἄλαλος, κωφός, χωλός, δαιμονίζομαι) that were semantically related directly to δαιμόνιον or to one of the semantically related spheres of exorcism and miracle stories and sickness. The other words seem to be related simply because they happened to appear in an important, semantically related context or to co-occur with a semantically related word. And though this is only a small sample of the data, this seems to suggest that Word2Vec, on a corpus as small as the New Testament, tends to be affected more by the relatively random occurrences of low-frequency words in important contexts than the Log-Likelihood method. And this observation perhaps goes hand-in-hand with the observation above that more lower-frequency words tend to appear on the Word2Vec lists than on the first list. If we were to continue our investigation of the results of these three language models, these would be thoughts that we should keep in mind as we move forward.

In the end, all the three language models returned the same central semantic representation of δαιμόνιον as a word that is related to Jesus' miracle stories and, thus, serves to demonstrate his power as a wonder worker. And even though we think that this central representation is most clearly shown in Table 5.5, the other two tables served to strengthen it by introducing important words that did not appear in Table 5.5, such as λεπρός, δαίμων, χωλός, κακῶς, ἄλαλος, and κωφός. We would also like to remind the reader here that the Log-Likelihood language model scored significantly worse on the Gap Score metric than either of the other models did. And despite this, it seems to have returned a clearer picture of the semantics of δαιμόνιον than either of the other two models.

4 Conclusion

In this paper we have demonstrated on the basis of a small sample of data the usefulness of having a more hands-on and task-related method to assess the results of distributional semantic extraction algorithms. We discovered that for our relatively small corpus of the New Testament that the language model that scored the lowest on the Gap Score metric (the Log-Likelihood method) actually seemed to return the most straightforward representation of the semantics of δαιμόνιον. And even though it is possible that a broader investigation of the data would actually reveal that the opposite is true, we believe that we have shown that by taking the time to actually do in-depth analyses of the data returned by any algorithm, as we did in above, scholars will be better able to choose which algorithm and which parameters will return data that is most useful to their own purposes.

To actually put this assessment method into practice, we would suggest that a scholar choose a small and varied subset of words from their corpus that are as unrelated as possible to the subject under investigation to analyze. So if we were investigating the semantics of the word πίστις in the New Testament, the investigation that we carried out above could be useful since we would consider δαιμόνιον to have only a marginal semantic relationship to πίστις. If, however, we were investigating the concept of exorcism in the New Testament, then δαιμόνιον would be a poor word to choose since it has a very close semantic relationship with exorcism. The thought behind this restriction is that if one is trying to choose the best parameters for an algorithm by actually considering words related to the subject under investigation, one is likely to introduce one's own biases and expectations into the data production process. This is the reason behind the computational linguistic maxim of not training on the data that you wish to test.

We would also suggest choosing words from different syntactic categories (at least from noun, adjective, and verb) and with differing occurrence counts (some with high counts, some with low counts, and some in the middle). Such a wide variety of words will give a better picture of the algorithms and parameters under investigation than just looking at, e.g., frequently occurring verbs or infrequently occurring adjectives would. And we would also like to stress that this form of investigation does not in any way preclude standards-based testing, such as the TOEFL question test or the Gap Score test that we have used here. On the contrary, we believe that such testing is a precondition of being able to engage in the qualitative assessment that we propose here. One should first test the data using one or more such standardized tests and only then carry out a qualitative investigation of those models that look the most interesting. And finally we would like to stress that even though this qualitative assessment requires a significant amount of attention to detail, it is not as time- and labor-intensive as it might look. We were able to complete the qualitative part of the assessment of these three language models in approximately

16 hours, basically two full days of work. So if one did something similar for a list of 10 different words, one could expect to be finished with the qualitative part of the analysis in less than a month. And if this qualitative analysis comes at the beginning of a larger research project, then we believe that this time spent in quality control will pay dividends throughout the life of the project.

References

Bullinaria, John A., Levy, Joseph P., "Extracting Semantic Representations from Word Co-Occurrence Statistics: A Computational Study," 2007, <http://www.cs.bham.ac.uk/~jxb/PUBS/BRM.pdf>.

Bullinaria, John A., Levy, Joseph P., "Extracting Semantic Representations from Word Co-Occurrence Statistics: Stop-Lists, Stemming and SVD," 2012, <http://www.cs.bham.ac.uk/~jxb/PUBS/BRM2.pdf>.

Dunning, Ted, "Accurate Methods for the Statistics of Surprise and Coincidence," *Computational Linguistics 19*, 1993, 61-74.

Goldberg, Yoav, Levy, Omer, "Word2vec Explained: Deriving Mikolov et Al.'s Negative-Sampling Word-Embedding Method," *CoRR* abs/1402.3722, 2014, <http://arxiv.org/abs/1402.3722>.

Harris, Zellig, "Distributional Structure," *Word* 10, no. 23, 1954, 156.

Harris, Zellig, "How Words Carry Meaning", Language and Information: The Bampton Lectures, Columbia University, 1986, <http://www.ircs.upenn.edu/zellig/3_2.mp3>.

Jurafsky, Daniel, Marin, James H., *Speech and Language Processing: An Introduction to Natural Language Processing, Computational Linguistics, and Speech Recognition*, Second Edition, Prentice Hall Series in Artificial Intelligence, Upper Saddle River, NJ: Pearson Education, 2009.

Louw, Johannes P., Nida, Eugene A., *Greek-English Lexicon of the New Testament: Based on Semantic Domains*, Second Edition, 2 vols., New York: United Bible Societies, 1989.

Manning, Chris, Schütze, Hinrich, *Foundations of Statistical Natural Language Processing*, Cambridge, MA: MIT Press, 1999.

Mikolov, Tomas et al., "Distributed Representations of Words and Phrases and Their Compositionality," *CoRR* abs/1310.4546, 2013, <http://arxiv.org/abs/1310.4546>.

Mikolov, Tomas et al., "Efficient Estimation of Word Representations in Vector Space," *CoRR* abs/1301.3781, 2013, <http://arxiv.org/abs/1301.3781>.

Mikolov, Tomas, Yih, Wen-tau, Zweig, Geoffrey, "Linguistic Regularities in Continuous Space Word Representations," in: *Human Language Technologies: Conference of the North American Chapter of the Association of Computational Linguistics, Proceedings,*

June 9-14, 2013, Westin Peachtree Plaza Hotel, Atlanta, Georgia, USA, 2013, 746-751, <http://aclweb.org/anthology/N/N13/N13-1090.pdf>.

Munson, Matthew, *Biblical Semantics Applying Digital Methods for Semantic Information Extraction to Current Problems in New Testament Studies*, Theologische Studien, Aachen: Shaker Verlag, 2017.

Nida, Eugene A., *Componential Analysis of Meaning*, The Hague: Mouton, 1975.

Nida, Eugene A., Louw, Johannes P., Smith, Rondal B.,"Semantic Domains and Componential Analysis of Meaning," in: *Current Issues in Linguistic Theory*, ed. Roger William Cole, Bloomington: Indiana University Press, 1977, 139-167.

Schnabel, Tobias, et al., "Evaluation Methods for Unsupervised Word Embeddings," in: *Proceedings of the 2015 Conference on Empirical Methods in Natural Language Processing, September 17-21, 2015, Lisbon, Portugal*, 2015, 298-307, <http://www.aclweb.org/anthology/D15-1036>.

Test Sets

For reasons of space and readability, this table includes only the number and letter identifying the domains. In order to find a fuller description of these domains, as well as all the words that belong to the domain, please visit <http://www.laparola.net/greco/louwnida.php>.

Domain 1	Domain 2	Domain 1 words	Domain 2 word
67 E	23 A	μακρός, χρόνος, πάντοτε	Ψωμίζω
14 F	74	φωτίζω, λάμπω, φέγγος	δύναμις
33 Q	16	διδαχή, σωφρονίζω, παιδεία	ἀποτινάσσω
15 D	23 C	ἐκβαίνω, ἐκπορεύομαι, ἀπολύω	Τεκνογονία
12 A	10 B	ἐλωΐ, θεός, αββα	γονεύς
12 A	11 B	ἄθεος, παντοκράτωρ, θεός	ἀδελφότης
20 C	6 P	ὄλεθρος, πορθέω, συναπόλλυμαι	ἄγγος
33 Q	28 C	παιδεία, κατηχέω, παιδεύω	φανέρωσις
4 A	33 O	ἀγέλη, ζῷον, θηρίον	ἀγγελία
37 A	13 D	συλαγωγέω, ἐνέχω, βραβεύω	Προγίνομαι
3 C	2 F	βάτος, χόρτος, σίναπι	Χαλκηδών
7 B	15 D	σκηνοποιός, σκήνωμα, σκηνή	ἀπέρχομαι
20 C	53 I	ὄλεθρος, συναπόλλυμαι, φθορά	προφῆτις
25 U	54	προμεριμνάω, μέριμνα, καταπονέω	ἀνάγω
43	87 C	ἀροτριάω, ἀμάω, σπείρω	Πρωτεύω
4 A	37 D	θηρίον, τετράπους, θρέμμα	ἡγεμονεύω

Domain 1	Domain 2	Domain 1 words	Domain 2 word
41 A	25 U	κατάστημα, ἀγωγή, διάγω	ἀμέριμνος
64	15 D	ἔοικα, ὁμοίωσις, ὁμοιόω	ἐκβαίνω
25 U	87 C	ἀμέριμνος, μετεωρίζομαι, προμεριμνάω	εὐγενής
23 A	37 A	βρώσιμος, τρώγω, βιβρώσκω	αὐθεντέω
85 E	30 A	ἐγκατοικέω, κατοικητήριον, κατοικία	Διενθυμέομαι
43	25 U	σπείρω, ἐπισπείρω, ἀμάω	Μέριμνα
87 C	33 J	ὑπεροχή, μεγιστάν, εὐγενής	ἑρμηνεία
53 A	67 B	ἱεροπρεπής, θεοσέβεια, εὐσέβεια	ὁπότε
67 I	8 B	φθινοπωρινός, θέρος, διετία	τρίχινος
28 E	23 A	κρυφαῖος, βαθύς, κρύπτη	Θηλάζω
37 A	23 G	βραβεύω, δαμάζω, εὐπερίστατος	Συζωοποιέω
28 E	11 B	βαθύς, ἀπόκρυφος, κρυφαῖος	Χριστιανός
14 F	64	ἐπιφαίνω, φέγγος, ἐκλάμπω	οἷος
67 B	53 A	πρότερος, πρῶτον, προφθάνω	Δεισιδαίμων
60 B	25 C	ἐννέα, δύο, τέσσαρες	φίλανδρος
49	28 C	σπαργανόω, ἐγκομβόομαι, ἐνδύω	ἀποκάλυψις
41 A	25 C	βίος, χράομαι, ἀναστρέφω	φιλόθεος
23 G	67 I	συνεγείρω, ζάω, ζῳογονέω	θέρος
23 G	24 F	ἀνάστασις, ζάω, ζῳοποιέω	παθητός
3 C	24 F	χλωρός, βοτάνη, βάτος	Πάσχω
54	33 E	ἀποπλέω, εὐθυδρομέω, πλοῦς	ἀπογράφω
33 F	67 I	προσαγωγή, λαλέω, προσλαλέω	Παραχειμάζω
67 B	5 A	προφθάνω, πάλαι, καινός	Διατροφή
20 D	30 A	κατασφάζω, θανατόω, σφαγή	ἔννοια
33 J	7 C	ἐπίλυσις, μεθερμηνεύω, ἑρμηνεία	Γαζοφυλάκιον
85 E	64	περιοικέω, κατοίκησις, κατοικία	τοιοῦτος
33 O	23 I	ἐκδιηγέομαι, ἀναγγέλλω, ἀγγελία	Λέπρα
10 B	74	μάμμη, ἀπάτωρ, προπάτωρ	ἰσχύω
8 B	5 A	θρίξ, μέλος, κόμη	Χόρτασμα
11 B	41 A	ἄδικος, ψευδάδελφος, Χριστιανός	ἀναστροφή
11 B	3 C	ποίμνιον, ψευδάδελφος, νεόφυτος	ἄψινθος
3 C	67 F	χλωρός, χόρτος, ἀκάνθινος	ἕως
23 C	15 D	γέννημα, τεκνογονέω, ἔγκυος	Μεταίρω
85 E	11 C	παροικέω, ἐνοικέω, περιοικέω	ἔθνος
53 I	85 E	ψευδαπόστολος, ἀπόστολος, συμπρεσβύτερος	Παροικέω
88 X	67 E	ὀργή, θυμομαχέω, θυμός	ἀεί
2 F	67 F	χαλκηδών, σμαράγδινος, ἴασπις	ἀναβολή

Domain 1	Domain 2	Domain 1 words	Domain 2 word
33 Q	7 B	παιδεύω, διδασκαλία, θεοδίδακτος	Κατάλυμα
10 B	6 P	προπάτωρ, πατρικός, πατήρ	Θήκη
23 A	3 C	βρῶσις, τρώγω, ἐσθίω	ἀκάνθινος
33 Q	43	παιδεύω, διδάσκω, διδασκαλία	ἐγκεντρίζω
74	88 X	ἰσχύω, κατισχύω, ἐξισχύω	ὀργίζομαι
53 A	6 P	ἱεροπρεπής, δεισιδαιμονία, θρησκός	ἄντλημα
24 F	4 A	πόνος, συνωδίνω, πάθημα	κτῆνος
2 F	85 E	σμάραγδος, χαλκηδών, χρυσόπρασος	οἰκητήριον
11 C	33 J	ἔθνος, πολίτης, ἐντόπιος	διερμηνευτής
20 C	57 H	ἐξολεθρεύω, ἀπόλλυμι, πορθέω	Παραδίδωμι
53 I	28 C	ψευδαπόστολος, εὐαγγελιστής, ἀπόστολος	ἐπίσημος
33 Q	4 A	θεοδίδακτος, παιδεύω, διδασκαλία	ἀλώπηξ
30 A	43	ἀναλογίζομαι, λογίζομαι, ἔννοια	Σπείρω
60 B	41 A	δέκα, ἑπτά, τέσσαρες	Χράομαι
23 I	6 Q	λεπρός, κάμνω, μαλακία	ὀθόνιον
67 B	2 F	προφθάνω, ὁπότε, ἔκπαλαι	σάπφιρος
13 D	87 C	ἐπεισέρχομαι, ἐπιγίνομαι, συγκυρία	Κυρία
67 I	12 A	παραχειμάζω, διετής, χειμών	Παντοκράτωρ
7 C	53 A	οἴκημα, κοιτών, ἀνάγαιον	θεοσεβής
20 D	88	θανατόω, κατασφάζω, ἀναίρεσις	Πταίω
67 A	30 A	προθεσμία, εὐκαιρέω, εὔκαιρος	λογισμός
28 E	67 A	μυστήριον, βάθος, ἀπόκρυφος	Προθεσμία
41 A	60 B	ἀναστρέφω, στοιχέω, προσφέρω	τέσσαρες
13 D	15 D	πληροφορέω, ἐνίστημι, προγίνομαι	ἐξέρχομαι
16	23 C	ἀπομάσσομαι, τρόμος, ῥιπή	ὠδίν
64	25 U	ὁμοίωσις, οἷος, ἔοικα	ἀνασκευάζω
4 A	14 F	ὑποζύγιον, ἄρκος, θρέμμα	ἐπιφαίνω
23 C	12 A	γέννημα, γενετή, ἔγκυος	Μαράνα
20 D	10 B	σφάζω, ἀποκτείνω, διαχειρίζομαι	πατρῷος
14 F	3 C	ἐπιφαύσκω, λάμπω, φῶς	ἄψινθος
11 B	25 C	ἐθνικός, ἐθνικῶς, ψευδάδελφος	Φιλία
33 J	20 D	διερμηνεύω, ἑρμηνεία, ἐπιλύω	Θανατόω
23 C	85 E	ἀρτιγέννητος, γέννημα, τίκτω	Περιοικέω
49	33 Q	περίθεσις, ἐνδιδύσκω, ἐγκομβόομαι	Διδάσκω
33 Q	57 H	θεοδίδακτος, ὑποτίθημι, διδασκαλία	Δόμα
25 C	53 A	φιλόθεος, φιλάδελφος, φιλόστοργος	εὐσέβεια
37 A	2 F	ζωγρέω, συλαγωγέω, συνέχω	ἴασπις

Domain 1	Domain 2	Domain 1 words	Domain 2 word
11 C	54	ἐντόπιος, πολιτεία, πολίτης	Πλέω
88	33 F	ἁμάρτημα, ῥᾳδιουργία, προαμαρτάνω	Λέγω
6 P	37 A	νιπτήρ, ἄντλημα, θήκη	Ζωγρέω
8 B	54	κόμη, κρανίον, ἔριον	εὐθυδρομέω
33 O	23 C	ἄγγελος, σπεκουλάτωρ, ἀγγελία	ἀρτιγέννητος
60 B	16	τρεῖς, ἕξ, ἑπτά	Σείω
16	53 I	τρέμω, ταράσσω, σαλεύω	ἀποστολή
12 A	24 A	αββα, κύριος, θεός	Βλέπω
15 D	8 B	ἀπέρχομαι, ἔξειμι, ἀποβαίνω	τρίχινος
15 D	67 A	ἀποβαίνω, ἐκπορεύομαι, ἐξέρχομαι	εὐκαιρέω

CHAPTER 6

Using Natural Language Processing to Search for Textual References

Brett Graham

1 Introduction

In natural languages, as opposed to computer languages like C or Pascal, the words and syntax are not artificially defined; instead, they develop naturally. Typical examples of natural languages are those that are spoken in human communication, such as the English, French, and Japanese languages. However, the term natural language can also refer to written text, such as Facebook postings, emails or even text messages. As well as changing over time, natural languages also vary among different cultures and people groups. So, for example, the words and syntax that a teenager might use to write a text message on their phone are likely to be different to the words and syntax that Shakespeare used to write Othello.

Within computer science, the term Natural Language Processing (NLP) refers to way computers are programmed to understand natural languages. At a basic level, NLP involves three steps – lexical analysis, syntax analysis, and semantic analysis. The complexity of each of these steps is perhaps best illustrated through looking at how three well-known programs incorporate NLP; namely, Microsoft Word, the Google search engine, and Apple's Siri.

If you were to type (or copy and paste) the following string – "Can I be worn jeens to church?" – into Microsoft Word then it will perform simple lexical analysis by grouping the characters into tokens (i.e. words) using the whitespace and punctuation as separators. Having done this, the program will then consult its dictionary and recognize that "jeens" is not a valid entry. As a result, it will place this word in red, somewhat like this:

> Can I be worn jeens to church?

If Microsoft Word's NLP was very intelligent, it would be able to detect that "jeens" is a misspelling of "jeans" and then automatically change the spelling for you.[1] Having made the correction, Microsoft Word will then recognize that

1 Word allows you to train it to do this correction via the Tools->Autocorrect menu option.

© BRETT GRAHAM, 2019 | DOI:10.1163/9789004399297_008

all the tokens in the string are valid, allowing it to move on to syntax analysis. It performs this analysis based on its understanding of English grammar, which is typically represented as a set of syntax rules. The sections of the string that violate the syntax rules are then placed in green and so the string will now look like this:

> Can I be worn jeans to church?

If Microsoft Word's NLP was even more intelligent then it would attempt to autocorrect the grammar of the sentence for you by scanning through all its syntax rules to find the closest match. In this case, it is likely to be a rule that looks like this:

> <question> = <adverb> <subject> <verb> <object> <prep phrase> <question mark>

It might then change the sentence for you in order to conform it to this closest rule, as follows:

> Can I wear jeans to church?

As complicated as this might sound, the next step, semantic analysis, is even harder. Such analysis would involve the program trying to understand the meaning of the sentence. Subsequently, the program might be intelligent enough in order to suggest a more formal alternative, such as:

> What type of clothing is appropriate for church?

While Microsoft Word is not yet able to perform such complicated analysis, the Google search engine attempts to do this when it responds to a user's request. For example, if you were to copy and paste the string "Can I wear jeans to church?" into this search engine, it will attempt to find the answer to this question by searching for web pages that might be relevant. Typically, the set of matching pages will be large, so the search engine will rank the results by its own criteria, such as, "most matching keywords", or "most recently uploaded", or "most visited page" etc. At the time of writing, the highest-ranking answer (i.e. one at the top of the displayed list) is an entry from <http://www.wikihow.com/Dress-For-Church-Services>, which reads as follows:

> Black dress pants are the best option for a person attending a church service. If you don't have a pair, you can wear clean and wrinkle free casual slacks or khakis as an alternative. Avoid shorts.... And [if] you do wear jeans, do not wear ones with patches or holes.[2]

Although the response does appear to answer this particular question, it only works because the same question has been asked before and the answer has been posted on the Internet. As such, the search engine is not really working out the answer; rather, it is relying on existing research. This means that the search engine's semantic analysis will only ever work for old questions, not new ones. This is demonstrated by the fact that if you ask it a question that has not been asked before, such as, "Can I wash jeans at church?" then the search engine is unable to find an appropriate answer. Instead, it simply returns the set of Internet postings that it thinks are the best matches for the words in the question, which in this case turns out to be a similar set of pages to the first question.[3] Thus, the search engine is not doing true semantic analysis (because this task is beyond the limits of current computing); it is just approximating semantic analysis to the best of its ability.

While Microsoft Word and the Google search engine perform NLP on written (or typed) text, the latest generation natural language processors are able operate on spoken text.[4] These include programs like Apple's Siri,[5] as well as Amazon Alexa[6] Google Assistant,[7] and Microsoft Cortana.[8] The reason why such technology is so popular is that it has the potential to answer almost every question and perform almost every request. That is, not just existing questions, but new ones as well! Not only can you ask, "How far is it to the moon?" but you also say, "Please order me a pizza." This is because Siri is not simply looking at web postings on the Internet (though it can do this) but it is asking other computer programs to perform actions on its behalf. These programs can either be running on the same device/computer or they can be running on other platforms across the Internet. In computer science, this second type of program is known as a "web service". In order to answer new questions (i.e. questions that

2 This is the response of the Google search engine on June 3, 2017.

3 This is the response of the Google search engine on June 3, 2017.

4 The application Google Assistant allows the Google search engine to have a voice activated interface. See, "Google Assistant", *Wikipedia*, May 17, 2017 <https://en.wikipedia.org/wiki/Google_Assistant>, accessed on 10.04.19.

5 "Siri", *Wikipedia*, May 18, 2017, <https://en.wikipedia.org/wiki/Siri>, accessed on 10.04.19.

6 "Amazon Alexa", *Wikipedia*, May 18, 2017, <https://en.wikipedia.org/wiki/Amazon_Alexa>, accessed on 10.04.19.

7 "Google Assistant", *Wikipedia,* May 17, 2017, <https://en.wikipedia.org/wiki/Google_Assis tant>, accessed on 10.04.19.

8 "Cortana (Software)", *Wikipedia*, May 31, 2017, <https://en.wikipedia.org/wiki/Cortana>, accessed on 10.04.19.

do not have their answer posted on the Internet), such as, "When is Peter's birthday?" programs like Siri might consult another application, like Apple Contacts, in order to find the birthday field of Peter. For more complicated requests, such as "How many recent Facebook postings are influenced by Shakespeare?" where there is no relevant Internet posting, Siri would need to ask a web service to do the research for it.

This paper explains how these recent advances in NLP technology can be harnessed to search for allusions and influences to ancient texts. We will begin by investigating the variety of reference forms that were used in ancient literature. Subsequently, we will analyze the recent projects in the Digital Humanities with the aim of determining how effective these projects are in detecting the different reference forms. After recognizing the similarities of these projects, the paper proposes a generic NLP algorithm for detecting textual references. The algorithm is designed to be generic so that can be used to detect any type of textual reference in any type of text (or even a oral allusion to an oral speech). It is suggested that the best way to implement this algorithm is as a web service so that it can be invoked by any Internet search engine, like Google's, or by any virtual personal assistant, like Siri or Cortana etc. This implementation would suit the intention of the algorithm, which is to answer new questions that have not being asked before.

After briefly explaining how this new algorithm works, the final section of this paper will describe how it can benefit biblical (and other textual) studies. The most significant of these benefits is the ability to highlight potential references that are not found by other models, whether automated or manual. In this regard, several examples will be given from applying the algorithm to the Pastoral Epistles. Furthermore, the new algorithm also shares several of the benefits that have been highlighted in recent attempts to automate the detection of textual references. In particular, computers can not only broaden the scope of which documents are searched, but they can also gather metadata from these searches, such as which source texts that a particular author was more inclined to reference, or when and where a particular source text has been most influential in history.

2 The Variety of Reference Forms

The onset of the digital age has brought with it the potential to automate the search for textual references, thereby allowing large databases of source texts to be quickly scanned. However, in order to find as many references as possible, it is important to know exactly what to look for. Therefore, this present section catalogues some of the different reference forms (i.e. the various ways that words are borrowed) in ancient literature.

It has been said that one of the characteristic features of the work of Clement of Alexandria is "the presence of borrowed material [...] taken more or less accurately from other authors' and "culled from every nook and cranny of the nearly thousand-year span of Greek literature."[9] The difficulty of identifying this "borrowed material" is compounded by the fact that he rarely acknowledges his sources; instead "most of the time Clement connects a thought from outside by no more than a single word, a brief formula, a hidden allusion or a mere hint."[10]

While this Early Church Father may be an extreme case, Clement's habit of borrowing from previous literature was certainly not unusual. The Jewish and Christian Scriptures, for example, contain numerous links to earlier texts, both in the form of marked citations as well as un-marked parallels and echoes of their predecessors.[11] Meanwhile, students of the ancient rhetorical schools were explicitly encouraged to embellish their writings with quotations from and allusions to famous authors. According to Quintilian, this involved imitating "the practice of the greatest orators, who [appealed] to the poems of the ancients [...] for the support of their arguments" (Inst. 1.8.10).[12] Likewise, Philo is said to have "borrowed" from a large number of other authors including the Greek philosopher Plato;[13] and the works of Eusebius of Caesarea have been described as "a rich mine of fragments of Greek literature."[14]

Not only was borrowing from earlier works commonplace, there was also a variety of ways in which this was done. Apart from the authoritative quotations that were encouraged by the rhetorical schools, a number of other methods were also employed. Many of Philo's references, for example, are paraphrases rather than quotations, based apparently from memory rather than from a physical text.[15] Similarly, the hymns of Qumran (known as the

9 Van den Hoek, Annewies, *Clement of Alexandria and His Use of Philo in the Stromateis: An Early Christian Reshaping of a Jewish Model*, Leiden: E.J. Brill, 1988, 1.

10 Van den Hoek, *Clement of Alexandria*, 1.

11 Hays, Richard B., *Echoes of Scripture in the Letters of Paul*, New Haven: Yale University Press, 1989, 14. For support of this claim, see "Appendix IV – Loci Citati Vel Allegati" in: *Nestle-Aland Novum Testamentum Graece* (28th edition), Aland, Barbara, et al., eds., Germany: Deutsche Bibelgesellschaft, 2012. See also, Louden, Bruce, *Homer's Odyssey and the Near East*, Cambridge: Cambridge University Press, 2011. Louden finds evidence to suggest that the Jewish and Christian Scriptures also contain 'allusions' to Homer's Odyssey.

12 Quintilian, *Institutio Oratoria Books I-III with an English Translation by H.E. Butler*, Cambridge, Massachusetts: Harvard University Press, 1920), 151.

13 Runia goes as far as saying that 'one can read the whole of Philo's works without coming across a single original thought', Runia, David T., *Philo of Alexandria and the Timaeus of Plato*, Leiden: E.J. Brill, 1986, 9.

14 Van den Hoek, Annewies, *Clement of Alexandria*, 1.

15 Runia, David T., *Philo of Alexandria*, 369. Likewise, Hartog says of Polycarp, "[his] habit of loose quotation demonstrates that he usually quoted from memory and that he felt free

Hodayot) refer to other texts either by summarizing their ideas and themes or by drawing structural parallels.[16] Likewise, the so-called "Testamentary Literature" seeks to gain acceptance by imitating the structure of Jacob's last word (or testament) to his sons.[17] Different again is the book of Jubilees, which interweaves short phrases and groups of verses from the narrative of Genesis and Exodus with "extensive material from other books, in the form of quotation, but also, and more frequently, allusion."[18] A similar approach is adopted in the Prayer of Manasseh, which alludes to the events of 2 Chronicles 33, as the following comparison illustrates:[19]

2 Chronicles 33	Prayer of Manasseh
[Manasseh] ... provoking his [Yahweh's] anger	I provoked your fury (or anger)
	I set up idols
... placed ... the idol ... in the Temple.	I am ensnared,
... Manasseh with hooks	I am bent by a multitude of iron
... in chains ...	chains
humbling himself deeply	I am bending the knees of my heart
before the God of his ancestors.	before you, God of our fathers.

These few examples highlight the variety of reference forms that were used in ancient literature. Not only were citations and quotations common, but more subtle references such as paraphrases, keywords and structural parallels were also used. The following table summarizes these reference forms.

---

to creatively edit his sources". Hartog, Paul, *Polycarp and the New Testament the Occasion, Rhetoric, Theme, and Unity of the Epistle to the Philippians and Its Allusions to New Testament Literature*, Tübingen: Mohr Siebeck, 2002, 172.

16 Hughes, Julie A., *Scriptural Allusions and Exegesis in the Hodayot*, Leiden: Brill, 2006, 51. Hughes also makes a helpful distinction between allusions and mere "coincidences in vocabulary": the former being *intentional* references to *specific* texts, whereas the latter are unconscious repetitions of Scriptural language that were also adopted by the wider Qumran community.

17 Charlesworth, James H., "The Pseudepigrapha as Biblical Exegesis", in: *Early Jewish and Christian Exegesis: Studies in Memory of William Hugh Brownlee*, Evans, Craig A., Stinespring, William F., eds., Atlanta: Scholars Press, 1987, 139-152, 145.

18 Crawford, Sidnie White, *Rewriting Scripture in Second Temple Times*, Grand Rapids: William. B. Eerdmans Publishing Company, 2008, 64. Jubilees has the rare distinction of being found at Qumran as well as being preserved through Christian scribes, especially via the Abyssinian (Ethiopian) Orthodox Church which granted the book canonical status.

19 This example is noted in Charlesworth, James H., "The Pseudepigrapha as Biblical Exegesis", 144.

TABLE 6.1 The different reference forms; ©BRETTGRAHAM

Reference Form	The Way that the Text is Borrowed
Quotation	Verbatim
Paraphrase	Re-wording of a single clause
Single Keyword	One word
Multiple Keywords	Words from multiple clauses that are copied to a single clause
Structural Parallel	Words from multiple clauses that are copied to multiple clauses

This above table serves to highlight that the references come in a variety of forms. This list of reference forms is unlikely to be exhaustive; it is, however, illustrative in that it reveals the complexity involved in trying to detect every reference.

3 Combining Modern Computers and Ancient Texts

In the past, the task of identifying textual references was the domain of individual scholars who each manually searched the set of source texts that he/she was familiar with. However, the onset of the digital age has meant that searches can now be performed on any source text, whether familiar or not, at the click of a button. Event-driven software programs, like Accordance and Logos, and Internet search tools, like Bible Gateway and the *Thesaurus Linguae Graecae* (TLG), enable biblical scholars to perform word searches at a much faster rate than the traditional paper-based approach. For a complex query with multiple search words, it usually takes more time to type in the search string than for the computer to return the result. This difference becomes even more pronounced when large numbers of searches are involved, such as when searching for allusions and influences across an entire document. Thus, over the last decade several projects in the Digital Humanities have attempted to overcome this problem by introducing a level of automation to the generation (and running) of searches. These projects usually involve the adaptation of algorithms that are commonly used in NLP, including the Bag-of-Words, Greedy String-Tiling, and Sequence Alignment algorithms.

The Bag-of-Words algorithm uses a "hashing function"[20] to convert a line of text into a vector (represented as a set of numbers), where the entries of the vector contain the number of occurrences of each different word in that line.[21] Two lines of text can then be compared based on the similarity of their vectors,[22] with those above a specified threshold being marked as related in some manner, such as one being a paraphrase of the other. The vector entries (i.e. the word counts) are indexed based on the value returned by the hashing function rather than their original order in the text, making this algorithm particularly useful for languages such as Greek where the word order can vary, or when the borrowed text has been paraphrased or modified through word insertions/deletions. The Bag-of-Words algorithm has already been used effectively to study the possible use of Mark in Luke's Gospel.[23]

The Greedy String-Tiling algorithm divides a source string (such as a line of text) into "tiles"(i.e. sequences of words) and then places them on top of a target string in places where the words match.[24] Then, if a specified percentage of the target string is covered with tiles, one string might be dependent on the other. This algorithm is described as "greedy" in that it tries to make each tile as big as it can be, even though two smaller tiles placed in the same location might cover more words in total. Hence the algorithm may not always achieve the best solution (since not all permutations are considered), but it finds a good result in a shorter timeframe. The Greedy String-Tiling algorithm is used in the METER project at the University of Sheffield[25] and is most effective when the words are borrowed in sequences (such as in quotations).

The third type of algorithm, Sequence Alignment, divides the source and target strings into overlapping sets of consecutive words. These sets are called "shingles"or "n-grams", where n is the specified number of words in each set

20 The hashing function converts each word into a number, or index, which is then used to order the words. An example of a simple hashing function is to sum the unicode of each letter in the word.

21 The algorithm can also be applied to a sentence or a verse, or even to a whole document. It is commonly used to filter messages in email accounts by defining a vector for a typical spam message (such as having one or more occurrences of the word "Viagra") and comparing this with the vector of each new message.

22 This comparison is made using a "cosine measure". See Dale, Robert, Moisl, Hermann, Somers, Harold, eds., *Handbook of Natural Language Processing* (1st edition), New York: CRC Press, 2000, 471; Lee, John, "A Computational Model of Text Reuse in Ancient Literary Texts," *Proceedings of the 45th Annual Meeting on Association for Computational Linguistics*, Prague, Czech, June 23-30, 2007, 472-479, 475.

23 Lee, John, "A Computational Model of Text Reuse in Ancient Literary Texts".

24 Tiles, or words, that do not match are discounted.

25 Clough, Paul, et al., "METER: MEasuring TExt Reuse," *Proceedings of the 40th Annual Meeting on Association for Computational Linguistics*, ACL'02, Stroudsburg, PA, USA: Association for Computational Linguistics, 2002, <http://eprints.whiterose.ac.uk/78530/>, accessed on 10.04.19..

and is usually two or three words ("bigrams" or "trigrams").[26] The comparison of the two strings begins by searching for one common n-gram between the source and target, after which the surrounding context is searched for other matches. Then, if a minimum number of n-grams are found together within a maximum distance of each other (or context), the algorithm signals a potential dependency.[27] Like Greedy String-Tiling, the Sequence Alignment algorithm works best when the words are borrowed in sequence, such as quotations, but it can also be used to detect paraphrases if n is small (e.g. one or two). This flexibility has contributed to its use in several recent studies, including being used to search for text re-use across the TLG database.[28]

In summary, there have been a number of recent projects in the Digital Humanities that have sought to detect textual references across a particular set of source texts. In essence, each of these projects is a natural language processor that automates the first two steps of NLP, lexical and syntax analysis. Due to the complexity of NLP, these projects involve written (rather than spoken) texts where the lexical analysis can be largely pre-determined. Each of these projects has a slightly different form of syntax analysis (i.e. determining which combination of words could be valid reference) that is an adaptation of three types of algorithms (as mentioned above), all of which are aimed at detecting verbal similarity. Only potential references with a minimum level of verbal similarity are passed on for semantic analysis (which is done manually on account of the complexity of this task). This approach is inclined to prefer quotations and paraphrases as opposed to single keywords. The syntax analysis can be configured to detect single word matches but that would mean all such matches would need to be passed to the manual semantic analysis phase, which is not practical for large databases of texts.

Furthermore, these programs assume that the syntax of references (i.e. the arrangement of the borrowed words) is static. However, the form of textual references in poetry, for example, need not be the same as those in prose. Likewise, the way that the Early Church Fathers make reference to the New

26 So for example, the string "Shakespeare wrote many plays about love" would be divided into four trigrams: "Shakespeare-wrote-many", "wrote-many-plays", "many-plays-about" and "plays-about-love". Some adaptations of this algorithm omit certain classes of words, such as articles and prepositions. See, for example, Olsen, Mark, Horton, Russell, Roe, Glenn, "Something Borrowed: Sequence Alignment and the Identification of Similar Passages in Large Text Collections", *Digit. Stud. Champ Numér.* 2/1, May 17, 2011 <https://www.digitalstudies.org/articles/10.16995/dscn.258/>, accessed on 10.04.19.

27 Both the minimum number of n-grams required, or "span", and the maximum separation between them, or "gap", are configured as parameters of the algorithm.

28 Büchler, Marco, et al., "Unsupervised Detection and Visualisation of Textual Reuse on Ancient Greek Texts", *J. Chic. Colloq. Digit. Humanit. Comput. Sci.* 1/2, June 16, 2010, <https://knowledge.uchicago.edu/record/133>.

Testament is likely to be different to the way that way that modern pop music does. As such, reference forms are not fixed but context dependent. Therefore, the following section outlines a generic NLP algorithm that is designed to detect references in a variety of contexts.

4 A Generic NLP Algorithm

A generic algorithm for detecting text references using NLP is simple; it is just three basic steps:

Lexical analysis,
Syntax analysis,
Semantic analysis.

The goal of the first step, lexical analysis, is to parse a target text in order to produce subsets of words that are then passed on to the syntax analysis phase. For a traditional natural language processor, each subset is a sentence as delimited by punctuation. However, the "maximum subset size" is treated as parameter of the algorithm because the optimum value of the parameter is dependent on the target text. For example, the optimum value for detecting how Ancient Greek literature makes references to other Ancient Greek literature will be different to the optimum value for detecting how modern English novels refer to the same literature. Thus, the optimum value for the parameter for a particular type of target text is learnt rather than being fixed. This process of learning the optimum value is achieved by training the algorithm to detect known textual references that occur in target texts of the same type.[29]

The lexical analysis phase also involves parsing each word of the target text[30] and then determining the lexical alternatives of the words.[31] These alternatives are a set of one or more words in the language of the source text that can match the word in the target text during a search. They are used in the syntax analysis phase to find potential references between the texts. The target and

29 This training of the algorithm is explained further below.

30 If the source texts were not previously parsed, these would need to be processed as well. The parsing involves finding the root word and determining the lexical form of the word. The recently released natural language processors, like Siri or Cortana, are able to perform this type of lexical analysis on a spoken target text.

31 While the parsing of the target text might need to be performed at run-time (unless it is an existing written text), the lexical alternatives for each word in a language can be preprocessed and then retrieved at run-time.

source texts can be in different languages (such as the target texts being in Ancient Greek and the source texts being in Hebrew) and the lexical alternatives make the translation between the languages possible.

The algorithm has a parameter called "level of alternatives" that is used to fine-tune the search process for each different reference form. This parameter has three different values: "one word,"[32] "same root,"[33] and "synonyms." The level that is selected will influence the amount of matching source texts for each search. When the source texts are large, setting this value to "synonyms" will make it difficult to find a combination that is unique to one passage (or even potentially unique). Therefore, in testing the algorithm (see Section 4 below), the value of "level of alternatives" for the keyword reference form was set to "one word' and value for the other reference forms was set to "same root."

Syntax analysis on each subset of words involves scanning through all the syntax rules to find the rule (or set of rules) that matches the words. If the algorithm were implemented as a web service, these syntax rules could be passed to the algorithm through a file (or data stream) in a standard format called XML. Like the syntax rules of a traditional language like English, the syntax rules for references are relatively simple, but the number of rules is quite large. Every form of reference (like the ones listed in Table 6.1 above) needs several rules for every different length subset. Like the "maximum subset size" parameter, the "syntax rules" are a parameter of the algorithm in order to make them context dependent. This feature allows the algorithm to be used to learn the most effective set of rules for each particular context.

When a matching syntax rule is found, the potential reference is passed on to the semantic analysis phase. While a syntax rule defines a legitimate way that the words can be arranged in order to form a reference, not all of these arrangements will constitute an actual reference (i.e. the semantic analysis will reject potential references that are not meaningful). Due to the current limitations of semantic analysis (i.e. it needs to be done manually to be truly accurate) the algorithm only investigates syntax rules where the matching words are rare.[34] This is based on the assumption that intentional references

32 When the target and source texts are in the same language, the 'one word' is the same word. For differentlanguages, the "one word" is a word from the source language that is commonly translated as that word in the target language.

33 For example, words on the same root of σῴζω ("I save") are σωτηρία ("salvation"), σωτήριος ("saving"), and σωτήρ ("savior"). Where appropriate, some very common synonyms might also included amongst a word's 'same root' lexical alternatives, such as κύριος ("lord") as an alternative for θεός ("God").

34 This is analogous to the logic of Inverse Document Frequency (IDF).

usually appeal to particular passages.[35] To achieve this goal perfectly, the borrowed words in the target text would need to be "perfectly singular". That is, the words would only be found together in just one source text – the text being referred to. However, not all references achieve this perfect singularity.[36] For example, calling someone a "good Samaritan" was originally meant to be a reference to the kind person in Luke 10:25-37, but the word "Samaritan" (Gk. Σαμαρίτης)[37] is found in seven passages of the New Testament, two of which contain someone who could be considered "good".[38] So, while a reference might intend to refer to single passage, in some cases this goal will not be achieved.

Therefore, the algorithm uses a parameter called "potential singularity" as a way of identifying which of the syntax rules to perform semantic analysis on. Like the other parameters, the optimum value for potential singularity is context dependent and needs to be learnt for each type of target text.

```
The algorithm is summarized below:
Parse the target text into subsets of words
For each subset
  Scan the syntax rules
  For each matching rule
    If the words are potentially singular
      Perform semantic analysis
```

The following section now describes how this algorithm was tested in the field of biblical studies.

35 Perri, Carmela, "On Alluding", *Poetics* 7, 1978, 289-307.This paper refers to "intentional" references since the task of NLP is essentially to determine the speaker's/author's intended meaning. The algorithm that is presented in this paper will actually detect both "intentional" and "unintentional" potential references, but only those where the matching words are rare, or "potential singular". This limitation is based on the theory of allusions as described by Perri and is used to reduce the amount of semantic analysis that is required by the algorithm.

36 Contra Hartog and Kittel who require perfect/absolute singularity. See Hartog, Paul, *Polycarp*, 174; Kittel, Bonnie Pedrotti, *The Hymns of Qumran* Ann Arbor, Michigan: Scholars Press, 1981, 51.

37 The word "good" is not found in Luke 10.

38 As well as Luke 10, Luke 17 describes a Samaritan who is the only one of the ten healed lepers who returns to thank Jesus.

5 Testing the Algorithm

This paper presents a generic NLP algorithm for detecting potential textual references. The algorithm itself is not particularly novel since it is in essence just the three steps of NLP. It was developed and tested during the research phase of a PhD in the field of biblical studies. The research looked at how the Pastoral Epistles (i.e. Titus and 1 & 2 Timothy) might have been influenced by the Septuagint and Jewish Pseudepigrapha. Implementing the algorithm as a computer program was not possible (nor necessary) in this context because a database of these texts was not available in the public domain. Since the semantic analysis (the most complicated aspect of NLP) needed to be manually performed, the lexical and syntax analysis was also simulated manually. This was possible because the algorithm is essentially very simple. The complicated parts of the process were the development of the syntax rules and the semantic analysis of the potential references.

In order to test the algorithm, a broad set of syntax rule definitions were developed that would seem to cover the different reference forms in Ancient Greek literature (see Section 2 above). The algorithm was initially used to detect potential references between the Pastoral Epistles and the Septuagint. The parameters of the algorithm were trained so that algorithm would detect all the potential references listed in the standard Greek editions of the New Testament (i.e. the UBS5 and the NA28) that the semantic analysis deemed to be meaningful. During this training, additional reference forms were added to the original set (including a definition of emphatic keywords). Other reference forms (such as multiple keywords) were taken out of the list because they were deemed not necessary for the Pastoral Epistles. The syntax rules were effective for the Pastoral Epistles. Future studies might test their effectiveness for other Ancient Greek texts.

Having trained these parameters to work for one set source texts (i.e. the Septuagint), the algorithm was then applied to a relatively new question, namely, "What are the potential references between the Pastoral Epistles and the Jewish Pseudepigrapha?". The algorithm was able to detect 36 potential references, which is substantially higher than the number detected by all previous studies (i.e. 12, of which only 6 were deemed as meaningful by the semantic analysis). The average verbal similarity of the algorithm's references (2.5 root words and 3.2 total words) was also higher than previous studies (2.2 root words and 2.8 total words). These results highlight the potential benefits of this approach.

6 The Benefits of the Algorithm

In recent years, several projects in the Digital Humanities have sought to introduce a level of automation to the search for textual references. In the context of these studies, this paper proposes a new algorithm that uses NLP. It is proposed that this algorithm be implemented as a web service so that can be used with the latest NLP technology, like Siri or Cortana, in order to perform new research. This algorithm presents three significant benefits for the study of the humanities.[39] Firstly, because it can be configured to detect potential references with low verbal similarity, it enables a systematic approach to the detection of allusions and influences. Secondly, it can search through large collections of source texts, even unfamiliar ones, so that more potential references can be considered. Then thirdly, this ability to perform large-scale searches means that metadata can also be collected, including which source text is used most frequently.

The primary benefit of this algorithm is its ability to be configured to detect a variety of reference forms (including those that have low verbal similarity) without overburdening the task of semantic analysis. This is particularly helpful for allusions, which can be signaled by a single keyword like Μελχισέδεκ ("Melchizedek"), as well as for influences, which might borrow only one or two words from their source text (or perhaps just synonyms of those words). As such, the detection of these references is frequently subjective and difficult to evaluate.[40] For example, the opening words of 1 Tim 1:15 (πιστὸς ὁ λόγος καὶ πάσης ἀποδοχῆς ἄξιος[41]) indicates that what follows (ὅτι Χριστὸς Ἰησοῦς ἦλθεν εἰς τὸν κόσμον ἁμαρτωλοὺς σῶσαι[42]) might contain a reference to another text,[43] but because there is no obvious quotation, it is difficult to determine which text this might be. However, by analyzing the frequency of different combinations of the words, such as how often ἔρχομαι ("I come") and σῴζω ("I save") are found together in the Septuagint, this algorithm can indicate which source text might have been the most influential.[44]

39 The first benefit applies only to this new algorithm. The remaining two benefits also apply to other methods of automation.

40 This subjectivity is highlighted by the observation that the NA28 lists as many as thirty-two potential references to the Septuagint in 1 Timothy, while the UBS5 has only twenty.

41 Eng. Trans. – "This word is faithful and worthy of all acceptance."

42 Eng. Trans. – "that Christ Jesus cam into the world to save sinners."

43 The UBS5 and NA28 both suggest a possible influence from the words of Jesus in Luke 19:10. The other possible influences are discussed in Towner, Philip H., *The Letters to Timothy and Titus*, USA: William B. Eerdmans Publishing Company, 2006, 145.

44 The idea of the messiah coming to save (ἔρχομαι and σῴζω, or their synonyms) is surprisingly rare in the Septuagint. Interestingly, one of these occurrences, Zech 9:9, is quoted

TABLE 6.2 Comparison of potential references from Titus to the Septuagint; ©BRETTGRAHAM

	Potential references	Average root words / reference	Average total words / reference
New Algorithm	38	2.5	3.2
UBS5	7	2.3	2.9
NA28	12	2.3	2.9

TABLE 6.3 Potential references from Titus to Septuagint – categorized by type; ©BRETTGRAHAM

	New algorithm	Those not in UBS5 or NA28
Quotations	8	5
Paraphrases	9	5
Single Keywords	1	1
Multiple Keywords	8	8
Structural Parallels	12	10
TOTAL	38	29

The efficiency of the new algorithm is demonstrated by analyzing the potential references from Titus to the Septuagint (see Table 6.2 above).

The new algorithm detected substantially more potential references compared to both the UBS5 and NA28 and yet these references also have greater verbal similarity, both in terms of matching root words and total matching words (i.e. including synonyms). The increase is partly due to the inclusion of more reference forms, with over 55% of the algorithm's references (i.e. 21 of 38) being keywords and structural parallels (as illustrated in Table 6.3 above). However, there were also five new paraphrases and five new quotations detected.

The additional references also make the total references more evenly distributed, both in terms of the places in Titus where they are found, as well as the locations of the relevant source texts in the Septuagint. This highlights that the algorithm functions equally well across all source texts, including those that are less familiar.

twice in the Gospels when Jesus makes his final entry into Jerusalem, suggesting that it was well known (and influential) within the Early Church.

This feature leads to the second major benefit of the algorithm for the study of humanities: namely, its ability to ask new questions. For example, the statement in 1 Tim 2:14, Ἀδὰμ οὐκ ἠπατήθη ("Adam was not deceived"), is usually understood by Biblical scholars as an allusion to Gen 3:13, where Eve explains, Ὁ ὄφις ἠπάτησέν με ("the serpent deceived me").[45] This connection comes from recognizing that this is the only verse in the Septuagint where the verb ἀπατάω ("I deceive") appears in the context of the noun Ἀδάμ ("Adam"). However, if the intertextual framework (i.e. the familiar source texts) of the author of 1 Tim 2 included the texts of Jewish Pseudepigrapha that were extant in the first century, then this same statement could instead be a rebuttal of Apoc. Sedr. 5:1 – ἠπατήθη [...] ὁ Ἀδάμ ("Adam was deceived"; c.f. LAE 16:5; Hist. Rech. 7:8; 3 Bar. 4:8; and Sib. Or. 1:39-40). Thus, by simply changing the set of source texts to search, the new algorithm can simulate a different intertextual framework and thereby provide insight into another possible context.

Finally, the third major advantage of automating the search for potential references is the ability to gather metadata. Although this is also possible for manual analysis, computers increase the scale by which it can be done. This then allows statistics to be collated, such as the number of times an author appears to refer to each source text, which in turn indicates which ones were most influential. Alternatively, by recording references to a particular source text across centuries (or domains), this data can highlight when (or where) that text had the greatest impact. This data can then be used in further analysis, such as tracking the usage of a text before and after certain major events, like wars and revivals, or even to study which texts have been the most influential in legal decisions. Consequently, the ability to record metadata provides a wealth of possibilities for more scholars to investigate further.

In summary, this new algorithm offers three significant benefits to the study of the humanities. The foremost of these is that it can detect any reference form, including those with low levels of verbal similarity. Furthermore, by varying the set of source texts to search, it can simulate different intertextual frameworks, thereby allowing it to highlight potential references in large databases of source texts, even those involving in less familiar texts. While doing so, metadata can also be collected that can in turn provide a better understanding of the way different source texts are used.

---

45 See, for example, Knight III, George W., *The Pastoral Epistles, New International Greek Testament Commentary*, Marshall, Howard, Gasque, W. Ward, eds., USA: William. B. Eerdmans Publishing Company, 1999, 143; Aland, Barbara, et al., eds., *Greek New Testament* (5th edition), Stuttgart: German Bible Society, 2014, 694; Aland, Barbara, et al., eds., *Novum Testamentum Graece: Nestle-Aland* (28th edition), Stuttgart: German Bible Society, 2012, 637.

References

Aland, Barbara, Aland, Kurt, Karavidopoulos, Johannes, Martini, Carlo M., Metzger, Bruce, eds., *Greek New Testament*, (5th edition), Stuttgart: German Bible Society, 2014.

Aland, Barbara, Aland, Kurt, Karavidopoulos, Johannes, Martini, Carlo M., Metzger, Bruce M., eds., *Nestle-Aland Novum Testamentum Graece*, (28th edition), Germany: Deutsche Bibelgesellschaft, 2012.

"Amazon Alexa". *Wikipedia*, May 18, 2017, <https://en.wikipedia.org/wiki/Amazon_Alexa>, accessed on 10.04.19.

Büchler, Marco, GeBner, Annette, Eckart, Thomas, Heyer, Gerhard, "Unsupervised Detection and Visualisation of Textual Reuse on Ancient Greek Texts", *Journal of the Chicago Colloquium on Digital Humanities and Computer Science 1/2*, June 16, 2010, <https://knowledge.uchicago.edu/record/133>, accessed on 10.04.19.

Charlesworth, James H, "The Pseudepigrapha as Biblical Exegesis", in: *Early Jewish and Christian Exegesis: Studies in Memory of William Hugh Brownlee*, Evans, Craig A., Stinespring, William F., eds., Atlanta: Scholars Press, 1987, 139-152.

Clough, Paul, Gaizauskas, Robert, Piao, Scott S.L., Wilks, Yorick, "METER: MEasuring TExt Reuse", *Proceedings of the 40th Annual Meeting on Association for Computational Linguistics*, ACL'02. Stroudsburg, PA, USA: Association for Computational Linguistics, 2002, <http://eprints.whiterose.ac.uk/78530/>, accessed on 10.04.19.

"Cortana (software)", *Wikipedia*, May 31, 2017, <https://en.wikipedia.org/wiki/Cortana>, accessed on 10.04.19.

Crawford, Sidnie White, *Rewriting Scripture in Second Temple Times*, Grand Rapids: William. B. Eerdmans Publishing Company, 2008.

Dale, Robert, Moisl, Hermann, Somers, Harold, eds. *Handbook of Natural Language Processing*, (1st edition), New York: CRC Press, 2000.

Gamble, Harry Y., *Books and Readers in the Early Church: A History of Early Christian Texts*, New Haven: Yale University Press, 1995.

"Google Assistant", *Wikipedia*, May 17, 2017, <https://en.wikipedia.org/wiki/Google_As sistant>, accessed on 10.04.19.

Hartog, Paul, *Polycarp and the New Testament the Occasion, Rhetoric, Theme, and Unity of the Epistle to the Philippians and Its Allusions to New Testament Literature*, Tübingen: Mohr Siebeck, 2002.

Hays, Richard B., *Echoes of Scripture in the Letters of Paul*, New Haven: Yale University Press, 1989.

Hays, Richard B., *The Conversion of the Imagination: Paul as Interpreter of Israel's Scripture*, Grand Rapids, Mich.: William B. Eerdmans Publishing Company, 2005.

Van den Hoek, Annewies, *Clement of Alexandria and His Use of Philo in the Stromateis: An Early Christian Reshaping of a Jewish Model*, Leiden: E.J. Brill, 1988.

Hughes, Julie A., *Scriptural Allusions and Exegesis in the Hodayot*, Leiden: Brill, 2006.

Kittel, Bonnie Pedrotti, *The Hymns of Qumran*. Ann Arbor, Michigan: Scholars Press, 1981.

Knight III, George W., *The Pastoral Epistles, New International Greek Testament Com*, Marshall, Howard, Gasque, W. Ward, eds., USA: William. B. Eerdmans Publishing Company, 1999.

Lee, John, "A Computational Model of Text Reuse in Ancient Literary Texts", *Proceedings of the 45th Annual Meeting on Association for Computational Linguistics*, Prague, Czech, June 23-30, 2007, 472-479.

Louden, Bruce, *Homer's Odyssey and the Near East*, Cambridge: Cambridge University Press, 2011.

McLean, Bradley H., *Citations and Allusions to Jewish Scripture in Early Christian and Jewish Writings through 180 C. E*, Lewiston, NY: The Edwin Mellen Press, 1992.

Olsen, Mark, Horton, Russell, Roe, Glenn, "Something Borrowed: Sequence Alignment and the Identification of Similar Passages in Large Text Collections", *Digital Studies / Le Champ Numérique 2/1*, May 17, 2011, <https://www.digitalstudies.org/articles/10.16995/dscn.258/>, accessed on 10.04.19.

Perri, Carmela, "On Alluding", *Poetics 7*, 1978, 289-307.

Runia, David T., *Philo of Alexandria and the Timaeus of Plato*, Leiden: E.J. Brill, 1986.

"Siri", *Wikipedia*, May 18, 2017, <https://en.wikipedia.org/wiki/Siri>, accessed on 10.04.19.

Stanley, Christopher D., *Arguing With Scripture*, New York: T & T Clark, 2004.

Towner, Philip H., *The Letters to Timothy and Titus*, USA: William B. Eerdmans Publishing Company, 2006.

CHAPTER 7

Electronic Transcriptions of New Testament Manuscripts and their Accuracy, Documentation and Publication

H.A.G. Houghton

1 Introduction*

The adoption of digital tools to edit the Greek New Testament has fundamentally changed the methodology of creating such an edition. In the past, data was painstakingly gathered in the form of collations of manuscripts against a standard printed text, which were then combined to create an apparatus of readings.[1] The base text used for collation was a fixed point against which everything was measured; once the apparatus was constructed, the individual collations were no longer required. In contrast, electronic editing software (in particular, the widely-adopted *Collate program* and its successors) is based not on a single apparatus but on multiple files, each of which consists of a complete electronic transcription of a single manuscript witness.[2] The apparatus is compiled automatically from these files, using an algorithm to improve alignment and creating meta-files to assist with the normalisation of the data. This has at least four distinct advantages over the previous method: the performance of the mechanical task of compilation by a computer is much quicker, less susceptible to human error, reproducible and reconfigurable. A collation can be re-run from the same files with different settings or a different selection of witnesses. It is therefore the complete electronic transcriptions rather than

* I would like to thank my colleagues Amy Myshrall, David Parker, Bruce Morrill and Catherine Smith for sharing their experience in comments on a draft version of this chapter, and Ulrich Schmid for the invitation to present it at the 72nd annual meeting of the SNTS in Pretoria in August 2017.

1 For a description of how to make a paper collation, see Parker, David C., *An Introduction to the New Testament Manuscripts and their Texts*, Cambridge: CUP, 2008, 95-100.

2 Robinson, Peter, *Collate: Interactive Collation of Large Textual Traditions, Version 2*, Computer Program distributed by the Oxford University Centre for Humanities Computing: Oxford, 1994; see also Houghton, H.A.G., and Smith, Catherine J., "Digital Editing and the Greek New Testament," in: *Ancient Worlds in Digital Culture* (Digital Biblical Studies 1), ed. Clivaz, Claire, Dilley, Paul, Hamidović, David, Leiden: Brill, 2016, 110-127; especially 118-120.

collations of variants (and the apparatus created by collating these collations) which become the building blocks of editing a text.

The result is that the first generation of digital editors have a double task, as I have observed elsewhere:

> First of all, they must edit the individual documents, creating an electronic archetype of each witness for the required biblical book. Only then can they proceed to use this information to edit the text itself.[3]

This procedure of making electronic transcriptions is fully integrated into the workflow of the *Novum Testamentum Graecum Editio Critica Maior* (ECM) and has also been adopted in other editorial projects relating to the New Testament, such as the *Vetus Latina Iohannes* and the *Digital Codex Sinaiticus*. In the light of the experience gained on these projects, it is now appropriate to reflect on the creation and use of electronic transcriptions of the New Testament and make some recommendations for good practice. This chapter will briefly outline the process of making electronic transcriptions and the ways in which they can be used, before turning to consider three areas in which further clarity or standardisation may be beneficial. These are, in turn: the accuracy of transcriptions; the documentation of transcription practice; and finally, the publication of electronic transcriptions, especially with regard to authority and availability.

2 Making and Using Electronic Transcriptions

The principle of making an electronic transcription of a New Testament manuscript is remarkably similar to creating a paper collation, even though the result is different.[4] Because the textual agreement between almost all manuscripts and editorial reconstructions is around 90% (and even higher in many cases), the most efficient way for transcribers to proceed is to take an electronic file of an editorial text, compare it with the manuscript, and intervene at every point of variation, in this case by adjusting the file to match the reading

3 Houghton and Smith, "Digital Editing", 115.

4 A description of how to make an electronic transcription is given in Parker, *An Introduction,* 100-106. Parker's comment that "the transcription process is very different from collating" (104) refers to the incorporation of layout information, as explained below.

of the manuscript.[5] Selecting a base text close to that of the witness, such as the *Textus Receptus* for transcribing Byzantine manuscripts, means that the transcriber has to introduce fewer changes. The choice of base text should be unimportant, since the resultant transcription file should reproduce the text of the manuscript: it is only if the transcriber overlooks a discrepancy that a reading of the base text will persevere unchanged.[6] One instance where the base text is likely to affect the transcription is in the transcriber's interpretation of unclear characters or treatment of damaged portions, so the use of a base text similar to that of the manuscript could assist with this.[7]

For an edition of the text of a particular book of the New Testament, an electronic transcription need only represent the biblical text copied by the original scribe and any subsequent corrections. Where this is absent or somehow doubtful, the relevant text should be correspondingly marked as lacunose, reconstructed or unclear. In practice, however, transcribers for the ECM also introduce basic information about the layout, recording page, column and line breaks: the benefits of this include the easy comparison of transcription and image, especially useful in proofreading, and ensuring that transcribers are constantly engaged with the manuscript through regular intervention in the file, rather than losing attention if the differences between the base text and manuscripts are scarce. The amount of information recorded in a transcription can easily be increased, such as the inclusion of abbreviations, punctuation, decoration or paratext.[8] A balance must be struck in order to enable

5 This high agreement between manuscripts and the majority text is the main reason why few resources have so far been devoted to the development of optical character recognition methods for reading New Testament manuscripts: the complex systems of abbreviation, the challenge of interpreting corrections, and the presence of paratextual material also present significant obstacles, especially in the majority of manuscripts written in minuscule script. Nevertheless, the large body of scholarly transcriptions of New Testament manuscripts created for the ECM would provide an excellent set of training data for those wishing to develop such a system, which could also be extended to Greek manuscripts more broadly.

6 In practice, however, variants are often overlooked by transcribers: for example, careful review of the eight places of variation between the *Textus Receptus* and the majority text of John led to the correction of many transcriptions. For Galatians, the IGNTP has experimented with using different base texts for the two initial transcriptions, but this has not yet been evaluated.

7 The practice of the INTF, however, is that lacunae in electronic transcriptions should be filled with the reading of the Nestle-Aland base text unless this is clearly wrong (INTF, *Dokumentation der Funktionen des Transkription Editors und Richtlinien zur Transkriptionen neutestamentlicher Handschriften,* Version 1, August 2013; see especially 19).

8 For an illustration of the practices adopted for the ECM, see INTF, *Dokumentation,* and the equivalent IGNTP document, *Guidelines for the Transcription of Manuscripts Using the Online Transcription Editor* (2016), available at <http://epapers.bham.ac.uk/2161/>.

transcribers to work with maximum effectiveness and not become distracted from textual accuracy by recording additional features.[9] It may also be noted in passing that the degree of engagement with a manuscript required to make a full electronic transcription places a researcher in a strong position to assess its textual evidence, given Hort's maxim that "Knowledge of documents should precede final judgment on readings."[10]

The first generation of electronic transcriptions, created for use with the original Collate software, were plain-text files with basic tags for markup, produced in a standard text editor.[11] These were converted in a separate process to a more advanced format for publication (first SGML, then XML). The Workspace for Collaborative Editing project produced the browser-based Online Transcription Editor in 2013. This enabled transcribers to work directly on XML files in a display which matched the published transcriptions, the markup being hidden behind the scenes.[12] Not only was the aim to standardise the markup and deliver formally correct files, but this procedure also meant that transcriptions could be published online and distributed immediately. One of the strengths of XML encoding corresponding to the TEI Guidelines is that each file is complete in itself, with a standard form of markup which is not only largely readable by humans but also actionable by machines. This is vital for the long-term sustainability of these files as well as their availability for re-use, as discussed below. The Online Transcription Editor supports a wide variety of TEI-compatible features which can be added as enhancements to standard transcriptions, such as formatting, annotations and other paratextual features.

Unlike printed transcriptions and collations, electronic files may be re-used or developed in a variety of ways. A transcription created as part of a study of

9 Experience in reconciling transcriptions shows that even the recording of a single correction may often lead transcribers to overlook other textual variations on the same line. Similarly, initial transcriptions of commentary manuscripts are frequently less accurate due to transcribers having to count the number of lines between sections of biblical text.

10 Westcott, Brooke F., Hort, F.J.A., ed. *The New Testament in the Original Greek. Introduction and Appendix,* Cambridge: Macmillan, 1881, 31.

11 For more on this markup and its subsequent development, see Houghton, H.A.G., "The Electronic Scriptorium: Markup for New Testament Manuscripts," in: *Digital Humanities in Biblical, Early Jewish and Early Christian Studies*, Clivaz, Claire, Gregory, Andrew, Hamidović, David, Leiden: Brill, 2014, 31-60, especially 33-35.

12 The Online Transcription Editor was produced by Martin Sievers and Gan Yu at the Trier Center for Digital Humanities, and has been integrated into the New Testament Virtual Manuscript Room and the Workspace for Collaborative Editing. For further information, see Houghton, H.A.G., Sievers, Martin, Smith, Catherine J., "The Workspace for Collaborative Editing." in: *Digital Humanities 2014 Conference Abstracts, EPFL-UNIL, Lausanne,* Switzerland, 8-12 July 2014, 210-211 (online at <http://dharchive.org/paper/DH2014/Paper-224.xml>), and Houghton, "Electronic Scriptorium", 36-37.

an individual manuscript may be incorporated into an edition.[13] A transcription created for one edition may be used in another.[14] A transcription produced for an edition may be adopted by a holding institution and displayed alongside images of the manuscript, perhaps with the addition of further information.[15] A transcription produced by a research project may be adapted by a commercial software provider and included on their platform.[16] All these scenarios have taken place in recent years, and demonstrate how a single electronic file can be redeployed in ways which are impossible for printed texts. Electronic files may also be easily adjusted if errors are spotted, or improved as new images or processing techniques become available. When investigating the biblical text of a particular manuscript, my own practice has been to make a transcription as this requires little more effort than a collation: the file can then be used to generate a list of variants from a standard text or compare it with another manuscript, and the transcription is released through the Institutional Research Archive to complement the published study.[17]

3 The Accuracy of Electronic Transcriptions

The first area to be addressed more fully in this chapter consists of the measures taken to ensure the accuracy of electronic transcriptions. Given the key role these files play in the construction of scholarly editions, accuracy is paramount: as mentioned above, the apparatus is generated directly from these files and they can be used directly for various different types of analysis. In addition, the full transcriptions are normally incorporated into electronic editions, providing the user with the complete set of data on which the edition is

13 For example, the redeployment of transcriptions of Family 1 in John produced by Alison Welsby in the ECM of John: see further Welsby, Alison, *A Textual Study of Family 1 in the Gospel of John*, Berlin & Boston: De Gruyter, 2014, 4-5.

14 A good example of this is the transcriptions shared between the United Bible Societies' *Gospel according to John in the Byzantine Tradition* and the IGNTP volume of *The Majuscule Manuscripts of John* (see further Parker, *An Introduction*, 220-221).

15 As in the case of the Digital Codex Sinaiticus (www.codexsinaiticus.org; see further Parker, David C., *Textual Scholarship and the Making of the New Testament*, Oxford: OUP, 2012, 115, which refers to transcriptions "which have been used on four different websites, each in a different format") and the presentation of Codex Bezae in the Cambridge University Digital Library (<http://cudl.lib.cam.ac.uk/view/MS-NN-00002-00041/>).

16 As in the case of the Logos editions of Codex Bezae and Codex Sinaiticus (<https://www.logos.com/product/29619/codex-bezae-cantabrigiensis>; <https://www.logos.com/product/35581/codex-sinaiticus>).

17 See, for example, Houghton, H.A.G., "The Gospel according to Mark in Two Latin Mixed-Text Manuscripts," *Revue Bénédictine* 126.1, 2016, 16-58.

based. It is worth remembering at the outset that electronic transcriptions are an abstraction, a translation of a calligraphic artefact into the standard tokens of digital text; what is more, the transcriber's decisions regarding certain readings may remain open to interpretation, particularly if the original is damaged or hard to read.[18] Nevertheless transcribers, like manuscript copyists, are human and perform at different levels: even those who are normally reliable have off-days, so it is important to have a rigorous checking process to ensure that errors at this initial stage do not persist into the final edition.

The procedure for ensuring accuracy will vary from project to project, according to the resources at the disposal of each and the amount of information which each project chooses to record in its transcriptions. The current practice for Greek manuscripts in the ECM is that two transcriptions are made independently, which are then automatically collated with each other and the differences are reconciled by an experienced scholar, who alters one of the files with reference to the images of the manuscript.[19] Historically, this double-blind approach has been adopted by numerous projects for the creation of electronic text.[20] The high element of redundancy seems to have been counterbalanced by the relatively low cost of non-specialist labour. In the case of manuscript transcriptions, however, the situation is more complicated than producing a digital surrogate for printed text. It has even been claimed in one standard manual that the method of double keyboarding "has nothing to offer the scholar who wants to create an edition from manuscript material".[21]

Based on his experience with the International Greek New Testament Project (IGNTP), however, Parker states that:

---

18 On transcription as an abstraction, see Parker, *An Introduction*, 104-105.

19 This is described in Parker, *Textual Scholarship*, 114-115, which also underlines the importance of workflow; see too Wachtel, Klaus, "Editing the Greek New Testament on the Threshold of the Twenty-First Century," *Literary and Linguistic Computing* 15.1, 2000, 43-50, especially 47, and Müller, Darius, "Zur elektronischen Transkription von Apokalypsehandschriften: Bericht zum Arbeitsstand," in: *Studien zum Text der Apokalypse II* (ANTF 50), ed. Sigismund, Markus, Müller, Darius, Berlin: De Gruyter, 2017, 19-30. In practice, with small project teams, it is often necessary for the reconciler to be one of the two initial transcribers.

20 For example, it was used by both Wilhelm Ott and Vinton Dearing in the 1960s (see Ott, Wilhelm, "Transcription and Correction of Texts on Paper Tape: Experiences in Preparing the Latin Bible Text for the Computer," *LASLA Revue* 2 (1970) 51-66 and Gilbert, Penny, "Automatic Collation: A Technique for Medieval Texts," *Computers and the Humanities* 7.3, 1973, 139-146). I am grateful to Catherine Smith for these references.

21 Fenton Eileen G., Duggan, Hoyt N., "Effective Methods of Producing Machine-Readable Text from Manuscript and Print Sources," in: *Electronic Textual Editing*, ed. Burnard, Lou, O'Brian O'Keefe, Katherine, Unsworth, John, New York, MLAA, 2006, 241-253, quotation from 253.

> The double transcription is an effective way of eliminating error, so long as both initial transcriptions are of a sufficiently high quality for the two transcribers to be unlikely to make the same mistake independently.[22]

What constitutes a sufficiently accurate initial transcription? In criticising Abbott's collation of Codex Usserianus Secundus, Hoskier suggests that over the course of two gospels, "a good collator or copyist should make but half a dozen errors" rather than the one thousand he identifies in Abbott's work.[23] This seems overambitious, even when orthography is not taken into account. A figure which was informally suggested for postdoctoral transcribers working on the ECM of John was no more than two errors per biblical chapter. This would leave minimal work to be done at the point of reconciliation, but already represents an achievement comparable to many printed transcriptions.[24] Often, however, the initial electronic transcriptions are made by students or volunteers who are still in the process of developing their skills.[25] In terms of efficiency, the process would clearly be inadequate if it took an experienced reconciler more time to process a pair of transcriptions and reconcile the differences between them than to produce his or her own expert transcription.[26] Setting an acceptable level of accuracy beyond this is somewhat arbitrary, as transcribers normally improve over time and manuscripts vary considerably in legibility. Nevertheless, the more mistakes there are in one initial transcription, the more likely it is to agree in error with the other transcription used

22 Parker, *An Introduction*, 104. Elsewhere, Parker states that "the best way to achieve the greatest possible accuracy is by making two independent transcriptions, automatically generating a list of the differences, and then verifying the correct one." *Codex Sinaiticus: The Story of the World's Oldest Bible*, London: British Library, 2010, 177.

23 Hoskier, Herman C., *The Text of Codex Usserianus 2. r2 ("Garland of Howth"). With Critical Notes to Supplement and Correct the Collation of the Late Thomas K. Abbott,* London: Quaritch, 1919, iii.

24 For example, the *Vetus Latina Iohannes* edition identifies 29 textual inaccuracies in Tischendorf's transcription of John in VL 2 and 37 textual inaccuracies in Buchanan's transcription of John in VL 4, in addition to differences in format and punctuation; in contrast, there are only 6 textual errors noted in Vogels' transcription of VL 6 (see the linked files on <http://www.iohannes.com/vetuslatina/manuscripts.htm>).

25 See further Houghton, H.A.G., Parker, David C., Robinson, Peter M., Wachtel, Klaus, "The Editio Critica Maior of the Greek New Testament: Twenty Years of Digital Collaboration," *Digital Philology* (forthcoming). In addition, the Museum of the Bible Greek Paul Project trains students *ab initio* as part of an academic course (<http://ntvmr.uni-muenster.de/web/gsi-greek-paul-project>).

26 A spreadsheet prepared for the IGNTP in 2014 on the basis of previous work gave average rates of 600 words per hour for transcription and 750 words per hour for the tasks performed by the reconciler.

for reconciliation. This is especially the case if the initial transcribers have not worked independently but compared notes as they went along. As reconciliation only addresses differences between the two transcriptions, if both transcribers fail to adjust their base text at the same place, the error will not be visible to the reconciler and will therefore be allowed to stand. Furthermore, the more interventions a reconciler has to make in a transcription file, the greater the likelihood of him or her overlooking a discrepancy. For instance, if verses are not correctly identified or appear on more than one occasion, the entire verse will be highlighted as a difference, obscuring any internal textual variation.

Procedures for ensuring accuracy should also attend to the activities of the reconciler, who has a responsibility not to introduce any new errors and also a key role in file management. The file in which the corrections have been entered needs to be clearly identified. If not, there is a risk that one of the two initial transcriptions may erroneously be treated as the reconciled file, or even that an unaltered copy of the base text may be treated as a transcription. A belt-and-braces approach of both altering the file name at this point and recording its reconciled status in the body of the file is most secure. Procedural flaws may be picked up when unexpected data is returned, such as 100% agreement with the base text in statistical comparisons or typographical errors and unusual readings appearing in the apparatus prepared for the edition. Indeed, the process of editing a collation of new files almost always involves returning to the transcriptions themselves to make adjustments, such as changes to verse- or word-division, the treatment of lacunae, or the reconstruction of supplied text in the light of wider tradition as well as verifying (and if necessary correcting) any textual errors.[27]

A strong case may therefore be made for adding proofreading as a further stage in the transcription process, especially in cases where both transcriptions have been made by relatively inexperienced scholars or where one of the transcribers also served as reconciler. As mentioned above, a high number of differences between the transcriptions increases the probability that both transcribers may have made a similar mistake or that the reconciler might miss an alteration. The inclusion of page, column and line breaks in a transcription makes it a relatively straightforward task to compare it with the manuscript, and enables the proofreader to focus on the entire text rather than being

27 This may be illustrated by the fact that over half of the 254 Greek transcriptions prepared in conjunction with the ECM of John have been adjusted during subsequent work on the apparatus, even though few of these have involved a change to a reading: further details are available in the log of changes in the header to each of the files at <http://www.iohannes.com/transcriptions/>.

restricted to the points of variation thrown up during reconciliation. Indeed, if the whole manuscript is not examined by an expert, there is the possibility that significant information may be overlooked, such as an unindicated lemma in a catena manuscript or a set of marginal corrections.

When an initial transcription has been made by an experienced scholar, however, simply proofreading this is as likely to result in as accurate a transcription as the double-blind process, as well as being more economical of time. In this scenario, too, the entire manuscript will have been examined twice by experts, which is not the case for a reconciled and proofread file based on initial transcriptions made by inexperienced transcribers. This single-transcription approach was adopted in the COMPAUL project, and continued to result in improvements when compared with earlier published transcriptions.[28] It has also been employed by other projects, such as the *Piers Plowman Electronic Archive* and the Coptic editions at the *Institut für neutestamentliche Textforschung* (INTF); it is also the only method which is practicable for scholars working on their own.[29] Another advantage of a proofreading stage is that it promotes consistency across files, such as in the way that marginalia are recorded or editorial notes are added. Conforming such details to a standard format during the reconciliation process risks detracting from the focus on textual accuracy at this point.

One final observation on the accuracy of electronic transcriptions relates to the flexibility of electronic text and publication. The release of transcriptions on the internet enables a wide body of users to check them and provide comments. Feedback on both the Digital Codex Sinaiticus and the IGNTP transcriptions of the Gospel according to John has been received through a dedicated feedback page, emails, message-board posts and even published articles.[30] In several instances, this has led to an alteration to the transcriptions;

---

28 The XML files for this project are available at <http://www.epistulae.org/>, some of which include information about comparison with other editions. For instance, 8 textual errors in Tischendorf's transcription of the Latin text of 2 Corinthians in VL 75 (Codex Claromontanus) are listed in the header of the file.

29 For the *Piers Plowman Electronic Archive*, see Fenton and Duggan, "Effective Methods", 245-6. Robinson, Peter M., "The Collation and Textual Criticism of Icelandic Manuscripts. 1. Collation," *Literary and Linguistic Computing* 4.2, 1989, 99-105 describes his transcription process as a single transcription which was checked "at least three times" resulting in a maximum of eight errors per manuscript (an accuracy rate of 99.8%). The checking was assisted by including details of layout and a font which resembled that of the scribal hand.

30 The most extensive example of such a publication is Krans, Jan, "Codex Boreelianus (F 09) and the IGNTP Edition of John," *TC: A Journal of Biblical Textual Criticism* 15, 2010, <http://rosetta.reltech.org/TC/v15/Krans2010.pdf>.

for an edition eventually to appear in print, corrections at this preliminary stage will result in even more reliable data for the final publication. This broader engagement demonstrates the importance that electronic transcriptions have already achieved within the scholarly community and underlines how a single file in the digital sphere can be used and improved to support further research.

4 Documentation of the Transcription Process

The second area to be considered in this chapter is how the transcription process is documented. One of the strengths of XML is that all markup is included within the file itself, so that a single file contains the transcribed text of each manuscript, indications of layout and other non-textual data, and even the transcriber's own commentary.[31] The multiple layers of textual history in a single document can thereby be included in its electronic surrogate, beginning with the work of the original scribe and subsequent correctors or annotators as recorded on the page; to these may be added the observations of the transcriber responsible for translating the text into electronic form and those of other editors or correctors of the digital file. The result is a considerable gain in transparency, coupled with the benefit of having all information at the relevant place: the practice in many printed transcriptions of relegating corrections or comments to an appendix (as well as lists of errata appearing elsewhere) can make then very unwieldy in this respect.[32]

Most importantly, the file should include information about the practices adopted for the creation of the transcription itself. This chapter has already noted that it is advisable to record the transcription status, such as the date it was reconciled or proofread, as part of the file. While the primary purpose of

31 This was not the case with transcriptions produced for Collate, where transcriber notes were recorded in a separate file and indicated by pointers within the transcription (see Parker, *An Introduction*, 105). Although some scholars advocate "stand-off markup" in which the text is in one file and all metadata is in another, this requires a robust file management system to ensure that the two are always connected (see further Berrie, Phill et al., "Authenticating Electronic Editions," in: *Electronic Textual Editing*, ed. Burnard, Lou et al., New York, 2006, 269-276). On a procedural level, it might be suggested that the model of stand-off markup fails both to appreciate the complex interplay of text, presentation and use in textual artefacts and to recognise that a transcription itself is a work of interpretation (as already observed above).

32 Examples of such appendices may be seen in Tischendorf's transcription of Codex Claromontanus and Scrivener's transcription of Codex Bezae: these are almost the printed equivalent of stand-off markup described in the previous footnote.

this is for the internal monitoring of the project, there are many more details which external users may need to know, such as the sources used by the transcriber, the treatment of abbreviations and punctuation, and other principles on which the transcription was made.[33] Without this information, a certain amount of detective work would be required in order to work out the contents and scope of the transcription as well as reconstruct what may be known of the history of its production. This absence of these indications also compromises the value of the transcription as an authority, a topic to which we shall return shortly.

The TEI P5 guidelines require that, to be properly formed, each XML file should have a header with information about the contents of the file and its encoding.[34] The range of elements permissible within this header also enable the provision of extensive further information, if so desired. For example, in the "Source Description" section, a full bibliographic description of the manuscript can be given along with the sigla assigned to it in various catalogues, while in the "Declaration of Editorial Practices" section a free-text explanation can be given of the principles adopted for the transcription or a more structured description of how particular elements have been handled. Changes to the file can be logged individually in the "Revision Description" section, providing a full history of any later alterations. The TEI header is therefore the obvious place to document the creation and history of the following text, and should be considered obligatory for all electronic transcriptions when they are made available for further use.[35]

As part of the Workspace for Collaborative Editing project, an XML schema was developed for transcriptions of New Testament manuscripts.[36] This included a version of the TEI header, to which some adjustment now seems

33 For more on this subject, see Durusau, Patrick, "Why and How to Document your Markup Choices," in: *Electronic Textual Editing*, ed. Burnard, Lou et al., New York, 2006, 299-309.

34 See The TEI Consortium, *TEI P5: Guidelines for Electronic Text Encoding and Interchange*. Version 3.1.0, December 2016 (<http://www.tei-c.org/Guidelines/P5/>), specifically <http://www.tei-c.org/release/doc/tei-p5-doc/en/html/HD.html>, accessed on 10.04.19.

35 The need for such documentation for digital scholarly editing projects was also set out by Alexander Czmiel in a paper entitled "Sustainable Publishing: Standardization Possibilities For Digital Scholarly Edition Technology" presented at the DIXIT conference in Cologne in March 2016: see <http://dixit.uni-koeln.de/convention-2-abstracts/#czmiel> (and also <http://dh2016.adho.org/abstracts/132>).

36 This is described in Houghton, "Electronic Scriptorium", 39-41; for the latest version of the document, see <http://epapers.bham.ac.uk/1892/>. The subset of the TEI-P5 guidelines for transcribing New Testament manuscripts is set out in an ODD file created through the Roma tool, which is then used to generate RNG and XSD schemas for validation. It should be noted, however, that this customisation of the TEI only involves the selection of features, not the alteration of any elements or attributes.

appropriate. For a start, the transcription ought to include details of the images and any other sources used by the transcriber. A transcription based on digitised monochrome microfilm often has serious limitations, not least as it can be a challenge to identify corrections from such images. When new high-resolution colour digital images become available, these can enable much greater precision and even bring to light text obscured in the older photographic process, especially if the manuscript has been rebound in the interim.[37] Information about the use of the *editio princeps* or any other editions should also be specified, as, indeed, should any consultation of the original *in situ*. This material can be added in the section on manuscript description, using the <additional> and <surrogates> elements. It is also worth noting as a matter of good practice that the more information which can be added in the <msIdentifier> and <altIdentifier> elements about the identifiers of the manuscript in different catalogues, the easier it will be for the transcription to be located and used by other projects or even by automatic resource aggregators. The inclusion of the Diktyon number among the keywords of journal articles relating to Greek manuscripts has been encouraged, and if recently-announced proposals to create an International Standard Manuscript Number (ISMSN) bear fruit this too should be included in the header.[38]

Secondly, the declaration of editorial principles should be expanded from a general reference to the project's transcription guidelines to include specific information on the way in which the following aspects have been handled:

> The identification of correctors; layout; abbreviations (and nomina sacra); punctuation; capitalisation; rubrication and ornamentation; word-division; marginalia; non-biblical text.

Some of this information used to be included in the header to plain-text transcriptions but was not converted when they were translated into XML, or was imported as a single free-text editorial note at the beginning of the transcription. Given that the same project may treat certain categories of manuscripts differently, such as preserving all abbreviations in majuscule manuscripts but expanding them in minuscules, the structured provision of this information means that it is recorded on a case-by-case basis and offers a clear guide to the principles and limitations of the present transcription. This information

37 This is exemplified by Krans, "Codex Boreelianus".

38 For Diktyon numbers, see <http://pinakes.irht.cnrs.fr/>; the proposal for an ISMSN was put forward by the Biblissima project at a conference in Paris in April 2017. The current TEI header for the IGNTP includes a field for the identifiers in Trismegistos and the Leuven Database of Ancient Books.

would also be helpful for the later enhancement of transcriptions, when features not recorded by the original transcriber can be systematically added. A number of the categories suggested above are already catered for in the TEI P5 Guidelines by elements such as <interpretation>, <normalization>, <segmentation> and <punctuation>, while others can be expressed in free-text form.[39] The presence of this information within the header provides a clear statement about the scope of the following transcription, explaining the areas in which it claims to represent the manuscript and details which have not been consistently or fully recorded.

Thirdly, a strong case may be made for identifying contributors to the transcriptions by name. To date, the practice of the IGNTP has been to list all transcribers by name at the beginning of a published volume rather than connect them with particular manuscripts.[40] While this recognises the involvement of multiple people in each transcription, with the overall project taking responsibility for the accuracy of the data, it obscures any variation in the extent of the contributions made by each individual. Including details of transcribers in the TEI header when electronic transcriptions are published online provides immediate and demonstrable recognition, enabling transcribers to cite work in which they are expressly credited. This is especially important for students whose transcription forms part of an assessed portfolio, or who wish to show evidence of their wider involvement in the research field. At the same time, recording the names of those responsible for each stage of the process serves to confirm the status of the file within the workflow, indicating that it has been reconciled or proofread by an experienced scholar. Any errors remain a collective responsibility, and can easily be corrected once brought to the attention of the project: the driving force behind this proposal is to provide recognition and transparency, especially if the transcriptions produced for a particular project go on to be re-used elsewhere. In IGNTP work on John, individuals are already identified in the log of changes in each file; for transcriptions of the Pauline

39 See further <http://www.tei-c.org/release/doc/tei-p5-doc/en/html/HD.html#HD53>.

40 See The International Greek New Testament Project, *The New Testament in Greek. The Gospel According to St Luke. Part One. Chapters 1-12,* Oxford: OUP, 1984; Elliott, Bill W.J., Parker, David C., *The New Testament In Greek IV. The Gospel According to St John. Volume 1. The Papyri,* Leiden: Brill, 1995; Schmid, Ulrich B., Elliott, Bill W.J., Parker, David C., *The New Testament in Greek IV. The Gospel According to St John. Volume 2. The Majuscules,* Leiden: Brill, 2007; in addition, the following statement is found on the project website: "It is not IGNTP policy to attach names to individual transcriptions, since the editions are a collective effort worked on by a number of people." (<http://www.iohannes.com/IGNTPtranscripts/transcribers.htm>)

Epistles, contributors will be listed by name in the "Responsibility Statement" section which is part of the TEI header.[41]

5 The Publication of Electronic Transcriptions

The third section of this chapter deals with issues connected with the online publication of electronic files, in particular the authority they have and the manner in which they are made available. The matter of authority is highlighted by the many anonymous or inadequately documented biblical texts which are included in online portals: they are of no value for scholarly use until their provenance can be established.[42] The problem is not a new one: the reprinting of editions of the Bible with different title pages, sometimes without permission, was not uncommon in the early days of printing. The implementation of the changes to the XML header which have just been suggested, providing full details of the transcription principles and those responsible for the file's creation, will go some way towards ensuring that electronic transcriptions can be reused and cited in academic research, since their scope and origins will be expressly stated within the file. As indicated above, part of a transcription's authority derives from the transparency of its documentation: the systematic use of the "Revision Description" section in the XML header to record all changes is good practice in this respect.

The question of the availability of electronic transcriptions may be approached on two levels, the legal and the practical. Both the IGNTP and INTF have sought to encourage the re-use of their transcriptions by releasing them under Creative Commons licences since 2010.[43] This free general release of the data also acknowledges the contribution of public funds to their creation, a practice which has more recently been made obligatory by certain research agencies, including the European Research Council and UK Research Councils. A question remains as to whether the licences should restrict the re-use of these transcriptions to non-commercial activities. Until late 2017, this was the position of the IGNTP, due to a concern that profit should not be made from public-funded research; the re-use of the Codex Bezae and Codex Sinaiticus transcriptions on the commercial Logos platform was permitted on condition that they would be released without charge to users. In 2013, however, the INTF

41 This was first implemented for the transcriptions of Greek manuscripts of Galatians released in November 2017 at the website <http://www.epistulae.org>.

42 See, for example, Parker, *An Introduction*, 217.

43 See further <http://www.creativecommons.org>, and *Parker, Textual Sch*olarship, 114-115.

removed the non-commercial stipulation, specifying only that re-used files should have attribution to the original creator and be made available under the same licence (share-alike). This position has been endorsed in scholarly discussions about data sustainability, since the files will continue to be made freely available even if integrated into a commercial package.[44] However, even the share-alike requirement can work against the re-use of data, since a single resource which combines files from multiple contributors released under differing licenses cannot match the conditions set out for each one.[45] The expectation for the re-use of material from printed scholarly publications is that the original source is acknowledged, without restriction on the manner in which the subsequent work is made available (within the bounds of copyright law and fair-use policy). If a subsequent user has incurred costs in the enhancement of transcriptions, it is reasonable to allow them to seek to offset this expense if they so desire when releasing their own files: the initial data remains available free of charge and the original creators do not suffer any financial disadvantage. Following the original presentation of this chapter, a proposal was tabled that the IGNTP and other creators of electronic transcriptions should follow INTF's lead of removing the non-commercial stipulation from their licences and also dispense with the share-alike requirement, in order to allow for the widest possible re-use of this data. This was unanimously approved by the IGNTP committee in November 2017 and applied retrospectively with the release of 350 New Testament transcriptions under a Creative Commons 4.0 Attribution licence.

In reality, it is often practical measures for making transcriptions publicly available which can prove the stumbling block to their re-use. Earlier digital editions relied on a publishing model which served transcriptions as HTML generated from a database and provided no access to the original files: this is the case with editions of New Testament writings created with the *Anastasia* software as well as the transcription display in the Digital Codex Sinaiticus project, although the latter has the whole transcription file available as a separate download.[46] The adoption of a standard XML format has made it much

44 See, for example, Robinson, Peter M., "Some Principles for Making Collaborative Scholarly Editions in Digital Form," *Digital Humanities Quarterly* 11.2 2017, §§36-37 and <http://freedomdefined.org/Licenses/NC>.

45 See Robinson, "Some Principles", note 20, who also refers to Wiley, David, "Noncommercial Isn't the Problem, ShareAlike Is," *Open Content*, July 2007, <http://opencontent.org/blog/archives/347>. The HumaReC project on a trilingual New Testament manuscript, presented at the same seminar as the present chapter, does not specify share-alike in the licence of its transcription, <https://humarec.org/>.

46 On *Anastasia*, see further Houghton, "Electronic Scriptorium", 34-35. The download link for the Codex Sinaiticus transcription is <http://www.codexsinaiticus.org/en/project/

easier to provide direct access to raw transcription files, manuscript by manuscript, and establish repositories where these are made available. For example, all IGNTP transcriptions are published online as XML files once they have been reconciled, to enable their re-use and open them to public scrutiny.[47] Similarly, although no explicit information about this currently seems to be available for non-technical users of the website, transcriptions in the NT.VMR can also be accessed as XML through a call to the application programming interface (API).[48] Again, good practice calls for stable internet addresses and some form of version control, so that users can be clear that they are accessing the latest form of the file and are made aware of any differences from earlier versions through the log of changes.[49]

One aspect which has not been formally agreed is a default unit size for authoritative transcription files. In theory, this could encompass anything from a single page to a complete manuscript. The most practical and logical division, however, is by book. A book is a single, externally defined production unit, whereas the content of pages (and even of complete manuscripts) varies from document to document. The TEI header, too, is predicated at the level of the document or work rather than any smaller subdivision: attaching a full header to each individual page would not just double the size of the file, but result in partial information for many of the categories and make it very difficult to identify and link to a specific transcription. Conversely, it is straightforward to link individual page images to a transcription of the full book. The workflow for the ECM treats the book as a default unit, too, as the allocation of work to different teams in the project has been made on this basis. The main problem posed by this approach is how to join files when one book ends and another begins on the same page, but this is a matter of display rather than encoding.[50]

---

transcription_download.aspx>, although this has not satisfied all users, some of whom complained that they could not copy and paste overlines from the website while others wanted the download to be in Microsoft Word format.

47 See <http://www.iohannes.com/transcriptions> and <http://www.epistulae.org>.

48 The interface may be seen at <http://ntvmr.uni-muenster.de/community/vmr/api/transcript/ get/>. For example, the XML transcription of Mark in Codex Alexandrinus may be retrieved at the following page: <http://ntvmr.uni-muenster.de/community/vmr/api/transcript/get/?docID=20002&biblicalContent=Mark&format=teiraw>.

49 The University of Birmingham Institutional Research Archive (UBIRA; <http://ubira.bham.ac.uk>), on which many IGNTP transcriptions have been deposited, indicates to users if an updated version of the file exists. This repository is also planning to assign digital object identifiers (DOIs) to electronic files with effect from late 2017, which would make it even easier to locate and cite each transcription.

50 One workround could be to use the numbering of lines on each page to avoid overlap, or duplicating the entire page in each file. Lectionaries and catena manuscripts, too, require special treatment for display, although they are arguably a production-unit in themselves.

In terms of making transcriptions publicly available, each biblical book is the smallest intuitive unit and the most practicable in current project workflows, although there is no reason why these files cannot be joined together to create a single file per manuscript so long as the transcriptions are consistent and the header is suitably updated.

Finally, the emphasis in this section thus far has been on publication as the release of transparent, authoritative electronic files, which can be cited according to scholarly norms. Yet, as it has often been said, one of the innovations of digital transcriptions is the possibility for other users not connected with the original project to enhance them in some way. The problem with this is how to connect these updated files with their original sources and enable scholarship to develop in a cumulative way. Contributions by users through different forms of feedback have already been mentioned above. A more organic form of development, however, would be through the release of transcriptions in a public repository, such as the well-known GitHub site for software collaboration.[51] This site has extensive versioning controls, so that (as in Wikipedia) one can see which users were responsible for which changes. It also has the possibility for users to 'fork' files, copying them into a particular branch for specific development while leaving the originals untouched. One could imagine, say, that a project adding information to transcriptions about paratextual features, or editors wanting to use a defined set of files to create an edition, would develop their own forks. The strength of this approach is that there would be a single place to locate files, and users themselves would have the ability to link their files back to earlier versions of the same transcription. Given the practical problems of managing users and files, however, if such an idea were considered worth adopting, it may initially have to be implemented in parallel with the current, more specific, project-based approach.

6 Conclusion

In conclusion, as stated at the beginning of this chapter, full-text electronic transcriptions are now firmly embedded in the production of scholarly editions of the New Testament, as well as those in other disciplines. What is more,

---

51 One example of such a project is the Catalogue of Digital Editions maintained on GitHub by Greta Franzini since 2012 (<https://github.com/gfranzini/digEds_cat>). A presentation for a Society of Textual Scholarship workshop given in May 2017 by Hugh Cayless and Raffaele Viglianti, "Publishing Editions on GitHub Pages with the Text Encoding Initiative" can be downloaded from <https://go.umd.edu/STS-TEI>. The HumaReC project (see note 45 above) also uses GitHub.

a set of standards for the encoding of these files in TEI compliant XML has been widely adopted, and there is also a user-friendly interface for the creation and alteration of these transcriptions in the form of the Online Transcription Editor. This situation is to be celebrated, as it promotes collaboration towards a long-term goal.

This chapter has sought to look beyond transcriptions as the initial stage of an edition to their role as files in their own right which can be re-used and enhanced outside of the original context. While the procedures adopted by a specific project may seem self-evident to its members, they are not necessarily so transparent to other scholars or future generations. We do not know the uses to which these files may be put. Yet one of the particular benefits of electronic files is the potential they have to be redeployed, to enable others to start not from scratch but to be able to build on the best existing resources. It is this concern which underpins the suggestions made here about accuracy, full documentation, authority and availability. David Parker's comment that "part of the purpose of the electronic transcription is that it will not become obsolete" can only be justified if care is taken to ensure that they are created with wider usage in mind.[52]

Despite the proliferation of digital images of New Testament manuscripts, printed transcriptions and facsimiles from previous centuries continue to play a part in New Testament scholarship. Electronic transcriptions supersede these older publications in numerous ways, not least because of the way in which they can be processed, analysed and developed to inform a whole new generation of research questions. My hope is that, by encouraging full documentation in these files and clear standards for how they are made available, the work being undertaken today may prove to be as long-lasting as that produced by the earlier giants on whose shoulders we stand today.

References

Berrie, Phill et al., "Authenticating Electronic Editions," in: *Electronic Textual Editing*, ed. Burnard, Lou et al., New York: MLAA, 2006, 269-276.

Cayless, Hugh, Viglianti, Raffaele, *Presentation for a Society of Textual Scholarship workshop*, "Publishing Editions on GitHub Pages with the Text Encoding Initiative", May 2007, <http://go.umd.edu/STS-TEI>; accessed on 10.04.19.

Czmiel, Alexander, "Sustainable Publishing: Standardization Possibilities For Digital Scholarly Edition Technology" presented at the DIXIT conference in Cologne in

52 Parker, David C., *Textual Scholarship*, 115.

March 2016, <http://dixit.uni-koeln.de/convention-2-abstracts/#czmiel>; accessed on 10.04.19.

Durusau, Patrick, "Why and How to Document your Markup Choices," in: *Electronic Textual Editing*, ed. Burnard, Lou et al., New York: MLAA, 2006, 299-309.

Elliott, W.J., Parker, David C., *The New Testament in Greek IV. The Gospel According to St John. Volume 1. The Papyri,* Leiden: Brill, 1995.

Fenton Eileen G., Duggan, Hoyt N., "Effective Methods of Producing Machine-Readable Text from Manuscript and Print Sources," in: *Electronic Textual Editing*, ed. Burnard, Lou, O'Brian O'Keefe, Katherine, Unsworth, John, New York: MLAA, 2006, 241-253.

Gilbert, Penny, "Automatic Collation: A Technique for Medieval Texts," *Computers and the Humanities* 7.3, 1973, 139-146.

Hoskier, Herman C., *The Text of Codex Usserianus 2. r2. ("Garland of Howth"). With Critical Notes to Supplement and Correct the Collation of the Late Thomas K. Abbott,* London: Quaritch, 1919.

Houghton, H.A.G., "The Electronic Scriptorium: Markup for New Testament Manuscripts," in: *Digital Humanities in Biblical, Early Jewish and Early Christian Studies*, Clivaz, Claire, Gregory, Andrew, Hamidović, David, in collaboration with Schulthess, Sarah, Leiden: Brill, 2014, 31-60.

Houghton, H.A.G., "The Gospel according to Mark in Two Latin Mixed-Text Manuscripts," *Revue Bénédictine* 126.1, 2016, 16-58.

Houghton, H.A.G., Parker, David C., Peter M., Wachtel, Klaus, "The Editio Critica Maior of the Greek New Testament: Twenty Years of Digital Collaboration," *Digital Philology*, forthcoming.

Houghton, H.A.G., Sievers, Martin, Smith, Catherine J., "The Workspace for Collaborative Editing," in: *Digital Humanities 2014 Conference Abstracts, EPFL-UNIL, Lausanne, Switzerland, 8-12 July 2014*, 210-11, at <http://dharchive.org/paper/DH2014/Paper-224.xml>; accessed on 10.04.19.

Houghton, H.A.G., Smith, Catherine J., "Digital Editing and the Greek New Testament," in: *Ancient Worlds in Digital Culture* (Digital Biblical Studies 1), ed. Clivaz, Claire, Dilley, Paul, Hamidović, David, in collaboration with Apolline Thromas, Leiden: Brill, 2016, 110-127.

Krans, Jan, "Codex Boreelianus (F 09) and the IGNTP Edition of John," in: *TC: A Journal of Biblical Textual Criticism* 15, 2010 at <http://rosetta.reltech.org/TC/v15/Krans2010.pdf>; accessed on 10.04.19.

Müller, Darius, "Zur elektronischen Transkription von Apokalypsehandschriften: Bericht zum Arbeitsstand," in: *Studien zum Text der Apokalypse II* (ANTF 50), ed. Sigismund, Markus, Müller, Darius, Berlin: De Gruyter, 2017, 19-30.

Ott, Wilhelm, "Transcription and Correction of Texts on Paper Tape: Experiences in Preparing the Latin Bible Text for the Computer," *LASLA Revue* 2 (1970) 51-66.

Parker, David C., *An Introduction to the New Testament Manuscripts and their Texts*, Cambridge: CUP, 2008, 95-100.

Parker, David C., *Codex Sinaiticus: The Story of the World's Oldest Bible*, London: British Library, 2010.

Parker, David C., *Textual Scholarship and the Making of the New Testament,* Oxford: OUP, 2012, 115.

Robinson, Peter, *Collate: Interactive Collation of Large Textual Traditions, Version 2,* Computer Program distributed by the Oxford University Centre for Humanities Computing: Oxford, 1994.

Robinson, Peter, "Some Principles for Making Collaborative Scholarly Editions in Digital Form," *Digital Humanities Quarterly* 11.2 2017, <http://www.digitalhumanities.org/dhq/vol/11/2/000293/000293.html>; accessed on 10.04.19.

Robinson, Peter, "The Collation and Textual Criticism of Icelandic Manuscripts. 1. Collation," *Literary and Linguistic Computing* 4.2, 1989, 99-105.

Schmid, Ulrich B., Elliott, W.J., Parker, David C., *The New Testament in Greek IV. The Gospel According to St John. Volume 2. The Majuscules,* Leiden: Brill, 2007.

The International Greek New Testament Project, *The New Testament in Greek. The Gospel According to St Luke. Part One. Chapters 1-12,* Oxford: OUP, 1984.

Wachtel, Klaus, "Editing the Greek New Testament on the Threshold of the Twenty-First Century," *Literary and Linguistic Computing* 15.1, 2000, 43-50.

Welsby, Alison, *A Textual Study of Family 1 in the Gospel of John*, Berlin & Boston: De Gruyter, 2014, 4-5.

Westcott, Brooke F., Hort, F.J.A., ed. *The New Testament in the Original Greek. Introduction and Appendix,* Cambridge: Macmillan, 1881, 31.

Wiley, David, "Noncommercial Isn't the Problem, ShareAlike Is," *Open Content,* July 2007, <https://opencontent.org/blog/archives/347>; accessed on 10.04.19.

List of Internet Resources

Codex Bezae:

<http://cudl.lib.cam.ac.uk/view/MS-NN-00002-00041/>; accessed January 21, 2018.

<https://www.logos.com/product/29619/codex-bezae-cantabrigiensis>; accessed on 10.04.19.

Codex Sinaiticus:

<http://www.codexsinaiticus.org/en/>; accessed on 10.04.19.

<https://www.logos.com/product/35581/codex-sinaiticus>; accessed on 10.04.19.

Creative Commons licences:

<https://www.creativecommons.org>; accessed on 10.04.19.

Franzini, Greta, Catalogue of Digital Editions:
<https://github.com/gfranzini/digEds_cat>; accessed 10.04.19.
IGNTP transcriptions:
<http://www.iohannes.com/transcriptions>; accessed 10.04.19.
<http://www.epistulae.org>; accessed 10.04.19.
Museum of the Bible Greek Paul Project:
<http://ntvmr.uni-muenster.de/web/gsi-greek-paul-project>; accessed 10.04.19.
NTVMR:
<http://ntvmr.uni-muenster.de/community/vmr/api/transcript/get/>; on 10.04.19.
TEI P5: Guidelines for Electronic Text Encoding and Interchange. Version 3.1.0, December 2016:
<http://www.tei-c.org/Guidelines/P5/>; accessed 10.04.19.
The HumaReC project on a trilingual New Testament manuscript:
<https://humarec.org/>; accessed 10.04.19.
UBIRA:
<http://ubira.bham.ac.uk>; accessed 10.04.19.

CHAPTER 8

Visualizing Data in the Quantitative Comparison of Ancient Texts: a Study of Paul, Epictetus, and Philodemus

Paul Robertson

1 Introduction

In a recent monograph,[1] I argued for formal overlaps between several roughly contemporary texts in what I termed a shared "socio-literary sphere": the letters of the Christian apostle Paul, the Stoic popular philosopher Epictetus' *Discourses*, and the Epicurean scholar Philodemus' *On Death* and *On Piety*. Further, certain other writings – Seneca's *Natural Questions, Letter to the Hebrews,* and *4 Maccabees* – were likewise found to have formal similarities close to Paul's letters. These findings stood in contrast to several other types of texts often likened to Paul's letters, such as formal Greco-Roman orations (e.g., Aelius Aristides' *Panathenaic Orations*, Dio Chrysostom's orations) and sectarian Jewish literature (e.g., the Damascus Document), which were found in fact to be quite dissimilar to Paul's letters.

This comparative project was based on a polythetic approach to classification, whereby each text was defined not by essential terms such as genre or ethnicity but by a wide set of non-essential literary criteria. These criteria were inductively derived, formal, second-order characteristics that I hand-coded into spreadsheets and visualized graphically. In this way, providing second-order criteria that I inductively derived and empirically applied, I demonstrated that certain texts should be understood as closely related, based on methods and findings that were transparent, quantifiable, and therefore able to be visualized clearly. I further argued that this type of approach and conclusion was preferable to previous, existing approaches based on more essentialized understandings of literature.[2] In other words, I provided second-order theorization, application, and data-based conclusions from the digital humanities around biblical literature in its literary, ancient Mediterranean context.

1 Robertson, Paul, *Paul's Letters and Contemporary Greco-Roman Literature: Theorizing a New Taxonomy*, Leiden: Brill, 2016.

2 Robertson, *Paul's Letters*, 10-66.

The use of second-order characteristics, which is to say characteristics that are not native to the data in question but rather derived and created by the scholar for descriptive purposes and/or to answer particular types of questions, is essential. While categories native to the ancient world do exist that can productively characterize texts, notably those of advanced rhetorical theory such as found in Demosthenes, an attempt to connect data points which are subconsciously or indirectly related must use modern categories at some conceptual remove from the data.[3] In other words, while Paul, Epictetus, and Philodemus likely were aware of certain prescriptions of advanced rhetorical theory, they were probably unaware of how their social practices, beliefs, and writing style could be grouped into general types.[4] Indeed, categorization and classification is often a second-order operation, as our task as scholars is to seek patterns, overlaps, and connections not explicitly held or recognized within our data sets.

In my previous monograph, however, I provided only the general summary of these data sets and my empirical findings on them.[5] I did not show how each of the second-order, literary criteria comprising my polythetic classificatory framework manifested in my *comparanda* (Paul, Epictetus, Philodemus). In what follows below, I make a more specific case for my particular literary criteria, demonstrating how they manifest in texts written by Paul, Epictetus, and Philodemus, and then pairing this digital approach with qualitative analysis. This type of work is an essential supplement to my original monograph, as it details how second-order criteria can be derived from texts, and how these texts are understood specifically within my wider polythetic frameworks.

2 Socio-Literary Spheres: Theory and Classification

I contend that we should understand, describe, and compare ancient literature according to polythetic classification, a nuanced system of description allowing for comparison across such essentialized lines as ethnicity (Jew vs. Greek), geography (eastern vs. western), or genre (history vs. gospel vs. oratory). I have specifically argued that instead of these essentialized categories of literature (e.g., "Greek historical" vs. "Jewish apocalyptic"), texts and authors are better understood and categorized in what I've termed "socio-literary spheres", which are semi-autonomous fields of literate, cultural production that are

3 Robertson, *Paul's Letters*, 89-118.
4 Robertson, *Paul's Letters*, 77- 88.
5 Robertson, *Paul's Letters*, 121-169.

determined by particular intersections of texts' form, content, and social purpose.[6] These intersections are complex, as form, content, and social purpose are each comprised of many constituent elements. As such, we need a method of description that not only captures this complexity in a nuanced fashion, but also allows us to compare texts so described in this multifarious way. This type of comparison serves my wider contention, that we should be looking to describe pan-Mediterranean types of beliefs and social practices that can be generalized in terms of macro trends present across essentialized categories.

Essential to comparison is description and classification.[7] How any two things compare – i.e., in which ways, and to what extent – hugely relies on how the *comparanda* are understood and consequently described. My approach to comparison relies on the notion of polythetic classification. Polythetic classification, or polythetism, is a form of description whereby the object in question is classified according to a wide set of characteristics or criteria, no single one of which determines whether or not the piece of data belongs to a category. Instead, clusters of criteria are determinative for belonging to a particular category. Polythetism is thus a complex and nuanced form of description and classification: the issue is how many characteristics or criteria are needed to belong to a category according to a particular scholar's definition of that category. Polythetic classification around categories is a matter of "more and less", with no black and white determination, which makes it especially suitable for nuanced description and thus comparison of complex data sets.

---

6 The language of "fields" is drawn from Bourdieu, Pierre, *Outline of a Theory of Practice*, Cambridge: Cambridge University Press, 1977. My understanding of literature as existing within, and to be described through, embodied social practices (i.e., practice theory, or site ontology) is drawn particularly from Schatzki, Theodore, *The Site of the Social: A Philosophical Account of the Constitution of Social Life and Change*, Philadelphia, PA: University of Pennsylvania Press, 2002. Schatzki's work draws particularly from the work of Heidegger and Wittgenstein; for the latter, see further discussion below. Finally, Bourdieu's modern framework of literate fields should be paired with the Foulcauldian notion of "discourse" for work in the ancient world: while literate fields in the ancient world were even more rarified than they are in modernity, Foucault's notion of "discourse" as constructed entities via power relations usefully broadens Bourdieu's modernity-specific fields around aristocratic taste toward a more general explanatory framework pertaining to how groupings of the relatively educated and powerful create their own discourse conventions. See Foucault, Michel, *The Archaeology of Knowledge*, trans. A.M. Sheridan Smith, New York and London: Routledge, 2002. I thank Claire Clivaz for this essential theoretical broadening.

7 The desire for theoretical insights derived from description and classification (albeit of much different kinds of theories, data, and frameworks as discussed here) animated many of the early giants in religious studies' approach to comparative religion, See "Frazer", "Campbell" and "Eliade", in: Tarot, Camille, *Michel Despland, L'émergence des sciences de la religion. La monarchie de Juillet: un moment fondateur*, Paris: L'Harmattan, 1999.

When we describe a text's style, for instance, we use a host of descriptors, which can range from the technical and objective (e.g., "frequent use of metaphor") to the vague and subjective (e.g., "a loose, free prose"). What constitutes something like "loose, free prose", in turn, involves a whole host of other criteria, ranging from sentence length to word choice to clause complexity to types of imagery. There is no single, universally accepted point at which a sentence becoming slightly longer or an additional use of imagery turns a text's description from rigid into loose prose. Rather, a text can be described in a whole host of ways using explicitly stated criteria, which can be compared with another text described in the same terms, and the two texts can be then described as more or less "loose", for example, in their prose. Using a host of specific criteria also allows for further, more specific conclusions: where and in which ways the two texts are similar or different; the ways the two texts contain certain criteria clustered together or spread far apart; how the authors pair which criteria with their particular elements of content; and so on.

Polythetism contrasts with essentialized classification, whereby a single or a small set of criteria are considered "essential". Essential characteristics denote that their presence is necessary and sufficient for the object to be considered part of a category. Essentialized classification is thus simpler and clearer than polythetic classification: the issue simply becomes a yes-or-no question, namely whether or not a piece of data has all of the characteristics deemed "essential" to this category.[8] In the case of Paul's letters, an essentialized form of description or classification would describe his letters as Jewish or Greek or Christian, with a totalizing worldview ascribed to each.[9] Such essentialized approaches tend to think of these categories (Jewish, Greek, Christian) in mutual exclusion to one another (Paul, in this view, is notable as the rare figure

8 For further discussion of how essentialism is tied to underlying cognitive-epistemological processes, see Rehder, Bob, "Essentialism as a Generative Theory of Classification", in: *Causal Learning: Psychology, Philosophy, and Computation*, eds. Gopnik, Alison and Schultz, Laura, Oxford: Oxford University Press, 2007, 190-207. See further discussion of different theories of essentialism in Rehder, Bob, and Kim, ShinWoo, "Classifying with Essentialized Categories", in: *Proceedings of the 28th Annual Conference of the Cognitive Science Society*, eds. Run, Robert, Miyake, Naomi, Mahwah, NJ: Erlbaum, 2006.

9 Some scholars have attempted to reclaim Paul's "Jewishness", e.g. Boyarin, Daniel, *A Radical Jew: Paul and the Politics of Identity*, Berkeley: UC Press, 1994. And Nanos, Mark D., *The Mystery of Romans: The Jewish Context of Paul's Letter*, Minneapolis: Fortress, 1996. Underlying this approach is the general attitude that there is a divide between essentialized entities of Hellenism and Judaism, e.g. Sanders, E.P., "Paul between Judaism and Hellenism", in: *St. Paul among the Philosophers*, eds. Caputo, John D., Alcoff, Linda Martin, Bloomington & Indianapolis: Indiana University Press, 2009, 74-90.

straddling and combining these purportedly disparate worlds), instead of a wider ancient Mediterranean milieu with a host of types of beliefs and practices (gods as interested parties, piety linked to virtue, sacrifice, etc.) held in common.

Objects of study can be productively described via both polythetic and essential classification. In biology, for example, mammals are described according to a few "essential" criteria, such as the presence of hair and mammary glands with which they feed their offspring. Particular species, meanwhile, are often defined polythetically, due to the fact that species lines are often fuzzy, subject to hybridity, uncertainty, and change. Different dog breeds, for example, are typically defined as having a minimum of certain criteria, with outliers always possible. An entirely white German Shepherd, for instance, is still considered a member of that breed (i.e., category) despite lacking the typical coloration, as it possesses sufficient other characteristics that comprise that polythetic category.

Polythetism has been effectively deployed in not only biological taxonomies of speciation,[10] but also philosophical-epistemological typologies such as Ludwig Wittgenstein's notion of "family resemblances" in his "philosophical investigations" around the specific subject of language.[11] Indeed, while the notion of species has been increasingly questioned,[12] Wittgenstein's ideas have been productively applied to biological data as an epistemological foundation for retaining modified species concepts.[13] Polythetism has also been used in other spheres related to epistemology, such as cognitive psychology with respect to knowledge/concept formation.[14] Specific methodological

10 The touchstone introductory theorization comes from Mayden, Richard L., "A Hierarchy of Species Concepts: The Denouement in the Saga of the Species Problem", in: *Species: The Units of Biodiversity*, eds. Claridge, M.F., Dawah, A.H., Wilson, M.R., Allemagne: Springer, 1997. For biological epistemologies around taxonomy and speciation, see the useful introduction and discussion in Richards, Richard A., "Species and Taxonomy", in: *The Oxford Handbook of Philosophy of Biology*, ed. Ruse, Michael, Oxford: Oxford University Press, 1998, 161-188.

11 Wennerberg, Hjalmar, "The Concept of Family Resemblance in Wittgenstein's Later Philosophy", *Theoria 33.2*, Oxford: Blackwell Publishing, 1967, 107-132.

12 The so-called "species problem" in biology goes back at least decades: see the essays in Zachos, Frank E., *SpeciesConcepts in Biology: Historical Development, Theoretical Foundations and Practical Relevance*, Basel: Springer, 2016.

13 Pigliucci, Massimo, "Species as Family Resemblance Concepts: The (Dis-)Solution of the Species Problem?", *BioEssays 25.6*, United Kingdom: Wiley, 2003, 596-602.

14 Rosch, Eleanor, and Mervis, Carolyn, B., "Family Resemblances: Studies in the Internal Structure of Categories", *Cognitive Psychology 7*, Amsterdam: Elsevier, 1975, 573-605.

work has been done in applying notions from biological polythetism to literary studies,[15] notably given my research's focus around categories from literature.[16]

Polythetism, in other words, is useful in classifying and comparing complex sets of data whose particular boundary lines might be unclear. The analogy to the social, historical, and literary worlds is obvious, as society, history, and literature are extremely messy, complex, nuanced, and highly subject to change.[17] Essentialism, meanwhile, seems to fall short both in view of the evidence (with common practices and beliefs across the ancient Mediterranean)[18] and in light of long-standing methodological critiques.[19] Indeed, few scholars would still assert that Judaism and Hellenism are entirely mutually exclusive, or that they are distinct and perfectly bounded worldviews; all the more reason, it seems, to dig deeper into polythetic modes of description and classification.

3 Data: Findings and Visualization

In my fuller study, I compared Paul's letters with a host of texts, finding the closest similarities with Epictetus' *Discourses*, Philodemus' *On Death* and *On Piety*, and several others: Seneca's *Natural Questions*, *Letter to the Hebrews*, and *4 Maccabees*. These texts have little redactional overlap, meaning direct textual influence, with the exceptions of Paul's letters probably directly influencing the *Letter to the Hebrews*,[20] and Seneca's *Natural Questions* perhaps influenc-

15 Alastair Fowler has been a notable defender of the utility of biological analogy from the perspective of literary studies, e.g. Alastair Fowler, "Transformations of Genre," in: *Modern Genre Theory*, ed. David Duff, Harlow, England; New York: Longman, 2000, 232-249.

16 A lengthier discussion of methodological application can be seen in Robertson, *Paul's Letters*, 89-120.

17 Recently on classifying ancient orphic practices polythetically: Edmonds III, Radcliffe G., *Redefining Ancient Orphism: A Study in Greek Religion*, Cambridge: Cambridge University Press, 2013.

18 Becker, Adam H., and Yoshiko Reeds, Annette, eds., *The Ways That Never Parted: Jews and Christians in Late* Antiquity and the Early Middle Ages, Minneapolis: Fortress, 2007.

19 For a review of these methodological critiques, and a charitable conclusion regarding the utility of certain kinds of essentialist thinking, see Sayer, Andrew, "Essentialism, Social Constructionism, and Beyond", *The Sociological Review 45*, United Kingdom: Wiley, 1997, 453-487.

20 There is general consensus that *Hebrews* was written in direct imitation of Paul's authentic (as well as other, not surviving) letters: Rothschild, Clare K., *Hebrews as Pseudepigraphon: The History and Significance of the Pauline Attribution of Hebrews*, Tübingen: Mohr Siebeck, 2009.

ing Epictetus' *Discourses*.[21] The relationship between Paul's letters, Epictetus' *Discourses*, and Philodemus' texts, in other words, stems from their shared participation in what I term a socio-literary sphere, which is a shared social field of similar types of practices (text production, educated argumentation and group construction), knowledge claims (about the cosmos, about their personal exemplarity and authority), and literary style (use of examples, argument, exhortation) present across the wider milieu of the ancient Mediterranean.[22]

The socio-literary sphere containing Paul's letters, Epictetus' *Discourses*, and Philodemus' *On Death* and *On Piety*, as well as other texts, can be defined polythetically, through a set of twenty characteristics that I term "literary criteria". These characteristics include not only some formal, rhetorical criteria (metaphors) but also aspects of content (universal claims) and social purpose presumably indexed to the authors' activity in the social world (exhortation). These three elements – form, content, and social purpose – intersect in a complex fashion to constitute an author and text's overall style.[23] Derived inductively and tested deductively through many readings of the extant primary sources in Greek and Latin around Paul's time based on the general criterion of what was notable about any given text, the list is comprised of the following:

Universal Claims or Assertions – general knowledge claims about gods, cosmos, nature, etc.
Appeals to Authority – mentioning texts, authors, and/or divine beings that grant authority to the author's claims
Conversation – incidences where the author engages with his audience directly
Prosópopoiia/Éthopoiia – specific use of this ancient rhetorical tactic
Rhetorical Questions – use of questions for the same argument
Metaphors or Analogies – linking or explaining a situation or argument via these rhetorical tactics

21 Epictetus doesn't seem to mention Seneca directly; rather, the two draw from the same, earlier Stoic material such as Chrysippus: Bonhöffer, Adolf F., *The Ethics of the Stoic Epictetus*, translation Stephens, William O., New York: Peter Lang, 1996 (1894), esp. 3.

22 Note the important work of Glad, whose posited overlaps between Paul and Philodemus turn on certain *types* of ideas and social behavior present in their shared, ancient Mediterranean milieu, instead of a direct, specific influence: Glad, Clarence E., *Paul & Philodemus: Adaptability in Epicurean & Early Christian Psychagogy*, Leiden: Brill, 1995. Glad's work is a fine example of how certain types of ideas and social practices occur within a wider field that includes authors purportedly separable according to essentialized categories such as Jewish, Greek, Christian, etc.

23 Further discussion in Robertson, *Paul's Letters*, 72-120.

Anecdotes or Examples – use of concrete argumentative supports
Imperatives – commands for the audience to perform a type of action
Exhortation – general encouragement towards types of behavior
Caustic Injunctions – insults or strong critiques
Pathos – use of suffering and/or emotion as a rhetorical tactic
Irony or Satire – deployment of these within a wider framework
Hyperbole – over-emphasis of a given position or idea to make a point
Oppositions or Choices – framing an issue in binary terms, often in an overly generalized way
Figurations of Groupness – constructions of social groups, often around a particular attitude, belief, or behavior
Plural Inclusive versus Second Person Address – different types of address, either directly (their own word) or combined into a verb
First Person Reflection – author injecting their own voice and perhaps example or experience
Analysis of Potential Questions or Objections – specific examination and often refutation of contrary positions/ideas
Systematic Argument – careful logical analysis around an idea

To manifest an empirical comparison based on this polythetic description, each text in question needs to be coded according to the above criteria. Most simply, this can be done by citing where in the text each characteristic occurs. As the above categories are not specific words or grammatical constructions, they cannot be machine read and must be hand coded, which is to say this work needs to be done manually, with a trained eye carefully moving through each text. While much useful research has been conducted on feature selection in data mining that is applicable to digital humanities approaches,[24] such purely quantitative approaches cannot (yet) capture the type of qualitative judgment necessary to identify characteristics such as pathos, satire, systematic argument, or what constitutes an epistemological claim. As these kinds of second-order characteristics are thus identifiable only by a trained human reader, it is through combining digital tools with informed, primary source analysis that we can achieve proper coding.

For *1 Corinthians*, this is what this type of coding looks like:

24 E.g., Wrapper selection and Filter selection. Introductory discussion in Witten, Ian H., and Frank, Eibe, *Data Mining: Practical Machine Learning Tools and Techniques*, San Francisco: Morgan Kaufmann, 2005. Further discussion in Guyon, Isabelle, and Elisseef, André, "An Introduction to Variable and Feature Selection", *Journal of Machine Learning Research 3*, United States of America: MIT Press, 2003, 1157-1182.

TABLE 8.1 1 *Corinthians* hand-coded textual locations; ©PAULROBERTSON

Characteristic	Location
Universal claims or Assertions such as about the gods	1.8-9, 1.18, 1.21f, 1.25, 1.27f, 2.10f, 2.14-15, 3.19, 3.22-23, 4.1?, 4.5, 4.20, 6.13-14, 6.17, 6.18, 7.1ff, 7.10, 7.14, 7.19-20, 7.24, 7.31, 7.39, 8.4, 8.6, 8.8, 10.1-6, 10.13, 10.17, 11.3f, 11.8-9, 11.11-12, 11.27, 11.32?, 12.3?, 12.4-11, 12.13, 12.18, 12.27, 12.28, 13.4-8?, 13.13?, 15.2?, 15.3f,, 15.16f, 15.20f, 15.39-41, 15.42-4, 15.46f, 15.50, 15.51-54
Appeals to authority	1.1, 1.6, 1.17, 1.19, 1.31, 2.2f, 2.7, 2.9, 2.16, 3.10, 3.19-20, 4.1, 4.4, 4.6, 4.20, 5.4f, 6.16, 7.10, 7.15, 7.40, 9.2, 9.8-9, 9.16, 9.19-23?, 9.27?, 10.2, 10.7f, 10.18, 10.26?, 11.10?, 11.14, 11.23, 12.3?, 12.28, 14.21, 14.33, 14.37-8, 15.1, 15.3f, 15.8, 15.10, 15.27, 15.33, 15.45, 15.54-55, 16.15?
Conversation	1.12f, 3.4, 6.12-13?, 6.15, 10.23, 10.29-30, 14.15?, 15.29
Personification	6.15, 10.23?, 10.29-30, 12.3?, 12.21, 14.15?, 15.29
Rhetorical questions	1.13, 1.20, 2.11, 3.3-4, 3.5, 3.16, 4.7, 4.21, 5.2, 5.6, 5.12, 6.1-4, 6.5-6, 6.7, 6.9, 6.15, 6.16, 6.19, 7.16, 7.27, 8.10, 9.1, 9.4-12, 9.13, 9.24, 10.16, 10.18-19, 10.22, 10.29, 11.13-15, 11.22, 12.17, 12.19, 12.29-30, 14.6, 14.7-9, 14.15, 14.16, 14.23, 14.26, 14.36, 15.32
Metaphors	3.2, 3.6f, 3.10f, 5.6f, 9.7, 9.10, 12.12, 12.14f, 13.1, 14.7-9, 15.48?, 15.49?
Anecdotes or Examples	2.14f, 3.12f, 6.1, 7.21, 7.32-34, 7.36, 8.2-3, 8.7, 9.7, 10.27f, 12.3, 12.14f, 13.1-3, 14.2-4, 14.14, 14.24, 14.30
Imperatives	4.5?, 5.2?, 5.5, 5.13, 6.9f, 6.18, 6.20, 7.27, 7.36?, 10.12, 10.14, 10.25, 11.1, 12.31?, 14.1?, 14.20?, 14.39?, 15.34?, 15.58?, 16.2f?, 16.10f, 16.13-14, 16.18?
Exhortation	1.10, 3.21, 4.16, 6.18-20, 7.8-10, 7.17, 7.21, 7.24, 7.29-31, 8.9, 9.24, 10.7, 10.8f, 10.14, 10.24f, 10.29, 10.31-33, 11.1, 11.6f, 11.28, 11.33-34, 12.31, 14.1, 14.5, 14.12, 14.13?, 14.20, 14.26f, 14.31f, 14.39-40, 15.34, 15.58, 16.13-14, 16.16, 16.18
Caustic injunctions	5.2, 5.6, 6.3?, 6.5?, 6.7?, 11.22?, 14.36?, 15.34, 15.36, 16.22
Pathos	1.14?, 6.7?, 15.10, 15.31-32
Irony or Satire	4.8f
Hyperbole	4.8, 4.9f
Oppositions or Choices	1.22f, 2.14-15, 4.9f, 5.8, 6.3, 6.10-11, 7.22, 7.32-34, 8.1, 8.7, 10.8f, 10.20

TABLE 8.1 1 *Corinthians* hand-coded textual locations; ©PAULROBERTSON (cont.)

Characteristic	Location
Figurations of groupness	1.2, 1.22-25, 4.9-10, 9.13?, 9.19-22, 10.8f, 10.20, 11.16, 15.11?
Second person addresses	1.3f, 1.5, 1.9, 1.26, 2.1f, 3.9, 3.18, 3.21-22, 4.6, 4.14, 4.17f, 5.1f, 6.1-2, 6.4, 6.11, 6.20, 7.23f, 7.32, 7.35, 8.10, 9.2, 9.12, 10.1, 10.13, 10.15, 10.20-21, 11.2, 11.13, 11.17, 11.23, 11.30, 12.1f, 12.27, 12.31, 14.6, 14.37, 15.1-2, 15.11, 15.34, 15.50, 15.51, 16.1f, 16.23-24
Plural inclusive Addresses	1.2, 1.8, 1.18, 1.23, 1.30, 2.6, 2.12f, 3.9, 4.1, 4.9f, 6.3, 8.1, 8.4, 8.6, 9.4, 9.10, 9.12, 9.25, 10.1, 10.8f, 10.16, 10.22, 11.31-32, 12.13, 13.9, 15.19, 15.49, 15.51
First person reflection	1.4, 1.10-11, 1.14-17, 2.1f, 3.1f, 3.10, 4.3f, 4.14f, 4.17, 5.3, 5.7-8, 7.6-7, 7.8, 7.25f, 7.32, 7.35, 9.1, 9.8, 9.15f, 9.26-27, 10.1, 10.15, 11.1, 11.34, 14.18-19, 15.1-2?, 15.9, 15.10-11?, 15.32, 16.21
Analysis of questions or Objections	7.18, 7.21, 10.19-20, 15.12f, 15.29, 15.35-6
Systematic structure	3.11f?, 3.17, 4.17, 5.10f?, 7.1f, 8.1f, 8.4, 8.7, 8.11-13, 9.3, 9.10, 9.14, 9.19f?, 10.31?, 11.33-34, 12.1f, 12.12f, 12.14f, 12.26, 13.11-12, 14.2-4, 14.9, 14.11-12, 14.13f, 14.16f, 14.22f?, 15.21f, 15.27f, 15.42, 15.56, 16.1f

When the data have been thus compiled, further analysis is possible, the most rudimentary of which involves simply tallying the various incidences and then calculating which are most prevalent by comparing the percentage of total criteria any one given characteristic occupies. Where the presence of a given characteristic is uncertain, this was indicated by a question mark (recall the arguably desirable uncertainty of polythetism around the edges of formal categories), and a range of total appearances and therefore percentages appears. Where the presence of a given characteristic seemed to fulfill two categories, I double counted. This problem, of some characteristics being more homogeneous (e.g., analysis of questions/objections vs. systematic structure) while others are more discrete (e.g., first person reflection vs. metaphors/analogies), is inherent to this type of analysis. I have, perhaps inelegantly, here attempted to solve these two problems (uncertainty of appearance; double counting due to homogeneity) by simply taking the average of the aggregate numbers, with the understanding that I am seeking general trends and relationships, and that small differences in terms of counting will therefore not substantially change my findings and conclusions.

For *1 Corinthians*, this range of aggregate counting, with raw numbers and each characteristic's total appearances as a percentage of the total criteria, appears as follows:

TABLE 8.2 1 *Corinthians* numerical & percentage aggregates; ©PAULROBERTSON

Characteristic	Minimum #	Maximum #	Range (#s, %)
Universal claims or Assertions	44	50	44-50 / 11-14%
Appeals to authority	39	46	39-46 / 9-13%
Conversation	6	8	6-8 / 1-2%
Personification	4	7	4-7 / 1-2%
Rhetorical questions	42	42	42 / 10-12%
Metaphors	10	12	10-12 / 2-3%
Anecdotes or Examples	16	17	16-17 / 4-5%
Imperatives	12	23	12-23 / 3-6%
Exhortation	33	35	33-35 / 8-10%
Caustic injunctions	5	10	5-10 / 1-3%
Pathos	2	4	2-4 / 0-1%
Irony or Satire	1	1	1 / 0%
Hyperbole	0	2	0-2 / 0-1%
Oppositions or Choices	12	12	12 / 3%
Figurations of groupness	7	9	7-9 / 2%
Second person addresses	43	43	43 / 10-12%
Plural inclusive addresses	28	28	28 / 7-8%
First person reflection	28	30	28-30 / 7-8%
Analysis of questions or Objections	6	6	6 / 1-2%
Systematic structure	26	31	26-31 / 6-9%

Hand-coding all of Paul's letters can be done according to the same system. At that point, the relative percentages of each characteristic can be averaged to capture the shape of Paul's letters on the whole, here the seven undisputed letters along with *2 Thessalonians*:[25]

25 I include *2 Thessalonians* as I judge it to be an authentic Pauline letter, due to the ancient evidence (Marcion's alleged canon, the Muratorian Fragment, Irenaeus, Ignatius, Justin, Polycarp) and following certain modern scholars (e.g., Bruce Metzger). However, its status

TABLE 8.3 Paul's letters average percentages; ©PAUL ROBERTSON

Characteristics, high to low	Avg %	Rom	1Cor	2Cor	Gal	1Thess	2Thess	Phil	Philemon
Universal claims	12	15.5	12.5	10.5	12.5	13.5	7	9	0
Appeals to authority	11	12	11	15.5	8.5	7	6	13	25
Second person Addresses	10	8.5	11	7	8.5	4.5	38	4.5	8.5
Rhetorical questions	9	8.5	11	7	8.5	3	1.5	1.5	0
Plural addresses	8	10.5	7.5	8	8	4.5	25.5	3	0
Exhortation	8	5	9	8	7	15	8.5	14	17.5
Systematic argument	6	7.5	7.5	6.5	4.5	3	2.5	6	5.5
First person reflect.	6	5.5	7.5	5.5	7	3	1.5	10	23
Oppositions	5	2.5	3	5.5	7.5	12.5	7.5	8.5	0
Groupness	4	6	2	2	7	11.5	5	4.5	8.5
Examples	4	6	4.5	2.5	6	3	1	4.5	0
Imperatives	4	1.5	4.5	3.5	2	2	8.5	11	8.5
Pathos	3	0.5	0.5	8.5	2	8.5	1.5	11	14
Questions/Objections	3	5	1.5	3.5	3	0	0	1.5	5.5
Metaphors	2	1.5	2.5	4	2	7	0	0	0
Conversation	1	2	1.5	0.5	1	1.5	0	0	0
Hyperbole	1	0.5	0.5	2.5	3	0	0	1	0
Prosópopoiia	1	1	1.5	0.5	1	1.5	0	0	0
Caustic injunctions	1	0	2	0.5	2	0	0	0	0
Irony or Satire	0	0	2	0	0	0	0	0	0

This data can then be graphed to visually depict the overall "shape" of Paul's letters according to this particular polythetic description. The characteristics are arranged from low to high, according to the overall average of all Paul's letters, to show the extent to which each letter departs from this average. This somewhat rudimentary comparison of averages affords us an easily interpretable visualization of each text's shape, which allows for a generalized, comparative view across texts.

This bar-graph, focusing on counting the total incidences, shows the general trend from low to high and how each of Paul's letters roughly conform to the

as genuinely Pauline is strongly disputed, and below I discard the letter in my graphical comparisons in consideration of this debate to avoid distraction from my main points about overlaps/divergences between Paul's letters and other texts here discussed.

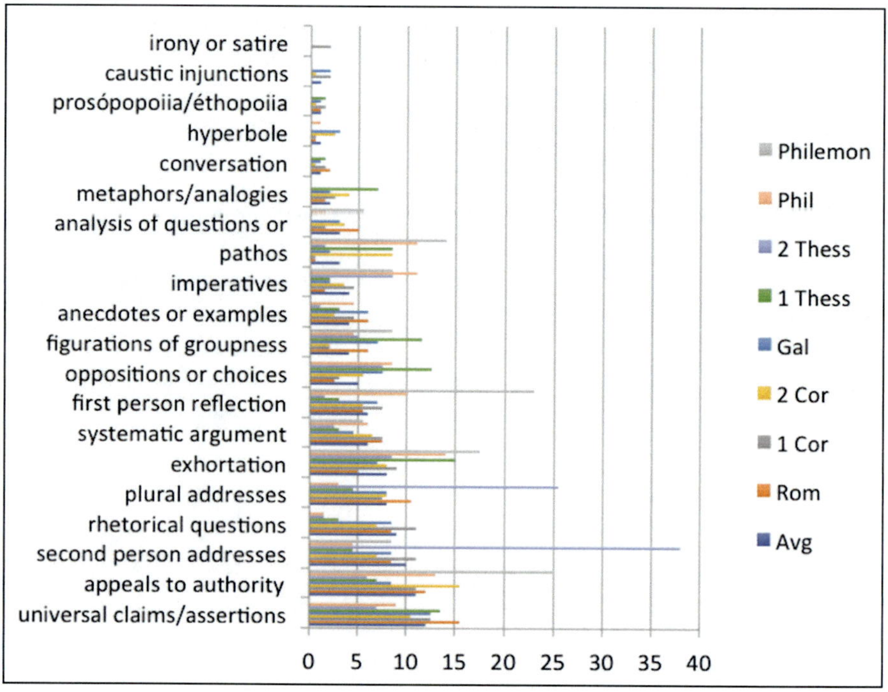

FIGURE 8.1 Paul's Letters Average Percentages: bar graph low to high

average, with notable outliers in *Philemon* and *2 Thessalonians*. The same data can also be visualized differently as a line graph, noting that this is not an expression of a mathematical function but rather still simply as counting total incidences.

Removing *2 Thessalonians* (contested authenticity) and *Philemon* (extremely short length resulting in data outliers due to small sample size) results in an even clearer picture of the way that Paul's letters cluster around each other. This clustering supports the contention that they are of a given type and belong all in the same socio-literary sphere. As a polythetic classification, meanwhile, we note some outlying data points in *1 Thessalonians* and *Philippians*, which in this understanding are less typical of Paul's overall style, while some data points in *Romans*, *1 Corinthians*, and *Galatians* more closely conform to the average and can be considered more typical of Paul's overall style.

With Paul's letters thus mapped, we can now turn to a comparison of other roughly contemporary texts, in the form of Epictetus' *Discourses* and Philodemus' *On Piety* and *On Death*. The same method for hand-coding these texts is performed, with the following results:

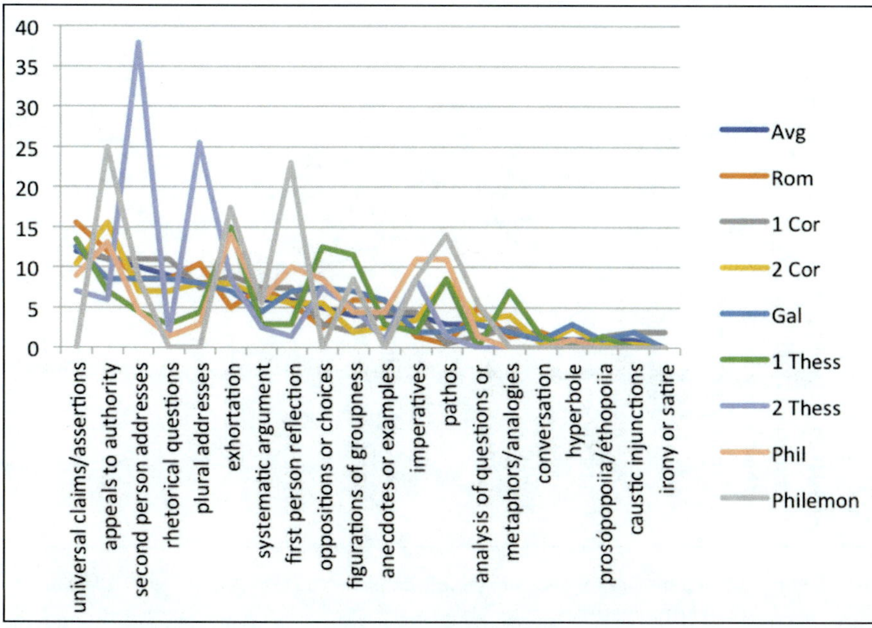

FIGURE 8.2 Paul's letters average percentages: line graph high to low

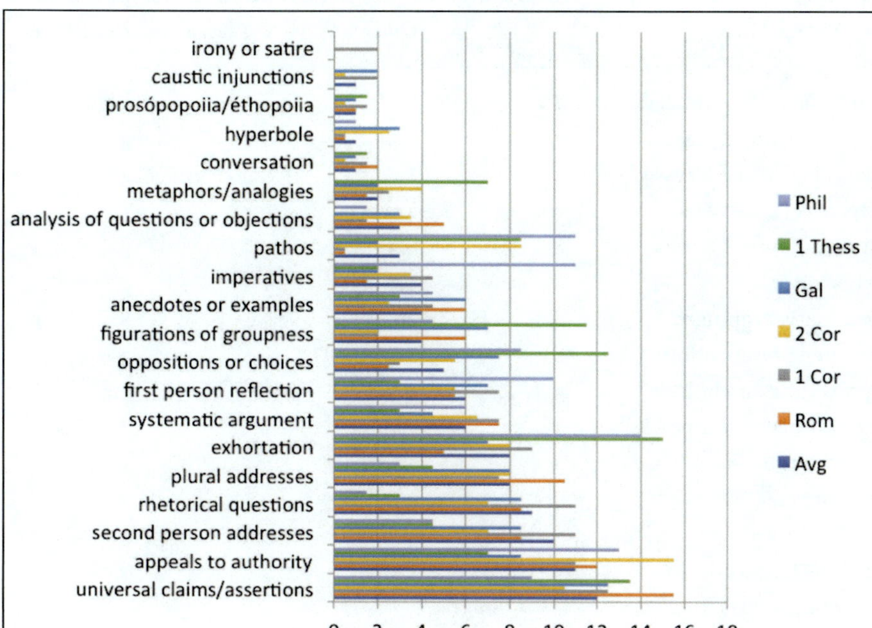

FIGURE 8.3 Paul's letters average percentages bar graph less 2 *Thessalonians* and *Philemon*

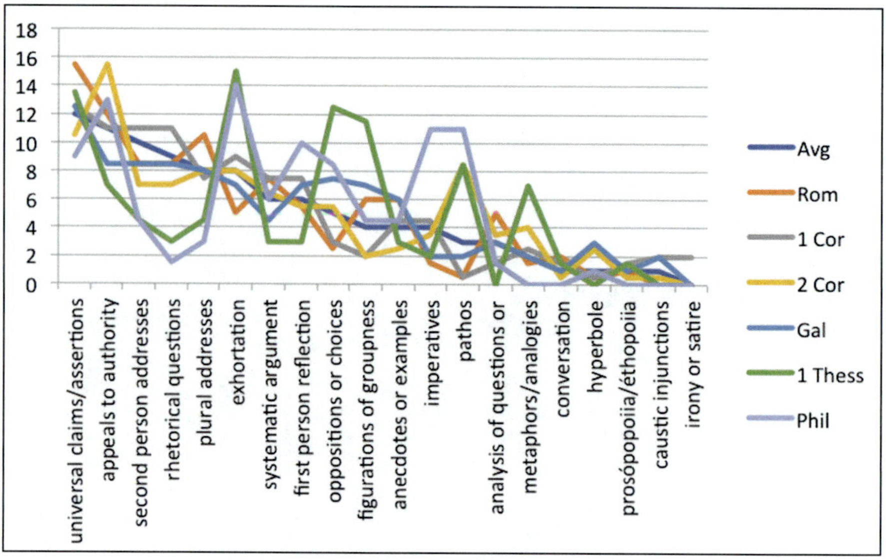

FIGURE 8.4 Paul's letters average percentages line graph less 2 *Thessalonians* and *Philemon*; ©PAULROBERTSON

TABLE 8.4 Average percentages: Paul's letters, Philodemus, Epictetus

Characteristic (w/average %)	Paul's letters	Philodemus' *On Death*	Philodemus' *On Piety*	Epictetus' *Discourses*
Universal claims/Assertions	12	6.5	7.5	4.5
Appeals to authority	11	6.5	13	4.5
Second person addresses	10	1	0	4.5
Rhetorical questions	9	4.5	0.5	14
Plural addresses	8	8.5	8	5.5
Exhortation	8	1	1	8
Systematic argument	6	20	21	8.5
First person reflection	6	1.5	6	2
Oppositions or choices	5	6.5	8	6.5
Figurations of groupness	4	12	19	3.5
Anecdotes or examples	4	18.5	5	10.5
Imperatives	4	0	0.5	2.5
Pathos	3	4	0.5	0
Analysis of questions/ Objections	3	11	2	8.5
Metaphors/analogies	2	0	1	1.5
Conversation	1	0	1.5	6.5

TABLE 8.4 Average percentages: Paul's letters, Philodemus, Epictetus (cont.)

Characteristic (w/average %)	**Paul's letters**	**Philodemus' *On Death***	**Philodemus' *On Piety***	**Epictetus' *Discourses***
Hyperbole	1	0	0.5	0.5
Prosópopoiia/Éthopoiia	1	0	0.5	3
Caustic injunctions	1	6	7.5	3.5
Irony or Satire	0	1	0.5	2.5

Visualized graphically, one can thus compare the shape of these texts in terms of the extent to which they belong in this polythetic category, what I've termed a "socio-literary sphere". Here there is a general, shared trend from low to high, following the average of Paul's letters.

Visualized differently, one can see the comparative shapes in a new light.

Here, Epictetus' *Discourses* are obviously closer to Paul's letters than the two texts by Philodemus. Philodemus' two texts have some clear outliers around the absence of Second Person Address (absent in both), and the relatively high incidences of Systematic Argument, Figurations of Groupness, and use of Anecdotes/Examples. Nonetheless, even with a graph so closely zoomed in to

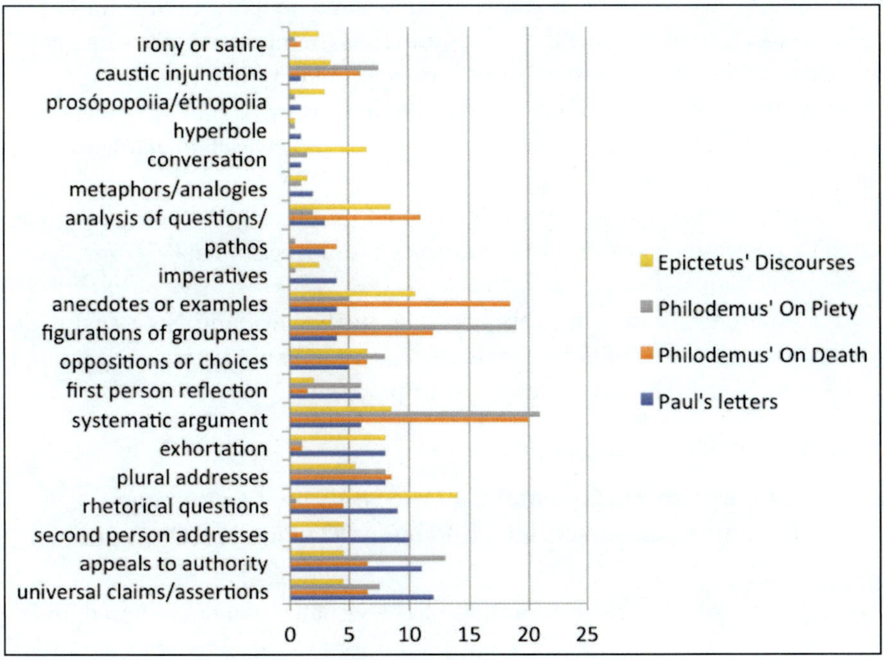

FIGURE 8.5 Average percentages bar graph: Paul, Philodemus, Epictetus; ©PAULROBERTSON

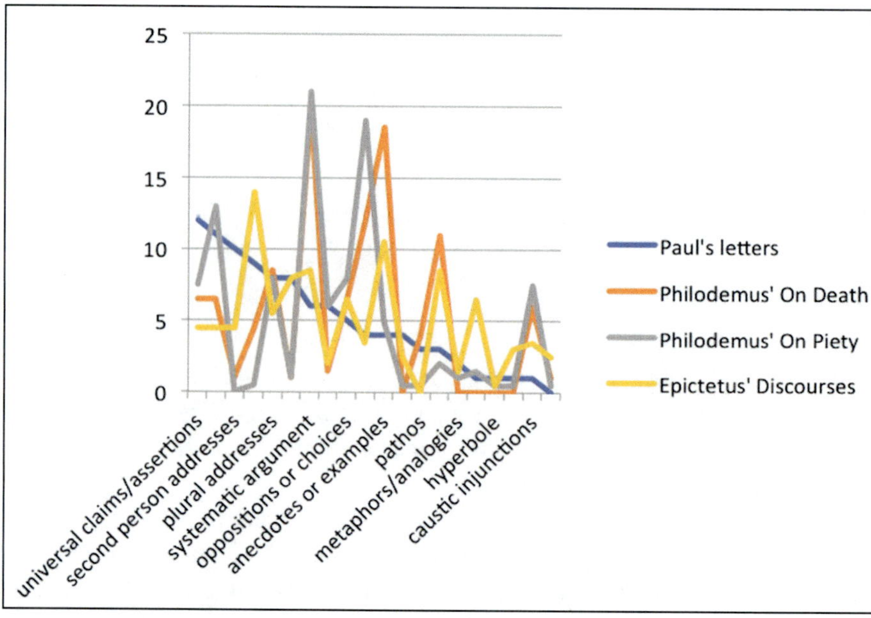

FIGURE 8.6 Average Percentages Line Graph: Paul, Philodemus, Epictetus; ©PAULROBERTSON

show differences, the general shape of these texts roughly align from left to right, speaking to their general overlaps and thus their belonging to same polythetic category. This conclusion is further strengthened when comparing Paul's letters with other texts, such as Greco-Roman oratory (Aelius Aristides) and Jewish sectarian literature (Damascus Document), likewise hand coded (Table 8.11).

This comparison can be clearly expressed graphically, by comparing the much wider scattering of the data relative to the average of Paul's letters, listed from low to high.

In a different visual form, this becomes further evident. Note again the much wider scattering of these two texts relative to Paul's letters as compared to the texts of Philodemus and especially Epictetus.

4 Literary Criteria in Context: A Case Study of 1 Corinthians, Epictetus' *Discourses*, and Philodemus' *On Piety* and *On Death*

It remains to provide specific readings of the visualized data. As noted, polythetic classification involves deriving second-order characteristics from the primary-source texts, and in this section I explain how this looks in literary

TABLE 8.5 Average percentages: Paul's letters, Panathenaicus, Damascus Document; ©PAULROBERTSON

Characteristic (w/average %)	Paul's letters	Aelius Aristides' Panathenaicus	Damascus Document
Universal claims/Assertions	12	23	21.5
Appeals to authority	11	3.5	19
Second person addresses	10	0	0
Rhetorical questions	9	0	0
Plural addresses	8	2.5	0
Exhortation	8	10.5	4
Systematic argument	6	17	11
First person reflection	6	0	2.5
Oppositions or choices	5	0.5	10.5
Figurations of groupness	4	0.5	2
Anecdotes or examples	4	0	0
Imperatives	4	0	0
Pathos	3	0.5	0
Analysis of questions/objections	3	3.5	13.5
Metaphors/analogies	2	0.5	19
Conversation	1	5	2
Hyperbole	1	4	0
Prosópopoiia/Éthopoiia	1	13	1
Caustic injunctions	1	0.5	0
Irony or Satire	0	14.5	7

practice, with specific examples from several of my criteria as they appear in Paul's letters, Epictetus' *Discourses*, and Philodemus' *On Piety* and *On Death*. To do so, I will investigate several of the characteristics most prominent in Paul's letters: Universal Claims/Assertions, Appeals to Authority, and Figurations of Groupness. For each, I will add qualitative analysis to my quantitative analysis from earlier, showing how each author and text manifests these specific literary criteria in the context of their unique content, as well as in the context of their use of the other literary criteria.

4.1 *Universal Claims or Assertions*

Representative Examples: *1 Corinthians*, 1:17-31; Epictetus' *Discourses*, 1.2, 1-4; Philodemus' *On Death*, 30, 1-17; Philodemus' *On Piety*, 31 (lines 878-892).

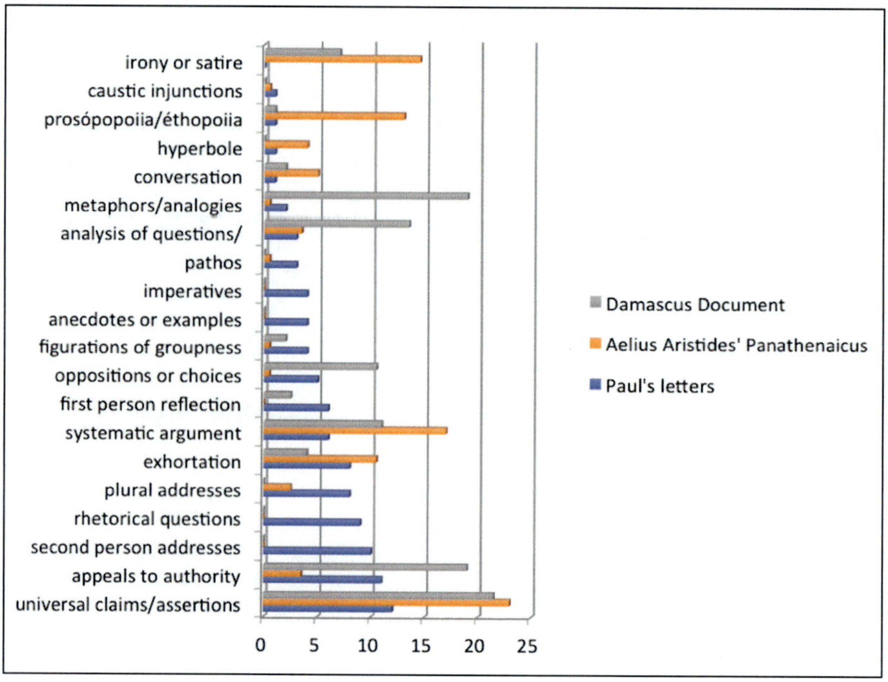

FIGURE 8.7 Averages Bar Graph: Paul's Letters, Panathenaicus, Damascus Document; ©PAULROBERTSON

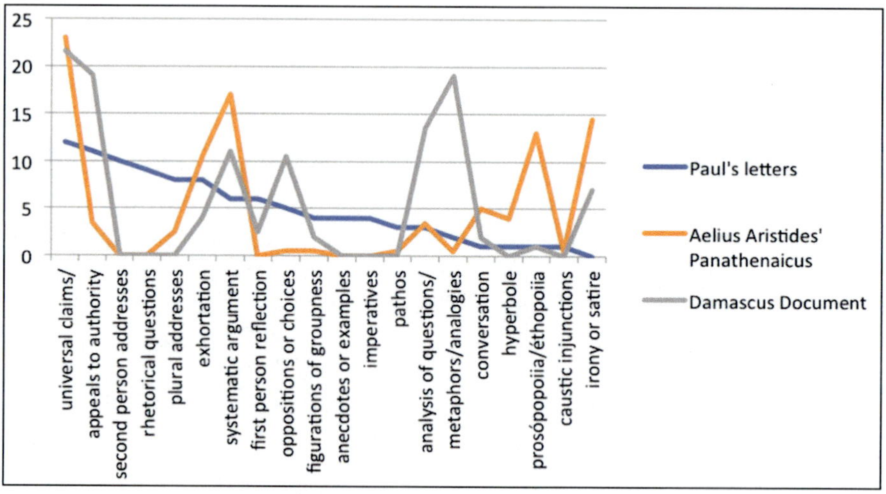

FIGURE 8.8 Averages line graph: Paul's letters, panathenaicus, damascus document; ©PAULROBERTSON

1 *Corinthians*, 1:17-31
For Christ did not send me to baptize but to preach the gospel, and not with eloquent wisdom, lest the cross of Christ be emptied of its power. For the word of the cross is folly to those who are perishing, but to us who are being saved it is the power of God. For it is written, "I will destroy the wisdom of the wise, and the cleverness of the clever I will thwart." Where is the wise man? Where is the scribe? Where is the debater of this age? Has not God made foolish the wisdom of the world? For since, in the wisdom of God, the world did not know God through wisdom, it pleased God through the folly of what we preach to save those who believe. For Jews demand signs and Greeks seek wisdom, but we preach Christ crucified, a stumbling block to Jews and folly to Gentiles, but to those who are called, both Jews and Greeks, Christ the power of God and the wisdom of God. For the foolishness of God is wiser than men, and the weakness of God is stronger than men. For consider your call, brethren; not many of you were wise according to worldly standards, not many were powerful, not many were of noble birth; but God chose what is foolish in the world to shame the wise, God chose what is weak in the world to shame the strong, God chose what is low and despised in the world, even things that are not, to bring to nothing things that are, so that no human being might boast in the presence of God. He is the source of your life in Christ Jesus, whom God made our wisdom, our righteousness and sanctification and redemption; therefore, as it is written, "Let him who boasts, boast of the Lord." (RSV)

This passage contains a host of claims alongside other characteristics, including argument expanding into further claims, first person reflection tied to appeals to authority creating parallel authority claims, examples and rhetorical questions as argument, and the shift between second person addresses when Paul is lecturing/exhorting and plural inclusive addresses when he concludes with general, abstract claims about Christ Jesus and God. We also see here specific groupness (Jews/Judaeans, Greeks, Gentiles) as well as implied groupness constructed around the unobjectionably positive characteristics of wisdom, righteousness, and sanctification, which Paul seems to frame in opposition to those who do not accept his claims ("Jews demand signs and Greeks seek wisdom, but we preach Christ crucified"). Paul here uses the plural inclusive to subsume this opposed groupness beneath his abstract claims ("but we preach Christ crucified ... but to those who are called, both Jews and Greeks, Christ the power of God and the wisdom of God"). This passage concludes with an abstract claim and appeal to authority, which opens up subsequent claims, argument, and first person reflection with appeals to authority (*1 Corinthians*, 2:1f.).

> Epictetus, *Discourses*, 1.2, 1-4
> To the rational being only the irrational is unendurable, but the rational is endurable. Blows are not by nature unendurable. How so? Observe how: Lacedaemonians take a scourging once they have learned that it is rational. But is it not unendurable to be hanged? Hardly; at all events whenever a man feels that it is rational he goes and hangs himself. In short, if we observe, we shall find mankind distressed by nothing so much as by the irrational, and again attracted to nothing so much as to the rational [...].[26]

Here we see a typical use of an abstract claim, the movement toward a specific ethical example in the context of argument in support of that claim, and then the move back toward an abstract claim framed in terms of a plural inclusive address. This passage shows the audience how to practically manifest this abstract knowledge about rationality. Clustered in this passage are a host of features standard to the claims-argument-claims form: claims, argument, examples, rhetorical questions, analysis of questions, conversation, and further claims. Epictetus draws a line between himself and his audience, answering a question and using an imperative to direct their attention, and also unites himself with his audience in his concluding, plural inclusive claims.

> Philodemus, *On Death*, 30, 1-17
> [...] they disregard (the fact) that all men, including those with as good a physique as Milo [the famous wrestler], become skeletons in a short period of time, and in the end are dissolved into their elementary particles [lit.: 'first natures']: and obviously, analogous points to those stated are to be understood also in the case of bad complexion and bad appearance in general. Now it is very foolish (for men) to be pained foreseeing (that) their burial (will be) not lavish and admired of al but simple and casual ... forgetting both that absolutely all of them are unconscious, or rather do not exist [...].[27]

---

26 *Epictetus' Discourses*, Books 1-2, trans. Oldfather, William Abbot, United States of America: Loeb edition, 1925.

27 Philodemus, *On Death*, translation and edition Henry, Benjamin W., Atlanta: Society of Biblical Literature, 2009.

Though we do not find a clear plural inclusive address paired with a claim, the opposition that Philodemus here draws between his opponents' group ("they") and his group comprised of those accepting his own claims is clear. We here see Philodemus bridging the abstract (his claim that death is a dissolution of particles) and the practical (one shouldn't fear death, and thus shouldn't worry about physical appearances or burial). For Philodemus, these claims and implied exhortations occur within an argument, accusing his opponents of disregarding and forgetting important points (a borderline caustic injunction in his allegation of foolishness), using concrete examples to underpin his further general claims and argument.

> Philodemus, *On Piety,* 31, 878-892
> [...] to conceive of their nature as accurately constituting the notion of benefit according to the epistemological standard. And, lest I extend my discussion, again: "Let us sacrifice to the god", [Epicurus] says, "devoutly and fittingly on the proper days, and let us fittingly perform al the acts of worship in accordance with the laws, in no way disturbing ourselves with opinions in matters concerning the most excellent and august of beings. Moreover, let us sacrifice justly, on the view I was giving. For in this way it is possible for mortal nature, by Zeus, to live like Zeus, as it seems".[28]

For Paul and Epictetus, proper claims are linked to proper behavior and unobjectionably positive qualities and conditions, and we see the same here in Philodemus with piety. The initial abstract claim here is slightly obscured, but seems to refer to the inherent goodness of the gods. Philodemus then immediately turns to Epicurus in an appeal to authority as his argument, showing how even though Epicurus in typical Epicurean fashion believed the gods cared little for humanity, it was still acceptable to worship the gods because they were the embodiment of goodness.

This passage also shows how general claims ('the gods are good') can move into the ethical realm, a bridging of the abstract and the practical likewise present in both Paul and Epictetus. The ethics here are both specific and generalized, as Philodemus (via Epicurus) advocates proper sacrifice to the gods but also generally correct attitude and thoughts regarding the gods. Abstract claims thus manifest in specific ethical matters (sacrificing on the right days) as well as vague but unobjectionably positive behavior (having the right attitudes toward the gods). The use of Epicurus as authority functions as argu-

28 Philodemus, *On Piety,* trans. and ed. Obbink, Dirk, Oxford: Clarendon Press, 1996.

ment for Philodemus' claim, and thereby constructs a parallel authority claim in support of Philodemus himself.

4.2 *Appeals to Authority*

Representative Examples: *2 Thessalonians* 2:9-15; Epictetus' *Discourses*, 1.29.3-8; Philodemus' *On Death*, 23.2-16.

> *2 Thessalonians,* 2:9-15
> The coming of the lawless one by the activity of Satan will be with all power and with pretended signs and wonders, and with all wicked deception for those who are to perish, because they refused to love the truth and so be saved. Therefore God sends upon them a strong delusion, to make them believe what is false, so that all may be condemned who did not believe the truth but had pleasure in unrighteousness. But we are bound to give thanks to God always for you, brethren beloved by the Lord, because God chose you from the beginning to be saved, through sanctification by the Spirit and belief in the truth. To this he called you through our gospel, so that you may obtain the glory of our Lord Jesus Christ. So then, brethren, stand firm and hold to the traditions which you were taught by us, either by word of mouth or by letter.

Paul here makes a series of abstract claims which he then supports by an appeal to authority, here to God, which Paul then ties to "our gospel" of "the glory of our Lord Jesus Christ" in a parallel authority claim. These claims involve a clear opposition in unobjectionably positive/negative terms, between those who do not accept Jesus and are thereby unrighteous and deluded, and those who accept Jesus and are thereby sanctified and pious. Paul then ties exhortation to the second person address ("stand firm and hold to the traditions which you were taught by us"), a common tie where he sees his audience falling short of his ideal and a tie that highlights his own authority and the ideal manifested in the plural inclusive address. The appeal here occurs in an ethical context, bridging his abstract claims (about Satan and Christ) with concrete behaviors (accepting Paul's teachings in person or in correspondence). Implied in such a formulation is Paul framing himself and his followers ("us") as imitable exemplars who manifest his general claims in the realm of ethics.

> Epictetus, *Discourses,* 1.29, 3-8
> For the judgments about the materials, if they be correct make the moral purpose good, but if they be crooked and awry, they make it evil. This is the law which God has ordained, and he says, "If you wish any good thing,

> get it from yourself." You say, "No, but from someone else." Do not so, but get it from yourself. For the rest, when the tyrant threatens and summons me, I answer "Whom are you threatening?" If he says, "I will put you in chains," I reply, "He is threatening my hands and my feet." ... [I]f I am afraid of any of these threats, it is me he threatens. Who is there left, then, for me to fear? The man who is master of what? The things that are under my control? But there is so such man.[29]

This passage contains a typical form where Epictetus makes a claim, then turns to an appeal to authority to support the claim in addition to a cluster of argument-based characteristics: examples, analysis of questions, rhetorical questions (as argument), and a first person reflection that constructs his own responses in parallel to his appeal to God. Here Epictetus firmly differentiates himself from his audience, faming himself as an imitable exemplar, who brings into the practical realm his abstract claims that are supported by divine appeal. Implicit in this account is Epictetus' exhortation to his audience to accept his abstract claims and put them into practice in examples like he provides here, thereby bridging the macro (general claims) and micro (specific ethical examples). Implicit in this account (and explicit in the lines following, 1.29, 9f.) is an opposition to those who fear a tyrants' threats (embodied in his second person interlocutor), as Epictetus constructs an oppositional groupness around those who accept his claims and thus embrace his exhortation to respond ambivalently to such threats.

> Philodemus, *On Death,* 23, 2-16
> But if one must judge by the results, who gained protectors such as Polyaenus and Metrodorus and Leonteus and Epicurus himself (gained) from (the moment of) death right up to now, and similarly all those who progressed in our school? And even among laymen we see many obtaining lawful and natural honor to the full extent from friends who displayed noteworthy goodwill, much more than those men (obtain such honor) who left behind the children of Danaus and of his brother and of him who [fathered an even greater number], Heracles, so that there is left over (?) to profit [...].[30]

Philodemus' appeal to authority is a list of the big names in the early Epicurean school. This appeal occurs in the context of an argument, which Philodemus

29 *Epictetus' Discourses,* Books 1-2, 1925.

30 Philodemus, *On Death,* 23, 2-16, trad. Henry, 2009.

supplements with a rhetorical question and examples. We here see those who behave properly, presumably due to adherence to correct claims, being framed with a plural inclusive address, which Philodemus opposes to the (majority?) group of people who put their stock in mythological examples of behavior. There also appears an implied exhortation, namely that even common people can and should have friends who display goodwill, which Philodemus links up with appeals to law and natural honor, i.e. nature. While we don't find an explicit first person reflection, the use of appeals here surely reinforces Philodemus' own wider argument and claims, which are aligned with those of Epicurus and other early Epicurean leaders. Proper adherence to these claims, in turn, has ramifications in the ethical world, specifically with friendship, as Philodemus uses the examples of his authorities in an appeal to demonstrate the bridge between the abstract and the practical.

4.3 *Figurations of Groupness*[31]

Representative Examples: *1 Corinthians*, 11:20-32; Epictetus' *Discourses*, 1.3, 1-4; Philodemus' *On Piety*, 75 (see also 77), 2158-2218.

> *1 Corinthians*, 11:20-32
> When you meet together, it is not the Lord's super that you eat. For in eating, each one goes ahead with his own meal, and one is hungry and another is drunk. What! Do you not have houses to eat and drink in? Or do you despise the church of God and humiliate those who have nothing? What shall I say to you? Shall I commend you in this? No, I will not. For I received from the Lord what I also delivered to you, that the Lord Jesus on the night when he was betrayed took bread, and when he had given thanks, he broke it, and said, "This is my body which is for you. Do this in remembrance of me." In the same way also the cup, after supper, saying, "This cup is the new covenant in my blood. Do this, as often as you drink it, in remembrance of me." For as often as you eat this bread and drink the cup, you proclaim the Lord's death until he comes. Whoever, therefore, eats the bread or drinks the cup of the Lord in an unworthy manner will be guilty of profaning the body and blood of the Lord. Let a man examine himself, and so eat of the bread and drink of the cup. For anyone who eats and drinks without discerning the body eats and drinks judgment upon himself. That is why many of you are weak and ill, and some have died.

---

31 For an understanding of this term and its utility in socio-historical research, see, among many others, the work of Brubaker, Rogers, *Ethnicity Without Groups*, Cambridge: Harvard University Press, 2004.

> But if we judged ourselves truly, we should not be judged. But when we are judged by the Lord, we are chastened so that we may not be condemned along with the world.

Paul uses the construction of groupness similarly to how he uses oppositions, in that both tend to underpin a shift from specific, concrete, ethical matters to abstract, generalized claims. Here we see Paul move from the discussion of meals and his audience's behavior therein to eating and drinking in memory of Christ generally, from which he then further moves onto the moral issue of judgment and being self-reflective. For Paul, groupness is constructed around specific ethical issues, but seemingly more important is the construction of groupness along general, moral, and abstract lines, specifically whether or not people acted in accordance with proper belief in Christ. Thus groupness constructed around ethical matters is given a deeper valence, tied to unobjectionably positive characteristics such as proper judgment and piety.

This move also extends Paul's authority from concrete, practical matters (who to dine with) to wider, abstract issues (what to believe, what is proper piety and judgment). We thus see the beginning of this passage, with non-ideal behavior, framed with argument, rhetorical questions, examples, appeals to authority, second person addresses, oppositions, and Paul's first person reflection and appeals to authority in a parallel authority claim. This turns, in a fashion common to Paul's letters and the other texts in this same sphere, into a concluding plural inclusive claim that is generalized, unobjectionably positive (judgment by the Lord), and in purportedly line with Paul's broader set of claims.

> Epictetus, *Discourses,* 1.3, 1-4
> If a man could only subscribe heart and soul, as he ought, to this doctrine, that we are all primarily begotten of God, and that God is the father of men as well as of gods, I think that he will entertain no ignoble or mean thought about himself. Yet, if Caesar adopts you no one will be able to endure your conceit, but if you know that you are a son of Zeus, will you not be elated? As it is, however, we are not, but inasmuch as these two elements were comingled in our begetting, on the one hand the body, which we have in common with the brutes, and, on the other, reason and intelligence, which we have in common with the gods, some of us incline toward the former relationship, which is unblessed by fortune and is mortal, and only a few toward that which is divine and blessed.[32]

32 *Epictetus' Discourses*, 1.3.1-4, trans. Oldfather, 1925.

This passage is a prime illustration of how Epictetus constructs a firm groupness based on the binary between those who accept his claims and those who do not. This binary is constructed along the vague but stark difference between the unobjectionably positive versus negative terms, here the difference between "brutes" ("animals", *ta zōa*) and those with "reason and intelligence" (*logos* and *gnōsis*). Epictetus often connects the acceptance of his claims with sound mind and piety, and broaches the ethical realm by talking about how one who has accepted his claims thinks about themselves practically.

We also see in this passage several other common themes, such as the plural inclusive and general claims regarding his ideal, the second person address when directing his attention to someone who may fall short of his ideal, the first person reflection used to foreground the author's authority, and the use of examples, questions, and argument to support a groupness constructed around his claims, which he subsequently expands with regard to claims, argument, examples, groupness, and exhortation (1.3, 4-9). Those who fall short of his ideal are subject to both censure and implied exhortation, both to accept his claims and to behave properly, which for Epictetus is a natural correlate.

> Philodemus, *On Piety*, 75 (see also 77), 2158-2181
> But the others of course introduced fabulous and terrible stories [about the gods], and did not seem to be introducing these things either in the same way as their predecessors [those who promulgated false tales to secure their own personal security] or as the sources of security to states; and what with, on the one hand conforming to currently prevailing opinions, on the other hand at the same time conceiving inconsistency and madness, they seemed not only impious but also dishonest; and they spoke in opposition (though a philosopher should speak freely) to no one at all; and they did not remotely perceive Epicurus' opinion about the gods, nor state it [...].[33]

In this passage Philodemus details how groups comprised of those with claims that differ from his own acted in the context of social life. This passage, in the context of Philodemus' wider argument about his claims, details the practical valences of these different groups. Groupness, in other words, is constructed around both claims (what people believe of the gods) and ethics (how people behave based on these claims), as groupness shows its ability to join the abstract to the practical.

33 Philodemus, *On Death,* trad. Henry, 2009.

Though Philodemus lacks the shift from the second person address to the plural inclusive claim, a lack that is relatively widespread in Philodemus compared to Paul and Epictetus, this passage does include the implied exhortation born of this type of groupness, here that people should eschew mythological stories and not speak in public unless they are contesting particular points. As is often the case with this and the other texts in this socio-literary sphere, Philodemus seems to construct this groupness as an opposition (in claims and behavior) and ties the sides of this groupness to unobjectionably positive and negative characteristics, here tying the opposed group to inconsistency, madness, impiety, and dishonesty.

5 Conclusions, Limitations, and Further Study

In sum, developing a polythetic classification of ancient literature has allowed an empirical, transparent, and quantifiable comparison of literature. This comparison has shown that certain texts by Epictetus and Philodemus are relatively similar to Paul's letters, while texts such as Aelius Aristides' *Panathenaic Oration* and the Damascus Document are relatively different from Paul's letters. To this quantitative analysis and visualization I added qualitative analysis, exploring how each author and text manifested certain characteristics in the context of their unique content as well as in the context of their use of the other characteristics that comprise the full polythetic classification of this socio-literary sphere.

Hand-coding the data is necessary in order to capture the complex nature of literature, literary style, content, and a nuanced classificatory framework. This hand-coding of the data, despite potential imperfections inherent to polythetic classification, subjective judgment, and the time-intensive nature of such work, nonetheless allows us to visualize a text's shape. This visualization is not only useful descriptively, however, as it also allows for a visual, empirical comparison with other data.

This type of comparative work, which in a certain way quantifies the notion of literary overlap, can test existing theories about literary typologies (e.g., how best to understand Paul's letters by analogy to other texts) as well as suggest new avenues of study (e.g., intersections between Paul, Epictetus, and Philodemus around literary production and their social goals). Given the volume and breadth of the data collected, in this and previous research, there remains a great deal of work to be done in visualizing, analyzing, and applying the data for projects both quantitative and qualitative. The present study provides biblical scholars another tool for understanding and approaching literary analysis and comparison.

More specifically, the analysis in this chapter and my previous work relies on univariate numerical description, which is to say I distill my data and figures into single numbers such as an average percentage. In some ways this over-simplifies the data and corresponding visualizations, but by choice: my goal here has been to show how straightforward, accessible tools in programs as simple as Excel can easily be used to test and/or suggest particular claims about literary overlaps and divergences. The data and graphs above, while simplified, are certainly suggestive in a variety of ways discussed above.

But this approach has clear limitations, which in turn opens the door for further analysis. In particular, the multiple-characteristic nature of polythetic classification points to the utility of multivariate (instead of univariate) statistical tools that make use of these robust data points and their potential relations. Potential statistical frameworks and tools are several, including correspondence analysis, biplots, and other types of graphical, fuzzy classification methods. Such tools would not only provide a richer visualization of the textual data as such, but ideally also of the relations between these characteristics and across these texts. As noted in my qualitative discussion above, certain characteristics in my socio-literary seem to cluster together. Multivariate statistical tools may well provide a clearer, and more quantitative, picture of these clusterings.

In particular, my current research program on this data focuses on correspondence analysis, which attempts to show how different categories of data (here my characteristics) correspond to each other in a wider structure.[34] Such data can be plotted in a variety of ways on two-dimensional graphs, showing both how characteristics cluster together in a given text and how the clustering of characteristics compares across texts. This type of analysis has a history of use in the humanities and social sciences, notably deployed by Pierre Bourdieu (recall my discussion of Bourdieu in my introductory discussion) in his analysis of how his notion of "distinction" manifested across particular social fields.[35]

34 Useful starting points: Michael, Greenacre, *Correspondence Analysis in Practice*, London: Chapman & Hall, 2007 (1993); Phillip M., Yelland, "An Introduction to Correspondence Analysis", *The Mathetmatica Journal 12*, Wolfram, 2010.

35 Pierre Bourdieu, *Distinction: A Social Critique of the Judgment of Taste*, Cambridge, MA: Harvard University Press, 1984 (1979); see discussion on Bourdieu's quantifying of social data, germane to my discussion here, in Frédéric Lebaron, "How Bourdieu "Quantified" Bourdieu: The Geometric Modeling of Data", in: *Quantifying Theory: Pierre Bourdieu*, eds. Karen Robson and Chris Sanders, New York: Springer, 2009, 11-30.

In addition to my own ongoing research, it is my hope that by making available my data and initial analyses, other scholars so inclined might make use of and build upon them with more sophisticated tools to redress some of the limitations and weaknesses noted here. Such analyses will likely strengthen and expand some of my findings and claims, undermine and reject others, and ideally provide new postulates and suggestions about the structure of these texts and their relationships with each other. These sorts of findings, in turn, will hopefully underpin new claims about the nature of ancient textual production and the foundational link between textual production, textual content, and social activity that I posit as fundamental to any socio-literary sphere.

References

Alastair, Fowler, "Transformations of Genre", In: *Modern Genre Theory*, ed. Duff, David, Harlow, England; New York: Longman, 2000, 232-249.

Becker, Adam H., and Yoshiko Reeds, Annette, eds., *The Ways That Never Parted: Jews and Christians in Late Antiquity and the Early Middle Ages*, Minneapolis: Fortress, 2007.

Bonhöffer, Adolf F., *The Ethics of the Stoic Epictetus*, translation Stephens, William O., New York: Peter Lang, 1996 (1894), esp. 3.

Bourdieu, Pierre, *Distinction: A Social Critique of the Judgment of Taste*, Cambridge, MA: Harvard University Press, 1984.

Bourdieu, Pierre, *Outline of a Theory of Practice*, Cambridge: Cambridge University Press, 1977.

Boyarin, Daniel, *A Radical Jew: Paul and the Politics of Identity*, Berkeley: UC Press, 1994.

Brubaker, Rogers, *Ethnicity Without Groups*, Cambridge: Harvard University Press, 2004.

Edmonds III, Radcliffe G., *Redefining Ancient Orphism: A Study in Greek Religion,* Cambridge: Cambridge University Press, 2013.

Epictetus' Discourses, Books 1-2, trans. Oldfather, William Abbot, United States of America: Loeb edition, 1925.

Foucault, Michel, *The Archaeology of Knowledge,* trans. A.M. Sheridan Smith, New York and London: Routledge, 2002.

Glad, Clarence E., *Paul & Philodemus: Adaptability in Epicurean & Early Christian Psychagogy*, Leiden: Brill, 1995.

Greenacre, Michael, *Correspondence Analysis in Practice*, London: Chapman & Hall, 2007 (1993).

Guyon, Isabelle, and Elisseef, André, "An Introduction to Variable and Feature Selection", in: *Journal of Machine Learning Research 3*, United States of America: MIT Press, 2003, 1157-1182.

Lebaron, Frédéric, "How Bourdieu 'Quantified' Bourdieu: The Geometric Modeling of Data", in: *Quantifying Theory*: Pierre Bourdieu, eds. Robson, Karen, Sanders, Chris, New York: Springer, 2009, 11-30.

Mayden, Richard L., "A Hierarchy of Species Concepts: The Denouement in the Saga of the Species Problem", in: *Species: The Units of Biodiversity*, ed. Claridge, M.F., Dawah, A.H., Wilson, M.R., Allemagne: Springer, 1997.

Nanos, Mark D., *The Mystery of Romans: The Jewish Context of Paul's Letter*, Minneapolis: Fortress, 1996.

Philodemus, *On Death,* translation and edition Henry, Benjamin W., Atlanta: Society of Biblical Literature, 2009.

Philodemus, *On Piety,* trans. and ed. Obbink, Dirk, Oxford: Clarendon Press, 1996.

Pigliucci, Massimo, "Species as Family Resemblance Concepts: The (Dis-)Solution of the Species Problem?", *BioEssays 25.6*, United Kingdom: Wiley, 2003, 596- 602.

Rehder, Bob, "Essentialism as a Generative Theory of Classification", in: *Causal Learning: Psychology, Philosophy, and Computation*, eds. Gopnik, Alison and Schultz, Laura, Oxford: Oxford University Press, 2007, 190-207.

Rehder, Bob, and Kim, ShinWoo, "Classifying with Essentialized Categories", in: *Proceedings of the 28th Annual Conference of the Cognitive Science Society*, eds. Run, Robert, Miyake, Naomi, Mahwah, NJ: Erlbaum, 2006.

Richards, Richard A., "Species and Taxonomy", in: *The Oxford Handbook of Philosophy of Biology*, ed. Ruse, Michael, Oxford: Oxford University Press, 1998, 161-188.

Robertson, Paul, *Paul's Letters and Contemporary Greco-Roman Literature: Theorizing a New Taxonomy*, Leiden: Brill, 2016.

Rosch, Eleanor, "Wittgenstein and Categorization Research in Cognitive Psychology", in: *Meaning and the Growth of Understanding: Wittgenstein's Significance for Developmental Psychology*, eds. Chapman, Michael., Dixon Roger, A., Hillsdale, NJ: Erlbaum, 1987, 151-166.

Rosch, Eleanor, and Mervis, Carolyn, B., "Family Resemblances: Studies in the Internal Structure of Categories", *Cognitive Psychology 7*, Amsterdam: Elsevier, 1975, 573-605.

Rothschild, Clare K., *Hebrews as Pseudepigraphon: The History and Significance of the Pauline Attribution of Hebrews*, Tübingen: Mohr Siebeck, 2009.

Sanders, E.P., "Paul between Judaism and Hellenism", in: *St. Paul among the Philosophers, edition Caputo, John D., Alcoff, Linda Martin,* Bloomington & Indianapolis: Indiana University Press, 2009, 74-90.

Sayer, Andrew, "Essentialism, Social Constructionism, and Beyond", *The Sociological Review 45*, United Kingdom: Wiley, 1997, 453-487.

Schatzki, Theodore, *The Site of the Social: A Philosophical Account of the Constitution of Social Life and Change*, Philadelphia, PA: University of Pennsylvania Press, 2002.
Tarot, Camille, *Michel Despland, L'émergence des sciences de la religion. La monarchie de Juillet: un moment fondateur*, Paris: L'Harmattan, 1999.
Wennerberg, Hjalmar, "The Concept of Family Resemblance in Wittgenstein's Later Philosophy", *Theoria* 33.2, Oxford: Blackwell Publishing, 1967, 107-132.
Witten, Ian H., and Frank, Eibe, *Data Mining: Practical Machine Learning Tools and Techniques*, San Francisco: Morgan Kaufmann, 2005.
Yelland, Phillip M., "An Introduction to Correspondence Analysis", *The Mathematica Journal* 12, United States of America: Wolfram, 2010, 1-23.
Zachos, Frank E., *Species Concepts in Biology: Historical Development, Theoretical Foundations and Practical Relevance*, Basel: Springer, 2016.

PART 3

Communication

CHAPTER 9

Teaching Epigraphy in the Digital Age

Heather Dana Davis Parker and Christopher A. Rollston

1 Introduction[1]

Fields of knowledge are always in transition, with data continuing to accumulate and analyses of the data constantly nuancing previous understandings. No exception to this is the field of Northwest Semitic epigraphy. Northwest Semitic epigraphy is the broad study of ancient inscriptions written in the daughter languages of Proto-Northwest Semitic (e.g., Hebrew, Aramaic, Phoenician, Moabite, Ammonite, Edomite, and Ugaritic). It is concerned with linguistic, grammatical, syntactic, lexicographic, onomastic, historical, palaeographical, and/or genre studies.[2]

Within this article, we will delineate certain aspects of the history of this field and will discuss the traditional means of studying ancient texts in light of new technological innovations. Our primary goal is to demarcate how these innovations are impacting the ways we do research, as well as how they can facilitate the presentation of our research and the ways we teach students in our field. The focus of this article is linear alphabetic Northwest Semitic scripts; nonetheless, similar techniques and methodologies can be used for other epigraphic fields.

2 The Epigraphic Toolbox of the Past

2.1 *Handbooks and Compendia, Images and Drawings*

Various handbooks and compendia have been produced for the study of Northwest Semitic epigraphy from the time of the field's early days in the late nine-

---

1 This article is an extended version of a previous one, reused in this volume with the kind authorization of the publisher, the journal *Near Eastern Archeology* that we thank a lot: Parker, Heather D.D., and Christopher A. Rollston, "The Epigraphic Digital Lab: Teaching Epigraphy in the 21st Century CE", *Near Eastern Archaeology* 79, 2016, 44-56.

2 See Naveh, Joseph, *The Development of the Aramaic Script*, Jerusalem: Israel Academy of Sciences and Humanities, 1970; McLean, Mark D, *Palaeography*, In: *Anchor Bible Dictionary* 5, New York: Doubleday, 1992, 58-60.

teenth century CE until now. Among the most important early works are *CIS*,[3] Lidzbarski's *Handbuch der nordsemitischen Epigraphik*[4] and *Ephemeris für semitische Epigraphik*,[5] and Cooke's *A Textbook of North-Semitic Inscriptions*,[6] which were points of reference for at least a generation. During the middle of the twentieth century, Moscati's *L'epigrafia ebraica antica: 1935-1950*[7] became a staple resource. Of course, Donner and Röllig's three-volume handbook entitled *KAI*[8] has been the gold standard for five decades now, and Gibson's *Textbook of Syrian Semitic Inscriptions*[9] has been considered very useful as well, though not as technical. More recently, Aḥituv authored a fine handbook of Northwest Semitic inscriptions entitled *Echoes from the Past: Hebrew and Cognate Inscriptions from the Biblical Period*.[10] Other useful works include Aufrecht's *A Corpus of Ammonite Inscriptions*;[11] *Hebrew Inscriptions* by Dobbs-Allsopp, Roberts, Seow, and Whitaker;[12] and Gass's *Die Moabiter*.[13]

It is also important to note that palaeography has become an important subfield within the broader field of epigraphy.[14] Palaeography can be described as the study of the morphology (shape) of the letters of a script, as well as the ductus of that script (i.e., the way in which letters are formed). Furthermore, palaeography focuses on the diachronic development of a script series

---

3 *Corpus inscriptionum semiticarum ab Academia inscriptionum et literarum humaniorum conditum atque digestum*(*CIS*), éd. Ernest, Renan, Paris: e Reipublicæ typographeo, 1881-1950.

4 Lidzbarski, Mark, *Handbuch der nordsemitischen Epigraphik,* Vols. I-II, Weimar: E. Felber, 1898.

5 Lidzbarski, Mark, *Ephemeris für semitische Epigraphik*, 3 vols, Giessen: Ricker, 1902-1915.

6 Cooke, George A, *A Textbook of North-Semitic Inscriptions: Moabite, Hebrew, Phoenician, Aramaic, Nabataean, Palmyrene, Jewish*, Oxford: Clarendon Press, 1903.

7 Moscati, Sabatino, *L'epigrafia ebraica antica: 1935-1950*, Rome: Pontifical Biblical Institute, 1951.

8 Donner, Herbert, and Wolfgang Röllig, *Kanaanäische und aramäische Inschriften* (*KAI*), 3 vols, Wiesbaden: Harrassowitz 1962-2002.

9 Gibson, John C. L, *Textbook of Syrian Semitic Inscriptions,* 3 vols, Oxford: Clarendon, 1975-1982.

10 Aḥituv, Shmuel, *Echoes from the Past: Hebrew and Cognate Inscriptions from the Biblical Period*, Jerusalem: Carta, 2008.

11 Aufrecht, Walter E., *A Corpus of Ammonite Inscriptions,* Ancient Near Eastern Texts and Studies 4, Lewiston, NY: Edwin Mellen Press, 1989.

12 Dobbs-Allsopp, Frederick W., Jimmy J.M. Roberts, Choon-Leong Seow, and Robert E. Whitaker, *Hebrew Inscriptions: Texts from the Biblical Period of the Monarchy with Concordance*, New Haven, CT: Yale University, 2005.

13 Gass, Erasmus, *Die Moabiter – Geschichte und Kultur eines ostjordanischen Volkes im 1. Jahrtausend v. Chr,* Wiesbaden: Harrassowitz, 2009.

14 Rollston, Christopher A., "Scribal Education in Ancient Israel: The Old Hebrew Epigraphic Evidence", *Bulletin of the American Schools of Oriental Research 344*, 2006, 47-74.

(i.e., the way a script develops through time) and the synchronic variation of a script series (i.e., the variations in a script that are present during a particular chronological horizon).[15] Among the most important palaeographic analyses of the twentieth century CE are Birnbaum's two-volume *The Hebrew Scripts*;[16] Cross's palaeographic analyses of the Old Hebrew script in a trilogy of *BASOR* articles;[17] McCarter's *The Antiquity of the Greek Alphabet and the Early Phoenician Scripts*;[18] Naveh's *The Development of the Aramaic Script*[19] and *Early History of the Alphabet*;[20] and Peckham's *The Development of the Late Phoenician Scripts.*[21] Parker recently completed a study of the early development of the Phoenician, Hebrew, and Aramaic scripts, *The Levant Comes of Age: The Ninth Century BCE through Script Traditions*.[22] Rollston has worked and published extensively on the palaeography of Northwest Semitic scripts. His studies include "The Script of Hebrew Ostraca of the Iron Age"[23] and *Writing and Literacy in the World of Ancient Israel*,[24] as well as various articles.[25]

15 Peckham, J. Brian, *The Development of the Late Phoenician Scripts*, Cambridge, MA: Harvard University, 1968; Naveh, Joseph, Early History of the Alphabet, Jerusalem: Hebrew Universit Magnes Press, reprint of second revised ed., 1997, 58-60.

16 Birnbaum, Salomo A., *The Hebrew Scripts Part 1: The Text*, Leiden: Brill, 1971.

17 Cross, Frank M. Jr, "Epigraphic Notes on Hebrew Documents of the Eighth-Sixth Centuries, BC, I: A New Reading of a Place Name in the Samaria Ostraca", *Bulletin of the American Schools of Oriental Research 163*, 1961, 12-14, reprinted in: *Cross* 2003, 114-115; ——–, "Epigraphic Notes on Hebrew Documents of the Eighth-Sixty Centuries BC, II: The Murabba'at Papyrus and the Letter Found near Yabneh-Yam", *Bulletin of the American Schools of Oriental Research 165*, 1961, 1962a, 34-46, reprinted in: Cross 2003, 116-124; ——–, "Epigraphic Notes on Hebrew Documents of the Eighth-Sixth Centuries BC, III: The Inscribed Jar Handles from Gibeon", *Bulletin of the American Schools of Oriental Research 168*, 1961, 1962b, 18-23, reprinted in: Cross 2003, 125-128; ——–, *Leaves from an Epigrapher's Notebook: Collected Papers in Hebrew and West Semitic Palaeography and Epigraphy*, Harvard Semitic Studies 51, 1961, Winona Lake, *Eisenbrauns*, 2003.

18 McCarter, P. Kyle. Jr, *The Antiquity of the Greek Alphabet and the Early Phoenician Scripts*, Missoula, MT.: Scholars Press, 1975.

19 Naveh, *The Development.*

20 Naveh, *Early History.*

21 Peckham, J. Brian, The Development of the Late Phoenician Scripts, Cambridge, MA: Harvard University, 1968.

22 Parker, Heather D.D., "The Levant Comes of Age: The Ninth Century BCE through Script Traditions", PhD diss., Johns Hopkins University, 2013.

23 Rollston, Christopher A., "The Script of Hebrew Ostraca of the Iron Age: 8th-6th Centuries BCE." PhD diss., Johns Hopkins University, 1999.

24 Rollston, Christopher A., *Writing and Literacy in the World of Ancient Israel: Epigraphic Evidence from the Iron Age*. Atlanta: Society of Biblical Literature, 2010.

25 Rollston, Christopher A., "Non-Provenanced Epigraphs I: Pillaged Antiquities, Northwest Semitic Forgeries, and Protocols for Laboratory Tests", *MAARAV 10*, 2003, 135-193; ——–, "Scribal Education in Ancient Israel: The Old Hebrew Epigraphic Evidence", *BASOR 344*, 2006, 47-74; Rollston, Christopher A., "Prolegomenon to the Study of Northwest Semitic

FIGURE 9.1
Samaria ostracon 16A (collection of the Istanbul Archaeology Museums) Note: The complete list of figures with the copyright information can be found on pages X-XII

Many of these resources have made superb contributions to the field. Still, many of them have not been without their limitations. Typically, they have included transliterations and translations of individual inscriptions but have often not included images of these texts. Furthermore, even if a photograph of an inscription has been included in a publication, it has often not been of a quality that would permit further independent analysis of that inscription by other scholars. Publications rarely include multiple images of an inscription that focus on areas that are difficult to read or that show the inscription in various light spectra or illuminated from various directions, images that might reveal important textual data.

Producing a drawing or facsimile of an inscription has long been a fundamental aspect of epigraphy. A drawing depicts the physical aspects of a text and its script, including both the letters of an inscription and any damage or wear on the physical object on which the inscription appears. It can also serve as a graphic representation of a palaeographic analysis of the script of an inscription alongside a written description of that analysis.

Paleography and Epigraphy." In: *"An Eye for Form": Epigraphic Essays in Honor of Frank Moore Cross*, edited by Jo Ann Hackett and Walter E. Aufrecht, Winona Lake, *Eisenbrauns*, 2014a, 1-4; Rollston, Christopher A.,, "Northwest Semitic Cursive Scripts of Iron II." In: *"An Eye for Form": Epigraphic Essays in Honor of Frank Moore Cross*, edited by Jo Ann Hackett and Walter E. Aufrecht, Winona Lake, *Eisenbrauns*, 2014b, 202-234; For other palaeographic studies of note, see Attardo 1984; Haines 1966; Kaufman (1966) 1982; Lemaire 2006; Renz (1995) 1997; and Yardeni 1997.

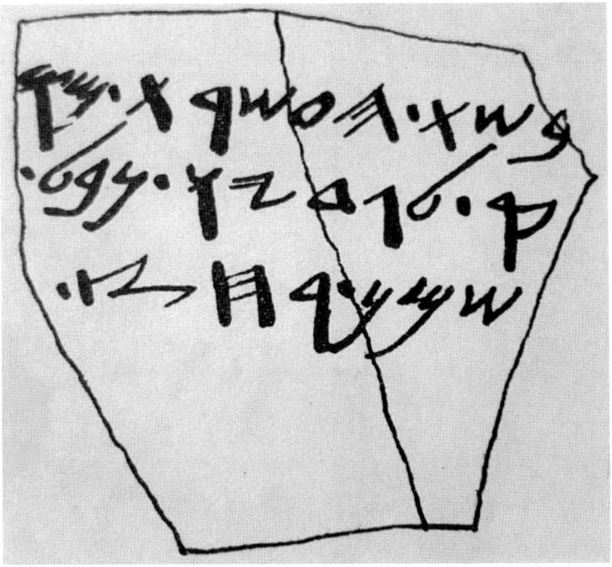

FIGURE 9.2
Samaria ostracon 16A (collection of the Istanbul Archaeology Museums) ; copyrights on page VIII.

Drawings or facsimiles of texts have likewise not always been included in publications, and when they have, they also have been of varying quality. Some scholars have made drawings "freehand," which is quite difficult to do with precision. Others have made drawings by placing a piece of Mylar paper on a photo of the inscription and then tracing it with pen and ink. This works tolerably well for inscriptions that are very clear, but not that well for inscriptions that have segments that are faded or abraded, as the Mylar further reduces the visibility of the text. Moreover, if scholars have not had quality images from which to work and/or have not personally seen and studied the inscriptions they are drawing, the accuracy of their drawings will be affected accordingly (Figs. 9.1-3).

Furthermore, the purpose of any drawing is to allow a particular scholar to represent his or her interpretation of an epigraph. Just as there can be differing interpretations of data in any field of study, various epigraphers might differ with regard to what they 'see' when they examine an inscription. For example, disagreement could occur regarding whether a particular spot on an ostracon (i.e., a pottery sherd reused as a writing medium) is a trace of ink or letter remnant or simply part of the hue of the pottery; or, for an incised inscription, whether a "rouge" is a natural pit in the medium or is a portion of an inscribed letter. Thus, as drawings are perforce interpretive, they are, to some degree, subjective, and the quality of a drawing stands in direct correlation to the quality of the interpretive skills of the epigrapher who executed it. It is important

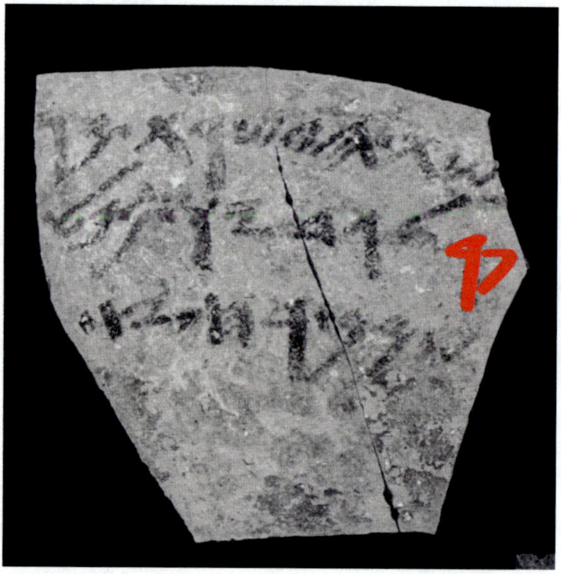

FIGURE 9.3
Samaria ostracon 16A (collection of the Istanbul Archaeology Museums) ; copyrights on page VIII.

to note here that the caliber of a drawing is more difficult to assess if no good images of the depicted inscription are readily available with which to compare it.

3 The Epigraphic Toolbox of the Twenty-First Century CE: Present Developments and Prospects for the Future

3.1 *Improvements in Imaging and Drawing, Technologies and Techniques*

During the past few decades, there have been a number of developments within the field of Northwest Semitic epigraphy, among the most important is the availability of high-quality photographic images as a resource for the study of inscriptions, as well as improvements in technologies that allow for manipulation of these images and for producing drawings.

As the need for more and better image resources for epigraphic study has become increasingly recognized, scholars have endeavored to meet that need and publications have begun to improve.[26] Of course, the quality and the avail-

26 See Arico, Ashley Fiutko, Nathaniel E. Greene, and Heather D.D. Parker, "Ancient Near Eastern Material Culture Studies and Reflectance Transformation Imaging (RTI)." In: *Proceedings of The Future of the Past: From Amphipolis to Mosul. New Approaches to Cultural Heritage Preservation in the Eastern Mediterranean. Conference at the Museum of Archaeology and Anthropology at the University of Pennsylvania*, Archaeological Institute of

ability of images are always subject to available technologies – these technologies impinge upon both imaging (data capture) and publication (data sharing). The advent of digital technologies has made easier and reduced dramatically the costs inherent in both procedures.

The use of digital images for epigraphic study has various benefits. For one, digital images can be manipulated with ease. Moreover, images produced with various photographic techniques, such as Multi-Spectral Imaging and Reflectance Transformation Imaging (RTI), that allow for enhanced capture of data – particularly data that cannot be seen with the naked eye – are also of great use. Multispectral Imaging, of use with texts written in ink or pigments, captures a sequence of images of an inscription in different wavelengths across the light spectrum, both visible and invisible, including ultraviolet and infrared. RTI, which is particularly helpful for viewing the textured surface of incised objects, captures a sequence of images of a text illuminated from various directions. A researcher may use the dynamic light source and special filters within RTI viewer software to reveal details of an inscription that are not visible in images wherein an object is lit only from a single direction.

America Site Preservation Program: Heritage, Conservation, and Archaeology. <https://www.archaeological.org/news/sitepreservationhcaspecialpubs/21700>, accessed on 10.04.19; Faigenbaum-Golovin, Shira, Christopher A. Rollston, Eli Piasetzky, Barak Sober, and Israel Finkelstein, "The Ophel (Jerusalem) Ostracon in Light of New Multispectral Images", *Semitica 57*, 2015, 113-137; Garfinkel, Yosef, and Saar Ganor, Khirbet Qeiyafa, vol. 1: *Excavation Report 2007-2008*, Jerusalem: Israel, Exploration Society and Hebrew University of Jerusalem, 2009; Greene, Nathaniel E., and Heather D.D. Parker, "Field of View: Northwest Semitic Palaeography and Reflectance Transformation Imaging (RTI)", In: *Epigraphy, Philology, and the Hebrew Bible*, edited by Jeremy M. Hutton and Aaron D. Rubin, Atlanta: Society of Biblical Literature, 2015, 209-235; Hanneken, Todd R., "New Technology for Imaging Unreadable Manuscripts and Other Artifacts: Integrated Spectral Reflectance Transformation Imaging (Spectral RTI)." In: Clivaz, Claire, Dilley, Paul, Hamidović, David, *Ancient Worlds in Digital Culture, Digital Biblical Studies* (*DBS 1*), Leiden / Boston, Brill, 2016, 180-195. Lemaire, André, and Benjamin Sass, "The Mortuary Stele with Sam'alian Inscription from Ördekburnu near Zincirli." *Bulletin of the American Schools of Oriental Research 369*, 2013, 57-136; see Lundberg, Marilyn., J. "New Technologies: Reading Ancient Inscriptions in Virtual Light." <http://www.inscriptifact.com/news/article.html>, accessed on 10.04.19; Parker, Heather D.D., and Arico, Ashley Fiutko, "A Moabite-Inscribed Statue Fragment from Kerak: Egyptian Parallels", *Bulletin of the American Schools of Oriental Research 373*, 2015, 105-120; See R.B. Toth Associates, <http://www.rbtoth.com/spectral-imaging--partners.html>, accessed on 10.04.19; Sober, Barak, Shira Faigenbaum, Itzhaq Beit-Arieh, Israel Finkelstein, Murray Moinester, Eli Piasetzky, and Arie Shaus, "Multispectral Imaging as a Tool for Enhancing the Reading of Ostraca." In: *Palestine Exploration Quarterly* 146, 2014, 185-197; see Tappy, Ronald E., and P. Kyle McCarter Jr., eds. 2008, *Literate Culture and Tenth-Century Canaan: The Tel Zayit Abecedary in Context.* Winona Lake, *Eisenbraun West Semitic Research Project* (*WSRP*), <https://www.eisenbrauns.org/books/titles/978-1-57506-150-4.html>, accessed on 10.04.19.

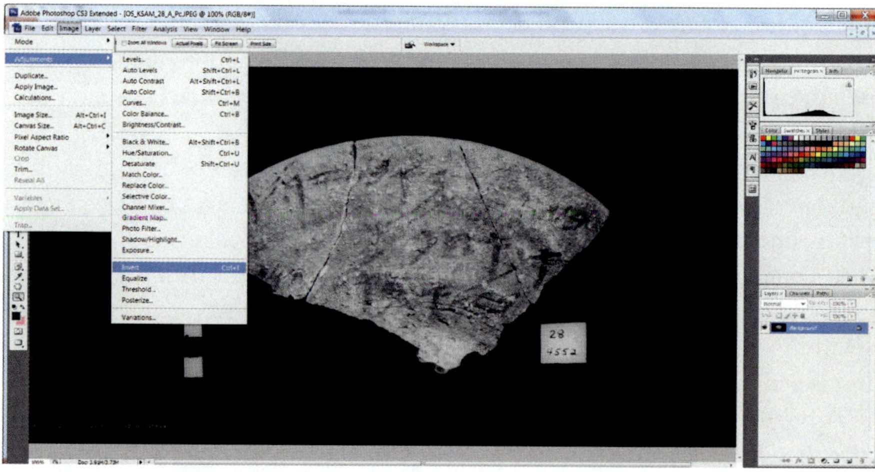

FIGURE 9.4 Adobe Photoshop's Invert tool being used on image of Samaria ostracon 28 (collection of the Istanbul Archaeology Museums); copyrights on page VIII.

FIGURE 9.5 Adobe Photoshop's Invert tool being used on an image of Samaria ostracon 28 (collection of the Istanbul Archaeology Museums); copyrights on page IX.

Just as technology has provided scholars with more precise images of inscriptions, it has also provided them with more options, and arguably more efficient ones, for using these images in order to obtain as much data from them as possible. One of the most commonly used software programs for working with digital images is Adobe Photoshop.[27]

27 See Adobe Photoshop, <http://www.photoshop.com/products/photoshop>, accessed on 10.04.19.

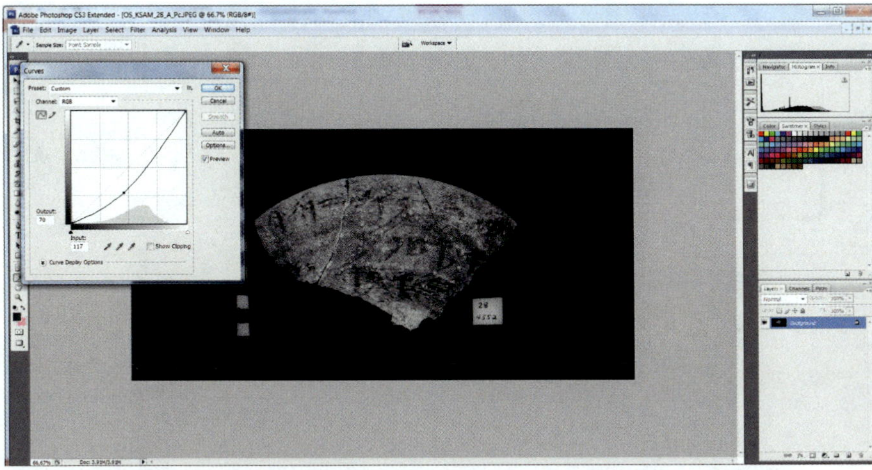

FIGURE 9.6 Adobe Photoshop's Curves tool being used on an image of Samaria ostracon 28 (collection of the Istanbul Archaeology Museums); copyrights on page IX.

The Photoshop "invert" tool (Figs. 9.4-5) or the "curves" tool (Figs. 9.6-7), which can lighten or darken an image, can maximize the legibility of writing on inscriptions. Images of seals can be flipped to facilitate epigraphic study. For the purposes of script analysis, it is often very useful to be able to measure the angles of certain letter strokes and to analyze the synchronic variation and diachronic development of stroke angles. Photoshop has tools that can be easily used to measure these developments (Fig. 9.8).

Just as Photoshop is a preferable program for the initial manipulation of digital images, Adobe Illustrator[28] is a preferable program for the production of digital drawings. While both Photoshop and Illustrator offer essentially the same basic digital drawing tools, such as brushes and pens, Illustrator, as a vector graphics creation application, facilitates the production of more precise and accurate drawings, and offers a higher degree of editing capabilities and limitless output resolution, than does a raster graphics program like Photoshop. Fortunately, both programs are designed to work interchangeably as part of the Adobe Creative Suite.[29] Though, as mentioned previously, drawings are not without their limitations, with the availability of good images (especially coupled with on-site study of an inscription itself) and the practice of sound

28 See Adobe Illustrator, <http://www.adobe.com/products/illustrator.html>, accessed on 10.04.19.

29 See Adobe Creative Suite, <http://www.adobe.com/products/catalog.html>, accessed on 10.04.19.

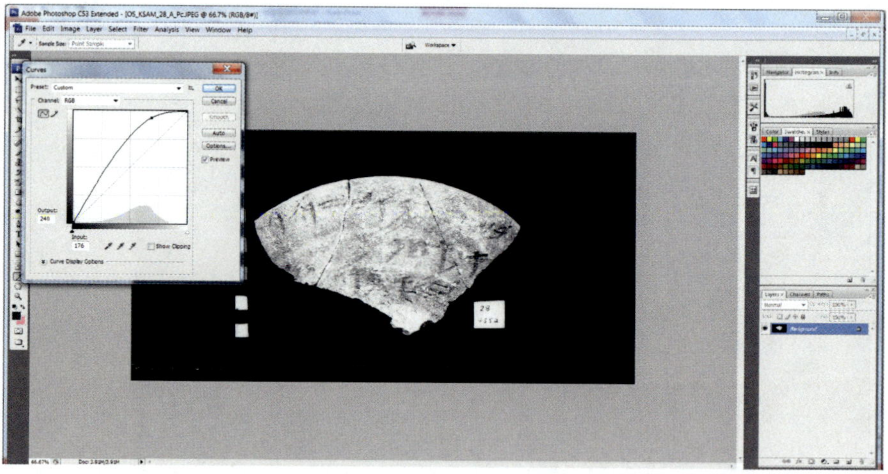

FIGURE 9.7 Adobe Photoshop's Curves tool being used on an image of Samaria ostracon 28 (collection of the Istanbul Archaeology Museums); copyrights on page IX.

FIGURE 9.8 Adobe Photoshop's measurement tools being used on an image of the Kerak fragment (Kerak Museum, No. 6807); copyrights on page IX.

epigraphic method,[30] there can be a substantial amount of objectivity and accuracy involved in the drawing process.

30 Parker, Heather D.D., "The Levant Comes of Age", Fig. 1, 9-44; Rollston, "Non-Provenanced", 150-157; Rollston, "Scribal Education", 50-54; Rollston, "Prolegomenon", 1-4; Rollston, "Northwest Semictic Cursive Scripts", 202-204.

FIGURE 9.9 Adobe Illustrator's Pen tool being used on an image of the Amman Citadel inscription (Jordan Archaeological Museum, No. J 9000); copyrights on page IX.

Digital drawings are normally produced in the following manner. High resolution digital images are placed in the base layer of an Adobe Illustrator file, and digital drawing tools are then used to trace the digital image with utmost precision onto a second layer in the file. The main Illustrator drawing and editing devices are the pen and paintbrush tool. By using these tools one can draw lines and create curves that define a shape, such as the outline of a letter. The shape of the tip of these tools can be formatted to match the shape of the incisions or strokes found on a particular inscription. That is, the digital tool can be adjusted to emulate the particular type of material tool that was used to make the inscription, as well as the weight of the strokes that form the individual letters (Fig. 9.9). Additional features such as the blob brush and live trace tools, allow for the rapid "roughing out" of letter outlines.

Digital drawing obviously allows for initial drawing speed and a high degree of precision in the finished product, but it is most strikingly different from drawing with pen and ink in its ability to permit an epigrapher to manipulate the drawing once made. First and most practically, it allows for easy correction and erasure while executing a drawing. Furthermore, it makes the epigraphic data in a drawing both easily comparable and easily transferable. This aids in both script analysis and in the publication and presentation of such analysis. The most obvious way is in the preparation of palaeographic script charts, which will be discussed in more detail shortly.

The drawing tools in Illustrator can be controlled through various means. The most basic is with the use of a standard computer mouse. However, we

FIGURE 9.10 Producing a digital drawing of KTU 1.46 with a tablet and stylus connected to a desktop computer; copyrights on page IX.

have found that using additional hardware, such as a tablet with a stylus, like those made by Wacom, affords an epigrapher greater control and, thus, facilitates more accurate drawing (Fig. 9.10). Using handheld tablets and Ultrabooks that allow one to draw with a stylus directly onto the screen, and thus directly onto the image of an inscription itself, is also advantageous. Drawing in this way is quite user-friendly and replicates as closely as possible the actual actions of a scribe. Furthermore, small, easily portable tools such as these provide particular convenience when working in inscription collections, as they allow for both the execution and correction of drawings on site. Certainly, there are a variety of tablets available.[31] Based on experience, we currently prefer to use the Microsoft Office Surface Pro. The Surface Pro is quite versatile and easily transitions between a standard word processor and a 'tablet', which makes it excellent for use in the field (Figs. 9.11-12). Most importantly, it is one of the few 'tablet-like' devices that is able to run the full versions of both Adobe Photoshop and Illustrator.

31 Holmstedt. Robert D., "Reading through the Noise: KAI 30 with Fresh Eyes (and Better Photos)", Paper presented at the annual meeting for the Society of Biblical Literature, Chicago, IL, November 21, 2012.

FIGURE 9.11
Producing a digital drawing of the Kerak fragment (Kerak Museum, No. 6807) on a handheld tablet with stylus; copyrights on page IX.

FIGURE 9.12
Producing a digital drawing of the Kerak fragment (Kerak Museum, No. 6807) on a handheld tablet with stylus; copyrights on page IX.

4 Teaching Epigraphy in the Twenty-First Century CE: Method and Tools

Because of the photographic and digital resources available, Northwest Semitic epigraphy can now be taught in a very refined and sophisticated manner. The "epigraphic digital lab" is a core component of this pedagogy. Having both inaugurated and conducted such a lab, in what follows we would like to highlight some of its constituent parts and to offer at least one model for replication.

A typical epigraphy class can be divided into two parts. In part one, students will be taught the methods and considerations necessary for making an epigraphic study of an inscription. Normally, this is the place to discuss things such as proposed readings, comparative Semitic philology, linguistic isoglosses, phonology, orthography, and palaeography. In part two, students will learn techniques for presenting such epigraphic analyses, particularly palaeographic analyses. They will learn the methods for making digital drawings and script charts. There will of necessity be overlap between the things taught in each part of the course; however, we have divided it into two sections for pedagogical purposes. Each member of the class will need their own computer, equipped with digital drawing software and with hardware that allows the user to manipulate the pen tool, such as a mouse or tablet and stylus.

4.1 *Part One: Epigraphic Analysis*

Typically, the handbooks and other resources previously mentioned have also been the standard references for epigraphy courses. Thus, students are often first introduced to the corpus of *Northwest Semitic Inscriptions* in transliteration. Transliterations that are, at times, accompanied by drawings and, less often, by images. Though studying inscriptions in transliteration alone is certainly serviceable, it is hardly ideal.

Without the presence of a high-quality image, students are unable to assess for themselves whether or not the transliteration, and drawing if present, offer the best possible interpretation of the inscription. Just as it was mentioned previously that drawings represent the interpretation of the text that is actually present in an inscription and are, therefore, somewhat subjective, transliterations are also interpretations. This is particularly important for a student to bear in mind when studying inscriptions that are particularly faded or damaged, and this is something that he or she will be less aware of without seeing an actual image of the text. A student should be presented and allowed to struggle with the complexities of actually performing a full epigraphic analysis. Now, because of the increasing availability of high-resolution images, it is possible to teach epigraphy in a more informative and instructive way, and instructors have begun to incorporate the use of images into their classes.

During class images of an inscription will be projected onto a screen and displayed on the monitor of each student. First, in order to establish a firm reading of the text, students will be instructed to read the letters of the inscription directly from the screen without notes. This approach is valuable and superior to reading inscriptions in transliteration alone. Students will become very familiar with the actual script tradition in which the text is written and also begin to understand the interpretive nature of reading an inscription, as they learn from experience the reasons that varying readings of a letter might occur – such as graphemic similarity between letters, idiosyncratic letter forms, or damage that has occurred to an inscription. After having established a secure reading of the text, students will then begin to work through the inscription line by line, offering a translation and discussing various lexical, syntactical, and comparative Semitic issues.

Also during part one of the class, the instructor will begin to discuss various palaeographic facets of the script of the inscription as well as the methodological principles being followed when conducting a palaeographic study. There are a variety of things that students will need to keep in mind when analyzing (and eventually drawing) inscriptions, as these data will provide important, diagnostic information for script analysis.[32] Students should consider the following with regard to the morphology of letter forms (Fig. 9.13):

- The placement of a letter in relation to the scribal guide line.
- The shape or form of a letter.
- The size of letters in relation to each other.
- Letter environment: the position of letters in relation to each other.[33]
- The stance of letters in relation to the vertical.
- Scribal ductus – the *way* in which a scribe executed a letter form, including the number of
- strokes with which he made it, the order in which he produced these strokes, and the
- direction in which he moved the writing instrument as he made them.
- Scribal media, whether stone, papyrus, velum or leather; chisel or ink with brush or pen.

32 Parker, Heather D. D, "The Levant comes", Fig. 1, 9-44; Rollston, "Non-Provenanced", 150-157; Rollston, "Prolegomenon", 1-4.

33 Zuckerman, Bruce, with Lynn Swartz Dodd, "Pots and Alphabets: Refractions of Reflections on Typological Method." *MAARAV 10*, 2003, 89-133; Rollston, "Non-Provenanced", 160-162; Rollston, "Scribal Education", 58-59.

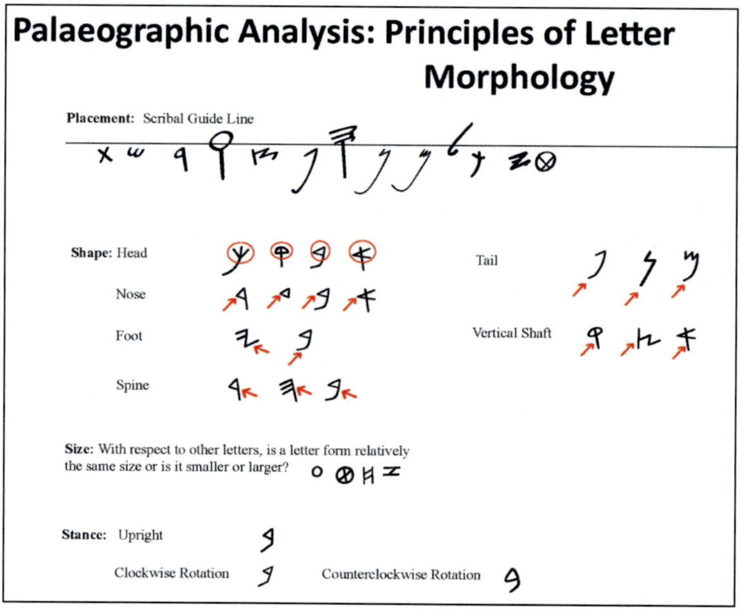

FIGURE 9.13 Principles of letter morphology related to the study of Northwest Semitic epigraphy and palaeography (linear alphabetic scripts); copyrights on page IX.

– he particular expression of a script that a scribe chose to use – whether formal or cursive.

4.2 *Part Two: Presentation of Epigraphic Analysis*

During the second part of class, the instructor will give assignments aimed at teaching the specific skills necessary for presenting an epigraphic analysis, such as the manipulation of digital images and the production of digital drawings and script charts. While drawing (and making decisions about how and what to draw), many methodological principles taught in the first part of the class will be exemplified and reinforced.

Students will first need to learn basic skills for using digital imaging and drawing software. Fortunately, both Adobe Photoshop and Illustrator come equipped with their own help documentation and/or video tutorials. The course instructor might also offer some basic lessons.

A most useful resource for many scholars and students at academic institutions are teaching and learning centers. For example, one component of Johns Hopkins University Sheridan Libraries is the Center for Educational

Resources.[34] This center partners with faculty and graduate students to connect innovative teaching strategies with instructional technologies. Some centers or department divisions will often readily provide basic instruction and introductory workshops in digital imaging and drawing software. In the early sessions of a course, an "expert" in such software could teach basic skills. After this initial instruction, the regular course instructor can then tailor future training and assignments to the way in which these programs can be used specifically in the field of epigraphy.

4.3 *Digital Drawings*

Students should first learn to make a complete drawing of an inscription. They should choose a base image of the text from which to execute their drawing. If multiple images of the inscription are available, especially images wherein the text has been photographed in a variety of light spectra and/or lit from a variety of directions, then students should be instructed to also consult these images for any additional data they might reveal.

As students begin the drawing process, various questions will arise naturally. Such as, "What constitutes important palaeographic information?" That is, "What should be included in a palaeographic drawing?" These questions develop as students encounter things like pockmarks, shadows, and abrasions on the surface of an inscribed object, and/or attempt to assess the "true" outline of a letter's form versus the wear or damage that might have occurred around the edges of that form. While most information or data found within an inscription or the image of an inscription is important, it is not all diagnostic. Students should be reminded of the purpose of a drawing, namely that it is not intended to be a snapshot of an inscription but rather a palaeographic interpretation of that inscription.

Students should start their drawings by focusing on an individual letter, such as *'alep*, and draw every example of that letter present within the inscription. Not only will this provide much essential practice in drawing technique, but students will begin to get a feel for the exact form of the letter that was in the mind of the scribe who executed the inscription. That is, students will begin to understand the basic shape of the letter that the scribe was trying to achieve and possibly the way he was moving his hand in order to achieve it, namely his scribal ductus.

34 See Johns Hopkins University Sheridan Libraries Center for Educational Resources, <http://www.cer.jhu.edu/>, accessed on 10.04.19.

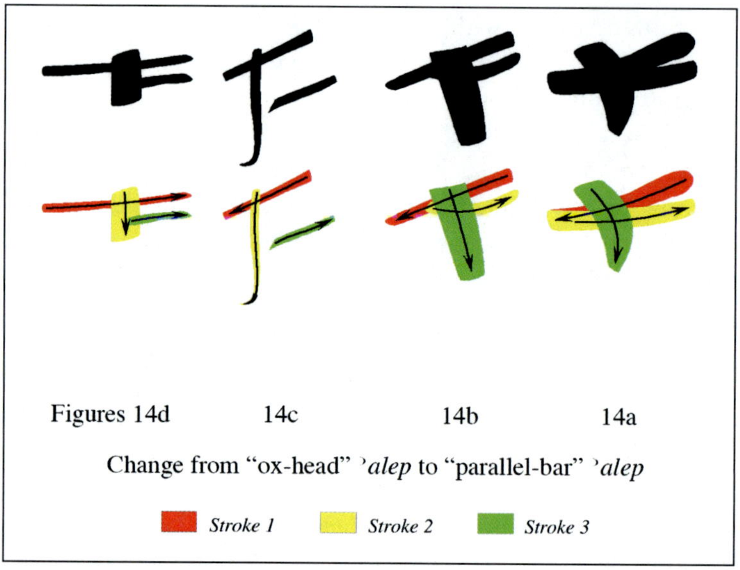

FIGURE 9.14 Producing digital drawings and script charts that indicate the ductus of a letter form; copyrights on page IX.

Sometimes ductus can be seen clearly, sometimes it cannot; and students learn much from being forced to struggle to ascertain it. If students are working with an inscription wherein in ductus can be determined, they should endeavor to indicate this ductus in their drawing. This can be done by superimposing a layer over their drawing whereon the order and direction in which strokes were made are indicated by numbers and arrows placed on top of each of the letter strokes, or by color-coding certain strokes (Fig. 9.14).

Digital drawing tools greatly facilitate the analysis of palaeographic data. One obvious way that examples of letter forms might be readily compared to each other is by copying and pasting them side-by-side. Examples might also be superimposed on top of each other, and Adobe Illustrator allows one to alter the transparency of one's drawing in order to perform quite detailed comparison (Fig. 9.15). This especially facilitates the comparison of solid, well-preserved letter examples and mere traces of a letter.

After students have drawn and begun to understand the morphology and ductus of the first letter of an inscription, they should repeat this process for each successive letter. They should make notes about these aspects as they draw, and based on these notes they should later be able to formulate a written description of each letter that corresponds to the form they have drawn.

FIGURE 9.15 Using Adobe Illustrator to facilitate detailed comparison of the letter forms of the Kerak fragment (Kerak Museum, No. 6807); copyrights on page IX.

4.4 *Digital Script Charts*

Palaeographers use script charts to show the ideal form of each of the letters present within an inscription. Script charts facilitate easy comparison of the script of an inscription with other inscriptions written in the same script tradition, in the same chronological period or over several periods. They also make it easy to compare an inscription (or multiple inscriptions) written in one script tradition with inscriptions written in a different tradition (Figs. 9.16-17).

Digital drawing tools allow for relatively easy construction of script charts, as letters can be copied directly from a digital drawing and pasted into a digital chart. They also enable a palaeographer to craft a chart with greater precision and to retain crucial diagnostic information about each letter in the chart. For example, when pasting a letter from a drawing into a script chart, one can more easily preserve the relationship of a letter to the scribal guide line by using various guides and measuring tools available within Adobe Illustrator (Fig. 9.18). Also, one can easily document the precise location from which a script chart letter example came (e.g., which inscription, which line of the inscription, or which example of the letter from that particular line). This can be done on a designated layer within an Illustrator file. The ability to 'copy and paste' letters from a drawing also facilitates the illustration of palaeographical discussions by enabling a scholar to paste letter examples (in the margins) directly alongside written letter descriptions (Fig. 9.19).

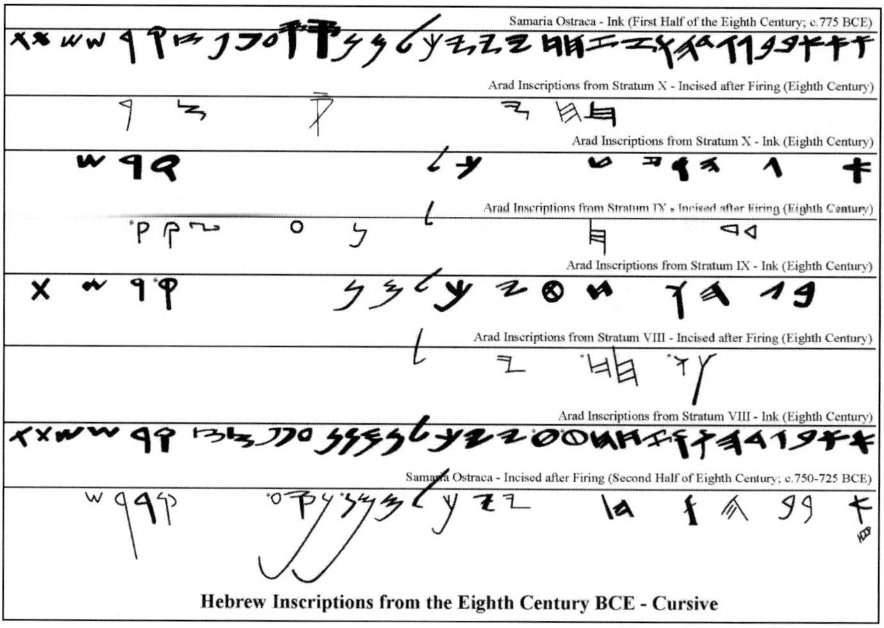

FIGURE 9.16 Digitally produced script chart of eighth-century BCE Hebrew cursive inscriptions; copyrights on page IX.

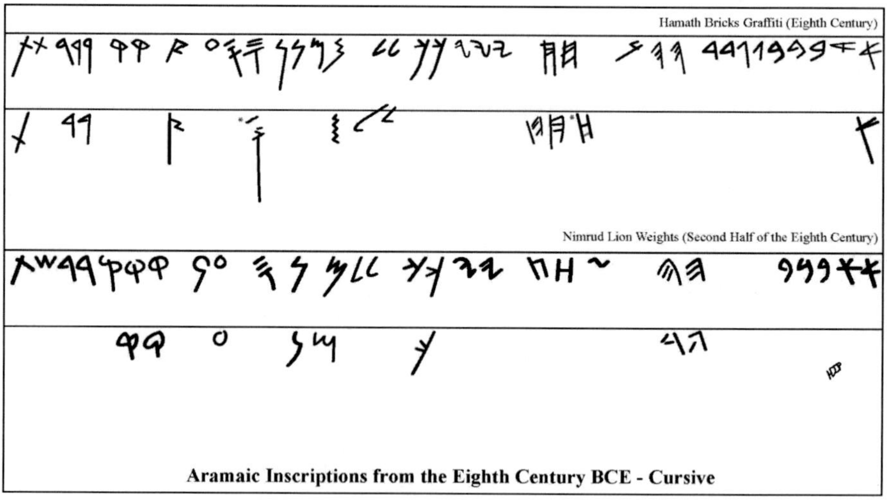

FIGURE 9.17 Digitally produced script chart of eighth-century BCE Aramaic cursive inscriptions; copyrights on page IX.

FIGURE 9.18 Adobe Illustrator's measurement tools being used on an image of the Honeyman inscription (Cyprus Archaeological Museum, No. 397); copyrights on page IX.

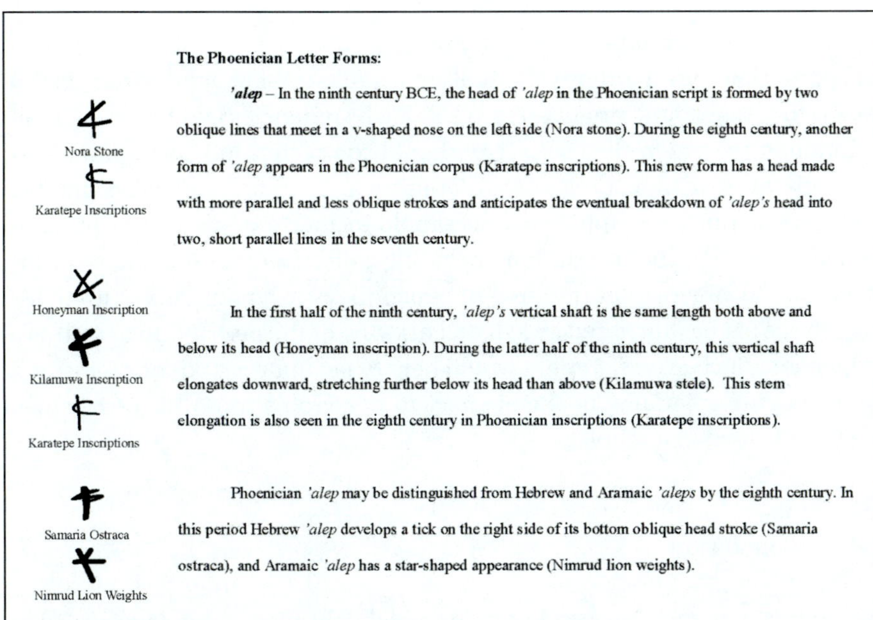

The Phoenician Letter Forms:

Nora Stone

Karatepe Inscriptions

'alep – In the ninth century BCE, the head of *'alep* in the Phoenician script is formed by two oblique lines that meet in a v-shaped nose on the left side (Nora stone). During the eighth century, another form of *'alep* appears in the Phoenician corpus (Karatepe inscriptions). This new form has a head made with more parallel and less oblique strokes and anticipates the eventual breakdown of *'alep's* head into two, short parallel lines in the seventh century.

Honeyman Inscription

Kilamuwa Inscription

Karatepe Inscriptions

In the first half of the ninth century, *'alep's* vertical shaft is the same length both above and below its head (Honeyman inscription). During the latter half of the ninth century, this vertical shaft elongates downward, stretching further below its head than above (Kilamuwa stele). This stem elongation is also seen in the eighth century in Phoenician inscriptions (Karatepe inscriptions).

Samaria Ostraca

Nimrud Lion Weights

Phoenician *'alep* may be distinguished from Hebrew and Aramaic *'aleps* by the eighth century. In this period Hebrew *'alep* develops a tick on the right side of its bottom oblique head stroke (Samaria ostraca), and Aramaic *'alep* has a star-shaped appearance (Nimrud lion weights).

FIGURE 9.19 Illustrated palaeographic discussion of the letter *'alep* in the Iron II Phoenician script; copyrights on page X.

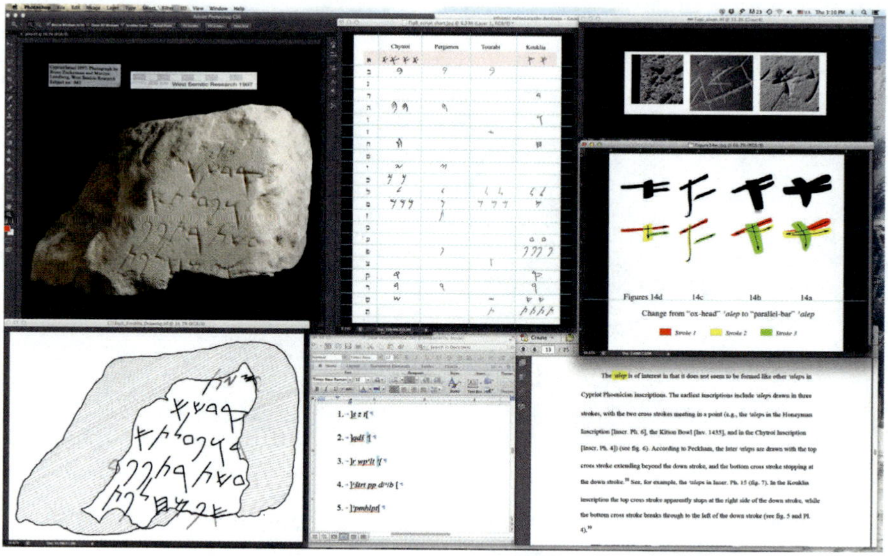

FIGURE 9.20 Example of a final project assigned during an epigraphic digital lab. Study of Phoenician dedicatory inscription to Astarte of Paphos (Cyprus Archaeological Museum, No. 399); copyrights on page x.

4.5 *A Final, Comprehensive Assignment*

An appropriate way to solidify the skills that students have gained from such a class is to assign a final project (Fig. 9.20). Each student should be given an inscription to present to the class. They should complete a full epigraphic treatment of the text, including a translation, vocalization, and palaeographic analysis. Their palaeographic analysis should include a written description of the letter forms of the inscription, including a discussion of how those forms fit within the larger script tradition of which they are a part. This written discussion should be illustrated by a digital drawing of the inscription as well as a script chart. Such an assignment would help to facilitate a student's transition from studying epigraphy in the abstract to being able to do his or her own analysis of a text as a scholar.

5 Conclusion

Within this paper we have endeavored to highlight new technology available for conducting epigraphic analyses and also for presenting such analyses. We have also offered a model for how to conduct an epigraphy course that incorporates and utilises this technology.

Obviously to become a skilled epigrapher requires more experience than one can acquire in a course or two. It takes much practice to hone the skills necessary to produce a sound epigraphic study. However, as with any course, students can be introduced to the methods and principles of a particular field and to the various issues inherent in producing sound analyses. By showing students how one might move from studying inscriptions theoretically in a classroom to producing an actual study of an inscription based on the use of high-quality images, one can greatly facilitate their transition to independent, authoritative scholarship.

Acknowledgments

This article is dedicated to our teacher, Prof. P. Kyle McCarter, Jr., "from whom we learned most and best." We would like to thank the following: Bruce Zuckerman, Marilyn Lundberg, Ken Zuckerman, and Johnna Tyrrell of the West Semitic Research Project (WSRP) for training Rollston and Parker in the use of Adobe Photoshop and Parker in Reflectance Transformation Imaging (RTI); Catherine Kiefe, graphic designer and Lecturer for the Johns Hopkins University School of Medicine, for training Parker in the use of Adobe Illustrator. We would also like to particularly thank Reid Sczerba, Multimedia Development Specialist of Johns Hopkins University Sheridan Libraries Center for Educational Resources (CER), for partnering with Parker and P. Kyle McCarter of the Near Eastern Studies Department of Johns Hopkins University to bring innovative technologies into the classroom, as well as for inviting McCarter to showcase this partnership in the CER's inner-university publication *The Innovative Instructor*. We are grateful to the following for their gracious hospitality during our on-site studies of various pieces showcased in this paper: Tammam A. Khasawneh, Museum Environment Specialist, The Jordan Museum; Fawwaz al-Khraysheh, former Director of the Antiquities of Jordan; Abdel Rahim al-Dwikat, Director, Jordan Archaeological Museum; Sate Massadeh, Director, Kerak Museum; Maria Hadjicosti, Director, and Despo Pilides, Curator of Antiquities, Cyprus Department of Antiquities; Suzi Hakimyan, Director of Beirut National Museum; Lawrence Stager, former Director of Harvard Semitic Museum; and Chang-Ho Ji, Excavator of Tell Ataruz. We greatly appreciate the various granting institutions whose generous support and ongoing commitment to academic research, specifically the study of the ancient Near East, is invaluable: the American Center of Oriental Research Harrell Family Fellowship; the Explorers Club Washington Group; the Johns Hopkins University: the Dean's Teaching Fellowship, the J. Brien Key Fund, Jewish Studies Department

Stulman Jewish Studies Award, Near Eastern Studies Department Schaefer Scholarship; and the West Semitic Research Project's Training Program in RTI, funded by grants from the Andrew M. Mellon Foundation and the Institute for Museum and Library Services; the Society of Biblical Literature; the Albright Institute of Archaeological Research; and the National Endowment for the Humanities. And we thank in particular the *Near Eastern Archeology* for its agreement to republish here an extended version of our 2016 article[35], as well as the Harvard Semitic Museum for its authorization to reproduce several photographs.

References

Adobe Creative Suite, <http://www.adobe.com/products/catalog.html>, accessed on 10.04.19.

Adobe Illustrator, <http://www.adobe.com/products/illustrator.html>, accessed on 10.04.19.

Adobe Photoshop, <http://www.photoshop.com/products/photoshop>, accessed on 10.04.19.

Aḥituv, Shmuel, *Echoes from the Past: Hebrew and Cognate Inscriptions from the Biblical Period,* Jerusalem: Carta, 2008.

Arico, Ashley Fiutko, Nathaniel E. Greene, and Heather D.D. Parker, "Ancient Near Eastern Material Culture Studies and Reflectance Transformation Imaging (RTI)." In: *Proceedings of The Future of the Past: From Amphipolis to Mosul. New Approaches to Cultural Heritage Preservation in the Eastern Mediterranean. Conference at the Museum of Archaeology and Anthropology at the University of Pennsylvania,* Archaeological Institute of America Site Preservation Program: Heritage, Conservation, and Archaeology, <https://www.archaeological.org/news/sitepreservationhcaspecialpubs/21700>, accessed on 10.04.19.

Attardo, Ezio, "La paleographia aramaica dagli inizi al 612 A.C." In: *Tesi di Laurea,* Padua University, 1984.

Aufrecht, Walter E., *A Corpus of Ammonite Inscriptions,* Ancient Near Eastern Texts and Studies 4, Lewiston, NY: Edwin Mellen Press, 1989.

Birnbaum, Salomo A., *The Hebrew Scripts Part 2: The Plates,* Palaeographia: London, 1954-1957.

Birnbaum, Salomo A., *The Hebrew Scripts Part 1: The Text,* Leiden: Brill, 1971.

Bordreuil, Pierre, and Dennis Pardee, *A Manual of Ugaritic,* Winona Lake, In: *Eisenbrauns,* 2009.

35 See footnote 1 above.

CIS = *Corpus inscriptionum semiticarum ab Academia inscriptionum et literarum humaniorum conditum atque digestum*, éd. Renan, Ernest, Paris: e Reipublicæ typographeo, 1881-1950.

Cooke, George A., *A Textbook of North-Semitic Inscriptions: Moabite, Hebrew, Phoenician, Aramaic, Nabataean, Palmyrene, Jewish,* Oxford: Clarendon Press, 1903.

Cross, Frank M. Jr, "Epigraphic Notes on Hebrew Documents of the Eighth-Sixth Centuries, BC, I: A New Reading of a Place Name in the Samaria Ostraca." *Bulletin of the American Schools of Oriental Research 163*, 1961, 12-14, Reprinted in: Cross 2003, 114-115.

Cross, Frank M. Jr, "Epigraphic Notes on Hebrew Documents of the Eighth-Sixty Centuries BC, II: The Murabba'at Papyrus and the Letter Found near Yabneh-Yam." *Bulletin of the American Schools of Oriental Research* 165, 1961, 1962a, 34-46. Reprinted in: Cross, 2003, 116-124.

Cross, Frank M. Jr, "Epigraphic Notes on Hebrew Documents of the Eighth-Sixth Centuries BC, III: The Inscribed Jar Handles from Gibeon." *Bulletin of the American Schools of Oriental Research 168*, 1961, 1962b, 18-23, Reprinted in: Cross, 2003, 125-128.

Cross, Frank M. Jr, *Leaves from an Epigrapher's Notebook: Collected Papers in Hebrew and West Semitic Palaeography and Epigraphy*, Harvard Semitic Studies 51, Winona Lake, 1961, *Eisenbrauns*, 2003.

Cultural Heritage Imaging, <http://culturalheritageimaging.org/Technologies/RTI/>, accessed on 10.04.19.

Dobbs-Allsopp, Frederick W., Jimmy J.M. Roberts, Choon-Leong Seow, and Robert E. Whitaker, *Hebrew Inscriptions: Texts from the Biblical Period of the Monarchy with Concordance*, New Haven, CT: Yale University, 2005.

Donner, Herbert, and Wolfgang Röllig, *Kanaanäische und aramäische Inschriften* (*KAI*), 3 vols, Wiesbaden: Harrassowitz, 1962-2002.

Ellison, John L, "A Paleographic Study of the Alphabetic Cuneiform Texts from Ras Shamra/Ugarit." PhD diss., Harvard University, 2002.

Ellison, John L, "The Ugaritic Alphabetic Script." In: *"An Eye for Form": Epigraphic Essays, in Honor of Frank Moore Cross*, edited by Jo Ann Hackett and Walter. E. Aufrecht, Winona Lake, Eisenbrauns, 2014, 56-71.

Ellison, John L, "The Ugaritic Alphabetic Script." In: *An Introduction to Ugaritic*, by J. Huehnergard, 179-188, Peabody, MA: Hendrickson.

Faigenbaum-Golovin, Shira, Christopher A. Rollston, Eli Piasetzky, Barak Sober, and Israel Finkelstein, "The Ophel (Jerusalem) Ostracon in Light of New Multispectral Images." *Semitica 57*, 2015, 113-137.

Garfinkel, Yosef, and Saar Ganor, *Khirbet* Qeiyafa, vol. 1: *Excavation Report 2007-2008,* Jerusalem: Israel Exploration Society and Hebrew University of Jerusalem, 2009.

Gass, Erasmus, *Die Moabiter – Geschichte und Kultur eines ostjordanischen Volkes im 1. Jahrtausend v. Chr. Wiesbaden: Harrassowitz,* 2009.

Gibson, John C.L., *Textbook of Syrian Semitic Inscriptions.* 3 vols, Oxford: Clarendon, 1975-1982.

Greene, Nathaniel E., and Heather D.D. Parker, "Field of View: Northwest Semitic Palaeography and Reflectance Transformation Imaging (RTI)." In: *Epigraphy, Philology, and the Hebrew Bible,* edited by Jeremy M. Hutton and Aaron D. Rubin, Atlanta: Society of Biblical Literature, 2015, 209-235.

Haines, Byron L., "A Palaeographical Study of Aramaic Inscriptions Antedating 500 BC." PhD diss., Harvard University, 1966.

Hanneken, Todd R., "New Technology for Imaging Unreadable Manuscripts and Other Artifacts: Integrated Spectral Reflectance Transformation Imaging (Spectral RTI)." In: Clivaz, Claire, Dilley, Paul, Hamidović, David, *Ancient Worlds in Digital Culture, Digital Biblical Studies* (*DBS 1*), Leiden / Boston, Brill, 2016, 180-195.

Holmstedt. Robert D., "Reading through the Noise: KAI 30 with Fresh Eyes (and Better-Photos)." Paper presented at the annual meeting for the Society of Biblical Literature, Chicago, IL, November 21, 2012, InscriptiFact, <http://www.inscriptifact.com>, accessed on 10.04.19.

Johns Hopkins University Sheridan Libraries Center for Educational Resources, <http://www.cer.jhu.edu/>, accessed on 10.04.19.

Kaufman, Ivan, "The Samaria Ostraca: A Study in Ancient Hebrew Palaeography." PhD diss., Harvard University, 1966.

Kaufman, Ivan, "The Samaria Ostraca: An Early Witness to Hebrew Writing." *Biblical Archaeologist* 45, 1982, 229-239.

Lemaire, André, "Aramaic Script and Its Role in Creating Cultural Links." In: *History of Script and Writing: Collected Essays of International Seminar of Tablet to Tablet* (*From Clay Tablet to Electronic Compact Disk*), Ministry of Culture and Islamic Guidance, Tehran: Chameh, 2006, 73-96.

Lemaire, André, and Benjamin Sass, "The Mortuary Stele with Sam'alian Inscription from Ördekburnu near Zincirli." *Bulletin of the American Schools of Oriental Research* 369, 2013, 57-136.

Lidzbarski, Mark, *Handbuch der nordsemitischen Epigraphik,* Vols. I-II, Weimar: E. Felber, 1898.

Lidzbarski, Mark, *Ephemeris für semitische Epigraphik,* 3 vols, Giessen: Ricker, 1902-1915.

Lundberg, Marilyn. J, "New Technologies: Reading Ancient Inscriptions in Virtual Light", <http://www.inscriptifact.com/news/article.html>, accessed on 10.04.19.

McCarter, P. Kyle. Jr., *The Antiquity of the Greek Alphabet and the Early Phoenician Scripts,* Missoula, MT: Scholars Press, 1975.

McCarter, P. Kyle. Jr., "Digital Labs: Drawing Ancient Inscriptions." In: *The Innovative Instructor: Pedagogy Forum,* Baltimore: Center for Educational Resources, Johns Hopkins University, 2011.

McLean, Mark D, Palaeography. In: *Anchor Bible Dictionary 5*, New York: Doubleday, 1992, 58-60.

Moscati, Sabatino, *L'epigrafia ebraica antica: 1935-1950*, Rome: Pontifical Biblical Institute, 1951.

Naveh, Joseph, *The Development of the Aramaic Script,* Jerusalem: Israel Academy of Sciences and Humanities, 1970.

Naveh, Joseph, *Early History of the Alphabet*, Jerusalem: Hebrew University Magnes Press, reprint of second ed., 1997.

Parker, Heather D.D., "The Levant Comes of Age: The Ninth Century BCE through Script Traditions." PhD diss., Johns Hopkins University, 2013.

Parker, Heather D.D., and Arico, Ashley Fiutko, "A Moabite-Inscribed Statue Fragment from Kerak: Egyptian Parallels", *Bulletin of the American Schools of Oriental Research 373*, 2015, 105-120.

Parker, Heather D.D., and Christopher A. Rollston, "The Epigraphic Digital Lab: Teaching Epigraphy in the 21st Century CE", *Near Eastern Archaeology 79*, 2016, 44-56.

Peckham, J. Brian, *The Development of the Late Phoenician Scripts,* Cambridge, MA: Harvard University, 1968.

Pitard, Wayne, "The Shape of the *'Ayin* in the Ugaritic Script." *Journal of the Ancient Near Eastern Society of Columbia University 51.4*, 1992, 261-79.

Reisner, George A, *Harvard Excavations at Samaria: 1908-1910*, Vol. I, Cambridge: Harvard University Press, 1924.

Renz, Johannes, *Handbuch der althebräischen Epigraphik*, Vols. I-III, Darmstadt: Wissenschaftliche Buchgesellschaft, 1995.

Renz, Johannes, *Schrift und Schreibertradition: eine paläographische Studie zum kulturgeschichtlichen Verhältnis von israelitischem Nordreich und Südreich*. Wiesbaden: Harrassowitz, 1997.

R.B. Toth Associates, <http://www.rbtoth.com/spectral-imaging--partners.html>, accessed on 10.04.19.

Rollston, Christopher A, "The Script of Hebrew Ostraca of the Iron Age: 8th-6th Centuries BCE." PhD diss., Johns Hopkins University, 1999.

Rollston, Christopher A, "Non-Provenanced Epigraphs I: Pillaged Antiquities, Northwest Semitic Forgeries, and Protocols for Laboratory Tests." *MAARAV 10*, 2003, 135-193.

Rollston, Christopher A, "Scribal Education in Ancient Israel: The Old Hebrew Epigraphic Evidence," *Bulletin of the American Schools of Oriental Research 344*, 2006, 47-74.

Rollston, Christopher A, *Writing and Literacy in the World of Ancient Israel: Epigraphic Evidence from the Iron Age,* Atlanta: Society of Biblical Literature, 2010.

Rollston, Christopher A, "Prolegomenon to the Study of Northwest Semitic Paleography and Epigraphy." In: *"An Eye for Form": Epigraphic Essays in Honor of Frank Moore*

Cross, edited by Jo Ann Hackett and Walter E. Aufrecht, Winona Lake, *Eisenbrauns*, 2014a, 1-4.

Rollston, Christopher A, "Northwest Semitic Cursive Scripts of Iron II." In: *"An Eye for Form": Epigraphic Essays in Honor of Frank Moore Cross*, edited by Jo Ann Hackett and Walter E. Aufrecht, Winona Lake, *Eisenbrauns*, 2014b, 202-234.

Sober, Barak. Shira Faigenbaum, Itzhaq Beit-Arieh, Israel Finkelstein, Murray Moinester, Eli Piasetzky, and Arie Shaus, "Multispectral Imaging as a Tool for Enhancing the Reading of Ostraca," *Palestine Exploration Quarterly 146*, 2014, 185-197.

Tappy, Ronald E., and P. Kyle McCarter Jr., eds. 2008, *Literate Culture and Tenth-Century Canaan: The Tel Zayit Abecedary in Context,* Winona Lake. In: *Eisenbrauns.West Semitic Research Project* (*WSRP*), <https://www.eisenbrauns.org/books/titles/978-1-57506-150-4.html>, accessed on 10.04.19.

Yardeni, Ada, *The Book of Hebrew Script: History, Palaeography, Script Styles, Calligraphy & Design*, Jerusalem: Carta, 1997.

Zuckerman, Bruce, with Lynn Swartz Dodd, "Pots and Alphabets: Refractions of Reflections on Typological Method," *MAARAV 10*, 2003, 89-133.

CHAPTER 10

HarvardX's Early Christianity: The Letters of Paul: a Retrospective on Online Teaching and Learning

Jennifer Aileen Quigley and Laura Salah Nasrallah

1 Introduction

The edX/HarvardX course Early Christianity: The Letters of Paul was developed in 2013 and launched in 2014. While at the time such an open-access online course in biblical studies was a relatively new phenomenon, it was concurrent with educational sites that require payment, such as The Great Courses.[1] Since the course, many other opportunities have emerged for free, open, and online scholarly study of ancient Christianity, the religion of antiquity, or Bible, such as Gary Anderson and John Cavadini's Jesus in Scripture and Tradition,[2] Barry Scott Wimpfheimer's Coursera course The Talmud: A Methodological Introduction,[3] Harvard's World Religions Through Their Scriptures,[4] which is organized by Diane Moore and includes scholars presenting the global impact and interpretation of a variety of scriptures, or the more exploratory and encyclopedia style Bible Odyssey from the Society of Biblical Literature.[5]

Our chapter takes up the theme of digital academic communication and publication by discussing the development and launch of the online edX/HarvardX course, Early Christianity: The Letters of Paul. This chapter offers a

1 <http://www.thegreatcourses.com/>, accessed on 10.04.19. The Great Courses is a subscription based service where students purchase access to individual courses. These courses are not live and interactive, but they do include lecture videos and other materials. Most courses, including offerings related to biblical studies, cost between $130-$225 per course.

2 <https://www.edx.org/course/jesus-scripture-tradition-notredamex-th120-1x>, accessed on 10.04.19.

3 <https://www.coursera.org/learn/the-talmud>, accessed on 10.04.19.

4 <https://www.edx.org/xseries/world-religions-through-scriptures>, accessed on 10.04.19. ScripturesX is a broad overview course, with 4 weeks dedicated to each of several major world religions' scriptural traditions, including Judaism and Christianity.

5 <https://www.bibleodyssey.org/>, accessed on 10.04.19. All of these courses are offered by scholars in the field of religion, theology, or biblical studies. The faculty for the Great Courses Bible courses include David Brakke, Cynthia R. Chapman, Bart Ehrman, and Luke Timothy Johnson. With the exception of pay-series such as the Great Courses, the proliferation of the courses mentioned above all have launched within the past three years, following the completion of Early Christianity: The Letters of Paul.

 DOI:10.1163/9789004399297_012

history of our project, quantitative data about registrants and those who received certificates, and qualitative data about the experience of the teaching staff and online students. Moreover, this chapter considers the centrality of pedagogical considerations to our project, reflecting upon our experiment in whether and how feminist pedagogies could be deployed in a MOOC.

Given the growth of online education in biblical studies and its relative newness, a broader conversation about its role in our field is needed.[6] Our chapter contends that this growth among organizations that can create and sustain MOOCs (Massive Open Online Courses) should keep as a key goal the crafting of a public, free, and critical space for students who express a desire, no matter their location on the globe, to learn about and to discuss the Bible. As one step toward this broader conversation, this chapter lays bare a key if publicly unexpressed learning goal of our course: to foster an online location for the development of peaceful conversation and critical knowledge in the face of both the violence and promise produced in the name of and because of religion.

2 Course Origin, Goals, Construction, and Pedagogy

In January 2013, an email from HarvardX to Harvard faculty invited ideas for an online massive, open course. This was at the time when faculty at San Jose State University were protesting their administration's decision to ask the faculty to pilot Professor Michael Sandel's HarvardX course, "JusticeX," which would functionally render their philosophy faculty as teaching support for an already existing course.[7] This was also a time when many expressed concerns about MOOCs as a phenomenon in the academy that threatened intellectual diversity, tenure track lines, and faculty jobs – the very things that most con-

6 For discussion of the potential of for-pay online education in the field of business, and a reflection on pedagogy and students' ability to teach each other, see "Education at a Crossroads" and discussion of the formulation and launch of HBS by its chief organizer, Anand, Bharat, *The Content Trap: A Strategist's Guide to Digital Change*, New York: Random House, 2016, 299-344.

7 <http://archive.boston.com/bostonglobe/ideas/brainiac/2013/05/san_jose_state.html>, accessed on 10.04.19; <http://www.chronicle.com/article/The-Document-an-Open-Letter/138937>, accessed on 10.04.19. See also Sandel's response, which indicates that he did not intend and did not want JusticeX to be used in such a way: <http://www.chronicle.com/article/Michael-Sandel-Responds/139021/>, accessed on 10.04.19. JusticeX is now archived on edX, although Sandel shares similar content through <http://www.justiceharvard.org/>, accessed on 10.04.19.

cern those of us who train doctoral students and who wish to preserve the ongoing life of academic freedom and intellectual diversity.

Nonetheless, Laura Nasrallah made the decision to go forward with a course for several reasons. First, HarvardX provided some photography and video equipment for graduate students to use during a seminar course that included travel to archaeological sites in Greece and Turkey, thus allowing the capture of high quality images for use in publications, for Harvard's New Testament Archaeology project, and for various other courses, including the HarvardX course. Second, HarvardX provided some funding and training of doctoral students. It seemed that doctoral students would benefit from experience in the preparation and execution of an online course. Such experience could be helpful in the current job market, providing an opportunity to think through a broad range of pedagogical issues not confronted in the brick and mortar classrooms of Harvard. Third, the larger educational landscape in the U.S. and abroad is experimenting with blended and online learning. Theological schools in particular, recognizing that their students do not have the luxury of a three-year residential Masters of Divinity program, increasingly utilize online courses. It was worthwhile for all teaching staff to understand better the benefits and consequences of online teaching. Finally, in early 2014, when the course was offered, there were few female faculty engaged in HarvardX (and edX more broadly) and few courses offered in the Humanities. Was it possible to create a space in emerging MOOC venues for the humanities and for the study of religion? Was it possible to create a humanities/study of religion MOOC while engaging some of the principles of feminist pedagogy, which emphasizes the importance of students' past knowledge and experience as helpful to the analysis of course materials, rather than something to set aside; the work of students and teachers as co-learners; the significance of sharing ideas and knowledge; and the goal of engaging course materials with an eye to attending to the voices of women and others who are marginalized in the historical record? MOOCs have a global reach, on the one hand, and often a "star" professor, on the other. Could one instead engage the experiment of feminist pedagogy in a MOOC, hoping that the course could engage with a diverse audience who could bring their own ideas and knowledge to the classroom? The course was organized to form and showcase a community of knowledge – a community among the faculty organizer of the course, teaching staff, and invited speakers, and also among the teaching staff and students.

In preparation for these goals, and in light of concerns about higher education in the United States, the possible monetization of MOOCs, and pedagogy, graduate students at Harvard, including the six graduate students involved in Early Christianity: The Letters of Paul, met with the instructor for an informal mini-course in the ethics of online education. The group read blogs and online articles debating the value and danger of MOOCs, as well as more programmatic essays such as "An Avalanche is Coming."[8] In addition, the teaching staff read texts that addressed broader questions of pedagogy.[9]

The teaching staff developed the course for approximately six months, and it launched in January 2014 for a five-week iteration through the edX portal, in partnership with Rap Genius, and using Facebook as an additional portal into the online course.[10] While edX has archived Early Christianity: The Letters of Paul,[11] the course materials, including all course videos, are still available online at a stable website,[12] including videos and time-maps that provide photographs of archaeological sites. We have not run the course again since.[13]

The Early Christianity: The Letters of Paul through HarvardX was a very simplified portion of an introductory course offered at Harvard for undergraduate, masters, and doctoral students. In sum, it adapted portions of roughly 2.5 weeks of the brick and mortar course, and paced these over 5 weeks online, with content launched three times per week.

---

8 Barber, Michael, Donnelly, Katelyn, Rizvi, Saad, *An Avalanche is Coming: Higher Education and the revolution ahead*, London: Institute for Public Policy Research, 2013, <http://www.avalancheiscoming.com/>, accessed on 10.04.19.

9 hooks, bell, *Teaching to Transgress: Education as the Practice of Freedom*, New York: Routledge, 1994; Schüssler Fiorenza, Elisabeth, *Democratizing Biblical Studies: Toward an Emancipatory Educational Space*, Louisville, KY: Westminster John Knox, 2009; Martin, Dale, *Pedagogy of the Bible: An Analysis and Proposal*, Louisville, KY: Westminster John Knox, 2008.

10 Some students participating in the course in locations without access to high speed internet requested discussions and course materials to be posted on Facebook, so the course team made the decision not only to allow students to participate in discussions through Facebook, but also to take the course through Facebook. Videos, discussion questions, and knowledge checks were all posted to the course page on Facebook. Students still needed to log in to edX (or link to Rap Genius) to access the readings, and students working toward a certificate of completion needed to log in to edX to complete their self-assessment (more on this below), but otherwise, the Facebook page allowed students to access a more limited amount of materials. Rap Genius took on the responsibility and liability for hosting course readings on their platform.

11 <https://www.edx.org/course/early-christianity-letters-paul-harvardx-hds1544-1x>, accessed, accessed on 10.04.19. All of the course materials, including discussion boards, student interactions, and all materials available to registered students, are still available at this website. The teaching team was updating the course both before and during the course, with the last update from the teaching team dating to March 7, 2014.

12 <http://div.hds.harvard.edu/lettersofpaul/>, accessed on 10.04.19.

13 At least two factors affected this decision. First, other Harvard Divinity School colleagues began preparing an overarching world scriptures course soon after the completion of Early Christianity: The Letters of Paul. Second, despite the intensive workload of creating, preparing, and running a MOOC, faculty are currently not offered standardized additional compensation, leave, or course relief for teaching MOOCs.

TABLE 10.1 Course components of Early Christianity: The Letters of Paul; ©JENNIFER QUIGLEY AND LAURA NASRALLAH

Course Component	Description
Readings	Primary and secondary readings offered both on the course website and through the Genius platform, which offered interactive text annotation
Short videos	Brief lectures offered by Nasrallah to introduce the day's topic, themes, and important historical context to the day's readings
Conversational videos	Long-form videos featuring Nasrallah interviewing scholars on particular topics or leading doctoral student discussions on a particular text
Bibliographies	Additional scholarly material to encourage student's further exploration
Discussion questions	Open-ended, interactive questions posted on discussion threads on the course website to encourage student interaction
Knowledge Checks	Content-based review questions posted on discussion threads on the course website to encourage student interaction

Each launch included combinations of six components as given in Table 10.1. Our teaching team of one faculty member and four doctoral students answered questions, stimulated discussion, and moderated discussion boards at all hours for five weeks in January-February of 2014. Student participation, especially at the beginning, overwhelmed both the website and the teaching staff, who were trying to respond to the crashing wave of student involvement, which sometimes blocked students from website use.[14] It also won the apostle

14 Within a few hours of launch, a discussion thread for Day 1 asking students to introduce themselves to one another accumulated 640 responses. *Letters of Paul Course Report*, 9. Archived discussion threads can also be viewed on the course website. At course launch, HarvardX did not nest discussion threads, which led to long site load times with discussion threads involving hundreds of comments. By the end of the course, nesting had been added to the discussion threads. Work still continues on enhancing features of online discussions and commenting, functions crucial to humanities courses but less utilized in MOOCs in other fields.

Paul a comparison with Beyoncé in the title of an online article, "More Popular than Beyoncé: The Apostle Paul at Harvard."[15]

Early Christianity: The Letters of Paul experimented with creating a feminist pedagogical space online.[16] The course was grounded in ideas from Elisabeth Schüssler Fiorenza's work, such as her *Democratizing Biblical Studies*. She argues that historical analyses of the context of the production of biblical texts should also speak to contemporary issues. Her work insists upon an ethics of interpretation that is attentive to how biblical texts are often deployed for injustice – to perpetuate racism, sexism, anti-immigrant attitudes, hatred of other religions, and homophobia. Schüssler Fiorenza, in part drawing on the work of Krister Stendahl, sees the work of bringing ivory tower biblical studies to communities that use and care about the Bible as a crucial "public health" issue.[17] The course also attempted to embody online the pedagogy espoused in bell hook's *Teaching to Transgress*, with its roots in Freire's *Pedagogy of the Oppressed.* hooks, offering a black feminist perspective, sees education as essentially dialogical, with classrooms co-constituted by those usually called teachers and those usually called students, and as working toward liberative purposes.[18] Education can be a practice of freedom if and where it teaches that anyone can learn and that anyone can contribute to the production of knowledge.[19] Could a MOOC, despite of its size and global reach, become a space that

15 McGovern, Celeste, "More Popular than Beyoncé: The Apostle Paul at Harvard." 2 April 2014, <http://www.thechristians.com>, accessed on 10.04.19.

16 These experiments are happening in a variety of online communities, including the creation of Distributed Open Collaborative Courses, or DOCCs. This movement, started by FemTechNet in 2013 began with a course called Dialogues on Feminism and Technology. The following is a description of DOCCs from FemTechNet: "A MOOC (massive open online course) is typically organized and branded by a single (elite) institution. A DOCC recognizes and is built on the understanding that expertise is *distributed* throughout a network, among participants situated in diverse institutional contexts, within diverse material, geographic, and national settings, and who embody and perform diverse identities (as teachers, as students, as media-makers, as activists, as trainers, as members of various publics, for example)." "Docc 2013: Dialogues on Feminism and Technology," FemTechNet Commons, <http://femtechnet.org/wp-content/uploads/2015/07/2013Fall_Pitzer_Juhasz.pdf>, accessed on 10.04.19. Since this first course in the winter of 2013, there are now a dozen "Nodal Courses" that have taken place. For larger issues in feminist pedagogy and biblical studies, see the work of Schüssler Fiorenza, Elisabeth, 2009.

17 See helpful discussion and citations in Marchal, Joseph, "To What Ends? Biblical Studies and Critical Rhetorical Engagement(s) for a 'Safer' World," *SBL Forum* n.p. Online: <http://sbl-site.org/Article.aspx?ArticleID=550>, accessed on 10.04.19.

18 hooks, bell, *Teaching to Transgress* 130. hooks of course offers many other important perspectives, including that of embodied knowledge, which were less immediately applicable to the MOOC setting.

19 hooks, *Teaching to Transgress* 13.

formed a "classroom" or community in which such learning and production of knowledge occurred? Ultimately, feminist pedagogy moves the classroom real or virtual toward a democratic forum in which all were producing as well as receiving knowledge, where all were gaining tools to adjudicate knowledge.[20]

These feminist pedagogical models were also enacted by organizing the course in such a way to decenter the faculty member who could be misunderstood as the sole star or "owner" of the MOOC. We chose to present the work on the topic of the Letters of Paul, and on issues in teaching the Bible more generally, as a community project. HarvardX gave us the opportunity to showcase other scholars. We filmed conversations among the full teaching staff demonstrating the ways in which individuals can develop knowledge together in a seminar-setting.[21] While the course did include short, mini-lectures by Nasrallah, these larger teaching staff conversations constituted the majority of film screen time, asking students to engage in longer-form videos modeling scholarly and reflective conversations. A filmed conversation with AnneMarie Luijendijk, of Princeton University, allowed us to show papyri from the Princeton collection and to learn from a scholar of early Christianity and papyrology. A discussion about teaching religion in the public schools highlighted the insights of Diane Moore, now head of the Religious Literacy Project at Harvard, alongside a former Harvard Divinity School student who teaches in a local high school. John Stendahl, a Lutheran pastor, discussed the life and work of his father, Krister Stendahl, a famous scholar of New Testament, bishop of Stockholm, Sweden, and former dean at Harvard; he also read one of his father's

20 Scholars from a variety of fields have reflected on feminist pedagogy and online education. On feminist pedagogy and MOOCs, see Callahan, Vicki, "Toward Networked Digital Scholarship: Mindful Media, Participatory Learning, and Distributed Authorship in the Digital Economy," *Cinema Journal* 53.1 (2013), 156-163; Chick, Nancy, Hassel, Holly, "Don't Hate Me Because I'm Virtual: Feminist Pedagogy in the Online Classroom," *Feminist Teacher*, Vol. 19, No. 3, 2009, 195-215. Even at the outset of online and distance education, feminist scholars have reflected on the pitfalls and promise of new technologies for women's studies and feminist pedagogy. See Whitehouse, Pamela, "Women's Studies Online: An Oxymoron?", *Women's Studies Quarterly*, Vol. 30, No. ¾, 2002, 209-225; Cronan Rose, Ellen, "'This Class Meets in Cyberspace': Women's Studies via Distance Education," *Feminist Teacher*, Vol. 9.2, 1995, 53-60. For work in the area of democratic online education, see Lockard, Joseph, Pergum, Mark, "Brave New Classrooms: Democratic Education and the Internet", in: Peter Lang, *Digital Formations 37*, New York, NY, 2007. On conversations related to critical pedagogies and the digital humanities more broadly, see Losh, Elizabeth, Wernimont, Jacqueline, Wexler, Laura, Wu, Hong-An, "Putting the Human Back into the Digital Humanities: Feminism, Generosity, and Mess," *Debates in the Digital Humanities*, Gold, Matthew K., Klein, Lauren F., eds., Minneapolis, MN: University of Minnesota Press, 2016, 92-103.

21 *Letters of Paul Course Report*, 18.

works to create a kind of podcast.[22] Finally, with each launch of a "day" of work we included a section titled "Go Further/bibliography" in order to mark publicly that our MOOC participated in and depended upon broader scholarly conversations, just as our students' work online participated in a broader conversation. The students' conversations with each other, conversations with the teaching staff and other colleagues, and the bibliographies as indications of sources and scholarly conversations were demonstrations of a larger pedagogical point: myriad communities have wrestled through time to understand and to attribute meaning to ancient authoritative texts, and in doing so have not come to one firm meaning, but instead have shown the possibilities for rich, effervescent, and multiple meanings in these historical documents. The course's very organization was developed from the pedagogical foundation that learning happens best in collaboration, that multiple viewpoints show the complexity of a topic, and that each learner must take on the ethical responsibility of weighing his or her conclusions amid a range of scholarly options.

The course's explicit goals, stated on the syllabus and in an introductory short video, were, first, to investigate Paul's letters as a key record of struggle and debate over social, political, ethical, and theological issues; to learn about the Roman Empire, in which the Pauline correspondence was penned, and the second century world in which people wrote about or even as Paul. A second goal was for students to come to their own understanding of what the Pauline correspondence reveals about first century debate over several key issues. The final course objective was to engage ancient texts with disciplined intimacy.[23]

The course taught that this disciplined intimacy involves learning and practicing close reading. This close reading produces intimacy – the feeling that the text is speaking to the current reader, or that the situations it engages are similar to one's own. This form of close reading also requires the discipline or *askēsis* of recognizing the cultural and temporal distance of the text, and of questioning whether the contemporary reader actually understands its terms at all. While students were not quizzed on particular pieces of information, such as the date of the book of Daniel, evidence for women's religious authority in antiquity, the definition of David Brakke's term "scriptural practices,"[24] or the socio-politics of the Roman colony of Corinth, the course asked them through several media to engage in and to practice certain reading strategies.

22 *Letters of Paul Course Report*, 19.

23 *Letters of Paul Course Report*, 5. See below for evidence related to learning outcomes (17-27).

24 Brakke, David, "Scriptural Practices in Early Christianity: Toward a New History of the Canon," in: Ulrich, Jörg et al., eds., *Invention, Rewriting, Usurpation: Discursive Fights for Religious Traditions in Antiquity*, Frankfurt am Main: Peter Lang, 2012, 263-280.

These strategies involved practicing how to read slowly and closely an ancient text, how to raise questions about its particularities, and how to avoid reducing one's questions to that of authorial intention, as if knowing what Paul really thought would fix the meaning of the text for those who received his letters in the first century CE or the generations who have received his letters since.[25]

To take a single example, on both the first and last day of the course, students were asked to respond to the Letter to Philemon. They were invited to annotate the text and respond to one another's annotations on the website Rap Genius,[26] to discuss with one another what they thought were the circumstances that produced the letter, and to watch doctoral students engage with one another in a similar discussion.[27] These assignments were designed to help students develop the academic practice of close reading strategies, to develop interpretations of ancient texts, and also, perhaps most significantly, to practice taking responsibility for their interpretations.[28] Thus a simple assignment of annotation requires reflection on the content of an ancient texts, engagement with that content, but also reflection on the ethics of interpretation and the ethics of reading and responding to others' interpretations.

3 Participation in Early Christianity: The Letters of Paul

edX captures significant data about its student registrants; they capture not only demographics but everything "from mouse clicks to time spent on tasks."[29] The teaching staff was not aware of this edX practice when the course began, nor that we could have engaged in a larger, meta-research process on learning processes and participation in the course. In the early days of HarvardX MOOCs in 2013, data researchers at HarvardX created individual end-of-course reports, including one for HeroesX with Prof. Gregory Nagy and JusticeX with Prof. Michael Sandel;[30] this research has since expanded to pedagogical and

25 See Johnson-DeBaufre, Melanie, Nasrallah, Laura, "Beyond the Heroic Paul: Toward a Feminist and Decolonizing Approach to the Letters of Paul," in: Stanley, Christopher, ed., *The Colonized Apostle: Paul Through Postcolonial Eyes*, Minneapolis: Fortress, 2011, 161-174; Marchal, Joseph, ed., *The People beside Paul: The Philippian Assembly and History from Below*, Atlanta: SBL Press, 2015; Nasrallah, Laura, *Archaeology and the Letters of Paul*, discusses these issues more fully.

26 The annotated text is still available: <https://genius.com/2636137>, accessed on 10.04.19.

27 *Letters of Paul Course Report*, 43-44.

28 See a classic statement in Schüssler Fiorenza, Elisabeth, "The Ethics of Biblical Interpretation: Decentering Biblical Scholarship," *JBL* 107.1, 1988, 3-17.

29 <https://www.edx.org/about/research-pedagogy>, accessed on 10.04.19.

30 <http://harvardx.harvard.edu/harvardx-working-papers>, accessed on 10.04.19.

demographics research across multiple edX classes and, at Harvard, the development of the Research Committee for the Harvard University Vice Provost for Advances in Learning.[31] At the time our course launched, HarvardX was no longer producing individual course reports. While we initially hoped to have the HarvardX research team help us create our own end of course report, instead we were given access to the raw data from the course, from which we created our own course report, which is available on the course website.[32]

Demographics data for all registrants for the course, as well as results from our end-of-course survey, completed by 2,748 course participants, allows us to gain some sense of whether and how our course met its learning goals. Our course had 32,036 enrollees as of March 2014 (see fig. 1).[33] This is less than a tenth the size of some popular STEM courses; CS50X, a computer science course, enrolled 358,223 after launching in Spring of 2014. Our course issued 1,548 certificates (4.8% of course registrants), while HarvardX averaged a certification rate of 6%.[34]

In keeping with our pedagogical goals as stated above, our course fostered diverse conversation in several ways. Geographical and linguistic diversity characterized the students. Enrollees hailed from 169 countries, and a number of active users created discussion threads in Spanish, Portuguese, and Korean, among other languages. Some students even created Portuguese subtitled versions of the lecture, which they posted on youtube, to help fellow students. The conversation was also more age-diverse than other HarvardX MOOCs. Our median student age was 35, while other HarvardX courses have a median age of 28, with a majority of students aged 20-30. The number of registrants of the Early Christianity: The Letters of Paul for the age categories 71+ represent more than 10% of total registrants in those age categories for all other HarvardX courses combined.[35] Many of these older students had never participated in

31 <http://harvardx.harvard.edu/research>, accessed on 10.04.19.

32 <https://div.hds.harvard.edu/lettersofpaul/course_report.pdf>, accessed on 10.04.19.

33 These numbers differ from those contained in the official course report, which captured data several months later, indicating that students continued to take the course beyond its "live" period. *The Letters of Paul Course Report*, 23 ff. All screen captures from edX websites are dated, because these sites continuously update with new statistics.

34 The certification rate varied widely from course to course, and also varied significantly over time, evidenced by a spike in registration and drop in certification following an appearance by an edX representative on Colbert, Stephen, et al., "HarvardX and MITx: The First Year of Open Online Courses, Fall 2012-Summer 2013," *HarvardX and MITx Working Paper No.1*, January 21, 2014) 13, accessible at <https://dspace.mit.edu/bitstream/handle/1721.1/96649/SSRN-id2381263.pdf?sequence=1>, accessed on 10.04.19.

35 *Letters of Paul Course Report*, 28.

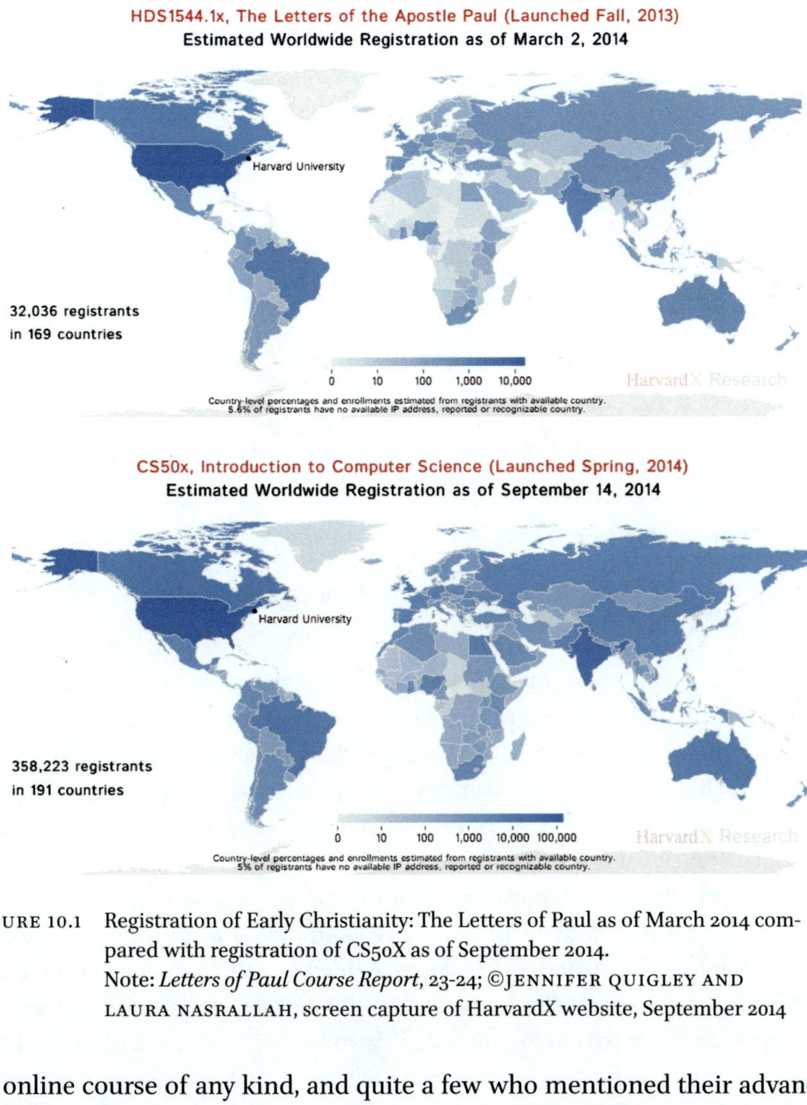

FIGURE 10.1 Registration of Early Christianity: The Letters of Paul as of March 2014 compared with registration of CS50X as of September 2014.
Note: *Letters of Paul Course Report*, 23-24; ©JENNIFER QUIGLEY AND LAURA NASRALLAH, screen capture of HarvardX website, September 2014

an online course of any kind, and quite a few who mentioned their advanced age were some of our most enthusiastic voices in discussion threads.

The student-registrants for our course did not evidence the gender and educational diversity for which we had hoped. HarvardX MOOC enrollment on the whole is male-dominated; the average course is close to 60% male.[36] Our course moved slightly more toward gender parity, at about 53% men.[37] One

36 Nesterkos, Sergiy O., et al., "Gender Composition," *HarvardX Insights*, 2014. <http://harvardx.harvard.edu/harvardx-insights/gender-composition>, accessed on 10.04.19.

37 *Letters of Paul Course Report*, 25.

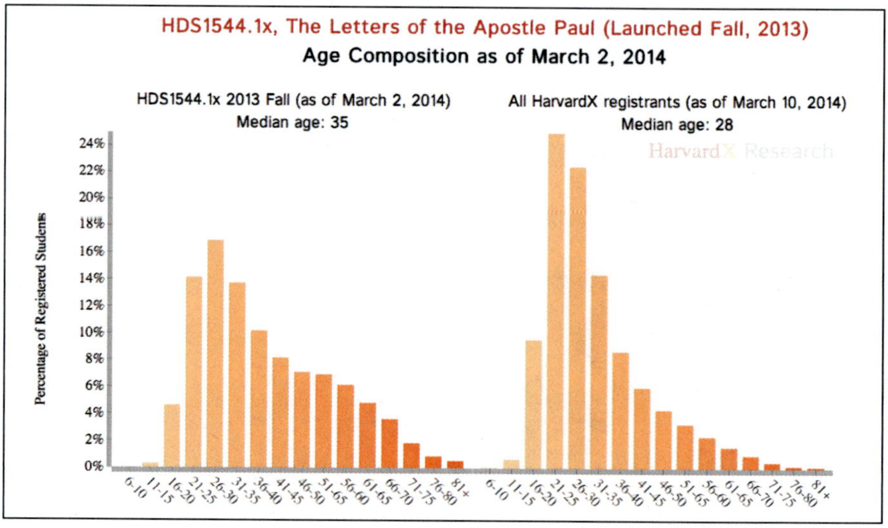

FIGURE 10.2 Early Christianity: The Letters of Paul, Age composition as of March 2014. Note: *Letters of Paul Course Report*, 28; ©JENNIFER QUIGLEY AND LAURA NASRALLAH, screen capture of HarvardX website, March 2014

other area where MOOCs, including our course, fall short is in a striking education gap.[38] 72.7 % of our students held undergraduate degrees, and 5.8% of our students hold doctoral degrees, while only 1.7% had less than a secondary level education. That is, three times as many Ph.D.s participated as persons without a high school degree or GED (United States educational terminology for General Education Development or high school equivalency degree).[39]

To return to our initial questions about feminist pedagogy and online education in our course, we have both positive and mixed results about whether and how our course formed a virtual space in which all could learn from each other. Early Christianity: The Letters of Paul created a truly global classroom and represented improvement in gender parity, in comparison with other HarvardX MOOCs. The education gap of our course, however, was a sobering

38 Rohs, Matthias, Ganz, Mario, "MOOCs and the Claim of Education for All: A Disillusion by Empirical Data" <http://www.irrodl.org/index.php/irrodl/article/view/2033/3527>, accessed on 10.04.19.

39 *Letters of Paul Course Report*, 26-27. This education gap varied depending on country of enrollment, ranging from 59.1% of South African enrollees to 88.9% of French enrollees holding a bachelor's degree or higher. Every country, however, had a significant majority of students who completed post-secondary education. This means that our course did not reach as broad or diverse of an audience as we would have liked; whether this had to do with our course offering or with the larger structures of edX/HarvardX is unclear.

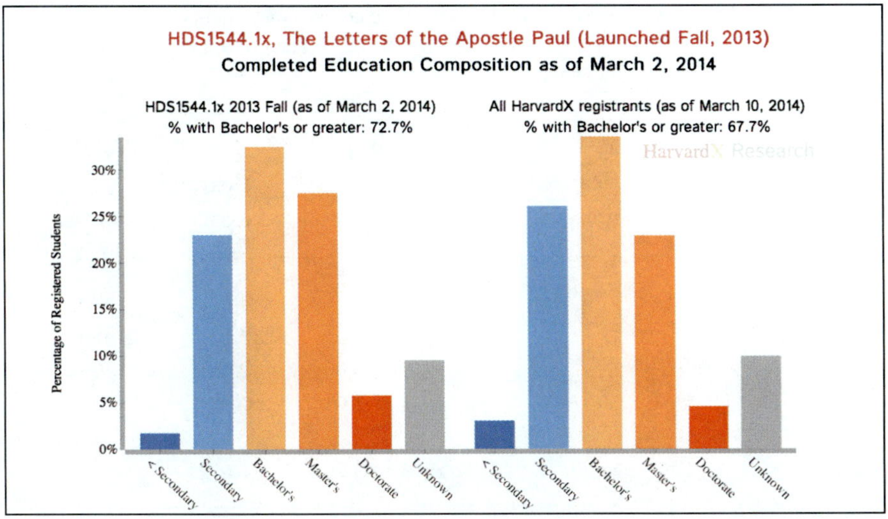

FIGURE 10.3 Early Christianity: The Letters of Paul, completed education composition as of March 2014; ©JENNIFER QUIGLEY AND LAURA NASRALLAH, screen capture of HarvardX website, March 2014

reminder that even when classes are free and online, that does not mean they are truly accessible to all learners.

4 Outcomes from Early Christianity: The Letters of Paul

The end of course survey proffered to students of our course was mainly formulated by edX according to the data that they wished to glean. We were able to add a few questions specific to our course concerns. 2,748 students took this end-of-course survey about their learning experience. Some of the questions on the survey asked students to respond about their learning. When asked how much students had learned in the course, 83% reported learning "a fair amount" or "a great deal." Only 4% of students reported learning little or nothing from the course. 66% of students said that the learning experience was "better" or "much better" than others they had had, 24% said that the experience was "about the same," and 10% said the experience was "worse" or "much worse."[40]

Students were asked to also rank the aspects of the course in which they perceived that they learned the most.[41] Options included videos, readings, assessments, and discussions. A table of student responses follows, with a scale

40 *Letters of Paul Course Report*, 29.

41 This section excerpts from the *Letters of Paul Course Report*, 31-34.

TABLE 10.2 End of course survey: Student learning and course components; ©JENNIFER QUIGLEY AND LAURA NASRALLAH, screen capture of HarvardX website, September 2014

Ranking	Answer	1 (learned most)	2	3	4 (learned least)	Total
1	Videos	995	307	58	34	1394
2	Readings	327	899	132	36	1394
3	Assessments	22	56	703	613	1394
4	Discussion Forums	50	132	501	711	1394
Total		1394	1394	1394	1394	

of 1 (perceived learning the most from this portion of the course) to 4 (perceived learning the least from this portion of the course) (Table 10.2).

Qualitatively, students were also asked open-response questions, including one soliciting what were the most intellectually transformative parts of the course. Both the quantitative and qualitative responses aligned well with the stated learning goals of the course, and students largely responded that learning about the historical, political, and literary context of the letters of Paul were the most intellectually transforming, often citing specific lessons, concepts, and course content. Not atypically, one student wrote:

> The lessons about historical, social and religious context were transforming. Learning about letter writing helped me to understand the purpose of the prescript and letter format, which had always confused me. Finally and perhaps most importantly lesson 11 on wisdom, knowledge and prophecy has given me insights that are still developing and may still develop for some time to come, for me.

Other students also reported being transformed by the aspects of the course that focused on material culture in antiquity; again, many mentioned specific sites, images, and concepts. Some students were even inspired to do additional research outside of the bounds of the course. One student wrote:

> Household Management discussion / Aristotle. Considering the veiled women section in Corinthians. Walking out here to read L. Nasrallah's article on Thessalonike and understanding the apse mosaics. (Empire and Apocalypse). Great article!

There were frequent positive responses to the lecture videos, doctoral student discussion videos, and the videos with Prof. AnneMarie Luijendijk and Rev. John Stendahl. One student wrote:

> I loved John Stendahl's reading of Krister Stendahl's lecture on "Why I Love the Bible." That lecture left me thinking and talking about the topics he raised for a couple of weeks and I could probably talk about it today too!

Many students reported being most transformed by interactions and conversation with fellow students. Students found interactions with one another to be both challenging and intellectually productive. One typical response follows:

> I was transformed by the discussions being so civil that it made my real life discussion also very civil and fruitful.

Lastly, many students reflected on their learning about taking responsibility for their interpretations, and quite a few reported feeling better equipped to read the Bible. Two particularly reflective responses follow:

> *Response 1*
> As an atheist enrolling in a course offered through a divinity school, I was understandably nervous about what I was getting myself into. Perhaps I shouldn't have been so surprised to see that the materials were presented in such a scholarly way. I expected to be told what Paul's letters meant from a theological standpoint; instead I learned how to read Paul's letters. Having an understanding the social/cultural/historical context is crucial for reading these ancient texts and now I have the tools to decipher them on my own.

> *Response 2*
> This course has helped me to do something different: to look at the texts themselves and notice the subtleties of language and vocabulary, read what I can of the history and social setting, and trust that these all of these things matter.
>
> Going forward, the experience of this course encourages me to do a couple of things:
>
> Read more slowly. I read and/or hear these texts all the time. I read one verse knowing the verse that comes next, which is to say that I am not paying close attention anymore. To do the work in this course, I had to read slowly and with a beginner's ear.

> Read the whole letter more often. The lectionary snippets are fine, but they are read out of context. Context matters: literary, social and political. Take guesses. All anyone has is the nutmeg grater:[42] everyone is guessing. Some guesses are better informed than others, BUT some guesses that now pass as certain knowledge were not good guesses at all. Junia[43] will always remind me of that.
>
> Check the data. More than once in this course I presumed my response to the Discussion Question would go in one direction, only to find that the data I could gather did not point in that direction at all.
>
> Pay attention to what I feel when I read. I was taught to do that in my first scripture courses, but one forgets and gets busy and opens the commentary too soon.
>
> Finally, there are those wonderful Bibliographies at the end of each Day's lesson. I originally planned to audit this course – just listen in – in the hopes that I would be able to figure out what folks are saying about Paul today, in 2014. By Day 1 or 2 I had changed my mind and decided to do the work. What a good decision. Seldom does it happen that the rewards are commensurate with the work, but that was the case in this course. I attribute that to careful planning in the course design. Bravo course designers! By the time we were mid-way through, I knew that if I put the time and effort in to the exercise, I would learn something. In fact, I learned a lot. AND I have these wonderful bibliographies to explore.

Turning to the question of whether and how our MOOC was able to create a pedagogical space in which students and teachers understood themselves as co-learners and producers of knowledge, the data reveals a remarkable level of connection and engagement for an online setting. 80% of respondents to our end-of-course survey (which included 2,748 of our more active participants) reported feeling somewhat, very, or extremely connected to the community of learners and instructors for the course, while 85% felt that the teaching team was somewhat, very, or extremely accessible.[44]

42 The Day 2 lecture quoted Carolyn Steedman on archives, saying, "Your craft is to conjure a social system from a nutmeg grater." Steedman, Carolyn, "Something She Called a Fever: Michelet, Derrida, and Dust," *The American Historical Review* 106, no. 4, October 2001, 1165.

43 Here the student refers to the lecture and discussion in our course about Rom 16:7. The phrase "Junia, remarkable among the apostles," which in Greek is clearly a female personal name, was emended in various manuscripts and translations to Junias, a male name. See Brooten, Bernadette, "Junia ... Outstanding among the Apostles," in: Swidler, Leonard and Arlene, eds., *Women Priests: A Catholic Commentary on the Vatican Declaration,* New York: Paulist, 1977, 141-144.

44 *Letters of Paul Course Report*, 29.

The students also produced their own subcommunities during the course. As mentioned before, language-specific groups formed themselves; for example, a Spanish-language group emerged on Facebook and one student translated the lectures into Portuguese. Community-building was not just virtual: students reported having in-person meetings with other students in the course. Moreover, students extended the community of learners: 40% of respondents completed the course or used some of its materials in face-to-face meetings with others.[45] From informal conversations with friends and family, to formal local meet-ups, to church and other faith community groups taking the course together, a significant number of students embodied the collaborative value of the teaching team by finding in-person communities with which to learn. Students who met face-to-face were asked to describe this experience. Two of these responses follow:

> *Response 1*
> There were so many in the class, so many ideas and points of views. We had a local group of ten who took the class and are still meeting to discuss the readings. I would have like to be placed in a group of ten from around the world. I think it would have been useful for me to have a specific group to respond to.
>
> *Response 2*
> I talked my church Bible study group into doing it, so we'd meet once per week for further discussion.[46]

In addition, some "super-users" of the various course venues, particularly the discussion thread, regularly engaged with one another, and even reached out to one another at the end of the course. We had quite a few closing comments that thanked not only teaching staff members, but also fellow students by name. One example follows:

> As lessons went by I found myself doing more research in internet on the subject then I would have expected at the beginning and in the end a new knowledge came to me and made me appreciate more and more the assignments and the discussion treads, even if I don't know why by the time I finished reading my assignments, all where full of posts and comments and I mostly restricted myself to comments on somebody also posts. How

45 *Letters of Paul Course Report*, 30.
46 *Letters of Paul Course Report*, 30.

> did they do it I don't know but my compliments to l****** – A********* – A************ and all others who supplied me with a lot of information. [*sic*]

On the whole, the teaching team was pleasantly surprised by the civility and deep engagement of these conversations. For example, on our discussion boards, an atheist and a born-again Christian disagreed respectfully (Fig. 10.4).

In other cases, students gently corrected one another and pushed each another to think more critically (Fig. 10.5).

Students thus practiced the goals of the course. As the course was concluding they also in their own words reflected some of the goals of the course. On February 17, 2014, one student posted on Facebook:

> Excellent video – my favorite quote is "In Paul's letters, theological language and … thought is a response to historical realities." Perhaps more than anything, this course has shown me that historians, no matter where they are coming from, still carry bias, and Paul's letters, like all of the Bible, must be understood (especially by people of faith), in their historical context, not just with the eyes of faith. Our bias does get in the way! Whether by omission of "small details" or facts, or history, or by myopia with issues of the time, our viewpoints can hinder an accurate (or more accurate) understanding of the truth.

This post gave Nasrallah the opportunity to expand, articulating a feminist hermeneutics:

> Thank you so much, —. And I want to expand a bit on what you said. Our biases can hinder, and they can also expand the range of questions that we can ask about the historical context (and theological potentials) of Paul's letters – that is, our standpoints both limit us and help us to see from new angles. That is one reason that studying in community, where others can push, correct, and learn from us, is so great! (posted February 23, 2014).

Some students articulated the feminist pedagogical claim that they were co-creators of learning in the course. On February 5, 2014, as the course was coming to a close, one student offered a post: "Thank you very much for the knowledge and experience gained through this course! Maybe there should be a sequel in the future, a part B perhaps!!!" Another responded to her post,

User P
2 months ago

I have to start this by stating that I am a very strong atheist with a rather negative view of Paul, but I wanted to take this course in order to learn more about him. In my first proper study of his prescripts, my view of Paul has become even more negative. I understand the need for the from and to aspects of letter writing, but his continual pointing out of his "apostleship" and "his calling by God" is no different that Vernon Wayne Howell changing his name to David Koresh. By changing his name to David Koresh, he was calling himself the spiritual descendant of King David and a messiah involved in the work of God. How is Paul any different? He didn't have the ability to change his name to something as meaningful as David Koresh, but he could continually point out his so-called commission by God, which is what he did.

Sorry, I'm not trying to ruffle anyone's feathers here, but I'm supposed to respond somehow and I'd rather be honest about what I see and feel.

Edit ✕ Delete

I think the difference between Paul and David Koresh is that Paul was humble and recognized that he was nothing without God, while David Koresh manipulated people and eventually his actions led to their deaths.

-posted 2 months ago by **User T**

I am born again. You have not ruffled my feathers. I think Paul makes such titles of himself for the benefit of the group to whom he writes. The titles I think made it easier for the ekklesai to relate to the message they were receiving. As for his name, and appointment they were given to him by God himself. He used the name in the commission of that appointment which was to spread the Gospel. I can't say about David Koresh, he wrote nothing I am remotely familiar with and if he did write something I most likely would not have wasted my time reading it.

-posted 2 months ago by **User B**

@UserT Very nice clarity

-posted 2 months ago by **User B**

I think Paul could appear humble when it suited him, but he wasn't really humble, particularly when he was angry. He spoke of himself as superior to other apostles; he called himself a father of the people when Jesus clearly said there is no father but one. Paul's teachings were of Paul, not those of Jesus. We only have his word of his appointment by God and he always seemed to use that as self-promotion, which is not humble at all.

-posted 2 months ago by **User P**

I think you bring up a couple of interesting points. However, I think we also need to understand that these letters are only a very small glimpse into Paul's life. I don't know if he is humble or not (and as a disclaimer, I am a Christian who tends to put Paul on the arrogant side of things), because we only have the letters. Additionally, we have to be careful not to read our own cultural interpretation of greetings into a 1st century Roman world. If there were common practices, especially in letter writing, then they likely were not intended or perceived as prideful or arrogant.
I think your claim that he used this for self promotion is interesting. I don't know if I'd compare it to David Koresh, honestly, but what evidence makes you think it was used in this way? I am curious as to why you think this because Paul is one of those people, especially when taken up in our own society, that tends to irk some (again, myself sometimes included).

-posted 2 months ago by **User A**

FIGURE 10.4 Sample student discussion 1; ©JENNIFER QUIGLEY AND LAURA NASRALLAH, screen capture of HarvardX website, September 2014

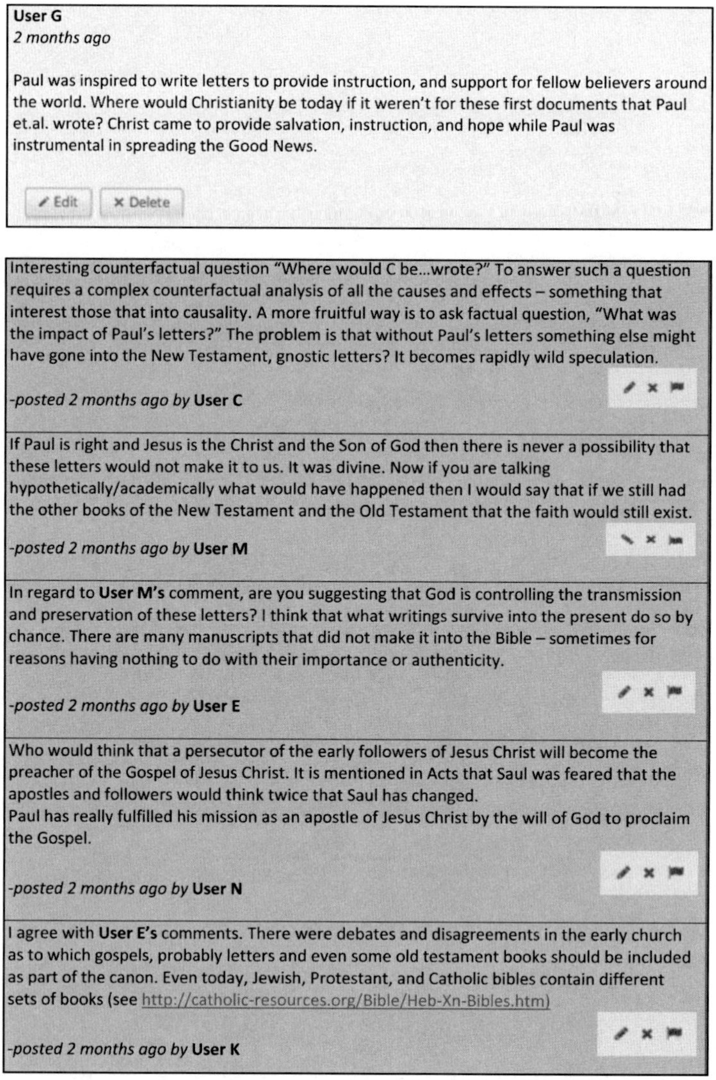
User G
2 months ago

Paul was inspired to write letters to provide instruction, and support for fellow believers around the world. Where would Christianity be today if it weren't for these first documents that Paul et.al. wrote? Christ came to provide salvation, instruction, and hope while Paul was instrumental in spreading the Good News.

Edit × Delete

Interesting counterfactual question "Where would C be...wrote?" To answer such a question requires a complex counterfactual analysis of all the causes and effects – something that interest those that into causality. A more fruitful way is to ask factual question, "What was the impact of Paul's letters?" The problem is that without Paul's letters something else might have gone into the New Testament, gnostic letters? It becomes rapidly wild speculation.

-posted 2 months ago by **User C**

If Paul is right and Jesus is the Christ and the Son of God then there is never a possibility that these letters would not make it to us. It was divine. Now if you are talking hypothetically/academically what would have happened then I would say that if we still had the other books of the New Testament and the Old Testament that the faith would still exist.

-posted 2 months ago by **User M**

In regard to **User M's** comment, are you suggesting that God is controlling the transmission and preservation of these letters? I think that what writings survive into the present do so by chance. There are many manuscripts that did not make it into the Bible – sometimes for reasons having nothing to do with their importance or authenticity.

-posted 2 months ago by **User E**

Who would think that a persecutor of the early followers of Jesus Christ will become the preacher of the Gospel of Jesus Christ. It is mentioned in Acts that Saul was feared that the apostles and followers would think twice that Saul has changed.
Paul has really fulfilled his mission as an apostle of Jesus Christ by the will of God to proclaim the Gospel.

-posted 2 months ago by **User N**

I agree with **User E's** comments. There were debates and disagreements in the early church as to which gospels, probably letters and even some old testament books should be included as part of the canon. Even today, Jewish, Protestant, and Catholic bibles contain different sets of books (see http://catholic-resources.org/Bible/Heb-Xn-Bibles.htm)

-posted 2 months ago by **User K**

FIGURE 10.5 Sample student discussion 2; ©JENNIFER QUIGLEY AND LAURA NASRALLAH, screen capture of HarvardX website, September 2014

saying: "We are the sequel … it's one thing studying and gaining knowledge but another to put it into practice. We are now in the fortunate position of being equipped to create our own 'Letters of Paul' II."

5 Final Reflections

As the teaching staff worked on the production of edX's Early Christianity: The Letters of Paul, we also engaged in a mini-seminar with readings that allowed us to consider broader issues in the industry of education.[47] A central conversation point of our mini-seminar was that many of us on the teaching staff were drawn to higher education because in the university we find a quasi-utopian space (as perhaps also in religious communities and activist communities) to think about the world differently: to experiment with means of liberation and with productive struggle, to learn lessons for transformation to take out and apply in broader contexts, as well as to further the work of disciplined attention to materials from antiquity.

As problematic as online education can be for as universities and for-profit ventures seek to monetize online learning, the MOOC also gave us some hope about transformative thinking and practices happening in the online teaching environment. The MOOC in particular and online education in general need not be primarily a concession to the expense and challenge of bringing students into one place. It can be a way to accommodate a hunger for knowledge, the longing for continuing education and broad communication and community. Ashon Crawley's *Blackpentecostal Breath* touches upon the topic of transforming the academy, focusing on "blackpentecostal aesthetic practice." This practice "'ruins' the normative, neoliberal university, 'ruins' such a zone of inhabitation in the service of producing otherwise possibilities," writes Crawley.[48] It is these otherwise possibilities that interest Crawley, the overflow of glossolalia, the university as "a great gathering of resources that should, it should be said, be exploited and put in the service of the search into the dark, dense folks of nothingness, the dark, dense folds of plentitude."[49] A MOOC, particularly one with feminist pedagogical frameworks and inspired by the theorizing of education and pedagogy by scholars like hooks and Crawley, has the potential for this effervescent glossolalic transformation of the university, drawing in a

---

47 Although the seminar's readings were largely focused on debates about MOOCs in 2013-2014, as well as feminist pedagogy and discussions about pedagogy in biblical studies, a broader seminar might include Veblen, Thorsten, *The Higher Learning in America: A Memorandum on the Conduct of Universities by Business Men* (1918), Baltimore: Johns Hopkins University Press, 2015. Veblen seems prescient in his concerns about the organizational scheme of universities and his analysis of and concerns about "this incursion of business principles into the affairs of learning" (217). For a critique of neoliberalism in the university, see Brown, Wendy, *Undoing the Demos: Neoliberalism's Stealth Revolution*, New York: Zone Books, 2015, chapter 6: "Educating Human Capital." For our mini-seminar syllabus, see Appendix A, *Letters of Paul Course Report*, <https://div.hds.harvard.edu/lettersofpaul/course_report.pdf>, accessed on 10.04.19.

48 Crawley, Ashon, *Blackpentecostal Breath: An Aesthetics of Possibility*, New York: Fordham University Press, 2016, 250.

49 Crawley, Ashon, 2016, 237. See also Harney, Stefano, Moten, Fred, *The Undercommons: Fugitive Planning and Black Study*, chapter 2: "The University and the Undercommons," Wivenhoe: Minor Compositions, 2013, 22-43.

diversity of voices, and spilling over the bounds of brick and mortar and into the larger world.

References

Anand, Bharat, *The Content Trap: A Strategist's Guide to Digital Change*, New York: Random House, 2016, 299-344.

Barber, Michael, Donnelly, Katelyn, Rizvi, Saad, "An Avalanche is Coming: Higher Education and the revolution ahead", London: Institute for Public Policy Research, 2013, <http://www.avalancheiscoming.com/>, accessed on 10.04.19.

Brakke, David, "Scriptural Practices in Early Christianity: Toward a New History of the Canon," in: Ulrich, Jörg et al., eds., *Invention, Rewriting, Usurpation: Discursive Fights for Religious Traditions in Antiquity*, Frankfurt am Main: Peter Lang, 2012, 263-280.

Brooten, Bernadette, ""Junia ... Outstanding among the Apostles," in: Swidler, Leonard and Arlene, eds., *Women Priests: A Catholic Commentary on the Vatican Declaration*, New York: Paulist, 1977, 141-144.

Brown, Wendy, *Undoing the Demos: Neoliberalism's Stealth Revolution*, New York: Zone Books, 2015, chapter 6: "Educating Human Capital." For our mini-seminar syllabus, see Appendix A, *Letters of Paul Course Report.*

Callahan, Vicki, "Toward Networked Digital Scholarship: Mindful Media, Participatory Learning, and Distributed Authorship in the Digital Economy," *Cinema Journal* 53.1, (2013) 156-163.

Chick, Nancy, Hassel, Holly, "Don't Hate Me Because I'm Virtual: Feminist Pedagogy in the Online Classroom," *Feminist Teacher*, Vol. 19, No. 3, 2009, 195-215.

Colbert, Stephen, et al., "HarvardX and MITx: The First Year of Open Online Courses, Fall 2012-Summer 2013," HarvardX and MITx Working Paper No.1, January 21, 2014, 13, accessible at <http://dspace.mit.edu/bitstream/handle/1721.1/96649/SSRN-id2381263.pdf?sequence=1>; accessed on 10.04.19.

Crawley, Ashon, *Blackpentecostal Breath: An Aesthetics of Possibility*, New York: Fordham University Press, 2016, 250.

Cronan Rose, Ellen, "'This Class Meets in Cyberspace': Women's Studies via Distance Education," *Feminist Teacher*, Vol. 9.2, 1995, 53-60.

Harney, Stefano, Moten, Fred, *The Undercommons: Fugitive Planning and Black Study*, chapter 2: "The University and the Undercommons," *Wivenhoe: Minor Compositions*, 2013, 22-43.

hooks, bell, *Teaching to Transgress: Education as the Practice of Freedom*, New York: Routledge, 1994.

Johnson-Debaufre, Melanie, Nasrallah, Laura, "Beyond the Heroic Paul: Toward a Feminist and Decolonizing Approach to the Letters of Paul," in: Stanley, Christopher, ed.,

The Colonized Apostle: Paul Through Postcolonial Eyes, Minneapolis: Fortress, 2011, 161-174.

Lockard, Joseph, Pergum, Mark, "Brave New Classrooms: Democratic Education and the Internet", in: *Digital Formations* 37, New York: Peter Lang, NY, 2007.

Losh, Elizabeth, Wernimont, Jacqueline, Wexler, Laura, Wu, Hong-An, "Putting the Human Back into the Digital Humanities: Feminism, Generosity, and Mess," *Debates in the Digital Humanities*, Gold, Matthew K., Klein, Lauren F., eds., Minneapolis, MN: University of Minnesota Press, 2016, 92-103.

Marchal, Joseph, "To What Ends? Biblical Studies and Critical Rhetorical Engagement(s) for a 'Safer' World," SBL Forum n.p. Online: <http://sbl-site.org/Article.aspx?ArticleID=550>, accessed on 10.04.19.

Marchal, Joseph, *The People beside Paul: The Philippian Assembly and History from Below*, Atlanta: SBL Press, 2015.

Martin, Dale, *Pedagogy of the Bible: An Analysis and Proposal*, Louisville, KY: Westminster John Knox, 2008.

Nasrallah, Laura, *Archaeology and the Letters of Paul*, Oxford: Oxford University Press, 2018.

Nesterkos, Sergiy O., et al., "Gender Composition," *HarvardX Insights*, 2014, <http://harvardx.harvard.edu/harvardx-insights/gender-composition>, accessed March 2014.

Rohs, Matthias, Ganz, Mario, "MOOCs and the Claim of Education for All: A Disillusion by Empirical Data", <http://www.irrodl.org/index.php/irrodl/article/view/2033/3527>, accessed on 10.04.19.

Schüssler Fiorenza, Elisabeth, *Democratizing Biblical Studies: Toward an Emancipatory Educational Space*, Louisville, KY: Westminster John Knox, 2009.

Schüssler Fiorenza, Elisabeth, "The Ethics of Biblical Interpretation: Decentering Biblical Scholarship," *JBL* 107.1, 1988, 3-17.

Steedman, Carolyn, "Something She Called a Fever: Michelet, Derrida, and Dust," *The American Historical Review* 106, no. 4, October 2001, 1165.

Veblen, Thorsten, *The Higher Learning in America: A Memorandum on the Conduct of Universities by Business Men* (1918), Baltimore: Johns Hopkins University Press, 2015.

Whitehouse, Pamela, "Women's Studies Online: An Oxymoron?", *Women's Studies Quarterly* 30, No. ¾, 2002, 209-222.

List of Internet Resources

<http://www.thegreatcourses.com/>, accessed on 10.04.19.

<https://www.edx.org/course/jesus-scripture-tradition-notredamex-th120-1x>, accessed on 10.04.19.

<https://www.coursera.org/learn/the-talmud>, accessed on 10.04.19.

<https://www.edx.org/xseries/world-religions-through-scriptures>, accessed on 10.04.19.

<https://www.bibleodyssey.org/>, accessed on 10.04.19.

<http://archive.boston.com/bostonglobe/ideas/brainiac/2013/05/san_jose_state.html>, accessed on 10.04.19.

<http://www.chronicle.com/article/The-Document-an-Open-Letter/138937>, accessed on 10.04.19.

<http://www.chronicle.com/article/Michael-Sandel-Responds/139021/>, accessed on 10.04.19.

<http://www.justiceharvard.org/>, accessed on 10.04.19.

<https://www.edx.org/course/early-christianity-letters-paul-harvardx-hds1544-1x.>, accessed on 10.04.19.

<http://div.hds.harvard.edu/lettersofpaul/>, accessed on 10.04.19.

<http://www.thechristians.com>, accessed on 10.04.19.

<http://femtechnet.newschool.edu/docc2013>, accessed on 10.04.19.

<https://genius.com/2636137>, accessed on 10.04.19.

<https://www.edx.org/about/research-pedagogy>, accessed on 10.04.19.

<http://harvardx.harvard.edu/harvardx-working-papers>, accessed on 10.04.19.

<http://harvardx.harvard.edu/research>, accessed on 10.04.19.

<https://div.hds.harvard.edu/lettersofpaul/course_report.pdf>, accessed on 10.04.19.

CHAPTER 11

Learning from Jesus' Wife: What Does Forgery Have to Do with the Digital Humanities?

James F. McGrath

1 Introduction

Early in the summer of 2016, interest in the papyrus fragment known as the Gospel of Jesus' Wife had begun to wane. Then investigative journalist Ariel Sabar published an article unveiling a great deal of truly fascinating evidence that he had uncovered, related not only to the Gospel of Jesus' Wife itself, but also the person who we can now say was almost certainly responsible for the forgery. The article told of connections with sex and pornography, scams and financial catastrophes, which made the real story behind the text seem even more sensational than the contents of the papyrus fragment itself.[1] Since then, still other new texts have come to light and made news headlines, including purported additional Dead Sea Scrolls, and what has been hailed as the oldest papyrus mentioning Jerusalem.[2] Israeli prime minister Benjamin Netanyahu appealed to the latter within days of the news of the fragment first appearing, as he responded to a proposed UNESCO declaration about the purported lack of ancient Jewish connection to the Temple Mount. Meanwhile, the Jordanian Department of Antiquities finally offered its assessment that the lead codices, touted by David Elkington as dating from the time when Jesus was alive, are modern fakes, a conclusion that most discussion of them online had already drawn.[3] These and many other examples illustrate how the work of scholarship on ancient history intersects with contemporary concerns,

1 Sabar, Ariel, "The Unbelievable Tale of Jesus' Wife," *The Atlantic*, July/August 2016, <https://www.theatlantic.com/magazine/archive/2016/07/the-unbelievable-tale-of-jesus-wife/485573/>, accessed on 10.04.19. On the broader context – the question of whether the historical figure of Jesus was married – see Le Donne, Anthony, *The Wife of Jesus: Ancient Texts and Modern Scandals*, London: Oneworld, 2013.

2 Moss, Candida, Baden, Joel, "Is Israel's Big New Find for Real?" *The Daily Beast*, 11th of June 2016, <http://www.thedailybeast.com/articles/2016/11/06/is-israel-s-big-new-find-a-hoax.html>, accessed on 10.04.19.

3 Jordan Times, "Antiquities agency chief says Jordan Codices fake", *Jordan Times* March 9th, 2017, <http://www.jordantimes.com/news/local/antiquities-agency-chief-says-jordan-codices-fake>, accessed on 10.04.19.

ranging from debates about celibacy in the Catholic Church to ongoing tensions in the Middle East. A successful forgery can make an enormous difference, but so too can an unsuccessful one – or one that is made intentionally with a view to it being exposed, since a forgery that claims to conveniently support some political or religious claim can further undermine it in the eyes of the public when the truth is revealed.[4] In addition to cyberwarfare and robotics, we may well also see forgery of antiquities increasingly used as an ideological weapon in the years to come. Mistaking a forgery for an authentic ancient artifact can also undermine public confidence in academic expertise. Whatever the motives happen to be, forgeries and fakes will undoubtedly continue to appear on the antiquities market, and scholars of antiquity will still have their work cut out for them.

The case of the so-called Gospel of Jesus' Wife provides an excellent test case around which to ask about the role of the digital humanities in not only the exposing but also the creation of forgeries. Our focus here will not be on the text itself, or the specific arguments for and against its authenticity, which have been rehearsed elsewhere, but rather on the principles and methods which characterized academics' reception of and engagement with the text – and with one another in discussing the text. The scholarly work on this particular papyrus fragment illustrates how scholarship is and can be done in the context of today's technology and social media, as well as highlighting both the potential and pitfalls of these methods. But the incident also provides opportunities for insights into the trajectories that forgery, the detection of forgery, and the digital humanities are likely to take moving forward into the future. The height of the discussion about this text is just far enough in the past that we can feel like we have enough information on the basis of which to comment, and yet not so far that it reflects a different technological setting, or something likely to be considered merely "old news".

2 Learning to Create Forgeries

It is appropriate to begin with what we can ascertain about the *creation* of the Gospel of Jesus' Wife, before moving on to the *exposure* thereof as a forgery. The Digital Humanities is not simply synonymous with the drive towards open access, and the placement of both primary texts and scholarship online where

4 Bak, János M., Geary, Patrick J., Klaniczay, Gábor (eds.), *National Cultivation of Culture: Manufacturing a Past for the Present. Forgery and Authenticity in Medievalist Texts and Objects in Nineteenth-Century Europe*, 1, Leiden: Brill, 2014.

the public as well as scholars can access them. However, digitization and access are major concerns of ours, and without continued progress and developments in these areas, the Digital Humanities in the full sense would be severely diminished. It may thus be disheartening to reflect on the fact that the Digital Humanities makes forgery easier. We saw this in the case of the Gospel of Jesus' Wife, in which the forger used Michael Grondin's interlinear of the Gospel of Thomas, which he had made available online, as well as utilizing Herbert Thompson's edition of the Qau Codex, which is in the public domain, to produce the accompanying forgery of part of the Gospel of John.[5] Images and transcriptions of manuscripts made available online will continue to provide forgers with things they can duplicate. This trend is likely to increase and expand in the future. It is likely that 3D analyses and descriptions of genuine artifacts will soon be fed into 3D printers to produce fake artifacts, whether exact replicas of the original or ones modified to appear even more significant and valuable. At present, such objects would be unlikely to pass authenticity tests, but this may change in the future.[6] Either way, if objects get news coverage before being tested, the public might be influenced by sensational headlines, never reading rebuttals that appear less prominently later. The very discussion of the issues related to the dating of the Gospel of Jesus' Wife and its identification as a forgery can potentially serve as an instruction manual for future forgers, helping them to produce more convincing fakes, as for instance

5 Askeland, Christian, "A Lycopolitan Forgery of John's Gospel," *NTS 61:3*, July 2015, 314-334, Askeland, Christian,, "A Fake Coptic John and Its Implications for 'The Gospel of Jesus's Wife'," *TynBul 65*, 2014, 1-10.

6 Rabinowitz, Adam, "The Work of Archaeology in the Age of Digital Surrogacy," in: Olson, Brandon R., Caraher, William (eds.), *Visions of Substance: 3D Imaging in Mediterranean Archaeology*, Grand Forks: The Digital Press @ The University of North Dakota, 2015, 29-30 suggests that we may not need to worry. See, however, the example of the Van Gogh replica that matched the brush strokes, frame, and even hand-written notes and labels on the reverse of the canvas of the original, using Fujifilm's process of Reliefography, as described in Liszewski, "3D Printing and Scanning." This was followed by the creation of a new painting created using software that analyzed the characteristics of the famous artist's works, as reported on by Brown, Mark, "'New Rembrandt' to be unveiled in Amsterdam," *The Guardian*, <https://www.theguardian.com/artanddesign/2016/apr/05/new-rembrandt-to-be-unveiled-in-amsterdam>, accessed <http://www.jordantimes.com/news/local/antiquities-agency-chief-says-jordan-codices-fake>. On other ethical issues related to the 3D printing of replicas of antiquities, see Schroeder, Caroline, "On Palmyra and 3D Modeling Cultural Heritage in the Middle East," *Early Christian Monasticism in the Digital Age* 6/12/2016, <http://earlymonasticism.org/2016/06/12/on-palmyra-and-3d-modeling-cultural-heritage-in-the-middle-east/>, accessed on 10.04.19, <http://www.jordantimes.com/news/local/antiquities-agency-chief-says-jordan-codices-fake>, and Bond, Sarah, "The Ethics Of 3D-Printing Syria's Cultural Heritage," *Forbes*, 22nd of September 2016, <https://www.forbes.com/sites/drsarahbond/2016/09/22/does-nycs-new-3d-printed-palmyra-arch-celebrate-syria-or-just-engage-in-digital-colonialism/>, accessed on 10.04.19.

when scholars have pointed out how forgers can recycle old papyrus and fake ancient ink. This potential for our work to be used by forgers might dishearten scholars, but it is in no sense an argument against the Digital Humanities. The same printed volumes that have served scholars in the past have also been available to forgers and con artists for them to use. It is inevitable that any products, digital or otherwise, which facilitate scholarship will be open to potential use and misuse by those seeking to profit through deceit. It is not a solution to restrict materials behind paywalls or limit their circulation online, as though that would prevent forgers from getting hold of them.

Moreover, the Digital Humanities has good reason to be working to develop precisely the technologies that forgers can (and inevitably will) utilize. Scholars will develop them for different ends, and will call them different things. But there are legitimate reasons to create high quality convincing replicas or facsimiles of texts and artifacts, such as allowing the originals to be preserved safely in optimal storage conditions, while simultaneously being visible to the public on display in the museum – or even in multiple museums simultaneously. The facsimiles of the Dead Sea Scrolls on display in the Shrine of the Book are not "forgeries," although if they had been produced in precisely the same way but with different intention, and sold to an unwitting customer for an inappropriate price as though genuine, they would be placed in that category.[7] Forgery has to do with the reason why an object is created, and what is done with it, and not its physical characteristics, composition, or date in and of themselves.[8] Facsimiles and replicas are important positive contributions that the Digital Humanities can and should be working to provide, even beyond the longstanding tradition of presenting facsimiles in museum exhibits (as well as their gift shops). Imagine if every archaeology and every ancient language classroom could have access to replicas of incantation bowls, 3D printed from clay, or manuscript facsimiles printed on papyrus. Imagine if producing such items became simple and inexpensive enough that one could give each class multiple collections of pottery or parchment fragments to work with, and for the next semester, simply print new ones. Imagine if museums

---

7 Another example of the blurring of such lines is the bust of Nefertiti. Stierlin, Henri, *Le Buste de Néfertiti. Une imposture de l'égyptologie?*, Gollion: Infolio, 2009, suggests that this famous object began in an effort to create a 3D rendition of the ancient queen, but was later mistaken for an authentic ancient artifact.

8 See further Lenain, Thierry, "The Narrative Structure of Forgery Tales," in: Kila, Joris, Balcells, Marc (eds.), *Heritage and Identity: Cultural Property Crime : An Overview and Analysis of Contemporary Perspectives and Trends*, 1, Leiden: Brill, 2014esp. 39, who emphasizes that forgery in the strict sense, by definition, has primarily to do with the *story* behind the creation of the object, rather than its physical characteristics. See also Ehrman, Bart D., *Forgery and Counterforgery: The Use of Literary Deceit in Early Christian Polemics*, Oxford University Press, 2012.

could more easily create replicas of important texts and artifacts for display, allowing them to be touched and handled by visitors, because they can now easily be replaced when they wear out. These are all legitimate and important positive goals within the framework of the Digital Humanities. The fact that they will inevitably be used by forgers does not make them less appropriate. But it does necessitate that scholars reflect on, discuss, and plan courses of action to respond to such use, and ideally that we do so before and while developing the technology, rather than only later, being proactive rather than allowing ourselves to be caught off guard when the technology is being put to troubling uses.

Most of the above points pertain to the artifacts themselves. As far as the content of manuscripts and inscriptions are concerned, some of the same Digital Humanities projects that have the potential to supply forgers with convenient resources on the internet also have the potential to help reveal forgeries for what they are. This is significant in and of itself, since it is important to the academic study of history that frauds and fakes be exposed, lest our reconstructions of the past be influenced by inauthentic objects and accounts. On the other hand, as academics reflect on the reasons why the digital resources that serve the needs of forgers cannot at present just as quickly lead to their exposure, it brings into focus some of the larger challenges confronting the Digital Humanities, and the role of academics in efforts to combat forgery, as well as in relation to media coverage of purported new finds.

One of the major shifts in the Digital Humanities in recent years is the transformation of a digital desert's economy of scarcity into a deluge that threatens to drown us with more raw data than we could ever hope to tame.[9] The overabundance of material – for instance, the sheer number of manuscripts and out of print books that have been scanned and made available – means we cannot manage it, cannot ever realistically hope to become personally acquainted with it all. This might appear to give the upper hand to the forgers: they need only find an obscure, neglected text online and copy it, and the likelihood of their being detected is minimal. This is not, however, discouraging news. It simply highlights the need to continue working to develop tools that can engage in optical character recognition of manuscripts in ancient languages such as Syriac, Greek, Hebrew, Aramaic, Coptic, and others with which we work. If the results of OCR scanning of older printed texts is imperfect, the

9 Michelson, David A., "Syriaca.org as a Test Case for Digitally Re-Sorting the Ancient World," in: Clivaz, Claire, Dilley, Paul, Hamidović, David (eds.), *Ancient Worlds in Digital Culture*, Leiden: E.J. Brill, 2016, <http://discoverarchive.vanderbilt.edu/handle/1803/8344>, accessed on 10.04.19, 59-66.

results of using OCR on handwritten texts will be all the more so. There will be a need for extensive proofreading of any such scans, work that will itself take decades if not longer. However, as educators who investigate plagiarism cases know, it does not take a precise match with an entire text in order for one to be able to trace copied material to its source. All it takes is verbatim reproduction in some sections, for searches on randomly-selected excerpts to produce positive results. We might therefore hope that one day, as digitization projects continue and OCR technology improves, whenever someone approaches an academic with a fragment of papyrus that they claim to have found, this could be followed on the spot by a Google search, which might fairly quickly suggest that the work too precisely matches another fragment or an online edition of a text, or reveal something else that should give a scholar pause. Of course, Google and most other widely-used search engines are commercial enterprises, and the results they provide may not be what are needed for these sorts of undertakings, even if OCR technology is developed that can accurately recognize ancient scripts, and even if the digitized manuscripts or transcriptions are online and not behind a paywall. Moreover, just as profit motivates forgers, the lack of profitability in the study of most ancient texts may prove to be a disincentive for corporations, keeping them from pursuing technology that would be useful in exposing forgeries for what they are.

It should go without saying that merely matching a known manuscript's contents does not make a new discovery a forgery, nor less valuable. It can be exciting for academics when additional copies of already-known works are found, regardless of how many we already have. However, such additional copies may not be especially valuable in financial terms. For forgeries to be profitable, therefore, it is not enough for them to appear to stem from a particular time and place. Their content needs to appear striking and unique. Nevertheless, the production of something unique yet convincing must inevitably build on existing knowledge of language and of texts. We saw in the case of the Gospel of Jesus' Wife that the forger drew heavily on known texts, making relatively minor modifications so as to make the contents more sensational. Just like students who plagiarize but change a few words, submitting the Gospel of Jesus' Wife to something like *TurnItIn* might have raised red flags immediately – if that database had included or searched online sources such as Grondin's Gospel of Thomas website. Once again, the point is not that this particular commercial tool would be the best one to rely on in such instances. But the same or a similar approach to maintaining and searching databases of texts might nonetheless prove useful in detecting some instances of forgery, just as tools like *TurnItIn* or even a Google search can detect some but by no means all instances of academic dishonesty.

Working to produce replicas, and to develop better and better technologies for doing so, is in the best interest of the education of students and the general public. The same is true for the making available of photos of the ancient artifacts and manuscripts themselves. Participation in the development of technologies and tools of these sorts is also likely to better situate us to recognize when others have used those same resources in an attempt to deceive and/or profit.[10] If those technologies become so advanced that it ceases, at some point in the future, to be possible to distinguish genuine ancient artifacts from forgeries, that will deal a serious blow to our prospects for learning new things about the past. But that technology will be developed, if indeed it can be developed, regardless of whether scholars participate in the process. And that will not change the situation for historians as radically as might first appear. Even today, the authenticity of unprovenanced artifacts is often uncertain.[11] In a future with even more advanced technology to create forgeries, just as in the present day, the most important element will be for academics to do their best to be the first to find ancient texts and other objects, and to document their discovery in a way that vouchsafes their authenticity. For, as Caroline Schroeder writes, "a thorough accounting of provenance is the only means of proving the authenticity of the fragment."[12]

If the mindset of the public (as well as many scholars and scholarly organizations) were to shift so that only texts and other artifacts whose provenance is clear were taken seriously, some of the issues related to forgery might no longer arise. However, the very fact that forgeries have occurred and continued to occur highlights the underlying problem, namely that human beings are not always trustworthy. For this reason, the question will still need to be asked whether and to what extent we can trust archaeologists, papyrologists, museum curators, and others who claim to have acquired items and maintained collections in a manner that safeguards their authenticity. In a context in which our ability to trust, and perhaps the appropriateness of trust, has been called into question or seriously undermined, scholars and the public will con-

10 See e.g. Bernhard, Andrew, "Postscript: A Final Note about the Origin of the Gospel of Jesus' Wife," *NTS* 63:2, 309-316.

11 See Schroeder, Caroline, "Institutional Responsibilities," *Early Christian Monasticism in the Digital Age* 6/23/2016, <http://earlymonasticism.org/2016/06/23/on-institutional-responsibilities-and-on-gender-final-thoughts-on-the-g-of-jesus-wife/>, accessed on 10.04.19, 3-22, on the way replication blurs the distinction between the real and the simulated.

12 Schroeder, Caroline, "Provenance Provenance Provenance," *Early Christian Monasticism in the Digital Age* 6/16/2016, <http://earlymonasticism.org/2016/06/16/provenance-provenance-provenance/>, accessed on 10.04.19.

tinue to hope that scientific tests will offer somewhat objective results that can settle matters, when assertions and even written documentation may not.[13]

3 Learning to Detect Forgeries

In a post on the American Schools of Oriental Research blog, Heather Parker addresses the point just made, as well as the second major point which now follows. She writes,[14]

> Forging an ancient document is difficult and requires expertise in several fields and a variety of resources. However, the same resources produced by scholars who study genuinely ancient texts are available to everyone. Handbooks and reference volumes on the languages and scripts of the Bible and its world are available in libraries and increasingly online. Software and digital fonts for replicating script forms are also readily available, as well as are volumes on the archaeology, history, and culture of the ancient world, complete with maps of archeological sites. The forger's job is easier than ever.
>
> Often forgers will inscribe a fake text on a genuine artifact such as a potsherd, stone object, or piece of papyrus. Such artifacts can often be stolen with relative ease while excavating – legally or illegally – ancient archaeological sites. Looters have ready illegal access to many archaeological sites throughout the Middle East where limited resources or political upheaval prevent adequate protection. Economic conditions also make the illegal antiquities trade particularly lucrative.
>
> [I]n the past, forgeries could be readily detected by scientific methods. For example, any ancient object recovered from the ground, as well as any ancient inscription written on such an object, will be covered with a patina – a film that accrues on an object over time as the result of various chemical processes, such as oxidation and calcification. Patinas can be analyzed spectroscopically to determine their precise chemical makeup,

---

13 See Meadows, David, "Oxyrhynchus and the First Apocalypse of James: Collection History Just Got Murkier," *Rogue Classicism* 12/13/2017, <https://rogueclassicism.com/2017/12/13/oxyrhynchus-and-the-first-apocalypse-of-james-collection-history-just-got-murkier/>, accessed on 10.04.19, for an example of questions being raised about a papyrus whose reputation and status most would consider solid; also Nongbri, "Provenance."

14 Parker, Heather Dana Davis, "Forging Ancient Texts," *The Ancient Near East Today*, vol. 4, n°10, October 2016, <http://www.asor.org/anetoday/2016/10/06/forging-ancient-texts/>, accessed on 10.04.19.

> and whether they include any modern elements. However, forgers, with the proper means, who wish to bolster the authenticity of their products, can now forge patinas using ancient organic materials that would pass various scientific rests, such as carbon-14 dating. Ancient organic materials can also be used to produce "ancient" inks with which to create inscriptions. As the resources for producing forgeries improve, forgers are better equipped than ever to defraud the unwary.

Parker's article was worth quoting at length because it highlights a number of key points that we have learned in connection with the Gospel of Jesus' Wife (as well as other cases). But most importantly, it is important to note the things, which, even though they are true about the Gospel of Jesus' Wife and its creator, are not the things which demonstrated it to be a forgery.

As Caroline Schroeder wrote in commenting on Sabar's Atlantic article, "A lot of the article focuses on the background of the owner of the fragment. This information is all important for understanding the story. I think it's dangerous, however, to imprint upon the fragment whatever 'sketchiness' or 'skeeviness' we attribute to the owner. Does the fact that the owner was involved in pornography necessarily mean the fragment is inauthentic? No. Does his knowledge of Coptic prove inauthenticity? No. Do his financial troubles prove it was a forgery? No."[15] One can add to this list the fact that the text was poorly written, and that it seemed to be a pastiche of material from other Gospels. As was pointed out early on, these same things are true of numerous authentically ancient texts. Some of those texts are so familiar to us, as is their extensive reproduction of earlier source material, that it is really quite shocking that any scholar would propose such features as unambiguously indicative of a modern forgery.[16]

Some scholars' immediate reaction to the fragment was that it is "too good to be true." But we ought never to say such things, and especially not say them as though they demonstrate forgery.[17] If the Gospel of Philip had come to light

15 Schroeder, Caroline, "More on Social Networks and Provenance," *Early Christian Monasticism in the Digital Age* 6/16/2016, <http://earlymonasticism.org/2016/06/16/social-networks/>, accessed March 19th, 2018.

16 See McGrath, James F., "Slow Scholarship : Do Bloggers Rush in Where Jesus' Wife Would Fear to Tread?" in: Burke, Tony (ed.), *Fakes, Forgeries, and Fictions: Writing Ancient and Modern Christian Apocrypha: Proceedings from the 2015 York Christian Apocrypha Symposium*, Eugene: Wipf and Stock, 2017, 326-340.

17 Heide, Martin, "The Moabitica and Their Aftermath: How to Handle a Forgery Affair with an International Impact," in: Lubetski, Meir and Edith (eds.), *New Inscriptions and Seals Relating to the Biblical World: Society of Biblical Literature archaeology and biblical studies*, Williston: Society of Biblical Literature, 2012, 193-241.

today for the first time via an antiquities dealer, one would have been inclined to say the same thing. A text that entices the reader by saying that "Jesus loved Mary and kissed her frequently on the…" only to have a convenient hole in the manuscript that can be filled with any sort of lurid imaginings one wishes? Isn't this "too good, too sensational, to be true"? Yet the manuscript is genuinely ancient–although it can still be considered an ancient *forgery*, since it was not in fact authored by the apostle Philip.[18]

There is thus a wisdom that we not only can but we need to learn from the case of the Gospel of Jesus' Wife, about how one demonstrates forgery, and how and whether one can do so in the present day. Carl Sagan popularized the phrase that "extraordinary claims require extraordinary evidence."[19] It can be argued that a find which would radically change our understanding of history ought to be held to a higher standard of evidence than a more mundane discovery. But be that as it may, the contents of the Gospel of Jesus' Wife did not really constitute an extraordinary claim. It might, if authentic, have represented another example of the kind of viewpoint found in the Gospel of Philip. But that hardly merits the sensation that arose over the fragment.

And so perhaps one tool in our arsenal as we seek to combat forgery is to work to make the public, through the media, more aware of the rather extraordinary things we already find in authenticated ancient texts. Some of those things are sensational, noteworthy, and interesting enough that, on the one hand, forgers will either have to ratchet up the kind of shocking content they include in their creations in an attempt to make them valuable, costing them credibility in the process. On the other hand, we can hope that the public might understand that there is no reason to treat a 4th-century text saying Jesus had a wife as especially newsworthy, which would lessen the financial value of a forgery of this sort, and thus undermine one motivation to produce something like it. To be sure, we should be under no illusion that a greater public awareness of authentic ancient texts will make forgeries go away – and we could be forgiven for pessimistically thinking that informing and persuading the public presents greater hurdles than determining the authenticity of a manuscript.

Many of the points made above have more to do with the prevention of forgeries than their detection, but the latter will never cease to be an important skill. The investigation of the case of the Gospel of Jesus' Wife highlighted the fact that there are limits to what existing scientific techniques such as Carbon 14 dating or Raman Spectrography dating can prove, since ancient materials

18 Ehrman, Bart D., *Forgery and Counterforgery*, 14, 19-20, 30-32, 43, 531.

19 He says this, for instance, in the 1980 Cosmos episode "Encyclopedia Galactica."

can be recycled.[20] That procedure of forgery – destroying ancient writing to make something else with either the ink or papyrus – is disturbing to contemplate in and of itself. Not only is a new object that sows historical confusion produced by the process, but genuine historical knowledge is destroyed as well, sacrificed in an effort to produce something that is fraudulent, but hoped to be more financially valuable. Future technology, however, may help us in our efforts to detect forgeries, beyond what they are currently capable of. For example, computer analysis may be able to identify common features and patterns in forgeries that the human eye and mind might not. The infrared and laser scanning technology that can now allow us to read a scroll without opening it, or one that is badly charred, may also detect aspects of modern forgeries that are currently being missed, and do so in a less invasive or destructive manner than is currently possible. If a technology in its current form cannot provide such insights, the next generation of the technology may. Moreover, even features visible to the naked eye may not be recognized as significant in detecting forgery until computer correlation of large data sets recognizes certain patterns. Yet this should not be an automated process. Automatic plagiarism detectors have failed to discern formatting and footnoting that made the agreement between two sources legitimate. Those detectors are helpful when they are used wisely by human beings. It is important not to jump to conclusions the way some did when the papyrus of the Gospel of Jesus' Wife was found to be ancient, since that result alone was not sufficient to determine whether the text written on the papyrus was also ancient.

As it turns out, however, we should not be too pessimistic about the value even of our current technologies and their usefulness in detecting forgeries, or about the value of newly-available texts and objects to serve as inspiration for the development of new tools of investigation. New technologies for detecting forgery were developed in order to study the Gospel of Jesus' Wife. Karen King has said that "'the most significant development' resulting from the papyrus was the formation of the Ancient Ink Laboratory at Columbia University and that lab's subsequent discovery of a nondestructive technique to date ancient inks. Director of the Ancient Ink Laboratory Jim T. Yardley said the lab created a 'totally unprecedented' method of dating manuscripts by analyzing tiny ink samples with a 'scanning electron microscope.'" When these new tests were carried out in conjunction with the more traditional method of Carbon

20 Compare Goler, Sarah, et al. "Characterizing the Age of Ancient Egyptian Manuscripts through Micro-Raman Spectroscopy." *Journal of Raman Spectroscopy 47.10*, 2016, 1185-1193 with Krutzsch, Myriam, and Ira Rabin, "Material Criteria and their Clues for Dating," *NTS 61:3*, July 2015, 356-367.

14 dating, the truth emerged: Yardley said, "The ink is from 200 AD, while the carbon 14 test says the document is from 700 AD. The age of the ink could be younger than the substrate, but it can't be older."[21]And so in this case, scientific methods *did* confirm the conclusions of investigative journalism and humanistic forms of analysis and argumentation.[22] Moreover, the simple fact that inks take much longer to dry completely than the typical forger will be willing to wait, makes some classic methods for detecting forgeries still very useful.[23] What we can hope for from future technology is not only better ways of detecting forgeries, but also less invasive and less expensive ways of undertaking the same kinds of verifications and analyses that are currently in use.[24] The takeaway message is that sometimes one method on its own may provide a clear answer, but in many cases, and perhaps most cases, a combination of approaches will be needed either to get at the truth, or simply to make the conclusions drawn by one approach more sound and secure.

4 Learning Collaboration and Cooperation

Academics sometimes express frustration about the media, in response to sensationalized headlines or misrepresentation as our nuanced explanations are edited into sound bites. Yet in the case of the Gospel of Jesus' Wife, journalists, professional scholars, graduate students, and interested laypeople all played an important role in carrying out the necessary investigations. Without the contribution of the kind of detective work that characterizes investigative journalism, we would not have as much clarity about this matter as we do. In his article for The Atlantic mentioned at the beginning of this chapter, Ariel

21 Bennett, Bonnie K., "'Gospel of Jesus' Wife' Researcher Says Frenzy Distracts from Larger Issues," *The Harvard Crimson*, 11th of November 2016, <http://www.thecrimson.com/article/2016/11/11/papyrus-christianity-divinity-school/>, accessed March 19th, 2018. The scientific work referred to here is published as Goler et.al., "Characterizing the age."

22 On the different methods and their relationship to one another over the course of the investigation, see Schroeder, Caroline, "Gender and the Academy Online: The Authentic Revelations of the Gospel of Jesus' Wife," in: Burke, Tony (ed.), *Fakes, Forgeries, and Fictions: Writing Ancient and Modern Christian Apocrypha: Proceedings from the 2015 York Christian Apocrypha Symposium*, Eugene: Wipf and Stock, 2017, 304-313.

23 Bell, Suzanne, *How to Identify a Forgery: A Guide to Spotting Fake Art, Counterfeit Currencies, and More*, New York: Skyhorse Publishing, 2013, 78.

24 The issue of how expensive tests are is mentioned in Burleigh, Nina, *Unholy Business: A True Tale of Faith, Greed and Forgery in the Holy Land*, New York: Smithsonian Books/Collins, 2008,186, citing Jean-Baptiste, Patrick, *L'affaire des fausses reliques: enquête au coeur des trafics de vestiges bibliques*, Paris: Albin Michel, 2005.

Sabar directly quotes from the American Association of Museums' Guide to Provenance Research, which in turn alerts academics and museum employees that investigation of provenance "is not unlike detective work." This point was also highlighted by Liv Ingeborg Lied in a conference paper about the Gospel of Jesus' Wife:

> The first point that deserves our attention, is the very fact that it was a journalist, using journalistic methods, that provided the last piece of the puzzle. Much work had already been done by scholars, but the provenance piece was still wanting. In later interviews, Sabar refers specifically to the importance of his experience as a news reporter for solving the case. He points out that journalistic methods, such as knocking on doors, talking to strangers, and following paper trails proved successful (Radio West – 8:21). He also notes that this is not something scholars would normally do. Scholars are used to working in the environment of the university, in archives and libraries, etc., but the methods he had used to track down Fritz and solve the case of the provenance of the fragment is a 'blind spot' in the repertoire of scholarly methods.[25]

Lied goes on to highlight that (1) "it was the combination of humanistic and journalistic methods that solved the case"; (2) it was the journalistic approach, which ultimately persuaded Karen King; and (3) the scientific methods were the least successful in setting the matter to rest. This last point is important, and reinforces our earlier point that matters of authenticity-testing should not be automated, while also highlighting the other side of that same coin: just as agreement with existing text does not automatically demonstrate forgery (any more than Matthew's agreement with Mark, for instance, makes the former a "forgery"), so too the antiquity of papyrus and ink can no longer be relied upon to safeguard the antiquity of the text written on that papyrus with that ink. Perhaps one day soon we may be able to use technology to recognize characteristics that distinguish forgeries made with recycled materials. But until then (and perhaps even then), we will need to employ historical/humanistic and journalistic/investigative methods along with scientific ones, and to allow the

25 Lied, Liv Ingeborg, "Media Dynamics and Academic Knowledge Production: Tracing the Role of the Media in the Gospel of Jesus's Wife Saga," paper read at the conference *Fragments of an Unbelievable Past? Constructions of Provenance, Narratives of Forgery, University of Agder, 14-16 September, 2016*, <https://www.academia.edu/28624547/Media_Dynamics_and_Academic_Knowledge_Production_Tracing_the_Role_of_the_Media_in_the_Gospel_of_Jesuss_Wife_Saga>, accessed on 10.04.19.

combination thereof to speak to the matter together, in a more effective manner than any one method can on its own.

5 Learning Patience

Demonstrating that the Gospel of Jesus' Wife was a forgery was not something that could be accomplished overnight. It happened more quickly than it would have in earlier decades, thanks to the kinds of collaborations that have only become possible in the internet era. But speed is not a virtue in and of itself, especially if accuracy suffers as a result.[26] Nor is the mere fact of eventually happening to be proven correct praiseworthy.[27]In an age of increasing speed, and emphasis on streamlining and productivity with rapid results, it is crucial for scholars to learn (or remember) patience, and to make sure that we proceed – and draw conclusions – only as rapidly as rigorous adherence to scholarly (and/or journalistic) methods allows us to. It is better to proceed carefully and cautiously, and then once we have done our due diligence and feel that our conclusions are sound, we can utilize online platforms to disseminate our arguments and results almost immediately. Perhaps most important is that scholarly interaction online not reflect the penchant for unbending dogmatism that characterizes so much of what passes for conversation on the internet. As long as we are committed to remaining open to correction in light of new evidence and new arguments, the speed of our own individual contributions may matter significantly less. The study of the Gospel of Jesus' Wife saw some quick judgments in a variety of directions, but on the whole, the scholarly process worked well, inasmuch as arguments were made and evaluated, investigations were undertaken, information was shared, and ultimately academics and the general public were reached and persuaded by the disseminated results of those efforts.

A particularly exciting aspect of the Digital Humanities in our time is also its biggest pitfall, and the case of the Gospel of Jesus' Wife illustrates this point well. We have moved from a situation of scarcity of information to one of

26 See Caraher, William, "Slow Archaeology: Technology, Efficiency, and Archaeological Work," in: Walcek Averett, Erin, Gordon, Jody Michael, Counts, Derek B.(eds.), *Mobilizing the Past for a Digital Future: The Potential of Digital Archaeology*, Grand Forks: The Digital Press @ The University of North Dakota, 2016, 422-423, 436-437.

27 McGrath, James F., "Slow Scholarship : Do Bloggers Rush in Where Jesus' Wife Would Fear to Tread?" in: Burke, Tony (ed.), *Fakes, Forgeries, and Fictions: Writing Ancient and Modern Christian Apocrypha: Proceedings from the 2015 York Christian Apocrypha Symposium*, Eugene: Wipf and Stock, 2017, 326-340.

overwhelming abundance. We have moved from a situation of painfully slow publication (think, for instance, of the Dead Sea Scrolls) to a situation in which a far greater number of ancient manuscripts are available in online repositories than the current number of scholars and students working in relevant areas could ever hope to translate. This might give a certain advantage to future forgers, who might be able to find and utilize (in other words, plagiarize) an obscure unpublished manuscript in creating a forgery, with or without making changes to the content to make it seem even more sensational and valuable.

But from another perspective, this ever-increasing abundance of digitized manuscripts also robs forgers of an advantage they might otherwise seem to have. Although we will always welcome new discoveries, we already have far more manuscripts that have already been discovered than we have time and academic personnel to translate them. There is enough to keep doctoral students in Syriac supplied with dissertation topics for countless decades to come, even assuming a major upturn in the number of students majoring in that field. There are so many exciting, newsworthy discoveries to be made among the current digitized manuscript collections of university libraries, that no one need feel compelled to give the benefit of the doubt to a private collector who approaches them with an unprovenanced manuscript or other artifact.[28] Technological tools and digitization projects are speeding things up so significantly in comparison with the way things had to be done mere decades ago, that we can hopefully afford to take an extra day or two, if not indeed an extra few months, in order to run tests, and still make incredibly fast progress. The potential to have one's name associated with a spectacular find is not worth the risk of having one's name associated with a forgery. Unless one pulls something from the ground oneself, therefore, we not only can afford to be patient, but must be patient. If the members of the scholarly community are consistently patient in this manner, that too may serve to deter certain kinds of forgery. It should, at the very least, lessen the extent to which forgers receive validation of their productions from established authorities, which may in turn deprive them of the profit and/or media attention which they so eagerly seek, but do not deserve.

28 On the many issues related to private collections see further Mazza, Roberta, "Papyri, private collectors and academics: why the wife of Jesus and Sappho matter", *Faces and Voices*, <https://facesandvoices.wordpress.com/2014/04/17/papyri-private-collectors-and-academics-why-the-wife-of-jesus-and-sappho-matter/>, accessed on 10.04.19 and Yates, Donna, "Some thoughts on the Hobby Lobby antiquities case," *Anonymous Swiss Collector*, 6 July 2017, <https://www.anonymousswisscollector.com/2017/07/some-thoughts-on-the-hobby-lobby-antiquities-case.html>, accessed on 10.04.19.

6 Conclusion

As this study has hopefully established persuasively, there are a number of the important lessons that we can learn from the case of the Gospel of Jesus' Wife which are relevant to those working in the Digital Humanities. The Digital Humanities has a long history of emphasizing the need for collaboration across disciplinary lines, online, in order to draw the most reliable conclusions that we can, in the most expedient manner possible. The case of the Gospel of Jesus' Wife illustrates and provides supporting evidence for the fruitfulness of this approach. We can point to the difference between assumptions and conclusions offered from a single perspective about the Gospel of Jesus' Wife, and the convergence and clarity that became possible using varied approaches, collaboratively, through conversations on blogs, which were also used to disseminate those conclusions and from there picked up by media sources.

The case of the Gospel of Jesus' Wife also provides an opportunity to teach our students information fluency skills. We can do this by producing replicas to increase their understanding of manuscripts and other artifacts, the originals of which we cannot conveniently bring into the classroom when we teach. But we can also do this by showing them how scholarship works: that it is a practice of fallible human beings, who are capable of deceiving and being deceived, and capable of jumping to conclusions rather than patiently waiting for the scholarly process to run its course. Determining authenticity is not merely a case of running a specific scientific test. Nor is it a case of merely consulting an authority from Harvard University or anywhere else. Scholarship works through the pursuit of consensus, using specific tools and methods to reach our conclusions. For some students, the application of scholarly methods to the Bible poses special hurdles because of the importance of those texts within their faith traditions. Precisely by providing an example that is outside the canon (and for some, at odds with their faith tradition's teachings), the Gospel of Jesus' Wife provides a counterbalancing example which may be pedagogically useful, as students' own instincts to jump to conclusions about such a text may lead to reflection on how motives and biases can interfere with the course of scholarship. The Gospel of Jesus' Wife also highlights that, even when a conclusion that we jump to later proves correct, it is not a scholarly conclusion except when certain procedures are followed, and followed rigorously.

The preceding exploration of forgery and Digital Humanities also provides an opportunity for reflection on whether and to what extent the detection of forgeries is a good use of scholars' time. For those working in history and related fields, the study of authentic evidence should be our priority, rather than focusing on the evaluation of authenticity for its own sake. It may be that, in some instances, the skills required for the latter sort of task will be more those of an investigative journalist than those of a typical historian. Yet it may also be that, to some extent, learning those related yet distinct skills can prove useful for the study of history proper. Likewise, the collaborative crowdsourcing that typified the interaction between academics during the high points in the discussion of the Gospel of Jesus' Wife may also be transferrable to other matters that ought to be more central to our work than the detection of forgery. The development of new technological methods and processes as a result of collaboration between scientists and historical scholars suggests that involvement in forgery detection can itself lead to worthwhile products and results. We need to remember, however, that the Gospel of Jesus' Wife did not really tell us anything that we did not already know or at least suspect about views held in certain circles in the fourth century, and would never have told us something important about the historical Jesus even if it had proved authentic. Academics (individually and collectively) therefore need to reflect seriously on the question of how much of our time ought to be devoted to evaluation of authenticity in cases such as this one.

There are other lessons that can be drawn, and it is to be expected that the Gospel of Jesus' Wife may not be done teaching us new things. But there is much that we can already learn, including that what from one perspective was simply an unfortunate and often frustrating incident of forgery, also provided an opportunity, a test case, the positive outcomes from which speak to the power and importance of those approaches that fall under the heading of the Digital Humanities.

References

Askeland, Christian, "A Lycopolitan Forgery of John's Gospel," *NTS 61:3*, July 2015, 314-334.

Askeland, Christian, "A Fake Coptic John and Its Implications for 'The Gospel of Jesus's Wife'," *TynBul 65*, 2014, 1-10.

Bak, János M., Geary, Patrick J., Klaniczay, Gábor (eds.), *National Cultivation of Culture: Manufacturing a Past for the Present. Forgery and Authenticity in Medievalist Texts and Objects in Nineteenth-Century Europe*, 1, Leiden: Brill, 2014.

Bell, Suzanne, *How to Identify a Forgery : A Guide to Spotting Fake Art, Counterfeit Currencies, and More*, New York: Skyhorse Publishing, 2013.

Bennett, Bonnie K., "'Gospel of Jesus' Wife' Researcher Says Frenzy Distracts from Larger Issues," *The Harvard Crimson*, 11th of November 2016, <http://www.thecrimson.com/article/2016/11/11/papyrus-christianity-divinity-school/>, accessed on 10.04.19.

Bernhard, Andrew, "Postscript: A Final Note about the Origin of the Gospel of Jesus' Wife," *NTS 63:2*, 305-317.

Bernhard, Andrew, "The Gospel of Jesus' Wife: Summary of Coptic and English Evidence of Forgery," academia.edu: <https://www.academia.edu/31775308/The_Gospel_of_Jesus_Wife_Summary_of_Coptic_and_English_Evidence_of_Forgery_March_8_2017>, accessed on 10.04.19.

Bond, Sarah, "The Ethics Of 3D-Printing Syria's Cultural Heritage," *Forbes*, 22nd of September2016,<https://www.forbes.com/sites/drsarahbond/2016/09/22/does-nycs-new-3d-printed-palmyra-arch-celebrate-syria-or-just-engage-in-digital-colonial ism/>, accessed March 19th, 2018.

Brown, Mark, "'New Rembrandt' to be unveiled in Amsterdam," *The Guardian*, <https://www.theguardian.com/artanddesign/2016/apr/05/new-rembrandt-to-be-unveiled-in-amsterdam>, accessed on 10.04.19.

Burleigh, Nina, *Unholy Business: A True Tale of Faith, Greed and Forgery in the Holy Land*, New York: Smithsonian Books/Collins, 2008.

Caraher, William, "Slow Archaeology: Technology, Efficiency, and Archaeological Work," in: Walcek Averett, Erin, Gordon, Jody Michael, Counts, Derek B.(eds.), *Mobilizing the Past for a Digital Future: The Potential of Digital Archaeology*, Grand Forks: The Digital Press @ The University of North Dakota, 2016, 421-441.

Craddock, Paul T., *Scientific Investigation of Copies, Fakes and Forgeries*, Amsterdam: Butterworth-Heinemann, 2009.

Ehrman, Bart D., *Forgery and Counterforgery: The Use of Literary Deceit in Early Christian Polemics*, Oxford University Press, 2012.

Goler, Sarah, et al., "Characterizing the Age of Ancient Egyptian Manuscripts through Micro-Raman Spectroscopy." *Journal of Raman Spectroscopy 47.10*, 2016, 1185-1193.

Heide, Martin, "The Moabitica and Their Aftermath: How to Handle a Forgery Affair with an International Impact," in: Lubetski, Meir and Edith (eds.), *New Inscriptions and Seals Relating to the Biblical World: Society of Biblical Literature archaeology and biblical studies*, Williston: Society of Biblical Literature, 2012, 193-241.

Jean-Baptiste, Patrick, *L'affaire des fausses reliques: enquête au coeur des trafics de vestiges bibliques*, Paris : Albin Michel, 2005.

Jordan Times, "Antiquities agency chief says Jordan Codices fake", *Jordan Times*, March 9th, 2017, <http://www.jordantimes.com/news/local/antiquities-agency-chief-says-jordan-codices-fake>, accessed on 10.04.19.

Krutzsch, Myriam, and Ira Rabin, "Material Criteria and their Clues for Dating," *NTS 61:3*, July 2015, 356-367.

Le Donne, Anthony, *The Wife of Jesus: Ancient Texts and Modern Scandals*, London: Oneworld, 2013.

Lenain, Thierry, "The Narrative Structure of Forgery Tales," in: Kila, Joris, Balcells, Marc (eds.), *Heritage and Identity: Cultural Property Crime: An Overview and Analysis of Contemporary Perspectives and Trends*, 1, Leiden: Brill, 2014, 39-60.

Lied, Liv Ingeborg, "Media Dynamics and Academic Knowledge Production: Tracing the Role of the Media in the Gospel of Jesus's Wife Saga," paper read at the conference *Fragments of an Unbelievable Past? Constructions of Provenance, Narratives of Forgery, University of Agder, 14-16 September, 2016*, <https://www.academia.edu/28624547/Media_Dynamics_and_Academic_Knowledge_Production_Tracing_the_Role_of_the_Media_in_the_Gospel_of_Jesuss_Wife_Saga>, accessed on 10.04.19.

Liszewski, Andrew, "3D Printing and Scanning Can Now Produce Near Flawless Art Forgeries," *Gizmodo*, August 26th, 2013 <https://gizmodo.com/3d-printing-and-scanning-can-now-produce-near-flawless-1201525111>, accessed on 10.04.19.

Mazza, Roberta, "Papyri, private collectors and academics: why the wife of Jesus and Sappho matter", *Faces and Voices*, <https://facesandvoices.wordpress.com/2014/04/17/papyri-private-collectors-and-academics-why-the-wife-of-jesus-and-sappho-matter/>, accessed on 10.04.19.

McGrath, James F., "Slow Scholarship : Do Bloggers Rush in Where Jesus' Wife Would Fear to Tread?" in: Burke, Tony (ed.), *Fakes, Forgeries, and Fictions: Writing Ancient and Modern Christian Apocrypha: Proceedings from the 2015 York Christian Apocrypha Symposium*, Eugene: Wipf and Stock, 2017, 326-340.

Meadows, David, "Oxyrhynchus and the First Apocalypse of James: Collection History Just Got Murkier," *Rogue Classicism* 12/13/2017, <https://rogueclassicism.com/2017/12/13/oxyrhynchus-and-the-first-apocalypse-of-james-collection-history-just-got-murkier/>, accessed on 10.04.19.

Michelson, David A., "Syriaca.org as a Test Case for Digitally Re-Sorting the Ancient World," in: Clivaz, Claire, Dilley, Paul, Hamidović, David (eds.), *Ancient Worlds in Digital Culture*, Leiden: E.J. Brill, 2016, <http://discoverarchive.vanderbilt.edu/handle/1803/8344>, accessed on 10.04.19, 59-85.

Moss, Candida, Baden, Joel, "Is Israel's Big New Find for Real?" *The Daily Beast*, 11th of June 2016, <http://www.thedailybeast.com/articles/2016/11/06/is-israel-s-big-new-find-a-hoax.html>, accessed on 10.04.19.

Nickell, Joe, *Real Or Fake: Studies In Authentication. Lexington: The University Press of Kentucky*, 2009, eBook Collection (EBSCOhost), Web, accessed November 11, 2016.

Nongbri, Brent, "Provenance and The Oxyrhynchus Papyri," *Variant Readings* 12/13/2017, <http://brentnongbri.com/2017/12/13/provenance-and-the-oxyrhynchus-papyri/>, accessed on 10.04.19.

Parker, Heather Dana Davis, "Forging Ancient Texts," *The Ancient Near East Today*, vol. 4, n°10, October 2016, <http://www.asor.org/anetoday/2016/10/06/forging-ancient-texts/>, accessed on 10.04.19.

Rabinowitz, Adam, "The Work of Archaeology in the Age of Digital Surrogacy," in: Olson, Brandon R., Caraher, William (eds.), *Visions of Substance: 3D Imaging in Mediterranean Archaeology*, Grand Forks: The Digital Press at The University of North Dakota, 2015, 27-42.

Rollston, Christopher, "Navigating the Epigraphic Storm: A Palaeographer Reflects on Inscriptions from the Market," *Near Eastern Archaeology 68*, n° 1/2, March – June 2005, 69-72.

Ruthven, K.K., *Faking Literature*, Cambridge: Cambridge University Press, 2001.

Sabar, Ariel, "The Unbelievable Tale of Jesus' Wife," *The Atlantic*, July/August 2016, <https://www.theatlantic.com/magazine/archive/2016/07/the-unbelievable-tale-of-jesus-wife/485573/>, accessed <http://www.asor.org/anetoday/2016/10/06/forging-ancient-texts/>.

Schroeder, Caroline, "On Palmyra and 3D Modeling Cultural Heritage in the Middle East," *Early Christian Monasticism in the Digital Age* 6/12/2016, <http://earlymonasticism.org/2016/06/12/on-palmyra-and-3d-modeling-cultural-heritage-in-the-middle-east/>, accessed on 10.04.19.

Schroeder, Caroline, "More on Social Networks and Provenance," *Early Christian Monasticism in the Digital Age* 6/16/2016, <http://earlymonasticism.org/2016/06/16/social-networks/>, accessed on 10.04.19.

Schroeder, Caroline, "Provenance Provenance Provenance," *Early Christian Monasticism in the Digital Age* 6/16/2016, <http://earlymonasticism.org/2016/06/16/provenance-provenance-provenance/>, accessed on 10.04.19.

Schroeder, Caroline, "Institutional Responsibilities," *Early Christian Monasticism in the Digital Age* 6/23/2016, <http://earlymonasticism.org/2016/06/23/on-institutional-responsibilities-and-on-gender-final-thoughts-on-the-g-of-jesus-wife/>, accessed on 10.04.19.

Schroeder, Caroline, "Gender and the Academy Online: The Authentic Revelations of the Gospel of Jesus' Wife," in: Burke, Tony (ed.), *Fakes, Forgeries, and Fictions: Writing Ancient and Modern Christian Apocrypha: Proceedings from the 2015 York Christian Apocrypha Symposium*, Eugene: Wipf and Stock, 2017, 304-325.

Stierlin, Henri, *Le Buste de Néfertiti. Une imposture de l'égyptologie?*, Gollion: Infolio, 2009.

Yates, Donna, "Some thoughts on the Hobby Lobby antiquities case," *Anonymous Swiss Collector*, 6 July 2017, <https://www.anonymousswisscollector.com/2017/07/some-thoughts-on-the-hobby-lobby-antiquities-case.html>, accessed on 10.04.19.

CHAPTER 12

Synagogue Modeling Project Report: a Multi-faceted Approach to 3D, Academic Modeling

Bradley C. Erickson

With the click of a button, my body is transported through time and space. A flicker of light catches my eye. I look up. Flames dance upon the plaster walls, casting eerie shadows on the mosaic floor upon which I stand. I am in a synagogue. An ancient synagogue. Yet at the same moment, in the same space, I am also standing in my office. I feel like I could reach out and touch the mosaic floor. As I try to do so, I notice another hand stretching forth, a hand that is stylized in the mosaic below me. It is the hand of God, reaching from the heavens to stay Abraham's sacrifice of Isaac. I am standing in the ancient synagogue of Beth Alpha on a mosaic scene depicting the Aqedah of Genesis 22. I get on my hands and knees to examine the scene more closely. Each tessera of the mosaic stands out more clearly as my eyes draw nearer to the floor. I can almost count each individual piece of stone. I begin to count, but a sound from another world snaps me back to reality. My phone is ringing.

I remove the virtual reality (VR) headset as my office comes back into focus. The light from the flicker of ancient oil lamps is overtaken by the luminescence of a lightbulb. I have removed myself from Beth Alpha but Beth Alpha has not yet left my memory. The distance between objects, the number of steps I traveled, and how the moonlight poured through the windows – these are some of the experiences I remember from my time exploring one of the 3D environments created for study with virtual reality.

1 Introduction

The production of 3D visualizations has vastly expanded beyond its original use by Boeing for airplane cockpit design in the 1960's.[1] Animation, architectural design, and engineering are a few of the occupations that have since adopted 3D toolsets for professional use. A modeler can produce a 3D visualization

1 Dreher, Thomas, *History of Computer Art*, 2011, IASLonline, trans. to English 2015, ch. 4: <http://iasl.uni-muenchen.de/links/GCA_Indexe.html>, accessed on 10.04.19.

using a variety of software packages that range in cost from free to tens of thousands of dollars. After producing a model, a user can experience the 3D visualization digitally on a computer or tactilely through fabrication with 3D printing, laser cutting, or CNC routing.

Biblical scholars and archaeologists, too, have embraced 3D modeling for its usefulness in providing visualizations of the past. In 2009, Robert Cargill published one of the first 3D-modeling based biblical studies projects in which he detailed a methodology "for using digital modeling to test various archaeological reconstructions" of Khirbet Qumran, the site of the discovery of the Dead Sea Scrolls.[2] In addition to Cargill's project, several archaeological teams excavating ancient sites throughout the Middle East have also used 3D technologies to record data in detail greater than photography allows.[3]

This article explores how 3D modeling addresses difficulties intrinsic to fields dealing with material culture through a survey of a recently completed Byzantine synagogue modeling project that produced scaled, virtual reality environments of the 4th–6th century CE synagogues of Beth Alpha, Hammath Tiberias, and Sepphoris.[4] For each synagogue in the project, a series of the following visualizations were produced: (1) an accurately scaled photogrammetric model of the synagogue's remains, (2) a high-definition, colorized image of the synagogue's mosaic floor, and (3) a suggested 3D reconstruction of how the synagogue may have looked in antiquity in which a user can explore via a first-person avatar using either an internet-connected computer or a VR device such as the HTC Vive. In what follows, I will identify a series of problems

---

2 Cargill, Robert, *Qumran through (Real) Time, vol. 1*, in: Cargill, Robert, *Bible in Technology*, Piscataway, NJ: Georgia Press, 2009, 4.

3 Two recent examples of archaeological excavations using 3D toolsets are the Jezreel Valley Regional Project in Israel (PRINS, Adam, "3D Modeling for Archaeological Documentation: Using the JVRP Method to Record Archaeological Excavations with Millimeter-accuracy": <http://www.jezreelvalleyregionalproject.com/3d-modeling.html>), accessed 21 March 2018 and the 'Ayn Gharandal Archaeological Project in Jordan ('Ayn Gharandal Archaeological Project: <https://religion.utk.edu/gharandal/>), accessed on 10.04.19.

4 These three synagogues were chosen due to the level of preservation of their mosaic floors. The Beth Alpha synagogue dates to the 6th c. CE; The Hammath Tiberias synagogue dates to the 4th c. CE; and the Sepphoris synagogue dates to the 5th c. CE. Please note that multiple synagogues were constructed on top of one another at Hammath Tiberias, but the synagogue I have modeled for my project is the "Severos Synagogue" from Stratum IIa of Moshe Dothan's excavation. For the dating methodology of each synagogue, please see the following excavation reports: Sukenik, Eleazar L., *The Ancient Synagogue of Beth Alpha: An Account of the Excavations Conducted on Behalf of the Hebrew University, Jerusalem: From the Hebrew*, New York: G. Olms, 1975, 44, 52; Dothan, Moshe, *Hammath Tiberias I*, Jerusalem: Israel Exploration Society, 2000, 67; and Weiss, Zeev, *The Sepphoris Synagogue: Deciphering an Ancient Message through Its Archaeological and Socio-Historical Contexts*, Jerusalem: Israel Exploration Society, 2005, 38-39.

that 3D modeling allows researchers working with material culture to overcome, provide a survey of the methods used to generate models in the synagogue modeling project, and conclude with a presentation of the final synagogue modeling data.

2 The Problem: Accessibility, Scale, and Dimensionality

Many items of scholarly interest sit on display in museums, reside in archival storage, or lie underground due to the need to backfill or build above former archaeological sites. If a scholar wishes to access a certain object, he or she must travel to its place of residence to do so. If a scholar cannot travel or access the needed objects, he or she must resign to view photographs of the objects.

Using photographs as a basis for interpretation presents a unique set of challenges, two of which are the problem of scale and static dimensionality. Once a photograph is taken, its sense of scale is largely lost. Though many pictures of artifacts and archaeological sites contain scale bars, such attempts to indicate scale within a photo requires viewers to visualize the re-scaled objects by imagining their correct size.

Photographs are two-dimensional representations of a three-dimensional environment. A viewer cannot step into the scene of a photograph and look behind any objects in the foreground that obscure the background. This problem of static dimensionality is similar to that of scale. A photograph requires a viewer to imagine how the two-dimensional image would have looked in three dimensions.

The problems of accessibility, scale, and dimensionality also affect the study of ancient synagogues. Concerning accessibility, the synagogues of Beth Alpha, Hammath Tiberias, and Sepphoris are all located in the Galilee region of Israel. For those living outside of Israel, visits to the synagogue sites prove expensive and time consuming. In lieu of a site visit, if a scholar wishes to view photographs of the site, he or she must rely on archaeological publications. The synagogues of Beth Alpha, Hammath Tiberias, and Sepphoris each contain mosaic floors upon which exist paneled images of the binding of Isaac from Genesis 22, the zodiac, and the Jerusalem temple. Scholars interested in studying the mosaic floors must rely on black-and-white or piecemealed photographs of individual panels and drawings of each mosaic since few aerial photograph of the entirety of any of the mosaic floors exist.[5]

5 For a drawing of the Beth Alpha mosaic, see Sukenik, Eleazar l., *Beth Alpha*, Plate XXVII; for a drawing of the Hammath Tiberias mosaic, see Dothan, Moshe, *Hammath Tiberias*, 34-35; for a drawing of the Sepphoris mosaic, see Weiss, Zeev, *Sepphoris*, 57.

The lack of holistic aerial images of these synagogue mosaic floors is due in part to conservation efforts and technological limitations. In 1929, Eleazar Sukenik excavated the synagogue of Beth Alpha and after the mosaic floor was brought to light, conservators built a protective structure over the remains.[6] The excavators of Beth Alpha took pictures of portions of the mosaic, but they did not take a photograph of the mosaic floor in its entirety.[7] The synagogue at Hammath Tiberias was excavated by Moshe Dothan from 1961-1965, and excavators took a holistic photo of the mosaic floor, which was printed in black-and-white.[8] In a volume detailing the more recently excavated ancient synagogue at Sepphoris, the authors provide a side-angled (i.e. not from above), low-resolution, excavation shot of the synagogue mosaic floor.[9] While helpful, the excavation shot does not provide enough detail for a close analysis of the mosaic floor or the narratives contained therein. Like Beth Alpha, the conservators of the synagogues at Hammath Tiberias and Sepphoris built protective, roofed structures above the sites' archaeological remains, rendering any high-definition, modern aerial shots of the synagogues impossible.

3D modeling, however, allows for the generation of scaled and rectified aerial shots from within a 3D model, which can be generated and studied remotely once a model is produced. So even though the synagogue remains of Beth Alpha, Hammath Tiberias, and Sepphoris sit under protective structures, with 3D modeling, detailed aerial images of each site can be produced.

In addition to the production of ortho-rectified aerial images, the synagogue models grant scholars remote access to these sites. With the introduction of playable avatars in VR, users can embody and explore the site from a true first-person perspective. In the following section on methodology, the means of producing each model will be surveyed.

3 Method of Production

3.1 *Photogrammetry*

The first goal of the project was to create both photogrammetric models of each synagogue's material remains and a high-resolution, colorized image of each synagogue mosaic floor.

6 Sukenik, Eleazar l., *Beth Alpha*, 5 and 7.

7 The partial images of the mosaic floor can be seen dispersed throughout Sukenik's excavation report.

8 For excavation dates, see Dothan, Moshe, *Hammath Tiberias*, 6; for the aerial photograph of the mosaic floor, see Plate 10; for a colorized photo of the mosaic floor, see Hachlili, Rachel, *Ancient Synagogues*, 255.

9 Weiss, Zeev, *Sepphoris*, 27.

FIGURE 12.1 An in-progress shot of generating the photogrammetric model of Beth Alpha with Agisof Photoscan; ©BRADERICKSON

Photogrammetric modeling is the process of photographing a site or object and from those photos generating a referenced, measurable 3D model of the subject. After making a photogrammetric model, a user can render a rectified image of the model from any angle, including an aerial shot otherwise known as an orthophoto.

To give an example of how a photogrammetric model and orthophoto are generated, I will use my work at Beth Alpha as an example. The photogrammetry project at Beth Alpha began with the taking of a series of 200 photographs of the synagogue's architectural remains and mosaic floor using a DSLR camera. Once all required photos were taken, each image was loaded into the photogrammetry program Agisoft PhotoScan.[10] Once in Agisoft PhotoScan, all necessary parameters were set and the model was processed.

To create models, Agisoft PhotoScan uses a set of algorithms that examines and compares every portion of each picture to every other portion of every other picture. The program detects and traces identical features of an object from photo-to-photo, such as the corners of a door. After identifying and tracing points often numbering in the thousands between photos, the software begins to combine those points in three dimensions, creating a 3D modeled object or environment. At this point in the process, a user is able to add internal scale bars or known GIS points to ensure that the final model is scaled accurately.

10 See Figure 12.1 for a screenshot of the Beth Alpha model generated by Agisoft PhotoScan.

FIGURE 12.2 Orthophoto of the Beth Alpha Synagogue; ©BRADERICKSON

Once the model is complete, a user can export the model and utilize it in a number of ways, including loading the model online for internet viewing or further processing the model in a video-game engine so that a user can walk around the site using a digital avatar.

The orthophoto of the Beth Alpha mosaic, along with the orthophotos of the mosaics of Hammath Tiberias and Sepphoris, can be viewed in the list of figures to this article and are labeled Figure 12.2, Figure 12.3, and Figure 12.4, respectively. Following the completion of the photogrammetric portion of the modeling project, it was time to move to the next stage: creating suggested reconstructions of each synagogue.

3.2 *3D Modeling*

As in the previous section on photogrammetry, the ancient synagogue of Beth Alpha will be used as an example to describe the methodology for 3D modeling ancient environments. The modeling of Beth Alpha began with a close reading of Sukenik's excavation report with an eye to details that relayed the dimensions and styles of recovered architectural features. Architectural top plans of

FIGURE 12.3
Orthophoto of the Hammath Tiberias Synagogue; ©BRADERICKSON

FIGURE 12.4
Orthophoto of the Sepphoris Synagogue.
Please note that the lights appearing on the synagogue floor are from modern light fixtures hanging above the synagogue remains and that the shadows appearing on the lower right of the image are due to modern railing; ©BRADERICKSON

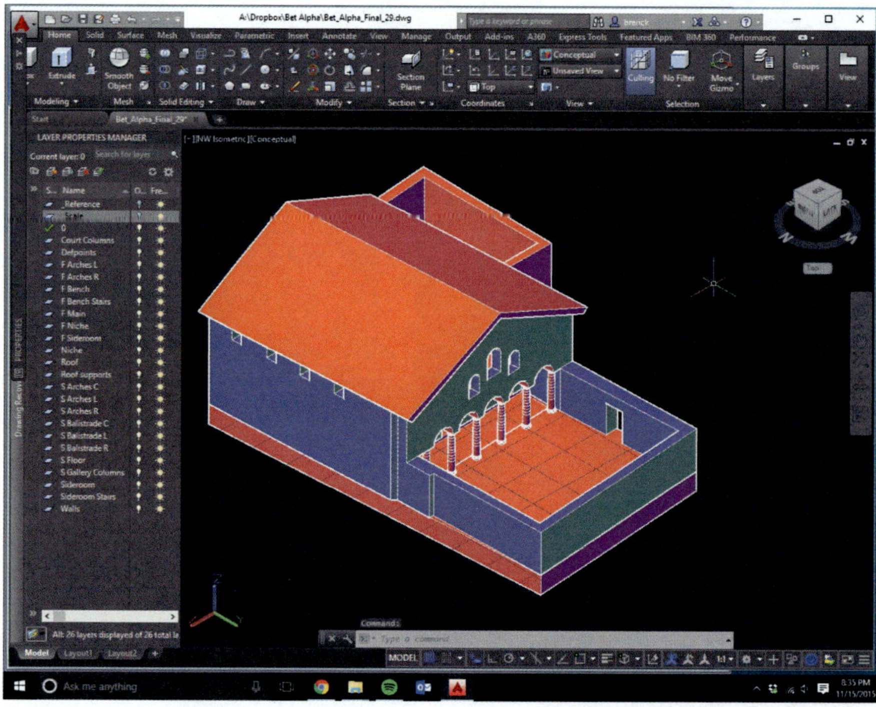

FIGURE 12.5 An in-progress screenshot of applying textures to the model of Beth Alpha in Blender; ©BRADERICKSON

Beth Alpha were scanned and loaded into AutoCAD, a drafting software application.[11] With the architectural top-plans loaded, a correct scale for the model was set and each feature of the structure (e.g. walls, benches, columns, etc.) was traced and extruded in three dimensions.

The next step in the modeling process was to export the scaled base model from the drafting software into a 3D modeling program. The drafting software is perfect for producing generic details, but a 3D modeling program is required to fine-tune the model and add unique aspects, such as fine details, animations, and textures. The open-source 3D modeling platform Blender was used.[12]

11 For architectural top plans, see Sukenik, Eleazar L., *Beth Alpha*, Plate XXVII; DOTHAN, Moshe, *Hammath Tiberias* 28-29; Weiss, Zeev, *Sepphoris*, 9 and 40. For a working screenshot of the Beth Alpha model production in AutoCAD, see Figure 12.5.

12 For a working screenshot of model production in Blender, please see Figure 12.6. For early renders of the outer and inner portions of the Sepphoris synagogue visualization, please see Figures 12.7 and 12.8. For a pre-textured render of the Beth Alpha synagogue, see Figure 12.9.

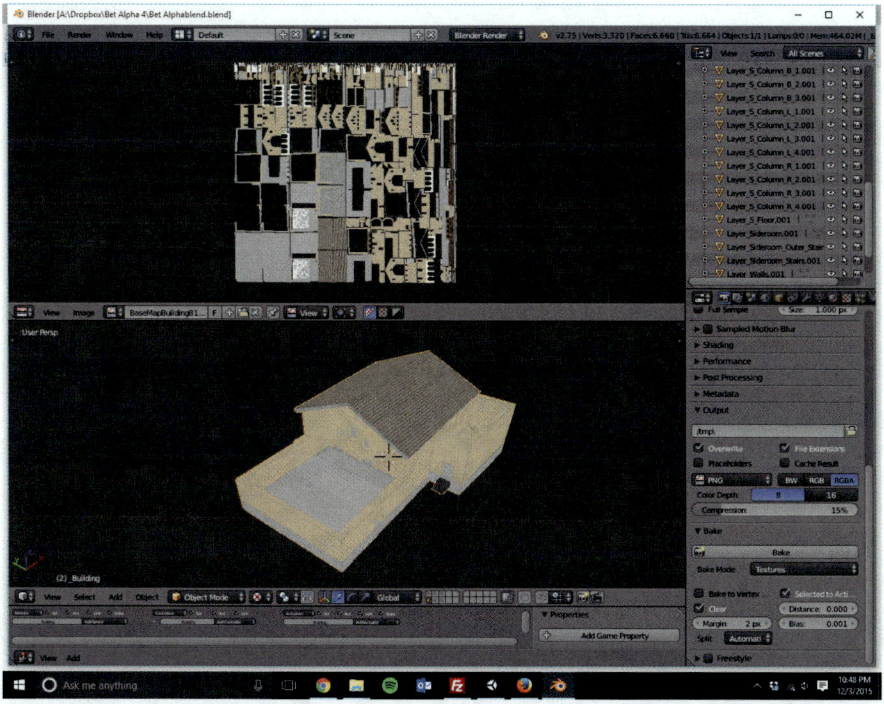

FIGURE 12.6 An in-progress screenshot of constructing the architectural model of Beth Alpha in AutoCAD; ©BRADERICKSON

Once each synagogue was modeled, interactive elements needed to be added to the model, including a playable character that a user could control and use to explore the synagogue from a first-person perspective. For this final interactive portion of the project, video-game engine software was used.

3.3 Game Engine

Video game engines are programs that aid game developers by taking care of large portions of needed computer code to create video games. So instead of having to program the effects of gravity or how light will reflect off objects in each model, Unity3D comes with a full suite of physics and environments preprogrammed into its system that saves developers time and effort. For this portion of the project, the photogrammetric model and suggested reconstruction of each synagogue was imported into Unity3D.[13]

13 For a working screenshot of model production in Unity3D, see Figure 12.10.

FIGURE 12.7 Early render of Sepphoris synagogue visualization, outside; ©BRADERICKSON

FIGURE 12.8 Early render of Sepphoris synagogue visualization, inside without Torah shrine; ©BRADERICKSON

Once loaded into Unity3D, a series of features were added to the model of each synagogue, including (1) a menu screen that allowed users to choose features for the character that they would embody in the virtual environment (e.g. height and walking speed); (2) a programmed sun to rotate around the model so that users could experience different lighting conditions within the synagogue through the model's day-night cycle; and (3) an option to toggle a collection of non-playable characters to fill the synagogue so that users could gain a sense of comparative scale.

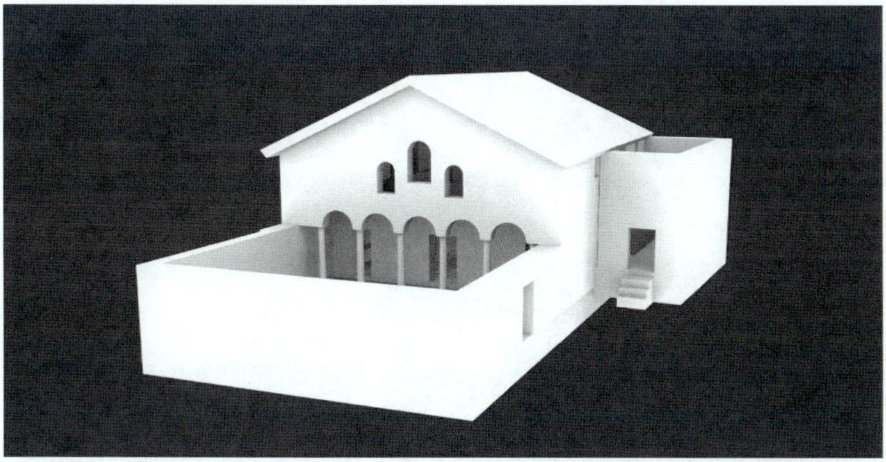

FIGURE 12.9 A render of the Beth Alpha synagogue visualization, Pre-Texture; ©BRADERICKSON

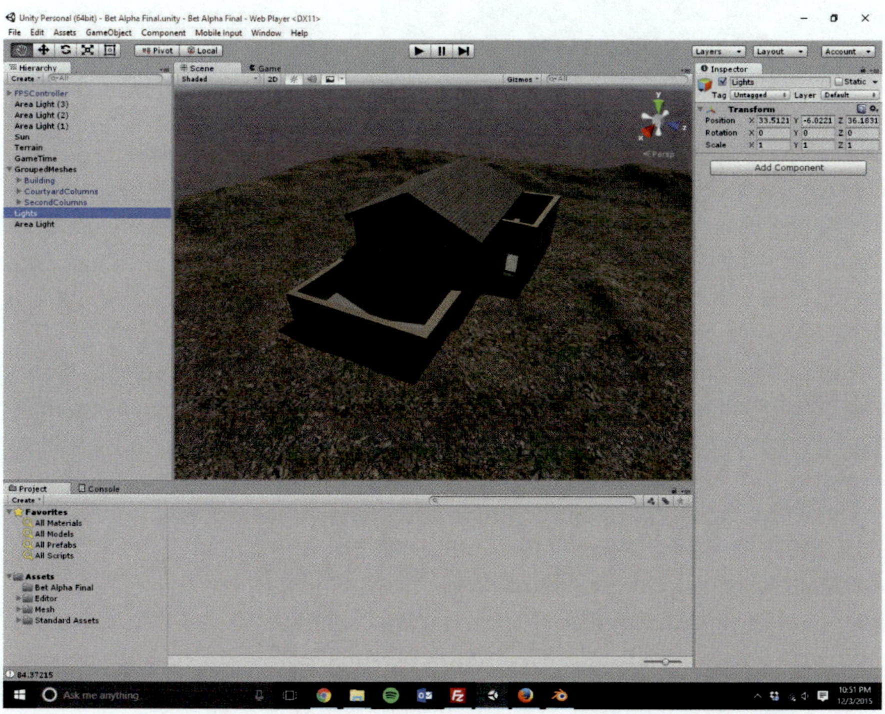

FIGURE 12.10 An in-progress screenshot of adding interactive elements to the model in Unity3D. Please note that the actual synagogue would have been surrounded by buildings and not an open field; ©BRADERICKSON

FIGURE 12.11
A user exploring the ancient synagogue of Sepphoris in VR with the HTC Vive. The user wears a headset through which he receives a first-person view of the synagogue. The hand-held controllers allow the user to interact with objects in the building. The television screen in the background projects what the user sees through the headset; ©BRADERICKSON

3D visualizations can often give the false impression of free, uninhibited experience. It is important to remember that designers are required to make decisions at every juncture of a modeling project. These decisions often establish boundaries to a player's experience. For example, concerning the playable character, a designer must input a number of pre-set features for the character, such as the character's height. In the synagogue models, I chose to make the basic, pre-altered avatar 1.6 m tall, which equates to roughly 5 ft. 7 in. This height setting might limit users wanting to experience the synagogue as someone taller or shorter. In order to combat my decision of a user's height as having an effect on his or her experience, I included a short computer script to allow the user to alter his or her avatar's height.

Once all scripted interactions and settings were programmed into the models in Unity3D, the final step of the production side of the project was to export the model as a single, useable package. Using Unity3D, the final versions of each models was exported so that the models could be accessed in two ways: online via a web portal and on a desktop personal computer via a VR headset – the HTC Vive.[14]

14 For a demonstration of someone navigating a synagogue model in virtual reality, please see Figure 12.11.

4 Results of Modeling and Final Products

I created my synagogue models with several goals in mind. First, I simply wanted a means through which I and others could embody ancient space. Through the embodiment of a virtual avatar questions such as how long would it take someone to walk from the entrance of the synagogue to the Torah shrine, how might different lighting conditions affect someone's experience of observing the synagogue's mosaic floor, and how many people could comfortably fit in the synagogue became questions answerable through observation within VR versions of the models. Second, through photogrammetry, I could generate the first high-resolution, holistic images of the synagogues' mosaic floors, which allowed for remote and detailed inspection of the mosaic remains.

In addition to my stated goals, other avenues of inquiry arose during the modeling process. It is important for the designer of an academic model to remain open to serendipitous discovery. For example, when adding windows to several of the synagogue models, I questioned how archaeological illustrators decided to place windows at certain heights in their architectural drawings of synagogue buildings. This led me to generate a set of models that allowed users to alter the height, size, position, and number of windows throughout the synagogue models so that users could observe how differently positioned and scaled windows affected natural light entering the building.

My synagogue models will be used in additional capacities to help visualize other theories in synagogue research. In Chad Spigel's recent volume on synagogue seating capacities, Spigel estimates a seating capacity of approximately 161 people for the Beth Alpha synagogue.[15] To test this theory, a user can populate a model with 161 non-playable characters, disperse them throughout the building, and explore the remaining space via the first-person playable character.

Photogrammetric models, orthophotos, and the navigable 3D visualizations of each synagogue can be accessed on my website at <http://bcerickson.com/synagogue-modeling-project/>. The photogrammetric models are hosted on Sketchfab and can directly be accessed at <https://skfb.ly/WBHQ>. The high-resolution versions of the orthophotos are hosted on Flickr and can be accessed at <https://flic.kr/s/aHskTQnvab>. All 3D models and images produced for this project have also been uploaded to the University of North Carolina at Chapel Hill Digital Repository to ensure that all models are preserved in case any website hosting a portion of the project goes down

15 Spigel, Chad, *Ancient Synagogue Seating Capacities: Methodology, Analysis, and Limits*, Tübingen: Mohr Siebeck, 2012, 158.

5 Conclusion

3D modeling in academia offers many unique avenues for research. Through digital avatars, scholars, students, and the public can embody and explore visualized ancient space, and explore the past from a first-person perspective.

While the ancient synagogue modeling project is in a technical state of completion, no digital project is ever truly finished. I am currently working on recording sounds that will play within each model when users approach certain areas of the models. I hope to add this sound feature both to provide audible guidance within the models and also to imagine what the background noise of ancient synagogues may have been. The project as it currently stands has allowed me to produce interactive models through which I can test hypotheses, teach others about ancient synagogues, and generate detailed photos of the mosaic floors.

To conclude this article, I want to share a story that conveys a powerful narrative of experience. At a recent research showcase, I setup my VR equipment and allowed university students to explore the model of the ancient synagogue of Sepphoris. A line quickly formed, and the first student stepped forward to try it out. After I instructed the student on how to navigate the model and explained the history of the synagogue and the project, the student put on the VR headset and hesitantly began to walk around the room.

After the student had walked for a few seconds, he looked down and noticed the mosaic floor for the first time. He gasped and apologized, asking if it was okay to walk on the mosaic floor – a floor that only existed in the digital environment rendered in the VR headset.

References

'Ayn Gharandal Archaeological Project, <https://religion.utk.edu/gharandal/>, accessed on 10.04.19.

Cargill, Robert, *Qumran through (Real) Time, vol. 1*, in: Cargill, Robert, *Bible in Technology*, Piscataway, NJ: Georgia Press, 2009.

Dothan, Moshe, *Hammath Tiberias I*, Jerusalem: Israel Exploration Society, 2000.

Dreher, Thomas, *History of Computer Art*, 2011, IASLonline, trans. to English 2015, ch. 4, <http://iasl.uni-muenchen.de/links/GCA_Indexe.html>, accessed on 10.04.19.

Hachlili, Rachel, *Ancient Synagogues – Archaeology and Art: New Discoveries and Current Research*, Boston: Brill, 2013.

Prins, Adam, "3D Modeling for Archaeological Documentation: Using the JVRP Method to Record Archeological Excavations with Millimeter-accuracy", <https://www.academia.edu/28587622/3D_Modeling_for_Archaeological_Documentation_using_the_JVRP_Method_to_record_archaeological_excavations_with_millimeter-accuracy>, accessed on 10.04.19.

Spigel, Chad, *Ancient Synagogue Seating Capacities: Methodology, Analysis, and Limits*, Tübingen: Mohr Siebeck, 2012.

Sukenik, Eleazar L., *The Ancient Synagogue of Beth Alpha: An Account of the Excavations Conducted on Behalf of the Hebrew University, Jerusalem: From the Hebrew*, New York: G. Olms, 1975.

Weiss, Zeev, *The Sepphoris Synagogue: Deciphering an Ancient Message through Its Archaeological and Socio-Historical Contexts*, Jerusalem: Israel Exploration Society, 2005.

Authors Index

Subject Index

Printed in the United States
By Bookmasters